A Shot At A Rose, To The Bite Of a Gator: The '75-'78 Ohio State Football Saga

THE BRAWNY PUG PUBLISHING CO.

Published by:

The Brawny Pug Publishing Co.
5829 Pinecone Court, Office One
Columbus, Ohio 43231-2940, USA

Library of Congress Cataloging in Publication Data
Skipton, Todd W.
A Shot At A Rose, To The Bite Of A Gator: The '75-'78 Ohio State Football Saga - Original softcover edition
Bibliography, includes index.
1. College Football - The Ohio State University
2. Biography - Wayne Woodrow Hayes
LC 93-072628
ISBN 0-9638057-1-1 $22.95 Softcover

W9-BEL-607

Cover photo work by Tom Skladany
Skladany Printing Center
6293 Busch Boulevard
Columbus, Ohio 43229
(614) 431-1144
Taken January 1, '77 Orange Bowl
Note Tom's #1 within the eyes of Woody

TABLE OF CONTENTS

FOREWORD

Woody Hayes will go down in sports history as one of the greatest college football coaches and molders of young men of all time. He will be remembered in the same breath as Pop Warner, Alonzo Stagg, Fritz Crisler, Bear Bryant, Bud Wilkinson, and Frank Leahy. His greatest tribute comes from the boys who played for him over his long career at Ohio State. They loved him, because they knew he cared for each and every one of them, not only during their college days, but long after. Woody never saw a mountain he couldn't climb - Mt. Michigan, Mt. Illinois, Mt. Iowa, and Mt. Southern Cal.

Sincerely,

JAMES A. RHODES
(Close friend of the Hayes family and former Governor of Ohio)

INTRODUCTION

This was a typical Ohio State football practice. The same play, a simplistic off-tackle dive by the tailback, had now been run numerous times, to the Head Coach's supreme dissatisfaction. After one final sub-par attempt of the same play, that Coach, Woody Hayes, let loose in a bombastic display of disappointment. Bellowing fiercely at the top of his lungs, Hayes lamented the terrible performance of "his boys." His speech was scattered with blue expletives, as he blistered the ears of his underachieving team.

In a climatic gesture of disapproval, Hayes ripped off his spectacles and sent them screaming to the damp practice turf. Before the disgruntled Hayes could stomp his lenses into oblivion, thereby purging his rage, they skidded off, undamaged, only to land precariously on the foot of an offensive lineman.

Normal practice drills had long since ground to a halt, as each of the more than one hundred OSU players, assistant coaches, and support staff of managers, trainers, and officials waited for Woody to calm down. The tension was tangible, even on the faces of the defensive unit across the field, as the assembled Buckeyes cringed on every breath of their disgruntled Coach.

Momentarily distracted by the unintended destination of his eyewear, Hayes ceased his demonstrative display. Still, no one dared move, and the lineman whose foot supported those glasses looked pleadingly toward his position coach, silently imploring, "What should I do?" The assistant, who was just as cowed and intimidated as everyone else on the huge field, merely rolled his eyes in a gesture of resignedness. In that brief moment, time stood still, and Hayes was the sole focus and center of each witnesses universe.

Eventually, Hayes wheeled around and walked away, his considerable anger at last spent. A student manager retrieved the eyeglasses, and practice picked up again, with a noticeably more intense pace. Yet, the prevailing mood remained applicable for each and every member of the Ohio State football program, beginning at their first encounter with Woody and usually extending well beyond any official association with the school: The presence and personality of Wayne Woodrow Hayes dominated their lives.

His thoughts, philosophies, wisdom, and good will, mixed in with a decidedly hands-on, vigorous teaching style, all sprinkled with flashes of a temper seldom matched, indelibly molded and fantastically influenced the lives of every person he came in contact with. *A Shot At A Rose, To The Bite Of A Gator* is the chronicle of this remarkable man's final four years of coaching, and is told largely through the day-to-day remembrances of the young men he had the privilege of leading during those eventful years.

Through their memories, the spirit of the Old Man, as his associates so affectionately called Woody (when safely out of earshot), continues to empower even those whom Hayes never met. Let us peer into the memories of the '75-'78 Buckeyes, beginning with...

CHAPTER ONE: PRE-SEASON '75

The freshmen class of '75 reported to an Ohio State University program brimming with cautiously optimistic expectation. Out of 108 candidates for the '75 team, only nine had started the narrow New Year's Day 18-17 Rose Bowl defeat to the University of Southern California. Woody stated after this heart-wrenching loss, "We got beat by a better team - one point better," and vowed to improve in this coming season. The defense had been hardest hit by graduation; overall, the '74 team sent 14 members into the NFL.

The '75 season offered perhaps the toughest schedule ever for an OSU team. The Buckeyes began the year against the Michigan State Spartans, their new nemesis, based on a controversial '74 defeat in East Lansing. This tense, much-anticipated showdown was followed by equally tough games against Penn State, North Carolina, and the University of California at Los Angeles.

For the first time in several years, a Woody Hayes squad could not point virtually exclusively toward the conference finale with Michigan. Ohio State traditionally placed the most emphasis on this final game, to the exclusion of other conference matchups. This year, the MSU game possibly sparked more interest than any Big 10 opener in history. The veteran Spartan team was expected to contend with the Buckeyes and Wolverines for national rankings, and was coming off five consecutive wins at the conclusion of '74.

One of those five wins, a stirring 16-13 victory at home over then top-ranked Ohio State, was so controversial that apparently it had sparked a National Collegiate Athletic Association investigation into alleged Spartan recruiting violations. After a disputed last second touchdown by Buckeye Brian Baschnagel was finally officially disallowed in that '74 thriller, a full 45 minutes following the final play, an extremely enraged Hayes decried the dirty tactics of MSU.

Hayes claimed the Spartan defenders deliberately laid on and prevented the OSU offensive players sufficient chance to run a play in the closing seconds. Indeed, film replays show OSU center Steve Myers being pinned, by his facemask, to the ground, struggling to get up and run the final play. Amidst a barrage of garbage and verbal missiles from Spartan fans which accompanied this protest, Michigan State was finally awarded the tainted victory.

As conventional wisdom reported, Hayes was so incensed at the loss that he turned MSU in to Big 10 authorities, sparking an investigation into a slew of supposed recruiting violations. The state of Michigan public sentiment, already against Hayes, became downright vehement as more news reports of the OSU Coach's involvement in the investigation emerged. These reports unanimously cited Hayes as prompting the investigation.

As yet, Hayes would neither confirm nor deny his role in alerting investigators, although NCAA president Walt Byers and Big 10 commissioner Wayne Duke each took the unusual step of swearing that Hayes did not prompt the probe.

Hayes himself had enough concerns regarding his own team. The offensive unit returned two senior co-captains: The third-year starting quarterback Cornelius Greene, and the defending Heisman Trophy winner, tailback Archie Griffin.

Also returning was senior wingback Brian Baschnagel, whom Hayes was pushing to be selected as a Rhodes Scholar. This achievement would be a first for an OSU football player. Baschnagel also was touted by Hayes as his best blocking back ever. Baschnagel had been All-Pennsylvania and All-America in high school, once compiling 450 yards rushing in a single game.

The younger Brian grew up in 17 different neighborhoods due to frequent moves by his family, yet had found his niche at OSU. He tremendously enjoyed his scarlet and gray days, especially, "...now that I know what Woody is all about and what kind of person he is."

The defensive side also featured two senior co-captains, linebacker Ken Kuhn and safety Tim Fox. Beyond both these strong seniors rested plenty of largely unproven talent. Junior defensive tackle Nick Buonamici was the only other returning defensive starter, although junior linebacker Ken (Ed) Thompson had started five '74 contests in relief of the injured Kuhn.

Senior Pat Curto and junior Bob Brudzinski would start at the defensive end spots, while sophomores Aaron Brown and Eddie Beamon would hold down the middle guard and defensive tackle positions, respectively, opposite Buonamici. Beamon stood out in the last-minute 18-17 Rose Bowl defeat, subbing for the injured Pete Cusick, one of the premier defensive tackles in the nation.

Kuhn was finally (almost) healthy at long last. A nagging assortment of injuries plagued him as a sophomore in '73, and in '74 a badly sprained ankle suffered during preseason camp caused him to miss most of the fall workouts. Later that year, a severely separated shoulder led to his five game absence. Though he returned and played, he was constantly in knife-like pain, so surgery was performed immediately following the Rose Bowl.

Regardless of his injuries, Kuhn always played with reckless abandon. "I love football," he enthused. "If I didn't, after all these injuries, I wouldn't be hanging with it." Construction work carrying cement blocks over the summer pared his hefty frame from 245 pounds to a more svelte 228, and the affected shoulder seemed able to handle the rigors of tackling.

Kuhn had a proud heritage of Buckeye ties, beginning with older brother Dick, who started for Woody in the late '60's on the offensive line. Brother-in-law Mark Stier was a Buckeye linebacker from '66-'68, and a Kuhn sister was recently wed to Tim Fox's brother. Ken, a former All-State fullback-linebacker from Louisville, Ohio, enlivened the locker room with wide grins and raucous barks befitting his colorful, fun-loving attitude. Like many free-spirited Buckeyes, Kuhn sported a tattoo, a "Kuhn-Dog" animal immortalizing his nickname.

The secondary was exceedingly green, excluding Fox. Fox exuded lots of leadership, and the newly-married journalism major from Canton (Ohio) Glenwood hurriedly began to merge his secondary mates into a unit. Junior Bruce Ruhl managed to squeeze in 123 hard-hitting minutes in '74, mopping up for Neal Colzie at safety. Ruhl was moving to halfback, to accommodate sophomore Ray Griffin's move from offense to the essential safety position.

Griffin saw little chance to supersede his established older brother Archie at tailback this year, so he agreed to ply his exceptional speed and athletic ability at the absolutely foreign position on the defensive side. The other defensive halfback had Heisman lineage in his blood as well. Howard "Hopalong" Cassady's son Craig was a two-time letterman who had earned the right to start as a senior.

The offense was in a little better shape, largely due to the presence of Greene, Griffin, and Baschnagel. Junior ball-busting fullback Pete Johnson was back as well, hoping to improve on a somewhat disappointing '74 season.

Senior Larry Kain was back at tight end, while outside speedster senior Lenny Willis returned at split end, after a very brief trial as a defensive back. Willis had been a junior college All-American at Fairbury (Nebraska), and was, according to best estimates, the first juco transfer in the Hayes reign.

The line looked to be the largest in sheer bulk and weight in all of Haye's years of coaching. Senior Scott Dannelly drew a starting nod at one tackle, and immense sophomore Chris Ward, an Ohio high school discus champion and the biggest Buck at 274 (a light estimate) pounds, held down the other tackle spot.

The center was senior Rick Applegate, in top shape after a summer painting houses, and the guards returned junior Ted Smith to the starting lineup. Smith began his OSU career as a linebacker, and retained his aggressiveness and extreme intensity. Juniors Ron Ayers, converted from tight end, and Bill Lukens hammered it out to each claim a portion of the remaining guard slot.

Lukens, who aspired to be a veterinarian, had worked with harness horses at a race track all summer, and was eager to improve on the '74 season, in which OSU was second nationally in total offense, averaging 437.6 yards each contest. Interestingly, Lukens' forays into the animal kingdom had produced unexpectedly beneficial results for many Buckeyes.

Lukens discovered that a certain liniment used to treat soreness in racehorses, popularly known as DMSO, also worked uncommonly well on human injuries. A player smeared the ointment on the affected area, be it shoulder, neck, thigh or whatever, and within minutes, the pain and soreness drifted away. Curiously, the application left a strong, repugnant, garlic taste in the mouth, which lingered for hours.

The side effects and future health concerns apparent in using this animal medicine were unknown and, at the time, not considered as important as the more immediate curative powers they contained.

With the overall team starting so many relative youngsters, in terms of playing experience, Hayes was very expectant of generous assistance from a strong freshman recruiting haul. Eighteen of the incoming youngsters had participated in some sort of All-Star tilt, and on sheer looks, the newcomers really stood out. The crop of almost thirty frosh was loaded with lineman and linebackers, as twenty of the class played in those spots in high school.

Tight end Jimmy Moore, a 6'5", 258 pound mass of raw athleticism recently of Tempe, Arizona, was perhaps the first to catch the coaching staff's eye. Reporting in good shape despite putting on around 35 pounds since the end of high school, Moore overcame some slight difficulties with the high humidity to dazzle with his soft hands and crunching drive blocks. Moore was an All-State selection in basketball and had also participated in track and field.

Fellow tight end Bill Jaco, a 6'5", 252 pounder out of Toledo, immediately impressed with his pass catching abilities. Six-foot five-inch, 244 pound Joe Robinson of Paulding, Ohio, lined up at tight end on his first day of practice and voluntarily stayed overtime in the intense heat for some much needed work on his pass catching skills. He had played tackle exclusively for the last three years in high school, and was reacquainting himself with handling the elusive pigskin. Explaining his penchant for the extra work, Robinson stated, "I'm a perfectionist. Besides, I don't like being yelled at."

Rest assured, there was always a lot of yelling at every practice. Stupendously large and equally gifted Doug France, a '74 senior who played brilliantly for OSU at both tight end and tackle, was a recent first round draft pick of the Los Angeles Rams. In an interview for a West Coast newspaper, France related his opinion of the '71-'74 team's sentiments regarding Hayes: "Really, we hated him. But we didn't let that hatred get in the way of winning football games."

France felt the OSU players banded together more closely than at other schools, uniting themselves in a supreme effort to show Hayes they were greater than he thought. France described each and every practice as a brutal war, with the constant fear of Haye's criticisms goading players to heretofore undiscovered heights. France himself found the mood before each game so tense, that it became a ritual for him to vomit twice just prior to a contest.

Though France did not totally agree with the Hayes methods, he did agree that Woody's foreboding, yet supporting presence spurred each player to constantly improve, or risk being trampled over, whether by teammates or occasionally the hyper-aggressive Coach himself.

Several other frosh impressed enough to mostly avoid a critical Hayes diatribe. Rod Gerald, listed at 6'1" and a generous 172 pounds, was a lithe, bony option quarterback from Dallas, Texas, who was immediately hailed as perhaps the quickest, shiftiest player ever at OSU.

Linebacker Tom Cousineau, out of Lakewood St. Edwards in Cleveland, Ohio, had recently starred in the Ohio-Pennsylvania battle of prep All-Stars. The 6'3", 225 pound piece of sculpted muscle drew notice for his work habits, exquisite conditioning, reckless joy for the game, and curly long hair which hung a good half foot beyond his helmet.

Fellow linebacker Richard Brown of Columbus (Ohio) Eastmoor lost 12 pounds in his first sweltering OSU practice, showing flashes of the play which made the All-State selection a standout in the just-played Ohio All-Star game in Ohio Stadium. Both Brown and Cousineau drew extended practice reps at the relatively thin linebacker corps, and Hayes liked what he saw.

Eventually, Brown's playing time tailed off, while Cousineau's took off. Such were the divergent paths of many prep stars once entering the collegiate big-time.

In one of his first public speeches of the season, Hayes spoke of the modern-day penchant for finding fault in public figures, insinuating that this predilection compounded the ouster of his personal acquaintance, the recently impeached Richard Nixon. "We've torn down all our heroes except Lincoln," Hayes lamented, and offered a new hero worthy of anyone's standards. Archie Griffin "...epitomizes everything that is fine in football," Hayes repeatedly gushed about this extraordinary player.

Griffin did seem virtually too good to be true, in an era when sporting and public heroes most often melted under the harsh glare of public scrutiny. Archie left the initial press photo session of the year, despite his obvious status as the most popular Buckeye and returning national player of the year, to attend an eleven a.m. class he refused to reschedule or miss. Griffin's older brother Daryle had received his degree from Kent State in less than the prescribed four years while playing football, and Archie wished to achieve the same feat.

To accomplish this, Archie took additional summer courses, while also doing extensive work with the Police Athletic League and their (mostly) elementary age student participants. Archie of course also kept his rock-hard conditioning work up, and bolstered his public speaking skills by taking every opportunity to especially address and impress young children.

With the addition of the freshman Duncan, there were now three Griffins playing for Ohio State. Duncan was a 5'11", 182 pound bundle of typical Griffin muscle. The hard-hitting defensive back out of Columbus Eastmoor was not as fast as brother Ray, who had turned in a 9.7 100 (yard) over the summer at a Dayton, Ohio, track meet, yet he could really lay the hurt on anyone venturing into his area. Duncan had been a standout linebacker as a prepster, though due to his undersized frame and quickness in getting to the ball, the OSU coaching staff soon converted him into a member of the secondary.

Fellow defensive back, sophomore Joe Allegro, drew attention for nailing the elusive Archie in the open field on several occasions early in fall practices.

Though not a name that showed up in the line score too often, senior backup tailback Woodrow Roach really pushed Archie to continually perform at his best each and every day. Roach intrinsically contributed immeasurably to OSU's offensive excellence in this manner, as did innumerable Buckeye reserves whose worth was proven on the practice field, if not in the games.

Equally underrated was converted tackle Greg Storer, a sophomore turning heads with his play at tight end. Incidentally, Storer and Mark Lang, a reserve defensive lineman for the Bucks, were the latest in a long line of prep standouts from Cincinnati (Ohio) Moeller, coached by the phenomenally successful Gerry Faust.

Fortunately, at this early part of the year OSU was blessed by a healthy lack of major injuries. Pete Johnson was battling a sore neck, though the massive one continued to hammer away in practice. Kuhn was fighting back courageously from his '74 knee injury, compounded by lingering soreness in his shoulder, brought on by a frightening summer water-skiing spill.

One major injury was to junior defensive end Don Coburn, who was apparently out for the year with a severe neck injury. Also apparently gone for the season was Dublin, Ohio, product sophomore linebacker Charles Simon.

Simon, who steadily rose to second team status, and performed as if a first-teamer, in early '74, nearly lost his life when complications set in after knee surgery in the fall of that year. Knee surgery at the time was not the tidy, somewhat convenient procedure it has gradually evolved into, and complete recovery, even without complications, was doubtful at best. Due to his additionally harrowing burden, Simon was not cleared for any contact in '75.

Eventually, Simon returned to the team, though his ability to pursue and generate momentum for a powerful tackle never bounced back after his layoff. Converted to the offensive line, regretfully, Simon's days of lettering were over. His unfortunate injury felled a very promising career. Several former teammates swear that the driven Simon would have made OSU fans forget about Randy Gradishar, had the aggressive 'backer not been stricken with his run of bad luck.

Other bad news in late August centered around a brand new National Collegiate Athletic Association mandate limiting home teams to a maximum of 60 players permitted to suit up each game, although 95 players per program were allowed to hold scholarships. More severely, only 48 players would now be allowed to make the journey to away games, meaning at least half of every team would have to stay at home, despite laying their time and efforts on the line all week in practices.

Amidst the uproar over this hotly contested legislation, the voice of Hayes boomed loudly and sharply. He downgraded the rule as extremely "foolhardy and silly," and hotly predicted that the move would backfire in terms of team morale. Particularly affected were non-scholarship walk-ons, who largely played in return for a chance to dress on game days.

Buckeye walk-ons still not on scholarship in '75 included Scott Wolery, a pre-med student playing safety; Todd Alles, a 27-year-old former Navy man (like Hayes) and a father of two; and Clarence Perry, who had dressed for home games each of the last three years.

Perry, a possessor of incredible defensive lineman talents, seemed every bit the player those ahead of him in the depth chart were considered. Yet, as shall be demonstrated time and time again in the case of numerous Buckeyes, he was forever relegated to a supporting cast status, no matter how well he performed in practices.

Needless to say, each of these unacclaimed parts of the Buckeye machine, plus so many others, were greatly discouraged by this new legislation. Each of the walk-ons mentioned above vowed their resolve to improve and earn the richly restricted right to wear the scarlet and gray in front of loyal home fans, regardless of the stringent new law. Hayes railed at the mandate, protesting that the volunteers such as Alles gained nothing and lost much, being adversely punished for no apparent reason.

A fellow voice in complaining about this NCAA law was former All-Big Ten Buckeye end Sid Gillman, who began his own estimable coaching career by serving four years as an assistant to legendary OSU coach Francis Schmidt. Gillman was a fierce sort, who once stated, "You know what football is to me? It's blood"; Schmidt proved a decisive, more intellectual influence on the excitable Sid. Perhaps to even a greater extent than Woody, Schmidt spent a lifetime possessed by football.

Stories abound concerning his singleminded devotion, including the time Schmidt drove his car to a mechanic and crawled into the back seat to diagram plays. As he temporarily finished his creations, Schmidt stepped out of his car, unaware that it had since been hoisted many feet above ground, while the mechanic tinkered underneath. After a rude fall into the already grease-splattered bay, the unruffled Schmidt retrieved his notes and resumed his work, this time in the waiting room.

According to Gillman, who had since worked with literally dozens of successful coaches at both collegiate and professional levels, Schmidt was, "The greatest football mind I've ever known." To his lasting detriment, Schmidt was so enamored of offense (he was credited with being the originator of multiple offenses utilized interchangeably during the same game) that he usually neglected the defensive aspect of the game.

Francis was eventually driven from Columbus for allowing teams, most damagingly Michigan, to run up scores of points and for failing to maintain adequate morale on his own team. Still, Gillman resolutely contended that had Schmidt cared even slightly more about defense, he would have coached at OSU for another 30-40 years. Gillman also pointed out these years would have been far more controversial and stormy than even the Hayes reign had proven, given Schmidt's uncommon feistiness.

The big happening in the vicinity of Columbus, prior to the start of this '75 football season, was the initial public unveiling of the one and a-half year old Muirfield Village Golf course, which was the brainchild of former OSU golfer Jack Nicklaus.

Hot on the heels of his amazing 16th major victory, captured in Akron, Ohio, at the Professional Golfers Association namesake tournament, Nicklaus hosted a Pro-Am tourney in Dublin, Ohio. This was the initial chance for most touring pros and prominent local citizens to play the universally acclaimed course. In a manner befitting almost all future professional events at the Muirfield course, it rained heavily on opening day.

On hand for the unveiling was fellow OSU alumnus and successful pro golfer Tom Weiskopf, who actually visited Hayes during this time, for advice on controlling his own, often out-of-bounds, temper. It seems Weiskopf admired the way Hayes was able to significantly rein in his own nasty outbursts, and of course Hayes eagerly counseled a fellow Buckeye.

Tennis star Stan Smith, a one-time USC student, also in town at this time for a Buckeye Classic Tournament, was equally enamored with Hayes. Smith heard a typically loquacious Hayes speech, which weaved patriotism and nationalism into a stirring oratory, and instantly became a convert to the W.W.H. train of thought. Smith readily admitted press clippings from West Coast newspapers did not prepare him for the in-person impact and persuasiveness of Hayes.

Just as outstanding was the OSU stable of kickers. Senior Tom Klaban, who booted the four field goals which proved the difference in OSU's heartwrenching 12-10 '74 squeaker over Michigan, was back to provide more heroics. Klaban, who was born in Czechoslovakia, had tied for the national lead among placekickers in '74 with 79 points, all the while not missing an extra point. Tom had recently visited Green Bay Packer kicking star Chester Marcol's kicking school, and seemed to be kicking with even more power and precision than in previous years.

Junior punter and kickoff specialist Tom Skladany also returned from '74, defending his national punting title. Skladany averaged an astonishing 46.6 yards each time he punted. By comparison, the NFL's leading punter, Oakland Raider All-Pro Ray Guy, averaged 42.2. Most astonishingly, the curly-headed striker's 31 punts were returned for a measly 78 yards, debunking the myth that Tom would "outkick" his coverage.

As a frosh, Skladany had some adjustment difficulties with the length of his kicks, averaging only 35.7 yards. Yet, his kicks were so high and hung for so long, that 37 punts were returned for an amazingly low 25 yards. Skladany really excelled in kickoffs as well. The smiling junior recalled that out of 80 kickoffs in '74, only 39 were returned. The majority of the rest sailed over and out of the end zone. George Hill, who doubled as special teams coach, surmised that only former OSU tackle and placekicker Lou Groza was a better kickoff performer.

Just as pleasing to Hayes was the fact that Skladany led all Buck coverage men in '74 tackles, with seven solo shots and an amazing 16 assists, providing a lot more than last-gasp containment. Skladany frequently was among the first Buckeyes to collide with the ballcarrier, and took great pride in showing off his athletic skills with an unexpected stick.

Senior Mike Keeton held the unenviable position of being the backup punter. According to Hayes, Keeton would perhaps be the best punter in the nation, if not for Skladany. "I doubt if anybody ever had two better ones," Hayes thought, and Keeton was slightly better in the occasional left-footed kicking contests which enlivened practice sidelines.

In '73, Skladany was apparently deliberately clipped from behind on a kickoff and broke his leg against Michigan. So, Keeton stepped up to average 41 yards on his two boots during the Buckeye Rose Bowl triumph.

One of Haye's few gripes at this early point in the year was the fact that Corny Greene, Craig Cassady and Ray Griffin were each, by the exacting estimation of Woody, too skinny, underweight, and undersized to stand up to the grinding, rigorous season. Each of the three tried valiantly to pack on additional muscular pounds, but the task was complicated by typically scorching 90 degree midwestern heat, which burned off any surplus pounds.

Judged as already beefy enough, freshman twin brothers Terry and Tim Vogler, the first pair of twins ever recruited by Hayes, drew many looks in practice. Terry was a rampaging linebacker, while Tim was a rough-hewn, rugged fullback. Sophomore defensive end Marty Cusick, sibling to departed strongman Pete Cusick, injured his knee in one of the few serious injuries of the pre-season camp.

Equally isolated was the solitary tailback among the recruited freshman. Les Gordon, a prep All-American out of New Rochelle, New York, was very impressive, though the talent at tailback was obviously so deep as to preclude much hope for any regular season action on his behalf.

As a result, after months and months of solely scout team action, Gordon asserted his considerable talents by deliberately changing assigned carry routes, successfully breaking long runs in the process, yet instantly drawing the vengeful wrath of Hayes, for altering the confines of the designed play. The purpose of the scout team offense was to prepare the defense for an upcoming opponent, so Gordon's undesigned creativity also invoked the considerable anger of defensive coordinator George Hill.

Deep talent at OSU had been a given at offensive tackle since at least '62. The litany of All-Americans started that year with the terrific tandem of Bob Vogel and Darryl Sanders, and continued unabated through James Davidson (All-American honors '64); Doug Van Horn (All-American honors '65); Dave

Foley and Rufus Mayes (each taking All-American nods in '68); to John Hicks (All-American recognition in 72-73, gaining third place in Heisman balloting as well in '73).

Less universally recognized names during this time, yet still masters at their craft, included Jim Tyrer, Mike Current, Dick Himes, and Doug France, who also starred at tight end his sophomore and junior years. The latest standout in this line of traditional distinction appeared to be senior Scott Dannelly.

Line coach Ralph Staub felt the 6'3", 255 pound Pennsylvanian could capably ascend to the level of his predecessors, after a career previously slowed by injuries and the wealth of considerable talent ahead of Scott. Dannelly missed nine games with various ailments in '72, saw limited action behind Hicks in '73, and played solidly as the right tackle in '74. In '75, all estimates pointed to the consistent Dannellys' further improvement into the sphere of the nation's elite. As a sign of his own seriousness and high expectations, Dannelly sheared his previously-long blond locks in preparation for a blockbuster campaign.

Hot on the heels in the rising star category was sophomore left tackle Chris Ward, who needed just a little seasoning before assuming the mantle of star. The huge youngster out of Dayton, Ohio, possessed all the tools, including foot speed, prodigious bulk, and a Herculean work ethic.

Defensive line coach Chuck Clausen had also seen his share of outstanding tackles during his five year tenure at OSU. In '74, Pete Cusick was OSU's first All-American defensive lineman since '58, when the untiring Jim Marshall captured said honors. Cusick had taken his bull-like strength and high tolerance for pain to the NFL, leaving a large void. Clausen also coached George Hasenohrl, who was still succeeding with the New York Giants. Hasenohrl was best recalled for his heroics in several Michigan games.

In '75, Nick Buonamici returned as a starter, ably carrying on the tradition of strong, overpowering, one-on-one bullrushers. The 6'3", 244 pounder had a knack for the spectacular pass rush, while also performing his run protection duties more than capably. Still just 19 years old, Buonamici was perhaps the youngest player ever to perform in a Rose Bowl, being all of 17 on January 1, '74.

Buonamici was not the perfect football specimen on paper, being somewhat slow, undersized, and often sporting some sort of a beer gut. On the playing field, however, Nick was relentless, unbelievably tough, and far exceeded his anticipated abilities.

Also returning at tackle, this time as a starter, was the quick, 6'2", 248 pound sophomore Eddie Beamon, who was really being challenged by Columbus (Ohio) Mifflin product Tyrone Harris. Tyrone was probably the fastest of the tackles, possessing extremely strong legs. Jim O'Rourke, from Brooklyn, New York, was a tough kid who also looked to contend for some playing time.

Freshman Byron Cato showed every indication of one day supplanting Cusick's feats. Cato had a burning desire to be the best defensive lineman in OSU history, and his 6'2", 238 pound frame and equally bountiful abilities certainly seemed capable of achieving that monumental task. Cato was a prep All-American from Lorain, Ohio, and he inherited the #71 so proudly worn by Cusick.

Another frosh lineman wreaking considerable havoc in early drills was New Bedford, Massachusetts, prep All-American Mark Sullivan. This 6'4", 238 pounder was relentless and explosive.

The talk of most early drills, though, remained Jimmy Moore, whose spectacular catches and piledriving blocks wowed everyone, including Hayes. Originally from Pittsburgh, Pennsylvania, Moore was a high school baseball teammate and buddy of sophomore Buckeye guard Darryl Weston. Weston exerted considerable influence in getting Moore recruited out of the often-overlooked football area of the Arizona deserts.

Fellow freshman Tom Taylor was an unwilling recipient of much attention when he was drilled and knocked out by Ray Griffin in an early-season drill.

A slightly more willing recipient of vast public notice was Hayes. Woody was feted in late August by nearly 1000 admirers, with an equal number turned away for lack of space. The salute began with a personal message from the President of the United States, Gerald Ford.

An ex-Michigan football player, Ford allowed how happy his playing days at Michigan were, since he played prior to Hayes' arrival at OSU. The Wolverines captured two consecutive victories over OSU during the President's undergrad days, a feat rarely achieved since the debut of Woody, as the President graciously conceded.

Beyond the many victories on the playing surface, Ford touched upon the true value and essence of the Hayes mystique, saying, "Woody, you have a wonderful capability to develop playing talent but more importantly, you inspire young men to achieve... not only on the field...[but] with life."

In that one sentence, Ford captured the greatest extent of the Coach's success: Football victories led to greater triumphs in life, if the lessons learned in the sport were applied beyond the playing field.

The above statement also encompasses the Hayes philosophy that Woody's beloved author, Ralph Waldo Emerson, so eloquently wrote of. "The indignation which arms itself with secret forces does not awaken until we are pricked and stung and sorely assailed," thought Emerson. Likewise, Hayes never chose the easy path in life, and he believed each defeat or disappointment always led to new victories. Woody lived aggressively, attacking life and bending it to his fierce will, habitually rising from the ashes of despair to greater heights than before.

Such were the principles and values Hayes taught, such as this stolid resiliency, they often never left his players. Bill Hess, longtime Ohio

University head coach and former Hayes assistant at OSU, postulated, "We're better men because we were with you." Many in the audience silently seconded that affirmation.

The ultimate Hayes legacy was in the lives his players and coaches went on to lead, with Woody serving both as guiding light and empowering motivator. (This is a concept more elaborately discussed by Woody and Paul Hornung in *You Win With People*.) The true love and respect that most of his former colleagues, players, and acquaintances felt for the Coach was highly evident on this evening. As fellow head coach Joe Paterno stated, a similar intention of Hayes was for his players, "... to [respect] me when it hits them what I've been saying all these years."

This is a common realization of many who endured the Hayes coaching style: When one is removed, both in time and maturity, from the follies of youth, it dons on the former player, "...Woody was right." Hayes was obviously extremely pleased and visibly touched by such a rare outpouring of public affection and thanks.

That night was not all teary-eyed and maudlin. Ken Kuhn told what he insisted was a true story, to much laughter and incredulous looks. It seems the Buckeyes had just conducted a practice, held under extremely threatening weather conditions. Despite the fearful threat of a storm, not a single drop of rain, clap of thunder, or peal of lightning was evident during practice.

As the team finished and ran off the field, the elements immediately unleashed in a vengeful torrent of rain, thunder, and godawful lightning. Kuhn happened to look over at Hayes as the squad ran off the field. Woody looked up to the heavens, winked, smiled, and mouthed "thanks" (almost this same tale was told in Jack Tatum's *They Call Me Assassin*). The fact that many of those influenced by Woody swear by the authenticity of this sort of tale speaks volumes about the Woody persona.

As the week of the MSU tilt approached, more freshmen stood above the crowd. Outside linebacker-defensive end Kelton Dansler, at age 19 the eldest in his class, began to assert his quickness and explosiveness. Though slightly undersized at 6'2" and barely 200 pounds, Kelton had been an outstanding fullback in high school.

Dansler improved rapidly as he acquainted himself with the complex, as compared to high school, defensive schemes. The Warren Harding (Ohio) graduate exhibited a penetrating pass rush and a pronounced knack for the big play. Scant days before the opening game, however, Dansler strained a knee.

Classmate Tim Burke, a burly lineman out of tiny Wapakoneta, Ohio, also hurt his knee and would miss at least ten days of contact. His knee troubles unfortunately followed him throughout his Buckeye career.

Joe Garcia, a 6'0", 218 pound linebacker culled from the sands of La Palma, California, showed some flashes of awesome potential.

Under the capable tutelage of new graduate assistants (and former OSU quarterbacks) Dave Purdy and Steve Morrison, the Bucks built to a fever pitch as game day drew closer. Former Buckeye tight end Mike Bartoszek also joined the grad assistant ranks, rejoining his former teammates after each of the three tried unsuccessfully to latch on with an NFL team.

The secondary in particular improved as the days of pre-season practice dwindled. The unit assimilated newcomers Griffin and frosh Leonard Mills into the fold. Mills was a speedy, helmet-popping 6'3", 189 pound converted middle linebacker out of Miami, Florida. The frosh was fresh off a summer living with the extremely popular Corny Greene, who never lacked for female company.

Interestingly, Mills and classmate Duncan Griffin had seen each other virtually every day at their respective places of employment in Columbus over the summer, yet never realized they soon would join forces and contend for playing time, until the first indoctrination meeting of the fall.

The evolving unit gained added depth as Tom Roche filled in for Cassady, who was slowed by a slight muscle pull.

A former Buckeye defensive back made headlines this week with his entry into the NFL. Tim Anderson was perhaps the original first round draft choice to eschew the NFL and opt for the Canadian Football League, way back in '71. Anderson's unusual move paved the way for the '72 Heisman winner, Nebraska's Johnny Rodgers, to receive big bucks for his similar decision to play up north several years later, along with Notre Dame quarterback Tom Clements, among scores of others who defected to the Canadian league.

Of course, Tom Cousineau, at this time just days away from his initial action as a Buckeye, later became the very first number one pick to choose the CFL.

Hayes was very pleased by his fullbacks at this stage as well. Junior Pete Johnson was in the best shape of his career, even allowing for his mild neck sprain. He careened madly over defenders in the first full-contact scrimmage of the fall to rack up four touchdowns. Back-up surprises were Bob Robertson and the superb blocker, Lou Williott. Sophomore Doug Bargerstock switched his sturdy 6'1", 239 pound frame from tackle to fullback and sent shock waves through unsuspecting tacklers.

Bargerstock was one of those rough, crazy-looking sorts who appear much older than they actually are. His stunning muscle maturity, foreboding air, and intimidating fu manchu facial hair contributed mightily to his menacing appearance.

In another position scramble, Jim Savoca and Cousineau continued to make strides at inside linebacker. With Simon out, Cousineau and Savoca battled for a backup slot, with the frosh earning a slight advantage over the intense sophomore.

As the brutal full contact work increased, virtually every running back was nursing a variety of nicks and bruises. Archie was banged up, per usual, as the hitting took a dreadful toll on the magnificent one's body. The pain and discomfort did not deter him from his goal of early graduation, however, as Archie hobbled to class no matter how much pain he was in.

Griffin also was a keynote speaker at the Hayes tribute, discussed previously. With humorous hints from former Buckeye fullback-kick returner-punter Tom Barrington, Archie now came off as a charming, articulate public speaker. The growth of Archie in this public capacity since his frosh year was nothing short of phenomenal.

Hayes showed off his own immense oratorical skills during a touching Buckeye Golf Association tribute to desperately ill long-time *Columbus Dispatch* photographer and central Ohio golf enthusiast Bill Foley. Despite his torrential flow of words that night, Hayes insisted "...the less talking and more listening I do, the more I learn." As former Notre Dame coach Knute Rockne proclaimed, "...if a coach talks too much, his words lose weight."

Later in this week Hayes met with the Skywriters, a conglomerate of roving midwestern sports scribes whose primary focus was Big 10 football. Under direct questioning, Hayes denied that he was tiring of his role as the elder statesman in the league. Hayes had been the senior coach in the loop since Ray Eliot retired from Illinois in '59.

Woody was also asked about retirement. His only response was an emphatic, "I'll retire at the end of a year," rather than announce his intentions prior to a season, which had been rumored about '75. Scribes theorized this early announcement might cunningly psych up his team even more than normal.

In some of the very best early-season scrimmages in Woody's memory, Gerald looked masterful. Greene sat out some of the brutal contact sessions, nursing a sore shoulder, so Gerald bore the brunt of an eager first team defense, as junior Jim Pacenta assumed the top spot. Gerald drilled passes and made numerous quick runs, bounding up instantly from a number of jarring tackles. After one especially ferocious lick from Pat Curto, Rod leaped up unaffected and smiled broadly for all to see. For a thoughtful English major, Curto really packed a wallop.

Gerald also impersonated MSU quarterback Charlie Baggett for the benefit of the defense, as Hayes stationed numerous loudspeakers on the sidelines to blare out simulated crowd noise. At MSU practices, walk-on tailback Nick Rollick assumed his impossible scout team task of imitating Archie.

The MSU Spartans expected to cram more than 80,000 people into their stands for this opening day battle. Additionally, the largest media contingent seen in East Lansing since their '66 clash with Notre Dame would be on hand. The game was not being televised, though ABC's *Wide World of Sports* promised to showcase all highlights later in the afternoon. The Spartan squad was led by supersonic fullback Levi Jackson, whose stunning 88 yard touchdown run provided the shocking margin of victory in MSU's upset of the Buckeyes in '74.

The aforementioned Baggett had assumed the titles of quarterback extraordinaire and team mouthpiece since transferring from North Carolina, where he was miscast as a tight end. Baggett was widely quoted in the several days leading to the showdown, brazenly predicting an easy Spartan blowout. Baggett supposedly felt that OSU, particularly the secondary, was too young and inexperienced to deal with the pumped-up East Lansing denizens. Spartan head coach Denny Stolz even boldly indicated Baggett would account for two or three touchdowns in the contest.

Most prognosticators felt the game would determine at least a co-champion of the conference, with the victor joining Michigan at the helm. By most accounts, momentum and recent history favored the home team, for the Spartans had won three of the last four times OSU visited, including the ill-fated '74 trip.

As an indication of the importance placed on this game, even mild-mannered Archie Griffin noted the vengeance and atonement opportunities this game presented, to partly make up for the '74 upset. Addressing the Buckeye booster organization Quarterback Club's opening dinner, Archie pointed out that OSU had concentrated solely on the Spartans in each practice, unlike previous years when Michigan occupied many pre-season hours. Griffin personified the steely, classy determination each Buckeye brought to the confrontation. Every member of the OSU program burned with the all-consuming desire to begin the '75 season on a winning note.

As Saturday approached, Hayes eased off in his workout demands. He eased up so much, OSU enjoyed perhaps the lightest practices ever for a Hayes team. Hayes began his so-called "fresh legs" system in '73, whereby at the tail end of the week physical work tapered off drastically in an effort to stave off fatigue and the state of over-training.

The highlight of the week came as nine freshmen were selected to make the road trip. The list of eligible frosh was topped by Moore, Mills, and Cousineau. The announcing of their selection was quintessential Hayes: Woody gathered the nine recipients together at the training table during breakfast, notified the nervous frosh of their traveling status, then made each youngster say, "Thank you, Woody," for allowing this privilege.

Of course, this respectful custom was foreshadowed in the very first organized meeting Hayes ever had with all of his '75 recruits. Woody opened the initial freshmen orientation with the phrase, "Just remember. I don't have to get along with you. You have to get along with me." Instantly, the frosh were aware of their status.

This welcoming speech was a little removed from the previous year's initial meeting. Hayes walked into the room, faced his nervous '74 freshmen, and remarked, "Make sure you do the thinking with this head (pointing to his cranium), and not with this head (gesturing beneath his belt)." With that, Woody turned and walked out of the room.

The new recruits initially thought the Old Man had gone nuts; at the end of their playing days, they realized just how wise this advice was. Recall, this was the era of the sexual revolution, and the temptations available to energetic, randy young men, many of them away from the confines of their parents for the first time, were plentiful.

As with many pronouncements from Woody, the initial impact of his statements often eluded the players. With time, however, and repeated emphasis, the intended message usually sunk in, almost imperceptibly. Hayes often spoke in generalized cliches to his players; the catch being, like his close friend Vince Lombardi said, "In coaching, you speak in cliches. But I mean every one of them."

Woody did possess a grand plan for his boys to live by, even if some of that plan's nuances, at first, seemed odd and offbeat. Hayes was a master at the change of direction in utilizing psychological methods on his team, who often were not aware of these methods until well after their playing days were done.

Unquestionably, though, with the eventual class of '78's unrestrained enthusiasm as an indication, OSU seemed visibly primed for the second straight journey to the unfriendly confines of East Lansing.

CHAPTER TWO: MICHIGAN STATE

Come Saturday, an unexpectedly polite MSU record crowd of 80,383 sat mostly silent through a largely listless first quarter. By contrast, on Friday night the Buckeye's motel was not nearly so quiet.

For several uncomfortable hours, until shortly past midnight, while the OSU team was tucked away in their rooms for the night, an MSU partisan disc jockey blared obnoxiously loud music in an effort to disturb the visitors slumber. There seems little doubt that Hayes was not lax in his protests, though it is doubtful that any Buckeye could have slept in their keyed-up state, regardless.

Lack of sleep or not, the young OSU defensive line badgered Baggett all next day, preventing the braggadocios signalcaller from ever establishing a successful rhythm. Craig Cassady became a hero in his very first start, picking off three Baggett passes. Oddly enough, secondary coach Dick Walker privately predicted this feat, just prior to kickoff. Two of the interceptions occurred in the critical opening minutes of the game, when each side was desperately fighting for field position. The Bucks battled a stiff headwind the entire first quarter, and the murky, moist field afforded poor footing for both side's running games.

The Buckeye offense finally got into gear late in the second quarter. OSU drove down the field on the fresh legs of Greene and Griffin, with help from a pass interference call against MSU which negated a disappointing third down incompletion. With 1:16 left in the half, Johnson jarred in from four yards out for the initial score of the year.

Though the Spartans were trailing by only seven at the half, the home crowd exhibited little of their usual crazy behavior which prompted each OSU coach not only to pack a batting helmet for sideline protection, plus to administer strict admonitions for each player not to remove his helmet while on the sideline. Gladly, neither precaution proved necessary.

Following the intermission, the OSU defenders continued to dog the big-play Spartan offense. Jackson never did break free, totaling a sparse 58 yards on 20 attempts. MSU's offense was virtually throttled throughout, held to 80 yards rushing and a mere 93 yards through the air. Baggett was continually haunted by the rampaging defensive front, and Cassady completed his troika of interceptions, squelching what little hope MSU had for a miraculous comeback.

The Michigan State defense, led by the esteemed front line of middle guard Kim Rowekamp, end Otto Smith, and tackles Larry Bethea and Greg Schaum, eventually wore down under the quick battering ram thrusts of the OSU line and backfield. Softened up by an increasingly effective Buckeye running game, the Spartans yielded a big passing play on a third and nine situation, late in the third quarter. Lenny Willis ran behind the secondary to make a spectacular snag of Greene's long pass, resulting in a 64 yard touchdown which considerably disheartened MSU.

Most of the Spartan fans filed silently out of the stadium a few minutes later, when Johnson capped a short march with a six yard touchdown burst. This fourth quarter score made the final a resounding 21-0. Three missed field goals by Tom Klaban were the sole blights to the OSU ledger.

Afterwards, Stolz and Baggett were surprisingly calm. Each claimed that this was the hardest-hitting, yet cleanest contest either had seen. Both admitted the game was veritably one-sided; almost a total domination on behalf of the Buckeyes. Hayes said simply, "This team plays like a typical Ohio State team." Prodded as to whether he had gained a modicum of revenge for the stunning '74 defeat, Hayes succinctly whispered, "...better to just be happy and let it go at that."

Hayes was especially proud of Greene, who was just now rounding into form following his earlier shoulder soreness and a recently revealed summertime clash with an ulcer. Cornelius finished with 12 carries for 48 yards, and struck on three of his seven pass attempts for 85 yards, including the backbreaking blow to Willis.

Later, in film reviews of the game, it was discovered that Greene so discombobulated one Spartan on an option keeper that the unfortunate MSU player crumpled to the ground, untouched, with a slightly fractured leg. Such was the elusiveness of Corny.

Johnson bulldozed his way for 69 yards on just eleven attempts, while Griffin weathered a harsh pounding to total 108 yards on 28 crunching carries. Defensively, middle guard Aaron Brown, along with Kuhn, Buonamici, and Beamon, sealed off the rushing lanes and pressured Baggett into his tide-turning interceptions. Beamon sliced and charged for three stops behind the line of scrimmage, spearheading the shutout of the explosive offense.

Following a day off for film review, Hayes proudly quoted English author William Wordsworth: "The old order changeth... give way to the new order..."; Hayes then threw in his own pointed addendum: "Well, the old order hasn't changeth yet!" Michigan State, thought to be an ascender to the league throne, was resoundingly shouted down as a pretender in an emphatic opening performance by Ohio State.

On Monday, Joe Falls, an acerbically-witted columnist for the *Detroit Free Press*, likened Hayes to Santa Claus. In his sarcastic article, MSU was characterized as an expectant child on Christmas morning, waiting for Hayes to giftwrap a Spartan victory. Falls concluded the column with this line: "When the fat man came down the chimney, he spat in their faces." No one ever put a game description so bluntly.

The big story emerging from the game was the shocking brilliance of Craig Cassady. The son of the legendary Heisman winner had endured three painful years of waiting for his opportunity at fame. A slender 5'11", 158 pound halfback-safety coming out of Columbus (Ohio) Whetstone, Cassady was not highly recruited, despite his All-City and All-District honors.

Finally, Hayes tendered a scholarship offer, yet Craig did not play at all as a frosh and was even briefly switched to split end. Appearing in four games the next season, Craig was mostly limited to special teams action. His sole moment of glory that year, '73, came on a flashy 38 yard punt return. As a junior, he effectively backed up Neal Colzie, garnering most of his game action in the waning minutes of blowout victories. Currently the third fastest player on the team, trailing only Willis and Ray Griffin, Cassady made an astonishing starting debut.

The history major, not surprisingly, admitted to more than a few marathon chats with his Coach concerning that mutual field of interest. (Each Buckeye spent mandatory time at a study table, practically nightly, during the season, and if one was studying history, a particular passion of Woodys', then the Coach often spent several hours in instructing far beyond the usual lesson plan). Amazingly, Craig almost elected to play only baseball for OSU in '75, deciding just before spring practice he was not yet ready to give up the gridiron sport.

So as not to impinge, Craig's illustrious father stayed out of his son's new limelight, trying to deflect as much attention from himself as possible while still providing behind-the-scenes support. Craig was proudly festooned with eight Buckeye leaves for his MSU heroics, while Beamon captured 8.5 for his outstanding play.

Though rightfully proud of the performance at MSU, Hayes tenaciously combated the normal tendency to relax following a big win. With the always-tough Penn State Nittany Lions coming to Ohio Stadium, Hayes ended his nice-guy persona on Monday. He summarily blistered his charges in preparation for the pride of College Station.

On Tuesday, Hayes increased the intensity even further. Woody considered Tuesday practices to be the most important of any week. Tuesday was early in the week, and allowed for adaptation to specific game plans and the timely correction of any apparent faults.

Alex Gibbs, newly arrived from West Virginia's Mountaineer football program, was in charge of the Buckeye centers and other offensive linemen. He readied his charges for a typically staunch Lion defense, led by the usual strong contingent of linebackers. This year's featured performer was Greg Buttle, an intelligent, 6'3", 228 pound, extremely mean middle linebacker.

Gibbs was assisted in his preparations by former Buckeye Dick Mack, who worked practice sessions around his grueling schedule of law school courses. Mack came from a very athletic family: His father Ray played second base with the Cleveland Indians, forming a wicked double-play combination with Lou

Boudreau, while brother Tom was an All-Pro offensive lineman with the L.A. Rams.

Injuries from the MSU tilt were slight, particularly considering the ferocity of the contact. Greene was on the mend from a slight concussion, and Dannelly persevered through a sprained neck. Cousineau continued to improve at linebacker, with his betterment pushing starter Ed Thompson's play to greater heights as well. Cousineau saw extensive kickoff coverage action at East Lansing, playing well. It seemed the longer Tom's hair grew, the better he played.

Surprisingly, in this era of longish hair and outlandish afros, Hayes contended, "If they can get it inside their helmets, they can wear it," and Woody refrained from placing restrictions upon facial hair. Hayes believed in ruling via attitudes, rather than by long lists of rules.

As always, Penn State featured a dominating offensive line, so OSU would need plenty of improvement from all parties to counterattack. Lion lineman Tom Rafferty was one of the best in the country. The startlingly quick 6'3", 238 pound Rafferty paved the way on running plays and ably protected quarterback John Andress.

Penn State utilized both the I and wing T formations, but would be somewhat limited offensively without the mercurial talents of sophomore wingback Jimmy Cefalo, still out of action with a broken thumb.

His replacement, Tom Donovan, rushed for 113 yards on ten carries in a 34-14 win over the Stanford Cardinal's. (The Lions had also eclipsed the Temple Owls by the narrow margin of 26-25, giving them one more game under their belt than OSU had.) Interestingly, Donovan's older brother Brian was a former Buckeye. The 6'1", 181 pound Tom eagerly looked forward to beating his brother's old school.

Penn State head coach Joe Paterno rightfully felt a defeat of OSU would catapult his team into national title contention. In four previous meetings, Penn State had never lost to Ohio State, and all four games had been played in Columbus.

Perhaps the most shocking PSU victory came in '64. The unbeaten and second ranked Buckeyes lost to a Penn State squad saddled with an ignominious four defeats. Paterno was the offensive coordinator for that Lion team, serving under the legendary Rip Engle, who guided the Lions to a 104-48-4 record between '50-'65.

Upon Engle's retirement, Paterno assumed the controls, continuing and actually improving the strong program. Paterno's record was a sterling 87-15-1, and Penn State was only a heartbeat away from being arguably the finest program in the country. Paterno felt one decisive strength of his '75 team was his slight-statured soccer style kicker, the wondrous Chris Bahr.

Bahr was the '75 National American Soccer League Rookie of the Year, and was equally talented at placekicking. Bahr had a 55 yard field goal to his credit, and his range and accuracy were unparalleled in all of college football.

As was the norm for Paterno teams, the Lions personified the term student-athletes. Indeed, the Lions would not arrive in Columbus until 7:30 p.m. Friday night, so as not to interfere with their normal class schedule.

Despite a deserved reputation as a masterful recruiter, Paterno somehow had neglected to court the favor of Aaron Brown. Brown grew up in Warren, Ohio, near the Pennsylvania state line, with a strong desire to play at Penn State, but was never recruited by his desired school. Reluctantly, Brown changed gears, ending up with a full ride to OSU.

Once in Columbus, the muscular Brown hoped to play linebacker, but changing needs of the personnel situations prompted the coaching staff to test him at a down lineman position. Placed in the middle, Brown flourished. Coach Hayes felt most adamantly, "Self-satisfied people never go very far," and Brown maintained a like attitude.

The shy 230 pounder was never satisfied with his performance, and was always looking to improve in every facet of his position. The Warren High School graduate envisioned a chance to sing with the OSU choir some day, and was known to occasionally hook up vocally with his more outgoing summer roommate, Cornelius Greene.

Affectionately coined "Chunky" for his squat, stout frame, Aaron was hoping to entice his younger brother Randall to matriculate to Ohio State. Randall was a massive 6'7", 260 pound prep senior lineman at Warren, and longed for the chance to team up with his older sibling.

CHAPTER THREE: PENN STATE

Come Saturday, Paterno rued his bypass of Brown during the recruiting process, for Brown was a prime ingredient in a stifling OSU defense. The Bucks limited the strong Lion offense to just three Bahr field goals, winning a tight contest 17-9. In front of a then-record Ohio Stadium crowd of 88,093, the home team wore down the seventh ranked visitors, making the '75 home debut a rousing success.

Sufficiently motivated by the capacity hometown throng and The Best Damn Band In The Land's humorous pre-game formation, "Block Woody" (a creative take-off on the traditional Block O formation), OSU grabbed the opening kickoff and marched 80 yards for a score.

Baschnagel took advantage of a rare carry from scrimmage, racking up 49 yards for the big play in this opening drive. Baschnagel was finally dragged down by the pursuit, yet that play established OSU as the aggressor, and Penn State was reeling early. Shortly following that long run, Johnson bulled his way across the goal line to put Ohio State on top by seven.

Penn State recovered quickly, scoring on their first possession as well. Bahr lived up to his hype by crushing a 55 yard field goal squarely through the uprights to put PSU down by only four. Just as decisively, the Buckeyes retaliated with a 45 yard Klaban kick for three points. This successful field goal position was achieved thanks to a 35 yard burst straight over center, by Griffin. Following an extended series of fine defensive stands on the part of both teams, OSU drove into place for a 47 yard Klaban attempt. This time, the boot was off.

Penn State reversed the momentum, marching downfield behind the runs of Rich Mauti and Duane Taylor. Taylor was especially effective the entire afternoon, bolting through an otherwise stringent OSU defense for 113 yards in 16 attempts. Bahr converted a short field goal opportunity, after OSU halted the Lions short of a touchdown, to tie the contest. With 1:24 remaining in the first half, OSU led by four.

Ohio State effectively ran out the remaining time, and Paterno ended the opening half with a typically sportsmanlike gesture. Joe made it a point to jog across the field to converse with Hayes about an earlier play in which Corny Greene was roughed up. Paterno assured a trusting Hayes that the tackle, which took place on the visitor's sideline, was not malicious or illegal. At the time of the brutal hit, Hayes ran onto the field in protest of what looked, from his extreme angle from across the way, to be an unnecessarily rough stick. Hayes thanked Paterno for setting the record straight, certain of Paterno's unflinching honesty.

The second half kickoff went to Penn State, and the trailing team wasted little time before carving into the lead. Two Andress flings, to tight end Mickey Shuler and split end Scott Fitzkee, respectively, quickly put the ball on the Buckeye nine yard line. Ohio State once more denied a touchdown, forcing Bahr to kick his third field goal.

The Buckeye offense got nowhere on their opening attempt of the final half, and PSU likewise was forced to punt on the ensuing possession. Baschnagel coughed up the ball on the kick, with Penn State recovering on the Buckeye 38. With the lead in jeopardy, Brown and Brudzinski stormed through to sack a scrambling Andress on two consecutive pass attempts. Forced into a long field goal attempt, Bahr this time narrowly missed from 57 yards out.

Ohio State eventually got the ball back with 12:12 remaining in the contest. Johnson continued his unrelenting battering of the Lion line. It was long since evident that Johnson's summer conditioning regime, presided over by his senior backfield partners, made the junior a much more potent force than in the preceding year. Pete ended the day with 23 runs for 112 yards, and applied many helpful blocks in paving the way for Griffin's 128 yards in 24 carries. Despite Applegate's premature exit with an unfortunate injury, Ron Ayers breached the gap with no letdown in effectiveness.

Following a critical pass interference call against Penn State for hitting Willis too soon on a third down pass attempt in this drive, OSU converted on the second chance. On the redemptive chance at the third and 11 play, Greene found Griffin for a spectacular, diving, 23 yard pickup. The amazing one-handed snag preserved the scoring march, and was a prime example of Griffin's vastly underrated value as a receiver.

This was Archie's 17th collegiate catch, and like the majority of his receptions, could not have come at a more opportune moment. Greene finished the day with unspectacular passing stats, hitting six of 13 for 59 yards, yet key conversions such as this Griffin delivery prolonged several drives. Johnson ended this march with his second score, making the tally 17-6.

The final PSU drive ended with a fumble, caused by a pigskin-stripping, combination tackle by Bruce Ruhl and Buonamici. Kuhn recovered the loose ball, icing the contest. As mentioned, Brown was at the apex of numerous Ohio State stars in the strong defensive showing which preserved the victory. Twice, Brown made tackles behind the line of scrimmage to take Penn State out of Bahr's considerable field goal range. Another Brown tackle forced Andress down for a large loss of yardage.

Buonamici played a magnificent game despite an injury to his hand. Kuhn and Beamon also lent their considerable efforts in keeping Andress and his charges out of the end zone. Andress was a sparkling 11 of 17 for 135 yards through the air, but failed to put the ball in the end zone.

Tim Fox made perhaps one of the finest defensive plays in the history of Ohio Stadium during this game. Nittany Lion fullback Duane Taylor broke free into the secondary late in the game, and seemed certain to go all the way, providing the go-ahead score. At a seemingly impossible angle, Fox sped in from out of nowhere to make a game-saving, fantastic, open-field hit. This many years later, several Buckeye eyewitnesses still contend this save was the greatest defensive play they ever witnessed. Coach Hayes nearly conceded as much, too, though he hesitated to call one play the unequivocal best.

Cassady also saved a potential score, batting down an Andress toss into the end zone in the last split second before reception. All these individual heroics meshed into a masterful, textbook clinic on the proverbial "bend-but-don't break" defense.

With the victory, OSU moved into the second spot in the national polls. In Haye's opinion, this recognition merely provided upcoming opponent North Carolina with an even greater incentive to upend the Buckeyes. The Tar Heels were in the midst of a rollarcoaster season, for they had soundly pasted William & Mary, only to be roundly clobbered by fellow Atlantic Coast Conference member Maryland.

The Tar Heels thrived on the remarkable offensive combination of tailbacks Mike Voight and Jim Betterson. In '74, the two backs became the first college teammates ever to each exceed 1,000 yards rushing in the same year. Ninth-year coach Bill Dooley alternated the two on every down, by utilizing each as a messenger to shuttle the play calls in.

The Tar Heels were reeling from the loss of 22 seniors from the '74 squad, which had played in the Sun Bowl. Among the few members still around and playing well were offensive linemen Mark Cantrell and Mark Griffin, who paved the way for Voight and Betterman's record rushes.

Defensively, the secondary was strong, with speedy halfback Russ Conley roaming the passing lanes. Joe Broadway and Bill Perdue applied pressure from their line positions. Interestingly, the last time the Tar Heels invaded Ohio Stadium, a little-known back by the name of Archie burst into the national spotlight, rushing for 239 yards in the 29-14 Ohio State upset victory. That setback was the only loss for North Carolina in '72.

Archie was aiming for another big day versus the Tar Heels, as Ohio State pursued their record 20th consecutive home victory. The previous record of 19 was established during a portion of the '67 season through a portion of the '71 season. That earlier record was greatly abetted, as no surprise, by a tremendous backfield; for such fantastic backfields were becoming a given on the Columbus campus. This outstanding tradition was evident from Haye's first national championship season, '54, at Ohio State.

The backfield that year consisted of quarterback Dave Leggett, halfbacks Bobby Hatkins and Hop Cassady, and fullback Hubert Bobo. This remarkable group led the Bucks to an unbeaten mark. Another great backfield was in '69, with Rex Kern calling the signals, handing off to halfbacks John Brockington and Leo Hayden, with fullback Jim Otis providing short-yardage punch. In '70, following the departure of Otis to the NFL, Brockington moved his massive frame to fullback and Hayden became the sole halfback.

Johnson was paving the way in '75, putting this Buckeye backfield on a par with any of those great combinations. Like a rampaging freight train, Johnson was pulverizing all in his path, including the unlucky Penn State safety who was knocked unconscious by Pete's pistoning thighs. In '74, Pete reported a little too large and somewhat out of condition. He suffered a sprained ankle in preseason and was never able to really shake the impairing effects.

Additionally, Pete alternated with senior Champ Henson, and it seemed both lost some effectiveness as they moved in and out of the lineup, unlike the twin Tar Heel terrors. Henson was so disappointed with the rotation, he passed up an opportunity for a final redshirt season, in '75. In fact, during the recent Rose Bowl, Henson was so displeased with his lack of playing time, that when he did enter, he played like a lunatic. Champ played amazingly well in that game, barreling downfield for a touchdown, absolutely pulverizing his man on the extra point attempt, then screaming obscenities at Woody as national television cameras whirred.

With Henson's jump to the NFL, Johnson was cemented as the lone fullback in '75. Presented with the chance, Johnson made a commitment to excellence that, according to running backs coach Mickey Jackson, was more than being fulfilled.

Another Buckeye playing at his peak level was defensive end Pat Curto, who had surpassed all competition since the start of the season to become the starter. In an unusually rugged workout during this NC week, Curto disappointingly, and severely, injured his right knee. He was diagnosed to miss at least ten days of contact work.

His backup, Farley Bell, a freshman from Toledo, Ohio, was also doubtful with a sprained knee, leaving the end spot rather thin. Brudzinski and frosh Joe Dixon did their best to fill in. Applegate continued to be sidelined, while sophomore defensive back Tom Roche was hobbling on crutches, nursing a severe ankle sprain.

Former Buckeye great "Deacon" Bill Willis began a slow recovery late this week, after a very serious tangle with viral spinal meningitis. Willis was released from the hospital to the comfort of his own home, but the doctors kept a careful eye on his condition.

Better news came in the form of Paul Ross, a Georgia high school teammate of Pete Johnson. The highly touted linebacker-fullback transferred from the University of Georgia to Ohio State, though he would not be able to play until '76. Beginning with that year, Ross would have three years as a Buckeye. The OSU coaching staff was very pleased with this addition, even though stringent NCAA transfer guidelines delayed his impact for another year. It was expected that Ross would play at a linebacker spot.

One transfer which did not materialize was nevertheless hot on the rumor grist mill. An anonymous tip claimed that retired Notre Dame coach Ara Parseghian, a former Miami (Ohio) grad and Hayes assistant, had purchased a home in Columbus. According to this source, Parseghian was waiting on Woody's retirement at the end of the year, whereupon Ara was to become the new Buckeye leader.

Despite vigorous private and public denials by Parseghian, this story continually made the rounds in Columbus, at office coolers and neighborhood bars alike. The rumor did not die out until the end of the year.

Despite this swirl of misinformation, Hayes managed to keep his attention focused solely on the upcoming game. The Coach was concerned about Greene, who was still struggling with his ulcer. Greene also was bothered by his slight concussion, and there was the recurring soreness in his shoulder bothering his play, too. As the week progressed, though, Greene looked sharper and felt better as his simultaneous ailments abated somewhat.

His NC counterpart at quarterback was Billy Paschall, who was having difficulties of his own, in adjusting from his summer success as an undefeated semi-pro baseball hurler. Paschall was finding it difficult to pitch footballs as well as he had pitched baseballs.

Continuing their college adjustment nicely were various OSU freshmen. Several drew raves for their play in the all-important scrimmage at weeks end. Reckless fullback Tim Vogler impressed the coaches, as did rampaging defensive ends Joe Hornik and Dansler. Improvement among the backup players was forever paramount to Hayes, for the ascending success of the non-starter prevented the starter from becoming complacent or lackadaisical.

CHAPTER FOUR: NORTH CAROLINA

On Saturday, the Bucks charged past NC by a score of 32-7, largely based on the exploits of Johnson. Johnson bulldozed his way for five touchdowns, on respective runs of one, five, one, two, and three yards. He ended the day with 148 rushing yards overall. Once more OSU began slowly, leading just 12-0 at the break, following a scoreless first quarter. This opening quarter saw the two teams essentially trade punts.

Skladany was coming off a phenomenal Penn State contest, in which he had averaged 47.6 yards on seven kicks. On this day he continued to kick deep and high. OSU did penetrate once to the NC 15, at which point the Tar Heels stiffened, stopping the Bucks short on a fourth down run. The second quarter began with an exchange of turnovers, as Greene fumbled the ball away; Fox thereupon intercepted a Paschall pass deep in OSU territory, at the 12.

The next time NC assumed possession, punt returner Mel Collins broke free from coverage containment. Only a lunging solo tackle by Skladany at the OSU 29 prevented a touchdown. The challenged Buck defense responded by yielding no ground, as Cassady, Curto (miraculously back in the lineup much earlier than anticipated), Brudzinski, and Beamon each came through with big plays. Tom Biddle was short on a 46 yard field goal try, and the scoreless tie was preserved a bit longer.

Inspired by the defensive stand, OSU now discovered an offensive punch. Johnson ripped off a 42 yard gain, Griffin followed with an 18 yard pickup, and Baschnagel hauled in a pass good for 20 yards. Following Johnson's initial score, Klaban surprisingly missed the point after.

Ohio State halted the Tar Heels following that kickoff, and the defense again held, with Fox fielding the resulting punt all the way up on the NC 45. Greene offset a sack on first down by zipping strikes of 21 and 27 yards to Larry Kain. Johnson ran the ball in from close range again, although Archie was stopped short in a bid for the two point conversion. Ohio State took only the twelve point lead into the locker room, although they had outgained the visitors 222 total yards to 41.

The Tar Heels reversed their offensive (mis)fortunes by marching 80 yards to paydirt in only nine plays, to open the second half. With fellow tailback Mike Voight benched prior to the game for undisclosed disciplinary reasons, "Boom Boom" Betterson utilized his doubled playing time. He charged for 32 yards in this drive alone. On the day, Betterson was the sole effective offensive threat for his team, finishing with 106 yards in 28 punishing carries. Paschall capped this lone scoring drive with a touchdown fling to fullback Brian Smith.

The Buckeyes responded to this mild threat with a 71 yard, seven play touchdown drive of their own. Griffin darted for 43 yards in three carries in the march, as Johnson bulled in for six points again. This time, Skladany was brought in to provide the PAT. Following this conversion, the Tar Heels could not get untracked, yet Ohio State was also halted on the next two possessions.

Early in the fourth quarter, OSU shook loose from the temporary offensive doldrums, romping 81 yards in 12 plays for another Johnson score. Skladany remained the placekicker, providing the conversion.

After the Tar Heel offense was again summarily stopped, Fox returned the punt 18 yards, once more giving OSU advantageous starting position. Greene found Baschnagel for a 20 yard gain, Griffin reeled off an 18 yard dash through the middle, and Johnson concluded the day's scoring with his 30th point. Continuing the strange kicking day, Skladany missed the extra point, making the final score 32-7, although over eight minutes remained to be played.

Johnson's astounding point total eclipsed the old school record of 24, held by seven different Buckeyes. Those seven included Bob White, who reached 24 points on two different occasions in '61. Griffin also enjoyed a record-setting day. Archie passed Rex Kern as the OSU career leader in total offense, and Archies' 157 rushing yards placed him just 502 yards from former Cornell running back Ed Marinaro's mark as the all-time major college rushing leader.

Hayes pulled his starters with this final touchdown, gaining his reserves some invaluable and deserved game experience. In a game in which the traditional Brutus Buckeye sideline costume was reintroduced in lieu of the unpopular modern design, OSU fans also saw the first Ohio Stadium appearance of Rod Gerald.

Though he failed to complete his only pass, Gerald electrified the crowd with dazzling option runs of seven, six, four, and five yards, although two of these gains were nullified by penalties. In comparison to Greene, an outstanding option quarterback in his own right, Gerald seemed almost impossibly quicker and threatened to break every carry for the distance.

Duncan Griffin ended the contest by intercepting an errant pass with nine seconds left, while Cousineau made five tackles in his allotted time. The only negative for the reserves was freshman offensive guard Ernie Andria's severely sprained ankle, painfully endured in the closing seconds.

Afterwards, Hayes and his counterpart Dooley both conceded that the powerful OSU ground game wore down North Carolina's overworked defense. Stacked predominately to defend the run, the Tar Heels showed a susceptibility to the play-action pass, as Greene spectacularly connected on seven of eight tosses for 132 yards. In all, the Bucks outgained the Tar Heels 535 total yards to 193, retaining possession for long stretches and limiting all but Betterson to little gain in return.

Beamon, Thompson, Buonamici, and Kuhn provided the brunt of the defense, and Tim Fox blocked a Tar Heel field goal attempt to further frustrate the visitors. Though he and Klaban each botched an extra point, Skladany almost atoned by just narrowly missing a 60 yard field goal.

Upcoming Buckeye opponent UCLA stumbled a bit on this particular Saturday, suffering through a tie game with the Air Force Falcons. More dramatically, Michigan's heretofore highly regarded squad endured their second straight tie. Stanford and now Baylor played the Wolverines to a standstill, to the uproarious protests of enraged UM fans. In response to this displeasure, head coach Bo Schembechler bellowed, "I don't give a damn about fans," nor did he care for their opinions. Schembechler cared only about his players: "These kids, they're the ones who make it so special."

Bo preferred to spend his time righting his team's fortunes, disregarding all outside opinions. Bo rapped what he termed, "negative external influences," which were proving detrimental to his program. These externals included disgruntled fans, newsmen, and television reporters. To help shield his young Wolverines from these detriments, Bo denied all public access to his practices.

Contrastingly, Hayes and his team were riding the high tide of success. Chief among these successes was the performance of the offensive line. For the first time since Ralph Staub had joined the OSU coaching staff, five of the six interior linemen graded out at 70% or better, after review of the NC game films. The lone member not to reach this height had a legitimate excuse.

Ron Ayers, a 6'4", 232 pound guard from Columbus Eastmoor, was still learning the new position of center he inherited when Applegate went down. No less an esteemed authority than Griffin proclaimed, "The line is better than last year."

A quick glance at Johnson's stats seemed to further confirm this reasoning. In all of '74, Johnson ran for 320 yards. His yardage total already in '75 was 329, though it should be recalled that Johnson himself was greatly improved and was no longer splitting time with Henson.

Perhaps the lineman performing the best was senior co-captain Ted Smith, an impressive 6'1" combination of quick feet, rugged drive blocking, and surprising down field blocking ability. Bill Lukens was performing at the most consistent levels, and was the most improved of all the interior linemen, too. His play had continued to surge, despite a painful motion-inhibiting ankle sprain.

Like many OSU players, Lukens and Smith were throwbacks to a long-gone era in football, when wounds were ignored in the quest for the greater glory of combat. Hayes liked the rough and tumble mentality, and this quality of play was paramount in all of his teams. Moore continued to shine, coming in at the tight tackle slot when the two-tight end set was utilized in short-yardage situations.

The UCLA Bruins had an accomplished offensive line, too. The Bruins averaged 6'5" and 250 pounds across their offensive front. This immense size translated into many holes for the speedy Bruin runners. The fine UCLA backfield was led by senior quarterback John Sciarra. This 5'10", 178 pound overachiever was often called, "The finest player in the country," by his head coach, Dick Vermeil. Sciarra had a proclivity for breaking runs in key moments of a game, and was a heady, virtually mistake-free option operator.

Fleet halfback Wendell Tyler led the squad in rushing, though he did not start in the experienced veer backfield set. The Bruins only drawback at this point in the season was an inexperienced and unproven defense. End Dale Curry was the lone returning starter on that side of scrimmage.

The 38-year-old Vermeil was in just his second year at the helm. Despite his tender years, Vermeil had coached under a long list of established coaches, for teams at both the collegiate and professional levels. Among those names and teams were Chuck Knox, Los Angeles Rams; John Ralston, Stanford Cardinal; George Allen, Rams; and Tommy Prothro, UCLA.

Vermeil spoke very highly of the discipline he learned at the feet of these masters, and recognized that same discipline in the OSU program. Vermeil said of Hayes, both truthfully and humorously, "I think maybe his players are scared to death to make a mistake." Vermeil hoped his own long years of service under similar situations could implant some of that same mind-set in his own program.

Like Hayes, Vermeil was a renowned workaholic as it applied to football. Dick often said, "My hobby is my work; I like it so much it's not even work." Immortal "Papa Bear" George Halas once acknowledged, "The only way I can sleep is to think of football," and Vermeil possessed a similar mindset. With the game being played at night, on the UCLA home field, and on a grass surface Hayes disliked so much, Vermeil felt he could possibly counteract the greater experience of Hayes.

Game experience was something Buckeye sophomore Tony Ross had none of. The quarterback of the weekly scout team did have an integral part in the preparations for each game, however. The 5'10", 182 pounder, like all scout team members, had to learn each opponent's tendencies and schemes, and execute that foreign philosophy against the first string each day in practice.

Hayes never underestimated the efforts of the scout team, for without their dedication, game-day success would be considerably reduced. Hayes lauded Ross directly, and the other scout-teamers indirectly, stating, "He makes a real contribution to our team, under very trying circumstances," especially since most members of the scout squad rarely appeared in an actual game. With Greene looking extremely sharp, Ross's chance at any game action remained dim, though Tony's effort never lessened.

One former Buckeye with plenty of scout team experience was now making quite a reputation for himself as the starting safety for the Chicago Bears. Ohio State '74 graduate Doug Plank did not start until the final five games of his collegiate career, yet became the only player drafted from that remarkably talented class to immediately start in the NFL. Perhaps Plank's reckless, indiscriminate tendency to knock himself out stone cold, in addition to opponents, teammates, and officials, concerned Hayes to the point of leaving

Plank primarily on the sidelines during his college days. Indeed, Plank routinely hit so hard on kick coverage units in college that he practically rendered himself useless the remainder of the game.

Though his knack at injuring himself had not abated (he knocked himself unconscious in each of his initial three NFL regular season games), the 12th round pick so impressed the Bear coaches that he became a vital cog in their revamped, rebuilding defense. Former OSU backfield mates Neal Colzie and Steve Luke also were making rookie waves in the NFL, with the Packers and Dolphins, respectively, though Plank, who performed custodial work at a brewery as an undergrad, was perhaps the most overjoyed with his higher-paid professional fortunes.

Similarly unproven until this year was sophomore Buckeye defensive tackle Eddie Beamon. The 6'2", 248 pounder was a definite surprise, to himself and the coaching staff. Beamon led all interior linemen in tackles thus far, and he was surrounded by outstanding talents, so this was quite an accomplishment. It seemed #67 was everywhere on the field. Beamon collared quarterbacks, nailed running backs, and chased down wide receivers with equal abandon and frequency.

Beamon dropped out of organized football at age eight, and did not play again until he was 13. Eddie never realized the importance of an education, at either the high school or undergraduate college level, until Hayes began recruiting him during Beamon's junior year in high school. Until that point, Eddie never realized the potential of his playing college football, or the disastrous effect his lack of scholarship could play on such potential.

After talking with Hayes, the talented tailback-middle guard-linebacker from Cincinnati (Ohio) Withrow dug into his schoolwork for the first time, and education became foremost in his plans. As an unheralded frosh, Beamon subbed infrequently for Cusick, flashing the 4.7 (forty) speed that carried him to fifth place in the campus-wide sixty yard dash intramural championship, and laid the foundation for his superb second season.

Of vital concern to Hayes on this West Coast road trip were three facets. Firstly, this was the maiden long, transcontinental voyage under the NCAA mandate limiting a squad to 48 players, so several substitutes practiced for multiple roles.

Jim Savoca, normally a linebacker, also prepared for work at offensive guard if necessary. Jim performed so well at this new slot that his days as a defenseman became numbered. His hard-charging style and attacking demeanor remained intact, even after his switch to the usually more sedate offensive side of scrimmage. Many other Buckeyes also practiced at completely new or somewhat unfamiliar positions.

Secondly, the Bucks were concerned enough about the grass playing surface in the LA Coliseum to change their accustomed shoewear. After consulting with Coliseum home teams the University of Southern California, the LA

Rams, and UCLA, Hayes outfitted the Buckeyes in special natural grass footwear.

Thirdly, this was also OSU's first game at night since '59. To prepare for the effect of lights, the Buckeyes worked out late in the week, at night, on Columbus Whetstone's high school illuminated grass field.

With OSU being in such great physical condition, Hayes did not think the infamous southern California heat, the third component of worry, would be a problem. After OSU's arrival on the coast, the Bucks underwent a light Friday afternoon run-through at the Coliseum. Hayes noticed no ill effects from the warm, 88 degree weather, since the humidity was actually very low, so, despite all of these unusual variables, Coach Hayes though his team's chances for a tiebreaking win in the series favorable. OSU won the initial matchup of the schools in '61, 13-3, though UCLA avenged that loss by winning 9-7 the following year. Now, Hayes had the opportunity to break that deadlock.

CHAPTER FIVE: UCLA

The assumptions of Hayes proved correct, in spite of a troubled start by the Bucks and a late Bruin rally. Taking the opening kickoff, OSU expertly marched to the Bruin 26. At that juncture, huge 6'6", 254 pound middle guard Cliff Frazier jarred the ball loose from Archie with a crunching hit, and the Bruins recovered. The Bruins capitalized on the turnover, as Sciarra led them 73 yards in a fast seven plays, ultimately passing to James Sarpy for the score.

When Griffin subsequently mishandled the ensuing kickoff, OSU began from their ten. The Coliseum crowd sensed an upset brewing. Greene burst that temporary thought, juking his way to a crowd-silencing 48 yard gain. Corny culminated the dominant 90 yard drive with a two yard option keeper across the goal line. On the successful PAT, the Bruins were penalized 15 yards, which was assessed on the kickoff.

Rather than waste the fortuitous field position, Hayes opted for an onside kick. Skladany recovered his own kick on the UCLA 34, as the shocked Bruins seemed perplexed by the derring-do of Ohio State. Greene promptly led OSU back into the end zone, as Johnson's three yard rumble put Ohio State on top 14-7.

The home team was forced to punt on their next possession, and OSU again quickly scored. The key play in the drive was a third and 15 conversion, via a 22 yard Greene pass to Kain. With the Bruins reeling, Johnson smashed into the end zone, with five minutes left in the half. The home team was foiled on offense once more, and OSU responded by traveling 61 yards in eleven plays.

This drive was a masterpiece in the use of the clock, thanks to the expertness of the game plan and Greene's cool leadership. The Buckeyes reeled off those eleven plays in an amazing span of just 1:40, as the touchdown came with 29 seconds left in the half. Griffin made a fantastic 22 yard catch in the drive, and Greene scampered the final 17 yards to carry a 21-7 lead into the locker room.

The smothering OSU defense forced another Bruin punt to open the second half. The OSU offense capitalized, charging 64 yards in only five plays. Greene hit Kain and Baschnagel for respective big gainers, and Griffin scored his very first touchdown of the year, from 18 yards out. Following another short-lived Bruin possession, Klaban ended a short drive with a 34 yard field goal. OSU had scored 38 straight points, steamrolling to a huge lead with 4:22 remaining in the third quarter.

The Bruins received the ensuing kickoff, at last responding with a long scoring drive. As the quarter came to a close, the margin was thus sliced to 38-13. The Bruin rally continued when Greene fumbled to end the next visitor's possession, with UCLA recovering on the OSU 22. Just minutes into the final period, Eddie Ayers scored, cutting the gap to a more manageable 38-20. The large LA crowd stirred in anticipation of a rousing, miracle comeback by the once-overwhelmed home team.

In an attempt to revive a suddenly dormant offense, Hayes uncharacteristically ordered a pass following the ensuing kickoff. Unfortunately, Greene's attempt to kick start the offense was picked off, putting the Bruins back in business at the State 37. Sciarra led the Bruins to the seven, where UCLA faced a first and goal situation. Four outstanding plays in a row by the Buckeye defenders kept UCLA out of the end zone. Vermeil went for the touchdown on the final down, and Beamon's ferocious rush kept UCLA off the scoreboard.

Ohio State assumed possession, yet appeared in desperate trouble as they were soon forced to punt. The Bruins received the kick on the OSU 44, with seven minutes left and still faintly smelling an upset. Deep into Buckeye territory, Sciarra went for the jugular, passing towards a Bruin near the goal line. The phenomenal athlete Kuhn stepped in front and grabbed the ball instead, squelching the scoring opportunity. On the strength of Archie's 23 yard run and 23 yard reception, OSU drove to a clinching 41 yard Klaban field goal.

With the score now 41-20, UCLA finally ran out of time and opportunities, as OSU staved off their determined comeback. Despite the late slump, OSU still emerged from the thrilling game with a three touchdown advantage.

Afterwards, a jubilant Hayes made an extremely rare admission. The Head Coach proclaimed his squad the number one team in the nation, particularly on the basis of the four straight convincing wins against top-notch opponents. Hayes could not stop the flow of superlatives for Greene, who in spite of the damaging late turnovers finished with 23 rushes for 120 yards and also connected on six of nine tosses for 98 additional yards. Each of the completions came at a critical juncture, prolonging several scoring drives in the process. With Greene leading the way, OSU outgained their foe 441-276 in total offense, as Sciarra passed for 134 of the Bruin total.

Griffin rebounded from his redoubtable beginning, providing big runs and bigger catches throughout. He almost singlehandedly kept the ball out of UCLA's eager hands on the final Ohio State scoring drive, finishing with 160 yards on 21 carries. His overall performance drew unique praise from his Head Coach. "He is a better young man than he is a football player, and he's the best ballplayer I've ever seen," Hayes announced to the huge array of assembled media, following this contest.

Immediately after his mellow post-game flings of praise, Hayes was informed that ABC-TV was in the OSU locker room interviewing players. Since all player interviews without both the consent and presence of Hayes were strictly forbidden, Woody charged into the small, dingy, cramped locker room to interrupt. As he burst angrily into the room, Hayes saw the offending sportscaster was his good friend, former Michigan pigskin legend Tom Harmon.

So pleased was Hayes with this West Coast win that he actually let Harmon and celebrated entertainer Bob Hope linger and talk freely with the players. The good spirits and the top rank proclamation of Woody proved prophetic on Monday as Ohio State vaulted past Oklahoma to become number one in the polls.

Despite the accolades, the Buckeyes did not let up at all in preparation for the winless Iowa Hawkeyes. Emerson wrote freely about the changing aspect of all things, and Hayes always believed similarly. Hayes forever admonished his players to look in the mirror at the tail end of the day, and ascertain if they had improved. According to Woody, if one had not improved, one had regressed, for change was constant. The Coach wanted to continue the improvement currently evident in his ballclub, to prevent a change in their high-ranking status.

The Buckeyes most dangerous foe for the next few weeks would probably be the psychological letdown that usually accompanies a gigantic, emotional win, let alone four such consecutive contests. The Bucks had captured ten wins in a row over the Hawkeyes, including a 35-10 victory in '74, though the outcome of that game was actually in doubt until OSU pulled away in the second half. The Hawkeyes won three games in '74 under new coach Bob Commings, yet were deep in the throes of a sophomore jinx in '75.

The history of the Iowa rivalry boasted several other interesting games. Hayes and former long-time Hawkeye helmsman Forest Evashevski were such bitter, heated competitors that Hayes once even challenged his counterpart to a physical battle. The personal confrontation thankfully never materialized, though few observers would have been surprised by such a tussle. Nicknamed "Ape" during his undergrad, captaincy days as a blocker at Michigan, Evashevski paved the way for Tom Harmon's Heisman award, and Hayes never forgot that Forest was originally of the hated maize and blue.

In '50, the year prior to the arrival of Woody, one of the most impressive single performances in all of collegiate history highlighted the matchup between the two schools. Ohio State halfback Vic Janowicz led the Bucks to an 83-21 blowout over Iowa, performing expertly in almost every facet of the game. Janowicz recovered fumbles, made tackles, threw four touchdown passes, returned a punt for a score, ran for a touchdown, kicked ten PAT's, and handled all the punting and prolific kickoff duties.

This game solidified the Janowicz reputation as a star, pushing him into the foreground of the national spotlight, which eventually resulted in a Heisman Trophy selection later in that year.

Several years later, in '58, the two squads played to a thrilling 38-28 offensive finale. The Hawks already had clinched a Rose Bowl berth that season, yet OSU emerged victorious in the slugfest. The Iowa coach had failed in his defensive motto, which was, "Score if you can, but don't pass." Evashevski deemed this shootout the greatest offensive game he ever saw in his lengthy career. The explosive '75 Buckeyes hoped for equal fireworks.

This '75 game seemed to be skewed favorably toward OSU, if only because Iowa used basic power fronts on both sides of the ball. Iowa featured a wing T power running game and a no-frills 5-2 defensive set, and these two formations played right into the similar Ohio State sets.

In man-on-man confrontations, OSU seemingly enjoyed an advantage over most college programs, for exactly the reason Vermeil cited: The exacting discipline meted out by Hayes, over the years, indelibly stamped his teams with an unmistakable aura of invincibility, for what pressure felt in a game could surpass having to please Woody on a daily basis in practice?

For instance, each daily practice session ended as Hayes stood literally inches away from the punters as they kicked five balls downfield. Skladany relates that next to this pressure, the game itself was a complete joy, and relatively relaxing.

The rigors of practice this week were fashioned around a battery of freshmen aptitude tests required by the university. These academic tests were inconveniently given during non-scheduled class times, but the forced, unusual hours for football practice did not diminish the normal intensity of the workouts.

The Thursday night scrimmage between the scout team and the backup units was among the fiercest and most spirited in years, according to the coaching staff. The regulars knocked off unusually early that night, as "all you others," the Hayes term for any player not in the two-deep lineup, stayed on. Kain and Lukens collected rewards for their play against UCLA, and took the early bus back to the locker rooms.

Shortly before those rewards were bestowed, Hayes reasoned that the especially tough early season schedule could only benefit OSU in the long run. "I believe you are only as good as you have to be," Hayes explained at midweek. This philosophy explained how OSU could rise to the occasion on four successive weeks, with no faltering. Hayes attributed much of these early victories to the fact that Ohio State was mostly able to avoid major injuries.

The fine pre-season physical condition of the squad had not diminished during what was judged the roughest skein in the schedule, and Hayes looked favorably to the remaining contests, since his Bucks were in such fine shape. Ted Smith and Bruce Ruhl were slightly banged up, and sophomore Garth Cox severely strained his knee, yet nothing of crisis status developed as the pattern of great fortune continued.

Maintaining his pattern of early interruptions of protocol this season, Bo Schembechler rightly lashed out at ABC television for determining the starting times of their Saturday NCAA telecasts, with little regard for the participant's wishes. Rather than conform to the completed football schedule, ABC often rearranged starting times to benefit and boost their potential television audience. Television was just beginning to shape, influence, and direct the college game toward the commercialistic big business it became within the decade, and the early growing pains were often severe.

Schembechler argued with characteristic aplomb that the welfare of the game and the participating schools themselves far exceeded any network concerns regarding scheduling or viewing patterns, but the lure of the ever-burgeoning dollar soon superseded Bo's protests. Michigan grudgingly was forced to conform with network demands to shuffle game times.

This situation was merely another step in the inexorable slide of college athletics, away from the simplistic, human, team conflict so loved by the likes of Woody and Bo. The game grew increasingly away from a sport and towards the mass marketed, overhyped, individualistic spectacle so manipulated by network programmers and advertisers. The game itself was no longer the primary focus; rather, the game became a key sideshow amidst commercial sponsorship, competing entertainment programs, and upcoming made-for-television events.

Television also contributed to the spread of a fascinating rumor this week. During the taping of a brand new concept in golf, a time-delay telecast of a skins game in Dublin, Ohio, between Professional Golf Association stars competing for purses proffered by monolithic Japanese corporations, an ebullient Lee Trevino turned to the whirring cameras and intoned "Hi, Woody". Simultaneously, word around Columbus town spread that Hayes had suffered a fatal heart attack. According to rumor, this was Trevino's way of saying goodbye. The rumor, as did most when Hayes was involved, flourished and spread rapidly, reaching all areas of the capital city within a few hours.

Hayes was delivering a speech to the Quarterback Club at the time, and his wife Anne was away at a speaking engagement in St. Louis, so refutation was not immediately possible. The seed of the rumor was never identified, though conventional wisdom had it that the hoopla surrounding the upcoming premiere of the ensemble comedy show "Saturday Night Live " prompted some jokester to get an early laugh. Whatever the basis, the lingering falsehood was finally squelched by OSU team doctor and personal Hayes family physician, Dr. Robert Murphy. Hayes himself had a good laugh over the incident, after he was finally located following his speech.

What a speech it was, too. Based on his considerable concerns regarding rising unemployment and the pressing need for increased energy conservation, Woody revealed that he had developed a new pass play for this season. The play was created and named in honor of the newest American-made compact car, as a reward to the manufacturer for putting people to work and saving fuel. Laughingly, Hayes disclosed that like most of his pass plays, this one still sat, unused, within his playbook.

CHAPTER SIX: IOWA

On Saturday, OSU overwhelmed Iowa as Greene enjoyed his second straight brilliant passing game. The Bucks were nearly perfect on offense, scoring touchdowns seven of the eight times they had the ball. Iowa's sole moment of defensive glory came as they halted Ohio State on downs at the Hawkeye 21, preventing an eighth touchdown. Sadly, this defensive stand did not occur until there was 1:05 left in the game.

On the other extreme, the OSU defense was so dominant that the Hawkeyes threatened to score on only one occasion. This moment of Hawkeye achievement did not occur until late in the third quarter, when the contest was already inescapably lost. On this solitary occasion, Iowa reached the Buckeye 11, whereupon OSU grew rankled at the threat to their shutout. Sufficiently inspired in the bid to extend their shutout string, OSU repelled the hapless Hawks, preserving the 49-0 final.

Iowa's afternoon began pleasantly enough. The visitors won the coin toss, and elected to receive. After the kickoff, the OSU defensive unit debuted the newest fashion among football teams, by holding hands in the huddle as a demonstration of unity. The practice had been recently popularized by the Denver Broncos in the NFL, whose swarming Orange Crush defense featured former Buckeye great Randy Gradishar. Iowa was quickly forced to punt, and the kick pinned OSU deep in their own territory.

From the line of scrimmage beginning at the nine, Greene continued his recent ultra-pinpoint passing as OSU drove 91 yards in 15 plays. Passes of 18 yards to Willis, and 22 and 11 yards, respectively, to Baschnagel, led to the familiar sight of a Johnson touchdown. On their second opportunity, the Bucks methodically ran on every down to another quick score. Not surprisingly, Johnson carried the ball across the goal line again. A Tim Fox punt return of 31 yards set up a third touchdown, scored on a brilliantly conceived and executed toss to the reliable Kain.

On the ensuing Iowa possession, Curto deflected a pass into the hands of Cassady, providing OSU with one more shot at points prior to halftime. Quick strikes of 17 yards to Baschnagel and 14 yards to Kain led to a prototypical Johnson score. Pete barged into the end zone with four Iowa defenders helplessly clinging to his impossibly huge frame.

Ohio State fielded the second half kick, with no letup in the virtuoso display. Greene continued his torrid passing, finding Willis for ten crucial yards, on a fourth and five situation, to keep the drive alive. Shortly thereafter, Cornelius darted his way in for the score, putting the tally to 35-0. The third quarter was barely four minutes old, and for all intent, the contest was decided.

Iowa showed a modicum of life following this kickoff, marching to the aforementioned isolated scoring threat. The Hawkeyes ran effectively on this drive, behind the efforts of Bobby Holmes, Butch Caldwell, and Jim Jenson.

Once the Buckeye defense ultimately stopped the Iowa threat, Hayes emptied his bench. Eventually, all 60 of the Buckeyes permitted to dress got into the game. Red II, the second team offense, and the Bombers, the defensive backups, acquitted themselves extremely well.

Interestingly, Hayes did keep one starter in the game, in an attempt to preserve a statistical string. Archie was aiming for his 26th consecutive 100 yard rushing game, and Hayes kept him in until the final quarter so he could pass the century mark. Griffin eventually reached 120 yards in 21 carries. Asked why he, for the first time in memory, seemed to put the personal glory of one person before the welfare of the team, Hayes explicitly pointed out the significance of this Griffin feat. "Nobody's done that in 100 years of football," Hayes noted. Woody went on to say that this Griffin record was the most significant individual mark in all collegiate annals.

Indeed, the consistency of the Griffin excellence week after week against defenses specifically designed to stop Archie amazed his Head Coach to no end, as did Archie's continual resiliency in absorbing the constant pounding inflicted upon him. Additionally, this streak assumed a team significance, for the entire OSU offense and particularly the offensive line took great pride in and accepted responsibility for the struggle to hit 100 yards each week.

This truly was a case where the record meant little to Archie, but was extremely significant to his teammates and coaches. Hayes went on to praise Archie and his fellow captains, saying "We've got great leadership, the best we've ever had."

Just a few days before this contest, assistant coach John Mummey raved about the crop of freshmen showing daily improvement. Cousineau, Moore, and Dansler were each making serious bids for playing time. Each of these three certainly played up to expectations against Iowa, with Cousineau taking "Specialist of the Week" honors, yet fellow frosh Rod Gerald stole the show.

On the opening play of the fourth quarter, Gerald twisted, cut, and swerved through the slower Hawkeye defenders for an electrifying 45 yard touchdown. Later in the quarter, Gerald continued his thunderous game, leading OSU on the final scoring drive of the afternoon.

After Griffin departed to a standing ovation during this drive, the unbelievably speedy Roach showed his awesome talents. Woodrow and sophomore Jeff Logan flashed glimpses of departing and approaching brilliance, respectively, as Logan darted and bulled his way for 58 yards on eight carries. Unfortunately, in this season, Jeff was reduced to hoping Archie got his 100 yards quickly, for until that milestone was breached, the exceptionally talented Logan stood virtually no chance of entering the contest. Gerald provided the finishing fireworks on a nifty 14 yard scoring jaunt.

Ohio State ended the powerful display with 70 offensive plays, totaling 495 yards, while Iowa was held to 207 total yards on 60 plays. Greene in particular was virtually perfect, connecting on all eight of his throws for 117 yards, including the beautiful scoring toss to Kain. Gerald displayed considerable speed, quickness, agility, and open-field maneuverability in his extended stint. His father, the Reverend Cornelius Gerald of the First Baptist Church in Dallas, flew in for the game, to see his son play in person for the first time in college. Rod certainly made the special occasion memorable.

Overall, the efficient OSU offense reached an incredible nine of their prescribed ten goals. Dannelly graded out to an equally astonishing 85% in another brilliant game for the senior. Iowa coach Commings said, without prompting, "That's the best team in the country!". Hayes modestly responded, "We're working like the devil to improve".

The following Monday, Hayes continued with his plaudits for Griffin. Woody extoled the oft-hidden blocking abilities of Archie, and raved about Griffin even carrying out fakes to perfection. Though Griffin had only 21 receptions in his career, his talents in that area really emerged in '75. All five of his catches thus far in this season were either critical conversions for a first down, spectacular circus grabs, or fairly long gainers.

As was soon to be evident in his professional career, Griffin was an excellent receiver with soft hands and a knack for not only freeing himself from coverage, but in gaining substantial yardage after the catch, too. Archie always enjoyed the chance to catch passes, all the way through his sandlot days to the practices of his now-dwindling college days. It was a little known fact, that OSU practices often devoted nearly as much time to the receiving game as was set aside for the favored running repetitions. The rousing success of the '75 aerial assault was a testament to the (often overlooked) huge emphasis put on the pass in practice.

Getting back on the subject of Archie, Hayes unveiled his classic statement concerning the magical tailback: "His actions speak so loudly, I can't hear what he says."

One of Griffin's leading competitors for Big 10 accolades was Wisconsin tailback Billy Marek, a little package of scoring dynamite. Marek was only 75 yards away from 3000 rushing yards in his fine career, and had actually led the conference in both scoring and rushing yards per game (for conference games only) in '74.

Marek ran successfully and often behind perhaps the best tackle in the land, 6'4", 270 pound Dennis Lick. Lick was certain to be a first round NFL draft choice, as he ably protected freshman quarterback Charles Green, as well as the recently demoted Mike Carroll, on Badger passing plays. Head coach John Jardine often used both quarterbacks interchangeably in an attempt to confuse defenses and keep his signalcallers fresh.

The 2-3 Badgers featured a swarming defense which had keyed the recent 17-14 upset win over Purdue. The undersized, overachieving 5'10", 209 pound middle guard-middle linebacker Dennis Stejskal garnered 23 tackles in that surprising toppling of the Boilermakers, including a vicious fumble-causing stick which led to the winning points.

Wisconsin was facing the number one team in the nation at Columbus, a city they had not emerged victoriously from since '18. Additionally, the Bucks had not lost in either Madison, Wisconsin, nor in Columbus to the Badgers since '59. The long winning streak seemed as likely to continue as Archie's string of 100 yard games did. The sadsack recent history of the series did include a tie between the foes in '51; a 23-14 upset victory by OSU in '52; while in '54, Wisconsin entered the contest ranked number one nationally, only to fall 31-14 to the resurgent Bucks.

This particular contest saw Wisconsin seize an early 14-0 lead, and they were driving towards a third score when Hopalong Cassady picked off a pass and somehow weaved 74 yards for a touchdown. That single play caused a huge momentum shift not only for that game, but on the fortunes of the season and the coming decades, for Ohio State. This shocking victory propelled OSU to their first national title under Woody, most likely saved the Coach's job, and sprung Cassady to the '55 Heisman award.

Perhaps recalling such an unlikely upending of a top-ranked team, Hayes really got mean on Wednesday in a dramatic attempt to ward off overconfidence or complacency. Woody did take time out from his remonstrations to fete Thompson and Fox for their achievements in the Iowa game, as Kuhn, Buonamici, and Beamon also drew praise. Not going unnoticed in all the hoopla was Dansler, who participated in ten tackles against Iowa, all coming in the second half.

Fellow frosh Cousineau moved into the starting lineup late in the week when Kuhn was unexpectedly hospitalized to combat a mysterious, pesky virus. Cousineau had displayed his outstanding pursuit skills brilliantly on specialty squads, so coach Hill felt few qualms about inserting him full force into the fray. On a lighter note, Skladany demonstrated his unique accordion playing skill late in the week, when he played several songs at the Casa di Pasta Italian restaurant, to commemorate his grandparent's 48th wedding anniversary.

Not celebrating at all this week was Schembechler. Once again he made headlines, this time by protesting the seemingly relaxed rules concerning offensive holding. According to Bo, the offensive lineman was being accorded unprecedented laxity in '75, in being able to extend his arms and grapple with the defense. This led to an unfair offensive advantage, particularly for offenses facing an exceptionally good defensive line. The defenses usual advantages were now offset by the lack of a holding call against the offense.

Hayes, certainly blessed himself with a preponderance of talented defensive linemen, wisely stayed out of this temporary tempest. Woody had for many years conducted daily practices under the supervision of Big 10 officials, who were hired at a great cost to the athletic department. This high cost seemingly paid for itself in eliminating gameday violations, for OSU was characteristically the least penalized team in the conference.

The Wisconsin game, although it was actually the second straight home game, formally ended a big week of homecoming celebrations. One unique honor accorded recent Buckeye gridiron All-Americans began this week. The aptly named Buckeye Grove, an area just outside the stadium, was designated as the spot to plant a tree for each player chosen to this lofty status. Hayes broke ground for the initial planting, with trees started in honor of Rex Kern, Jan White, Tim Anderson, Tom DeLeone, John Hicks, Randy Gradishar, Van DeCree, Kurt Schumacher, Pete Cusick, Steve Myers, Neal Colzie, Archie, and Skladany.

One former Buckeye of note, Jim Otis, though not included in this grove, was enjoying a standout year running the ball for the St. Louis Cardinals. Otis was the all-time leading rusher in school history when he left OSU, but had found the going somewhat rougher in the NFL.

Originally drafted by the New Orleans Saints, then acquired by the Kansas City Chiefs, Otis found a home and hit his stride upon joining the Cardinals, a full six tough years after entering the league. Paired with the versatile Terry Metcalf and running behind ex-Wolverine standout lineman Dan Dierdorf, Otis achieved his first 100 yard game in '75 and set his sights towards the benchmark of excellence, a 1000 yard season.

CHAPTER SEVEN: WISCONSIN

The Buckeyes delighted a packed homecoming crowd of 87,820 in continuing their string of excellence this Saturday. Throughout sporadic sprinkles of rain, OSU again dominated the entire proceeding with a balanced, overpowering attack from each side of scrimmage.

On their second possession, OSU ran roughshod over Wisconsin for 92 yards in 13 plays. The drive featured the power and dash of Johnson. Pete pulverized the Badgers for 65 yards on eight carries in the march, culminating his dominant display with a one yard scoring plunge. On the ensuing Badger possession, fullback Larry Canada fumbled and the opportunistic Curto pounced on the loose ball. Griffin rattled off a 26 yard gain, and the short drive ended with another Johnson score.

The crushing blow to the Badger's slim victory hopes was applied the next time Ohio State touched the ball. Tim Fox fielded the Wisconsin punt, and behind a smashing block administered by Duncan Griffin, sprinted his way 75 yards into the end zone, escorted by Cousineau and Woody Roach.

Fox, a former prep gymnast and high jumper, had long promised to perform a back flip if he ever scored a touchdown again as a Buckeye (he had returned a blocked punt two yards for a score in '73). Temporarily avoiding the congratulations of his jubilant teammates, Fox kept his promise. He later admitted that he was so fatigued from his touchdown trek that he almost couldn't complete his backwards revolution. Still, the capacity crowd went bonkers, as even Hayes cracked a quick smile about the stunt.

Just before the half Ohio State marched 89 yards in 14 plays for an additional score. Greene found Willis on two timing route patterns, and the elusive quarterback capped the long journey with a seven yard keeper on a daring fourth and one call.

The many woes of Wisconsin continued to mount following the brief respite. Canada fumbled once more on the Badgers opening play, with Ray Griffin recovering on the Wisconsin 24. On three successive runs, Archie finished what his brother began, as he lugged the ball into the end zone. After the Badgers received the ensuing kickoff, Ken Starch replaced Canada, with familiar results. Curto emerged from a big pileup after a Starch bobble, with his second recovery of the day. Ohio State took over, again deep in Wisconsin territory. Archie stayed in with the second team offense until he crossed the century mark, finishing with 107.

After Archie's cheered exit, seldom-used senior Lou Williott and the ever-improving Jeff Logan took control. Williot carried the brunt of the load as OSU marched in for the score. Following a brief Badger possession, Logan capped another Williot-dominated drive with a 16 yard touchdown romp.

Williott was a prep star from the football-mad environs of Youngstown, Ohio, who disappointingly was buried behind some fine backfield talent at OSU. Still, Lou was an outstanding blocker, perhaps the best of his position for the Buckeyes, and really shined in this, a rare Saturday opportunity. In the typical Buckeye offense, the fullback was essentially a "backfield guard" between the twenty yards lines, and Williott used his numerous blocking nods to really drill some Badgers.

The final tally in the 56-0 shellacking was a one yard Gerald sneak over the goal line, set up after a fourth down snap from center sailed over the head of Wisconsin punter Ray (Dick) Milaeger. The Buckeyes recovered in the shadow of the Wisconsin goal, and a Gerald touchdown finished the afternoon's scoring, although 10:07 remained in the rout.

The Badgers finally embarked on a decent drive in the closing minutes of the game, somewhat salvaging a modicum of pride. They somehow managed to move from their own 20 to the Buckeye 31, at which point any notions of ending the whitewashing were crushed by a Cousineau fumble recovery. On this ensuing final OSU drive of the day, Gerald darted down the sideline for a nifty 26 yard gain.

After Gerald was run out of bounds, Badger freshman safety Scott Erdmann popped him with a malicious late hit. Apparently the rage, hostility, and pent-up frustration caused by the embarrassing loss boiled over, for Erdmann viciously nailed Gerald very late, right near the Badger bench. The officials immediately tossed various penalty flags, and more revealingly, Erdmann's own teammates were so sickened and chagrined by the cheap shot they hurriedly pushed and loudly scolded the youngster. Coach Jardine hastily pulled Erdmann from the game, delivering a stiff lecture on sportsmanship in the process. Gerald characteristically bounced immediately up, yet limped off with a twisted ankle.

Later, the young quarterback humorously explained the ugly incident was his fault. "I should've outrun him," said the good-natured Texan.

With the blanking of Wisconsin, OSU achieved the third shutout of their early Big 10 season. The standard to aim for was four shutouts of conference opponents, accomplished in '73. The defensive effort against Wisconsin was even more impressive than it appeared, for the shutout was achieved with two freshman starters. Cousineau started in place of Kuhn, as mentioned, and Lenny Mills moved in for the injured Bruce Ruhl.

The unit suffered no lapses, fulfilling an amazing ten of ten announced criteria. A record 96 Buckeye leaves were doled out in the process. Cousineau finished with 13 tackles and was awarded six leaves, while Mills performed very solidly and garnered four leaves for his effort. Thompson led the way with 14 stops, as OSU shackled the prolific Marek. The Badger tailback was limited to 12 rushing attempts for just 38 yards.

Offensively, Ohio State outgained their Badger counterparts 406 total yards to 190, with Johnson totaling 98 yards on 13 early runs and Williot contributing 57 in 11 late rushes. Wisconsin never got untracked, fumbling ten times and losing possession on five of those blunders. Smith and Dannelly led the offensive line charge, grading at 80% and 79%, respectively, as OSU piled on the points.

Michigan enjoyed an even wider margin of victory this week, rushing past Northwestern 69-0. Bo was so embarrassed by the runaway victory that he could not talk to the Wildcat coach afterwards. That coach, John Pont, had been a roommate of Bo's at Miami of Ohio and was still a very close friend. The Wolverines compiled 573 rushing yards in racing to their most lopsided win since '47. Michigan was now rounding into expected form after enduring their very rocky start.

Part of the reason for their shaky beginning was a rash of debilitating injuries to the interior offensive line. Tackle Steve King and Guard Kirk Lewis were out for the year with injuries, while tight end George Pryzgodski was also sidelined, leaving the equipment manager some extra letters for other jerseys.

These experienced hands were replaced by an assortment of inexperienced substitutes, whose assimilation into the Michigan system was taking some time. Freshman quarterback Rick Leach was attempting to become the first starting frosh to ever quarterback his Big 10 team to a conference title. Leach had been All-State in football, baseball, and basketball as a prep legend in Michigan, and his supreme talents were starting to take hold as he grew more comfortable in his leadership role.

Senior tailback Gordon Bell was a tough, accomplished runner, while junior fullback Rob Lytle was the perfect complement of power and speed. Flashy freshmen Harlan Huckleby and Russell Davis provided solid backup in a marvelously deep backfield. The Wolverines were back on track in heading for the conference crown.

Ohio State now prepared for a showdown with the Boilermakers of Purdue, led in temperament and talent by the spirited, fiery Alex Agase. Purdue recently shocked Illinois 26-24, spoiling the Illini homecoming on a Mark Vitali touchdown pass with 2:32 left. The '75 team featured the rushing exploits of bruising fullback Mike Pruitt and halfback Scott Dierking, who often ran behind leading All-American prospect Ken Long, a 6'4", 255 pound center.

Vitali was back as the starting quarterback, after riding out a two game benching in favor of Craig Nagel. Purdue operated from as many as 70 different offensive sets, and Agase actually believed that the time off for Vitali beneficially allowed Mark the luxury of learning this complex offense without the added pressure of performing. Vitali hoped to continue the spate of clutch plays he engineered at Illinois.

Huge defensive lineman Ken Novak, 6'7" and 277 pounds, dominated the decent Boilermaker defensive scheme with his constant terrorization of opposing quarterbacks.

In preparing for the Boilermakers, OSU continued their very recent trend of being nagged by constant injuries. The defensive line was considerably dinged up, starting with the ailing Mark Lang. This versatile reserve was doubtful for the Purdue contest with a knee injury. Dansler and Buonamici were on the mend from an assortment of aches and pains, yet both were expected to be at or near full strength by Saturday.

Johnson left a practice prematurely at the start of the week after incurring a messy cut over his eye in a jolting scrimmage collision. The wound proved irritating but fortunately not disabling to the rampaging fullback. Kuhn was discharged from the hospital, allowed to begin light jogging but still not cleared for contact of any sort. Ruhl was fully recovered, although Mills retained his starting slot after the strong Wisconsin outing.

Fifth-year senior Larry Kain knew all too well the pitfalls of major injuries. The plucky receiver from Dayton (Ohio) Englewood had survived two operations, a broken ankle, numerous position switches, and numerous attitude adjustments before finally coming into his own in '75.

Kain was a high school All-American at linebacker-tailback, and began his Buckeye career as a linebacker. His outstanding speed prompted a position switch to defensive back; then came serious knee and shoulder operations. In mending from these surgical procedures, Kain cracked his ankle and missed his entire sophomore year.

During his exile from athletics, Kain concentrated heavily on his studies, in anticipation of a business career following graduation. As a junior, Kain switched to defensive end and played a limited backup role to the extraordinarily gifted Van DeCree. Still not satisfied with his role, Kain convinced Ralph Staub to try him as a tight end.

In '74, at this new position, Kain played often in the robust T formation, also relieving France and Bartoszek in other sets. By the close of the campaign, Kain was pushing the more seasoned vets to their limits. Kain bulked up by about 20 pounds in the off-season, without sacrificing any of his 4.7 (forty yard) speed, and was now an integral component of the dangerous, if relatively unknown, OSU passing attack.

With six catches for 108 yards and consistently high gradings for his blocking, Kain was entertaining modest thoughts of an NFL career, much in the manner of his more esteemed predecessors at the position. Kain and Dannelly were the old hands of the OSU team. The fishing and hunting buddies both arrived with the new stadium turf in '71, and each was enjoying his late delayed path to glory.

The familiarity with that turf brought the expectation of adjustment problems for OSU during the road trip to Purdue. The Boilermakers recently pioneered their breakthrough Prescription Athletic Turf, which was actually grass. The grass was planted above an elaborate system of plastic lining and pipes which pumped moisture into an underlying layer of sand, forcing the topsoil to develop long roots extending over one foot beneath the surface.

The prescription turf was designed to provide the comfort of grass with the convenience and drainage of conventional artificial turf. Consequently, the Thursday OSU practice was held at the Ernie Biggs athletic facility, on regular grass, which was the closest simulation of the prescription turf available.

Later that night, Hayes allowed quarterback coach Mummey and the quarterbacks themselves to leave a study session early so they could watch the stirring final game in the World Series between the Boston Red Sox and the Cincinnati Reds.

The first childhood love of Hayes was baseball. His passion for this game was aroused by the colorful homespun tales of retired pitcher Denton B. True "Cyclone" Young, whose reminiscences of 511 major league victories led Hayes to idolize Cy's contemporary, the gentlemanly Walter "Big Train" Johnson. Hayes believed that the World Series was, "Great for American morale...," seeing as baseball was the national pastime and the Fall Classic perhaps the pinnacle of the sport.

CHAPTER EIGHT: PURDUE

In front of the third largest Ross-Ade Stadium crowd in history to that point, Griffin reached the pinnacle of his sport, rushing for 130 yards, thereby passing Marinaro as the rushing leader for major colleges. Still within Griffin's reach was the all-time collegiate rushing mark of Howard Stephens, who ran for 5297 yards during his years at Randolph-Macon ('67 and '68), a division I-AA school, and Louisville ('71 and '72). Griffin was on pace to barely eclipse this mark, if he maintained his current pace. Archie's 23 yard blast over center with 8:30 left in the Purdue contest boosted him past the former Cornell star, immortalizing Griffin as one of the finest to ever lace up cleats on the collegiate level.

The Bucks began the day on an equally high note. Johnson burst 60 yards for a touchdown strike on the very first OSU play from scrimmage. Johnson appeared to shock the Purdue secondary with his speed, bursting through before any Boilermakers reacted.

Rather than demoralize the home team, the stunningly quick score evoked the Purdue ire. The Riveters drove right through OSU, breaking the conference scoring drought against the Bucks with a 22 yard field goal by Steve Schmidt. The OSU defense did tighten belatedly to prevent a tying score, yet the capacity crowd anticipated an upset.

Those thoughts soon dissipated, as Griffin took the ensuing kickoff 53 yards down the visitor's sideline, finally being tackled in front of his wildly exhorting brother Ray. Johnson capped a short scoring drive with a three yard run, following a clutch pass of 16 yards to Willis.

On the next OSU possession, Greene tossed a rare interception, deep in Purdue territory, stymying what seemed to be another scoring march. Purdue capitalized on the turnover by marching 66 yards in a marathon 16 play drive. Mike Pruitt repeatedly burst into the open on quick hitting, off-tackle power runs. Again, OSU denied a touchdown, forcing a second Schmidt field goal, this time from 27 yards out. The successful kick was the seventh of the year for Schmidt, establishing a new school record.

Ohio State soon regained the momentum, responding with an 80 yard drive consisting of 12 plays. The touchdown came on a Baschnagel catch deep in the right corner of the end zone, from 22 yards away. This score allowed OSU to carry a 21-6 lead into halftime. At this point, the consecutive string of 100 yard games by Griffin seemed in serious jeopardy, for Archie had just 36 yards in nine carries at the halfway mark.

Griffin responded to the challenge, asserting his dominance on the opening drive of the second half. OSU charged 80 yards in ten plays, with Willis hauling in a deep Greene pass for a 41 yard touchdown. Purdue immediately rebounded, driving downfield again, mainly on the strength of Pruitt. Upon reaching the Ohio State ten, the Boilermakers once more found paydirt very elusive.

On this occasion, a fourth down Vitali pass, intended for Jesse Townshend in the end zone, fell incomplete, and the Riveters came away with nothing. Airtight defense on this play, and numerous others throughout the contest, was supplied by Cassady. Craig broke up five passes on the afternoon, including this touchdown save.

The Bucks took over at the ten and trekked the 90 yard distance for the final score of the day. Griffin ran for 31 yards in the long drive, and also caught an eight yard pass. The score, a 28 yard scamper by Greene, came on the initial play of the final quarter, making the final score 35-6.

On the next OSU possession, Griffin gained the collegiate rushing record with his long run, shortly after surpassing the century mark. Ironically, the second team offense was poised and destined to enter the fray, on the very next play, regardless if the career mark was surpassed or not. Since the 100 yard mark had been reached, Hayes was ready to insert Red II. Greene glanced to the sideline, saw the assembled subs, and accordingly invoked a hasty prayer in the huddle. The record fell as if scripted, and the record crowd let loose with a long, gracious standing ovation. Archie's jubilant teammates carried the humble runner off the field on their shoulders, and the crowd noise swelled even larger.

Later, Hayes explained that Lenny Willis in particular convinced him to keep Griffin in the game until the record fell, especially since the contest was unquestionably settled. Hayes delayed the entrance of the second team, one of the few instances he ever acquiesced to a player wish in the heat of battle, and was happily rewarded with the phenomenal record.

The remaining eight minutes were admittedly anti-climatic, as Purdue again drove toward the OSU end zone, only to be denied by an Ed Thompson interception. Both the second team Buckeye units, offensively and defensively, were somewhat inconsistent, and Purdue actually finished with 22 first downs to 21 by OSU. The bulk of the Purdue offense was supplied by Pruitt, who accumulated 127 yards on 24 carries.

Freshman Mills recalls racing to the sideline and delivering a textbook hit on the big back after a short swing pass completion during this game, "...the best hit I ever had." So remarkable was the open field tackle, that as Mills unwrapped himself from the rugged Pruitt, Hayes was right there, praising the hard-nosed effort. Such exuberant face-to-face praise from the Head Coach was extremely rare, and each player lived for the moment that Hayes expressed such satisfaction, particularly in a game.

Woody especially enjoyed the player who fearlessly and with reckless abandon drove through a tackle, and this one such instance pleased the Old Man to no end. As Woody said, "Pursuit is taking the shortest route possible to the ball-carrier and arriving there in a bad humor." Times like these made the player almost forget the tantrums and pressure dealt with each day in practice, and really made the Buckeye experience worthwhile.

Middle guard Aaron Brown was knocked out with an early knee sprain in this rough game, and his backup Lang was of course already disabled. Buonamici moved into the unfamiliar center spot, and freshman Mark Sullivan took over the spot Nick vacated. Sullivan also went down to a knee injury, forcing the appearance of frosh Byron Cato. Cato took over at the unfamiliar middle guard spot, and the weakened defensive line understandably proved somewhat porous the remainder of the game. Pruitt continually found ample daylight up the middle, though the positive gains ceased as Purdue neared the OSU red, or scoring, zone.

With their backs to their own goal, the Buck defense rallied time and time again, led by the steady Thompson's 16 tackles. Cousineau provided 15 stops and Brudzinski had another big game with 14. Mills continued his sparkling play, thwarting two passes and providing a tackle for a loss. On the offensive side, Gerald juked his way for eight yards on three harried carries, while Roach reeled off a ten yard gain on his only attempt.

A beleaguered Agase was proud of the Purdue effort, yet conceded that his troops could not contain all of the vast array of OSU weapons. In the first half, Purdue effectively contained Griffin, yet Greene found open receivers instead, in the uncovered airways. In the closing half, Purdue primarily denied those passing lanes, so Greene and Griffin ran amok. Agase stated that big plays by the visitors provided the essential difference, particularly since Purdue came up empty in their repeated bids for big plays in return. Even Pruitt could not bust loose enough to score.

With this loss, many in West Lafayette lobbied for the dismissal of Agase, a serious sign of dissatisfaction indeed. Thankfully, the gruff coach survived the ouster movement.

On the OSU side, George Hill expressed his supreme dissatisfaction with the defensive line, promising their play would improve. In direct contrast to the week before, Buckeye leaves awarded to the defense were in sparse supply, though Thompson and Brudzinski did receive four apiece. Hard-hitting linebacker David Adkins was also praised, for his play on the second string unit.

As always, with a strong Hayes team, there was a very fine line between the first and second teams. Adkins was a perfect example of this subtle distinction, for, according to the OSU offensive coaching staff, David was consistently the hardest person to block during practices.

Despite the somewhat disappointing defensive performance, and in part because of their banged-up state, Hayes granted a very surprising day off on Monday. For most likely the first time in 25 years, a Hayes team was given reprieve from a scheduled practice, and the players were correspondingly grateful.

Following further review of the game films, offensive line play was judged excellent. Kain led the way, grading at 83% and earning 4.5 Buckeye leaves. Lukens graded out at 77%, keeping his play at a sterling level despite nursing a sore shoulder. Willis received an 84% grading for his often-overlooked blocking from the outside, while Smith also played well in the interior.

Amazingly, Griffin did not rate a leaf for his performance, though Hayes praised his achievement as "The greatest record in college football." Evidently, Hayes had trouble deciding which of the Griffin milestones was most deserving of this compliment, for this phrase was to be repeated concerning several different Griffin records. The duplication did not lessen the sincerity, however.

The rare day off allowed the coaching staff more time to review upcoming opponent Indiana. The Hoosiers had looked to improve on their 1-10 standard in '74, and '75 began promisingly enough with a 2-1 mark. However, the team had fallen on hard times since entering Big 10 play, and the Hoosiers were struggling badly enough to stand dead last in both total offense and total defense within conference play. Head coach Lee Corso humorously pinpointed the problem as not enough points and too little defense. Indiana was coming off a 55-7 trampling at the hands of Michigan.

Now, facing an OSU team which had not lost to the Hoosiers since '51, the mood in Bloomington was one of resignation and depression. Most of the attention around campus was centered on the basketball team, coached by Buckeye alumnus Bobby Knight. The Hurryin' Hoosiers were rated the number one hoop team in the nation in virtually every preseason poll, and an upcoming exhibition against a touring Russian national team pushed football to the back burner. Corso quipped: "We have one consolation [against Ohio State]. They only get to play with one football."

Indiana quarterback Terry Jones led the Big 10 in completion percentage in '74, but was not finding his receivers with the same frequency thus far in '75. The talented tight end-split end Trent Smock was the favorite target in the Hoosier game plan, especially as he was perhaps the sole deep threat. Smock also handled the prodigious punting tasks. Tailback Courtney Snyder was one of the finest runners in the annals of the school, with most every Hoosier record in jeopardy of being toppled by this large, powerful back. Defensively, IU was still adjusting to the damaging loss of defensive tackle Jack Hoffman, who was out for an indefinite period with a knee injury.

The OSU injury outlook brightened as the week went on. Lang resumed a normal practice regimen, and Kuhn also participated in contact drills for the first time in almost two weeks. Although Aaron Brown was running nicely on his sprained knee by Wednesday night, the coaching staff contemplated moving Kuhn to middle guard in order to keep Cousineau in the lineup.

Hayes created big headlines later in the week, advocating that the college game move the ball back five yards, to the 35, on kickoffs. The NFL adopted this rule two years previously, with favorable results. As Hayes so rightfully pointed out, 25 of Skladany's 49 kickoffs went for touchbacks, and though moving the placement of the kick back might prove detrimental to his ballclub, Hayes felt a need to keep the ball in the field of play more often, thereby providing more opportunities to alter the outcome of a game.

For all his usually deserved reputation as a stodgy, unimaginative keeper of the status quo, moments like these provided a rare, revealing glimpse into the cutting-edge facet of the wondrous Hayes personality. Woody realized that fan interests, and the opportunity for a trailing team to mount a comeback, marched hand in hand. The NFL results since their rules change indicated this simple step was an efficient way of stirring up both spectator interest and exciting comebacks.

It should be noted that Hayes was operating from an undisputed position of strength in this viewpoint, since the OSU kicking game was so strong, but his proposal actually was designed to hamper a team such as his. This possibility was acceptable to Hayes, if the greater good of the game was being served.

It is possible that the thoughts of Woody also turned this week to the words of perhaps his favorite writer, Emerson. "Our strength grows out of our weakness," writes Ralph Waldo. Hayes likely agreed, for the seeds of the '75 success were reaped from the ravages of the narrow Rose Bowl defeat which began the new year. Hayes habitually fought against complacency and self-satisfaction, never truly basking in glory and continuously seeking new challenges and new victories. Hayes lived an eternal quest, to find worthy opponents and to capture perfection within his team.

This philosophy is encapsulated in a war analogy, offered by the German philosopher Nietzsche. "The peace should be the means to new wars, and favor the short peace over the long. Let war be your struggle, and let peace be your victory and the means to a new war." Each game was indeed a war to Hayes, and even with his team ranked in the number one spot, Woody understood each game was an offering of fresh obstacles which had to be overcome. (Skladany and Baschnagel, on a team plane flight toward an opposing stadium, once discussed this war analogy, comparing themselves to mercenaries who flew in to wreak destruction, then were airlifted out after the battle).

This attitude was personified in the legendary Hayes work ethic, for he believed the one factor always in his control was how hard he worked. Hayes never felt any smarter or any better than an opposing coach. Rather, Hayes felt that his own unmatched, rigorous preparation propelled his team towards each of their hard-earned victories. Even when confronting a supposedly weaker team such as Indiana, and even as his Bucks neared peak performance levels, Hayes never lessened his all-consuming intensity and devotion. The Hayes passion for excellence never faltered, as fatigue was pushed aside to allow maximal work. No one kept up with the Old Man when it came to hard work, though many grew exhausted in the attempt.

Hand in hand with his philosophy toward hard work was the Hayes concept of daily improvements. Adopting a Japanese belief entitled "kaizen," which American business consultant W. Edward Demmings used to so fantastically rebuild the dismantled Pacific country's economy after World War Two, Hayes believed that seemingly insignificant, day-to-day improvements were a critical component in ultimate success.

Mickey Jackson recalls that Woody often used a barnyard fable to illustrate this concept. A small, young farm lad was given possession of a newborn calf, and instructed to bodily carry the animal from the barn to an outside spot every single day. In the beginning, the calf was small and its weight insignificant; over time, the calf grew into a huge cow. Over that same time, the young man increasingly grew larger and stronger, as the demands upon his work capacity increased. Taken over a small time frame, the young man did not visibly change, yet in the long run, these seemingly insignificant changes proved astronomical.

Following this brief lobbying for a new kickoff site, Iowa head coach Bob Commings and Minnesota head man Cal Stoll spoke out in a favor of a regressive, instead of progressive, change in college football. Each of these coaches favored a return to single platoon football, in which each player participated both offensively and defensively. With the NCAA limits on the size of teams, Stoll and Commings believed that parity among programs could only be reached by further limitations on team size. They believed the reduced pool of players would allow weaker teams to compete more effectively.

This line of reasoning thought the crucial difference between programs was the quality and quantity of the reserve players. By eliminating the advantage of that depth, a weaker school supposedly could compete at a higher level.

This retro-movement never received much support, least of all from Hayes. Hayes firmly believed in increasing participation, with few limitations on the opportunity to play (as long as reasonable academic performance standards were met), and thought that as a college fielded more players, the greater both school spirit and level of performance could be.

CHAPTER NINE: INDIANA

As Hayes had feared, OSU came out somewhat flat and relatively uninspired versus Indiana. Favored by nearly 50 points, OSU junked their normally diversified offense in favor of an almost exclusively two man attack. It appeared OSU was willing to button down their usual somewhat wide-open offense and eke out a win solely on the strength of the running game.

By contrast, Indiana pulled out all the stops in their bid for an unfathomable upset. Rather than being awed by an Ohio Stadium crowd of 87,835 hell-bent against them, the Hoosiers seemed invigorated and motivated by the challenge.

Ohio State was the top team in the land, with superior players led by a sagacious, experienced coach; Indiana relished this chance to upend a national power, and nearly pulled off an amazing road win. Corso explained his state of mind before the game: "...to see that great coach over there on the sidelines - to me he's a legend." Corso felt nothing, except possibly playing Notre Dame in South Bend, captured the essence of college football quite the same as a venture into Columbus.

The first Indiana drive of the game ended abruptly when Cassady pounced on a fumble, halting a consistent Hoosier drive. The Bucks capitalized on the turnover, marching to a 43 yard Klaban field goal, with 9:01 left in the first quarter. Undaunted with this early deficit, Indiana surprisingly ran the ball very successfully on their ensuing possessions.

Sophomore fullback Ric Enis was particularly effective in the early going, although IU was unable to generate a score as each drive was ultimately snuffed out just beyond field goal range. Cousineau contributed mightily, especially near the goal line, as he finished with a then school-record of 23 tackles.

Ohio State scored again with 10:01 remaining in the first half, on an unusually imaginative five yard dump pass to a wide-open Jimmy Moore. The unique call came out of a short-yardage set, and completely fooled the Hoosiers, who were stacked up to prevent the expected fullback plunge. The OSU game plan reverted back to an unimaginative running game following this score, although Greene did cushion their slim lead just prior to halftime. Greene followed a driving Griffin block into the end zone with just 1:32 left in the half, to cap a short drive, pushing the score to 17-0.

Following a rousing halftime exhibition by the bands of each school which was probably as exciting as the game itself, the Hoosiers emerged excitedly from their locker room. Enis compiled 109 yards rushing in the first half, and was eager to continue the damage. Indiana halted OSU on three downs to begin the second half, forcing a punt. Ohio State was levied a personal foul on the return, giving IU possession with very advantageous field position at midfield.

In an 11 play drive exhibiting the same diversity and unpredictable play calls shown in previous games by Ohio State, the Hoosiers pushed the ball into the end zone. Enis scampered four yards for the very first touchdown scored on OSU by a conference opponent all year.

Even more exuberant following the score, the Hoosier defense again shut down the simplistic Buckeye offense. Skladany blasted a 63 yard punt, seemingly pinning IU deep in their own end of the field, at the ten. On the first play, however, receiver Keith Calvin was interfered with, by an overeager Ray Griffin, and suddenly Jones was barking out signals from the IU 46. On a stirring drive of ten plays, Enis contributed 32 yards rushing, including his second touchdown of the day. His one yard plunge with 2:41 remaining in the third trimmed the lead to a precarious 17-14, after Walnut Ridge (Columbus, Ohio) product Frank Stavroff tacked on the extra point.

The two teams traded punts on their next two possessions, as the proud OSU defense finally began to play at their accustomed level. Tim Fox was out of action, exiting in the second quarter, but the speedy leaper Max Midlam stepped in to perform admirably. Brown and Lang were both knocked out, and the patched-up line finally began to solve the riddles of the unconventional Hoosier game plan.

Enis finished with 148 yards, and was particularly stifled following the second touchdown drive. This transplanted native of Union City, a small Ohio town near the Indiana border, frustrated OSU until the final quarter, although tailback Snyder never got going, ending up with only 44 yards. Leading receiver Smock was knocked out of the contest in the late going, further limiting Hoosier effectiveness.

Early in the closing period, Griffin and Johnson spearheaded a march from the OSU 31 all the way to the IU one. Just as it appeared the Bucks would ice the contest with a score, Johnson fumbled. The ball was recovered by linebacker Craig Brinkman (who later gained notoriety by catapulting himself over a steep balcony in Cincinnati's Riverfront Stadium, in pursuit of a foul ball. He lived), with just over nine minutes remaining in the game.

Attempting to spring a big play, Jones passed deep on the first play. Bruce Ruhl made a sensational, leaping, over-the-shoulder interception with his back to the line of scrimmage, giving the ball back to Ohio State on the IU 34. This time, Johnson held on to the pigskin, pounding in for the closing score. Ohio State put the defensive clamps on for the remaining minutes, emerging with a narrow, unimpressive 24-14 victory.

The two main cogs for Ohio State were Johnson, with 151 yards in 33 rushes, and Griffin, with 28 carries for 150 yards. These two carried the ball on virtually every single down, though Greene did hit on two of four passes for 19 yards and contributed 36 yards rushing on nine attempts. Indiana ended with 223 yards rushing, adding 76 through the air, in a performance hardly befitting the cellar dweller in virtually every conference category.

Corso pulled a fake punt, which was converted for a first down following a 17 yard scramble, from his bag of tricks, just one of many radical measures the eccentric coach employed in an attempt to engineer the upset.

In the end result, only the excellence of the OSU running game and a rejuvenated Buckeye defense allowed the favored team to prevail. Corso made it a special point to congratulate Griffin afterwards, especially singling him out since Corso had coached older brother Larry Griffin at Louisville. Hayes acknowledged the inspirational play of the Hoosiers, drawing upon the words of Napoleon to explain the near catastrophe. "From the sublime to the ridiculous is but one step," Hayes quoted, admitting that OSU was fortunate to escape without a defeat.

According to Archie, the near loss was actually beneficial to Ohio State. The squad was shaken from the doldrums of comfort, a feat Hayes wished to ward off prior to the slim escape. The team now realized that a number one ranking was not entrenched and could prove fleeting if not enhanced properly. As often happened, the players came to the belated conclusion that perhaps Woody was right, and his stern warnings should have been heeded in the first place.

Woody also always advocated that at the close of each day, a player look into the mirror and judge whether he had improved during that day, be it in football, school, or whatever. If the player could not honestly state he had extended the boundaries of his potential, then that player had to have regressed. According to Hayes, an individual was dynamic, either bounding forward or falling behind, with each passing day. If one was not working on getting better, right now, one had to be getting worse.

Brown, Lang, and Kuhn were all expected back for the road trip to Champaign, to face a rising Illinois team. With the addition of these veteran leaders, much of the confidence which dissipated early in the IU game began to re-emerge. Kuhn captured his starting spot back, though Cousineau expected to see plenty of action. The frosh linebacker played a solid game against IU, as did Ruhl, who also regained his starting role. Hayes and Hill each felt the defense was back to a peak level.

Offensively, Moore and Johnson received huge praise for their clutch performances against Indiana, and Illinois head coach Bob Blackmon lavished further attention on the Buckeye backfield, suggesting that it was the greatest collection of talent in the history of college football.

Taking exception to the relative anonymity of his own outstanding tailback, Bo Schembechler declared that Gordon Bell was the equal of any, including Griffin. The senior from Troy, Ohio, was a diminutive 5'9", 178 pounds, yet like Archie, ran a whole lot bigger than his program size might indicate. Bell had just surpassed Ron Johnson as the second leading career rusher in the distinguished line of Wolverine backs, and was currently performing at the best level in his outstanding career.

Bo heaped huge praise on his plucky senior, highlighting the considerable toughness of Bell, his wondrous ability to manufacture gains from seemingly busted plays, and Bell's unsurpassed propensity to instantly reverse his field and then bowl over unprepared tacklers. Bo could not wait to showcase Bell against Griffin during the November 22nd showdown in Ann Arbor.

Bo also made news for his outbursts against the officiating, following a slim 28-21 Wolverine victory at Minnesota. During this game, Bo stormed onto the field on numerous occasions, to protest what he considered terrible calls, and even bodily chased the officiating team down at the half to castigate them. Immediately after the game, Bo barred reporters from the locker room for a full 45 minutes, then unleashed a barrage of scathing criticisms. Bo said he was, "...surrounded by incompetence...," in this contest, meaning the performance of the officials, and was filing a protest of their actions.

On Wednesday, Big 10 commissioner Duke publicly reprimanded Bo for these criticisms, reminding Bo that he was already on probation for comments following a '73 clash with Duke and the '73 tie with Ohio State. Bo remained unrepentant, protesting, "When you're on the sidelines, you don't have time to worry about being polite." Minnesota coach Stoll also drew notice by railing against the leeway allowed Hayes and Schembechler during conference games, claiming that officials allowed these two to interrupt play with too long and too loud protestations.

Hayes steered remarkably clear of this boiling cauldron, sidestepping neatly all opportunities to comment. He did touch upon many other interesting subjects in a Wednesday night address to the Ladies (booster) Club in Columbus, including his suggestion of administering lie detector tests to collegiate coaching staffs, in order to root out and possibly forego many recruiting violations. Despite direct questions regarding the matter, Hayes refused to enter the Stoll/ Schembechler imbroglio.

Hayes was more concerned with the health of former Troy, Ohio, native and rampaging Buckeye fullback Bob Ferguson. The then-37 year-old Ferguson was recently felled by a severe circulatory ailment in Washington, DC, and remained hospitalized in serious condition. Ferguson slowly came back to full health, with plenty of support from both Woody and Anne Hayes.

Another former Buckeye great, quarterback Rex Kern, ended his injury-plagued NFL career this week, taking an administrative assistant position at his alma mater. Kern played in the defensive backfield with Buffalo and Baltimore, and could never quite shake a lingering series of nagging injuries. Hayes was happy to have the Lancaster, Ohio, native back within the fold, assuming a leadership role once more.

Bob Blackmon was beginning his fifth year at Illinois, since arriving from Dartmouth, which he departed as the winningest coach in Ivy league history. The '75 Illini were on the rise, their fortunes paralleling the improvement of sophomore signalcaller Kurt Steger, who was really coming on after a dreadfully slow start. Illinois was 4-4, with a 3-2 record in the conference, including an upset of Michigan State.

Jumbo-sized halfback Lonnie Perrin was fulfilling his tremendous potential after missing most of the last two years with injuries. Despite starting the '75 season with phlebitis, Perrin caught, passed, ran, and even kicked off in a continually amazing display of versatility. Scatback Chubby Phillips entered in spot situations, while fullback Steve Greene was rounding into form after missing all of '74 with a knee injury. Tackle Stu Levinick and tight end Joe Smalzer paved the way up front.

Defensively, tackle John DeFeliciantonio was as hard to handle as his name was to spell. Safety Jim Stavner finished off the few opponents not decimated by the brutal linebacking tandem of John Sullivan and Scott Studwell. Kicker Dan Beaver was extraordinary from long range, boasting four field goals of 50 or more yards in his career. His longest came from 57 yards out, displacing the old conference record previously held by former OSU kicker Gary Cairns. Interestingly, this kick by Cairns came against the Illini.

Historically, Hayes had his share of trouble with the Illini, with a career mark of four losses and two ties. It seemed OSU always had trouble putting the Champaign elite away. In '73, OSU won 30-0, though the halftime score was a modest 3-0. The Illini were fired up on that occasion by an emotional pre-game delivery by former coach Ray Eliot, whose fiery oration filtered into the packed Zuppke Field stands and kept the outcome in doubt for much of the game.

In '71, also at the unfriendly confines of Zuppke, head coach Jim Valek was fired just two days prior to the OSU game. Inspired by his dismissal, the home team nearly prevailed, finally going under by a respectable count of 24-10.

Similar resilience was expected this year, for former Illini star and NFL immortal Dick Butkus was being honored at halftime, with his induction into the Illinois Sports Hall of Fame. Illinois officials expected a crowd approaching 67,000, the most since a '67 contest with Notre Dame.

CHAPTER TEN: ILLINOIS

Come Saturday, the Illini did put up a tremendous fight in the early going, only to slowly fade under the onslaught of a resurgent Buckeye team. Beaver put the home team up first with a chip shot field goal of 36 yards, and soon after, Klaban missed a chance to tie as he was short on a 48 yard attempt. Shortly into the second quarter, OSU halted an Illini drive and received the forced punt on their own 43. Greene scrambled for a gain of 11, then Willis made a leaping, one-handed snare for a pickup of 14. Griffin outran the overpursuing Illinois defense to score from 30 yards out with 7:59 left in the half, a run which pushed him past the 5,000 yard mark in career rushing yards. Archie became the first major college athlete to reach this mark, and finished the day with 23 carries for 127 yards.

Most of the remaining time in the half was consumed by a battle of alternating punts, with Skladany winning the competition hands down. The active junior's leg was supercharged on this day, for he averaged 56.5 yards for his four punts. This average fell just short of the conference single game record, held by former Buckeye Fred Morrison, a tough fullback/punter who remained at the top of the books with a 57.3 yard average, achieved in a '49 contest.

The OSU defense completely dismantled the Illinois offense, who entered the game without Steger, a late scratch due to a painful back bruise. Despite an interception of Greene which yielded favorable field position, the Illini could produce no further points after the Beaver kick. With just minutes left in the half, OSU eked out a first down just across midfield. Greene had the wind jarred out of him on a pass attempt meant for Griffin, and Pacenta entered the game. Gerald was still limping from the late hit taken in the Wisconsin game, so Hayes was forced to go with his unseasoned junior. Pacenta passed incomplete, setting up a 59 yard field goal attempt.

Since the leg of Skladany seemed unusually lively on this afternoon, Hayes sent Tom out to try the prodigious boot. Two ticks remained on the clock. The curly-haired junior wound up and unleashed a low, line drive knuckleball which barely cleared the uprights, setting a new conference mark and vaulting the OSU lead to 10-3.

The Bucks charged out of the locker room after the half, eager to lay waste to the tenacious Illini. Despite the upwell of emotion, OSU was forced to punt. Illinois quarterback Jim Kopatz was immediately picked off by Thompson, who was brought down on the Illinois 42. Making only minimal yardage, OSU was forced to attempt another field goal. This time Skladany, still in for the leg-weary Klaban, popped the ball in from 40 yards away, increasing the lead to 13-3.

Illinois got possession, only to have Tim Fox step into a Kopatz pass and dash 20 yards unmolested into the end zone. The acrobatic safety furthered his tradition by again executing a daring back flip. This flip was more aesthetic than his first such celebratory tumble, probably since the touchdown run was shorter and Fox was less winded.

The Illini problem in retaining possession continued following the kickoff. Chubby Phillips could not come up with an option pitch as Cassady drilled him when the ball arrived. Brudzinski came up with the loose ball on the Illinois 21. In four plays, OSU pushed the ball into the end zone, with Johnson ramming in on the last play of the third quarter. Without the presence of big DeFeliciantonio, out due to an injury incurred just before the opening kickoff, Illinois simply was worn down by the aggressive Ohio State blocking.

The Illini erosion continued in the final quarter. This time Greene, back in after finally catching his breath, provided an exciting aerial display, finding Baschnagel open deep for a 51 yard gain. Greene then hit Griffin for a slight four yard pickup, Baschnagel again for ten, and following a sack of six yards, Greene connected with the open wingback Brian for another 17 yards. These passes led to a Johnson scoring plunge, his 21st on the year, which surpassed the school and conference record of 20, previously set by Champ Henson in '72. Klaban pulled the point after wide, continuing his strange one day slump.

After this tally, Hayes pulled his regulars, bringing in the second teams. The Red II offense responded with perhaps the finest drive of the year. Thirteen plays yielded 87 yards, not including an additional 15 yards, regained in response to a penalty. Jeff Logan capped the exquisite drive by sweeping in from 13 yards out, with a scant 36 seconds left.

Hayes was so enamored with the closing march that he awarded everyone involved with a Buckeye leaf. The drive was a telling punctuation to a 40-3 rout, in which OSU outgained the Illini 269 total yards to 54 in the second half. Greene finished the day eight of 11 passing, for 118 yards, with four of those completions going to Baschnagel for 87 yards. Griffin swung out of the backfield to catch three balls as well.

The one downer of the day was the loss of the formidable frosh Moore, who went down with a severe knee injury in the first quarter. The exciting, spectacularly improving frosh would miss the rest of the year. Moore went under the expert knife of team surgeon Dr. Mel Olix just a few days after this injury occurred. Brown re-injured his knee again, yet the prognosis had him missing just a few practices.

Lang stepped up to contribute ten tackles after Brown went down, leading a unit which Hayes claimed played the best it had in over a month. Woody felt his Bucks were back on the upswing, yet felt there was a need to improve the offense. "We had plenty of trouble out here," Hayes revealed, although the morale of the squad remained superb.

Asked afterward how long a victory celebration usually lasted, Hayes only half-jokingly responded, "...until I hit the locker room." Despite the upcoming clash with the upsurging Minnesota Gophers, the thoughts of Hayes could not help but turn to the impending showdown with Michigan. One daring reporter, obviously new to interviews with the Coach, brazenly asked of Hayes, "How many TD's are you going to beat Michigan by?" Surprisingly, Woody cracked a half-smile, as many reporters cringed in expectation of an outburst, and pleasantly promised that the game would be a "classic".

Hayes also remarked that the officiating crew made it a point to mention that this was the cleanest game they had ever officiated. Hayes loved hardnosed football, but he abhorred any hint of dirty play. Woody's squads lived by his admonishment, "It is hard to play dirty against a man who picks you up." This comment from the officiating crew was high praise indeed.

Hayes roundly applauded the performances of Johnson, Roach, and Ward after reviews of the game films. Hayes pointed out that each of these players demonstrated a wonderful work ethic during practices, particularly the immensely talented, yet still workmanlike Ward. Hayes recognized that Roach toiled in relative obscurity, yet was essentially a team leader, merely through his constant effort and upbeat attitude.

Johnson was praised for stepping forward and asserting his unbelievable physical skills in literally dozens of short-yardage and goal line situations. Nothing pleased Hayes more than a well-executed blast off-tackle by a plowhorse fullback, and nobody ever accomplished this better than Pete in '75. Hayes saved his loftiest platitudes for the tremendous kicking exhibition put on by Skladany.

It may be very significant to note that since '52, on every road trip to Champaign, Hayes enlisted the services of one special waiter, Charles Latham, in serving the traditional Friday night team meal. Latham utilized a novel technique while serving the Buckeyes' dinner: He gustily belted out songs as he delivered food and drinks. This style met with the hearty approval of Hayes, especially since on the day following the first singing experience, OSU intercepted ace Illini quarterback Tommy McConnel six times en route to a 27-7 victory. Thereafter, Hayes insisted that Charley sing at each squad dinner prior to an Illinois confrontation.

On this particular Friday, Charley made his usual appearance, but Hayes sensed his team needed further uplifting. He called upon Skladany to take the stage, and as Tom recalls, "No one ever said 'no' to Woody." Reluctantly at first, then with growing abandon, Skladany sang polkas and drinking songs. The mood of the team immediately changed into an uproarious, excited mode. The rousing ovations and boisterous chants of his name seemed to imbue Skladany with even more verve and energy than normal, and this wave of power obviously was manifested in his fantastic Saturday performance. This is another classic example of the ingenious methods Hayes called upon to empower his players.

The forthcoming game with Minnesota was especially noteworthy. Not only was it the final home game of the year; it was also the last home game for a remarkably talented and accomplished senior class, which had never lost an Ohio Stadium contest in their four year home career. The Gophers had not emerged victorious in Ohio Stadium since '66, and this unenviable task of confronting the illustrious departing seniors in front of a rabid home crowd held little promise for a road win this year, either.

Nevertheless, the Gophers were a rallying, improving club. Minnesota had evolved from an I formation running team into an almost exclusively passing unit out of the same I formation. Quarterback Tony Dungy was finally fulfilling the lavish potential he previously had only flashed intermittently. With three touchdown passes in his latest game, a rout of Northwestern, Dungy moved into the lead in virtually all conference and total yardage categories.

The talented 6'2", 204 pound receiver Ron Kullas was on a pace to exceed conference records for catches, yards, and touchdown receptions. Split end Mike Jones was possibly the most athletic Gopher, and was a bona-fide deep threat each snap.

Though their running game was now essentially shunned, the second leading rusher for Minnesota, junior Bubby Holmes, was coming on strong after a sophomore year in which he did not carry the ball even once. Enrolling out of high school from Monessan, Pennsylvania, Holmes was thought to be every inch the equal of then-Pitt Panther sensation Tony Dorsett. Holmes was just now showing some of that promise.

Defensively, tackle Keith Simons was the best Stoll had ever coached. The 6'5", 249 pound ruffian demonstrated agility, power, and great ball-hawking instincts. The makings of a fine defensive triumvirate was completed by middle guard George Washington and linebacker Steve Stewart.

Late in this week, Hayes and his wife were honored at a Buckeye Boosters dinner. Hayes left this avalanche of accolades to participate in a Si U party. Si U was a self-described non-fraternity of former OSU students who frequented various 16th and High establishments, just off the Columbus campus, during their undergraduate days. Hayes was an honorary member.

Woody gave a short speech in honor of the night's special guests, the several reunited members of the '35 Buckeye football team. This fine 7-1 team was remembered more for a legendary 18-13 loss to Notre Dame than it was for taking the conference title. In that game, OSU led 13-0 into the final quarter, only to fall victim to an Irish comeback which was the stuff of legend. To this day, this '35 contest is considered one of the finest collegiate games ever played.

After the atypically brief talk by Hayes, Governor James Rhodes addressed the prestigious gathering. "We little realize the greatness of Woody Hayes...

the great things he's done...," Rhodes intoned to enthusiastic cheers. The masterful politician was always outlandish in his praise of Woody, and this night was no exception. The keynote speaker, cartoonist Milton Caniff, was hard-pressed to follow Hayes and Rhodes, but pulled the feat off to his predecessors throaty approval.

CHAPTER ELEVEN: MINNESOTA

Hayes rested not at all on these laurels, focusing instead on the final sendoff to possibly his finest senior class. The visiting Gophers proved no match for the emotional Buckeyes, who leveled the invaders by a 38-6 margin. The contest began mildly enough, as Klaban capped a short drive late in the opening quarter with a 29 yard field goal. On the ensuing Gopher possession, Dungy was harassed unmercifully, and in the heat of several onrushing Bucks, tossed an interception to Cassady.

OSU cashed in, charging 64 yards to their first touchdown on the day. Greene faked into the line and swept past the charging Gophers for the 14 yard score on a daring fourth and inches call. This run was one of many in his illustrious career, some on much, much longer runs, in which Greene so befuddled the defense that not a finger was laid upon his skinny body. Eyewitnesses to this particular run, and numerous others, question whether Greene would have even been stopped had he been playing touch football.

The Minnesota passing attack was likewise so completely stifled by the hard-charging OSU defense, that Dungy did not complete a single pass in the opening half. He did throw two interceptions, though. Griffin reached the end zone just prior to halftime on an exquisite 19 yard sweep, putting the Bucks ahead 17-0.

Minnesota emerged out of the break with their sole sustained offensive thrust of the day. Mostly on the strength of Dungy, for on this drive he completed almost every pass, the Gophers moved 84 yards in a dominating 18 play march. Dungy connected with fullback Greg Barlow on a five yard scoring toss, and the OSU margin was trimmed to 17-6. Buonamici slapped away a Dungy pass on the bid for two, providing impetus for an OSU drive following the kickoff.

Ohio State chewed up plenty of real estate and time as the Bucks drove 80 yards to another score. Johnson rammed in for his 22nd TD of the year, putting OSU securely in the lead for good. Johnson ended another fine effort with 90 yards rushing. The offensive success of Minnesota was short-lived, and the Gophers were forced to punt. Fox broke the return for a 32 yard pickup, with his progress finally being halted at the Minnesota 41.

Just a few plays hence, Greene sprinted 31 yards off left tackle for his second astonishing score of the day. The moves of Cornelius never ceased to amaze, though often their true brilliance was not realized until stop-action film was viewed.

On this day dominated by graduating seniors, the freshman Mills provided his own personal highlight reel. Following the final Greene strike, the Gophers were summarily stopped by the overpowering Buck defense, and forced to kick.

Mills charged through the line, smothering the punt of Frank Mosko with his helmet and left arm. Mills recovered his own block on the Minnesota 21. In a fitting finale to the afternoon scoring, Baschnagel took a handoff on the very first play and ran a reverse around the confused Gophers for a fancy score.

Minnesota did manage one final threat, as Dungy passed and scrambled under pressure, moving the chains to the OSU 36. Again, Mills displayed his knack for the big play, stepping in front of the intended receiver to snare an errant Dungy toss at the home 22. Hayes used the extra time afforded with this possession to pull his senior starters on offense one at a time. Following each play, a senior ran off to the excited cheers of the adoring home crowd.

More meaningfully, as each senior exited to this thunderous applause, Hayes greeted him with a huge smile and a congratulatory handshake. Minnesota got the ball back, and Hayes accorded this same exiting privilege to his seniors on defense.

The virtually incomparable OSU backfield finished with 431 of the 491 total yards accumulated by the Bucks, and scored all five touchdowns. Griffin broke the 100 yard barrier for the 31st straight time in a regular season contest (the previous record was 17 consecutive games, held by the great Steve Owens of Oklahoma), compiling 124 yards before his exit with 3:52 left brought down the house. (The original intent of Woody was to pull the seniors following the Mills interception; the quick Baschnagel score pleasantly upset this schedule.)

Archie also hauled in two passes for 48 yards, concluding his home career in a typically virtuoso manner. Greene completed 7 of 13 pass attempts for 131 yards, contributing 63 yards rushing on 13 carries. Baschnagel added three receptions for 42 yards, and Kain grabbed one pass for an 11 yard gain. Willis broke free for 30 yards on his lone catch. The highly underrated Curto pressured Dungy unceasingly all day, as did Kuhn, closing out his home career in spectacular fashion. Ken made 13 tackles, sacked Dungy, and broke up two passes, all in typically demonstrative fashion.

Underclassman Thompson added 15 tackles, and Beamon finished with 13 stops. The OSU line ran roughshod all afternoon, nailing Dungy for a total of 39 yards in losses.

Just after the conclusion of this game, OSU learned that the matchup with Michigan would indeed be for the conference crown, since the Wolverines hung on to beat a stubborn Illinois team 21-15. Hayes declined any comment on the anticipated battle, citing '74 as the reason.

That year, Bo commented that the kicking game would determine the outcome. In response to this prophesy, Hayes accordingly drilled his placement man Klaban especially hard. The four field goals Tom contributed in the eventual game certainly proved to be the difference, so Hayes did not want to chance providing Bo with such an opening.

Instead of comments regarding the team up north, Hayes remarked that in the '74 game against Minnesota, all four backfield starters scored in the first half. Hayes jokingly claimed he was upset, since today this same feat took almost the entire game. Hayes spoke about saying farewell to this marvelous senior class, insisting there was no sorrow involved.

The passing of seniors was nothing but a joyous occasion. "Graduation is the most wholesome thing about a football team...," Hayes insisted, for graduation allowed new faces to make their mark on a program. Hayes felt rewarded each year as the seniors left, as graduation was the mission of the university itself.

Interestingly, on this same day, Yale head coach Carmen Cozza surpassed the immortal Walter Camp as the winningest Eli mentor. Cozza, who played for Hayes as a star halfback at Miami, and went on to coach with Woody on the Redskin staff, downplayed the significance of the wins. Cozza echoed his former coach and boss in stating the greater significance of his team's graduation rates. During his eight year reign at Yale, only four of his players had not achieved a degree, quite a feat considering the stringent academic standards of the Ivy League. Once more, the Hayes influence was far-reaching and everlasting.

Michigan entered the big game riding a seven game winning streak. The aptly coined "Baby Blue," christened because the roster was so heavily-laden with frosh and sophomore Wolverines, had righted their fortunes following the two early ties. As usual, this OSU-UM confrontation would decide the Big 10 Rose Bowl representative. Schembechler was eager to break the three year lock OSU enjoyed on the trip to Pasadena, especially since the last two OSU trips came via a vote of the conference council.

In essence, since then-in-vogue conference rules permitted just one team to participate in a bowl, UM was left empty-handed even though they were league co-champions in both '73 and '74. In '75, partly because the conference wished to avoid further controversy regarding bowl berths, commissioner Wayne Duke broke tradition and announced that the loser of this conference summit clash would also attend a bowl, in this case the prestigious Orange Bowl in Miami.

Duke rightly realized that allowing two conference teams into a bowl allowed greater publicity, and most importantly, more money to flow into the coffers of the conference. With the growth of televised games and consequent increased profits becoming possible from bowl appearances, the days of limiting post-season participation to only one, or even a few, conference teams were at an end.

Schembechler was very confident that his young team would emerge as the victor, especially since OSU had not won in Ann Arbor since '67. Michigan led the conference in both rushing and total offense, with Bell, Lytle, and Leach racking up stats comparable to those of Griffin, Johnson, and Greene. The southpaw Leach was now an acknowledged master of the tricky Wolverine option attack, although his passing remained streaky. A 218 yard aerial output against Purdue was his lone standout passing display of the year, for overall Leach had connected on just 18 of his 40 pass attempts in the season.

His infrequent completions did include several long connections with wingback Jim Smith, though the overall accuracy of Leach remained suspect. Besides the growth of his young pitcher, Bo listed the maturation of the extremely young offensive line as a prime factor in the ascendance of his team. Gigantic sophomore tackle Mike Kenn was particularly asserting his brilliance as the interior unit jelled.

Defensively, undersized middle guard Tim Davis was the crux of a patented, hard-hitting, ball-swarming, highly disciplined Wolverine bunch. The 5'10", 215 pound Davis was ably assisted by end Dan Jilek and linebacker Calvin O'Neal. Free safety Don Dufek roamed the field as the perfectly named monster back, a glorified linebacker playing in the secondary. Dufek dished out ferocious licks and provided essential field leadership. Dufek, and the entire Michigan team, played by legendary former New York Giant coach Steve Owen's credo: "Football was invented by a mean s.o.b., and that's the way the game is supposed to be played."

Once more, this game stacked up as two very similar, powerhouse running attacks vying to control two equally solid, walloping swarms of defenders.

Bo downplayed the seeming bitterness of the rivalry, attributing such descriptions to media overzealousness. Bo granted that traditionally, the contest was fiercely fought, albeit in a clean and sportsmanlike manner. Bo went out of his way to deny any personal rivalry between himself and Hayes, also his former coach and boss. Schembechler did jest, "Archie and I have a lot in common. We both played for the same coach. He brags about it, and I can't live it down."

Even Hayes made light of the so-called personal rivalry. "We're both left-handed, we've both had heart attacks, and we both have such wonderful dispositions," Hayes said, to the great amusement of assembled reporters.

Despite this jocularity, each coach closed practices to the media, with Hayes going so far as to liken possible practice espionage to the Klaus Fuchs spying incident, which revealed the secrets of the atomic bomb to the Soviet Union. In the estimation of Woody, this game meant that much - many others were inclined to agree.

Astonishingly, on Wednesday, free-lance United Press International photographer Andrew Sachs was caught snapping illicit pictures of a Michigan practice. A predictably angry Schembechler led the physical rush to confront the cameraman, whose film was confiscated by local police at the behest of the UM coaching staff.

Later, Bo's loving wife Millie allowed that her husband was learning to relax since his summer heart attack, but still blew up at certain provocations, such as this. His ill-temper was certainly quite understandable in this circumstance.

Ohio State continued their usual regimen of harsh Monday, Tuesday, and Wednesday practices, which lessened in intensity to just light run-throughs on Thursday and Friday. Wednesday evening, unaware of the Ann Arbor spying incident, Hayes politely discussed the mild weather conditions expected on gameday. The meteorological conversation lasted ten minutes; this amount of time was made more remarkable since a Tuesday press conference lasted all of 96 seconds.

As the week progressed, Hayes seemed in his most relaxed state ever prior to a Michigan game. Much of this calm emanated from his knowledge that his pet formation, the button-shoe robust T, was functioning at an unusually efficient level, in spite of the absence of integral cog Jimmy Moore. Hayes noted that the short-yardage and goal-line formation was successful on 39 of the last 41 opportunities, an unbelievably high percentage.

Just as successful in '75 was former Buckeye Tom Campana, enjoying a blockbuster campaign for the Saskatchewan Roughriders of the CFL. Campana led the league in punt returns, and had amassed an amazing 1936 yards rushing over the 16 game season. One of Campana's teammates was former Buck Ted Provost, whose interception return for a touchdown precipitated the shocking '68 upset of Purdue.

Such a victory over UM this week would not be considered an upset, but it would put OSU one step closer to the only football goal that mattered to Hayes: OSU must reach the Rose Bowl and win the national championship. The last-second loss to USC in the Rose prevented a national title in '74, and Hayes desperately wanted his fourth number one team. Only the tie against Michigan kept the crown from OSU in '73, and Hayes wanted no such happenings this year. As the Wolverine roster included 37 Ohio natives, nine of whom started, an OSU victory over such turncoats would prove even sweeter.

To those who contend that Woody was nothing more than a martinet, a man blind to all but this elusive national title, though, consider the story of Joel Laser. Laser was a prep star from Akron, Ohio, recruited as an offensive lineman in '75. His decision to attend Ohio State was based tremendously on the personal desire of his terminally ill mother, who unfortunately passed on before she could see her son step into Ohio Stadium.

With this traumatic loss of his wife, Joel's father slipped into a deep depression. Not surprisingly, Joel himself was sent into a downward emotional spiral, and somewhat lost interest in football. As the frosh of '75 arrived in the fall, Joel simply did not play up to his high school promise. Nonetheless, on the very first day off from fall workouts, Hayes approached his underachieving lineman and insisted Joel take off to visit and help his ailing father. Then, to ensure that the youngster could make such a journey, Hayes handed over the keys to his own El Camino, and forced Joel to make the beneficial trip.

Although Joel's play did not pick up too much through the course of the season, on Monday of this UM week, just after practice, Hayes called the scout team member into his office, to meet with Dr. Murphy. In this, the busiest, most intense week of the season, Woody wanted to know what further could be done to help Joel's dad. The grateful frosh was overwhelmed by the caring attitude of Hayes, who helped each of his boys, regardless of their level of contribution to the team. Thankfully, with the help of others like Hayes and Murphy, the senior Laser did eventually defeat his condition.

This generosity and openness was typical of Woody. Duncan Griffin recalls, despite often being at odds with the coaching staff over his shortage of playing time, that Woody encouraged similarly frustrated players to speak truthfully and forcefully to him, in private. Woody did not necessarily accommodate the request of said player; he did respond with his own honest comments and explanations. In this manner, many misconceptions and pent-up feelings were released, and team morale usually stayed high.

On Thursday of this week, OSU conducted the traditional senior tackle, whereby each senior ceremoniously leveled the tackling dummy one final time. On this day, TBDBITL provided musical accompaniment, much to the benefit of the already charged-up squad. Following this ritual, held in Ohio Stadium, Hayes led the kicking unit through waiting throngs of newsmen over to his home away from home, the Biggs Athletic facility. In remembrance of the crucial kicks in '74, Hayes put his placement crew through additional paces prior to the departure to Ann Arbor.

Once in the despised state up north, the Friday workout was delayed by an unwieldy, time-consuming tarpaulin removal. Expectedly mild weather conditions had given way to much colder temperatures, including swirling snow flurries, necessitating protection of the field.

At the team meal following the mellow workout, the team was especially uptight and tense, particularly in light of the national title implications surrounding the upcoming game. As the food was being delivered, the restaurant was eerily quiet. Suddenly, the shouts of Hayes shattered the uneasy silence. Woody was banging on his water glass, demanding to see the maitre d'. The head waiter hustled over, and Hayes animatedly instructed the man to immediately replace the nubile, lovely waitresses currently serving the team. As the co-eds were confusedly escorted out and replaced by greasy line cooks and less appealing bussers, Hayes explained the sudden switch to his hushed team, who were completely in the dark concerning the intentions of their Coach.

"It was a trick by Bo... softening you up with the attractive co-eds...," Hayes stated, and instantly, the team picked up the fabricated theme. Bo was trying to trick OSU into complacency and gentility by distractions of the flesh, but Hayes had foiled the lecherous attempt. Now the team was unified in their desire to pay Bo back, and confident since they had uncovered his clever attempt at psychological warfare.

The team rode this wave of induced emotion, with the ungodly pressure greatly eased, right up to kickoff time. Skladany recalls being in awe of the genius of Hayes, at his innate ability to motivate and bring the team together, especially amidst pressure situations, via such comedic intrusions.

CHAPTER TWELVE: MICHIGAN

Saturday dawned extremely chilly with intermittent hints of snowfall, yet the bone-cold weather failed to subdue a then all-time collegiate record crowd of 105,543 enthusiastic fans. Somewhat unexpectedly, the behavior of the teeming crowd was very much under control, their conduct unusually mild in comparison to recent antics during OSU-UM games. Of course, part of this mellowness was due to the somewhat predictable defensive tilt of the affair, excluding the initial OSU possession.

On their opening opportunity, the Buckeyes certainly looked the part of two touchdown favorites. The Bucks traveled 63 grueling yards in a 15 play drive, with the touchdown coming on an unconventional seven yard pass to a circling Johnson. This was one of those many plays Hayes kept under wraps until the big game, when they were sprung on an unsuspecting opponent. This lengthy drive ate up most of the first quarter, the score coming with 4:43 left, and cooled the partisan crowd down even more than the weather did.

The remainder of the first quarter and most of the second was chock full of defensive handiwork. Both offenses really struggled against the impassioned defenders. The OSU offense was virtually shut down, with only one first down following the touchdown, and that occurring in the first minutes of the second quarter.

From that point on, UM literally squashed the vaunted OSU running attack, as Griffin ended the half with a miniscule 25 yards rushing. Don Dufek and O'Neal shadowed and stalked the every move of Archie, who guttily rammed his way into the impenetrable maize and blue unit.

With 4:59 left in the half, UM took over after fielding a Skladany punt on their 20. Gordon Bell found precious running room between the tackles, propelling the Wolverines downfield. Leach came up with several crucial tosses to split end Keith Johnson, for gains totaling 42 yards. Ultimately, 11 yards from the OSU goal line, UM pulled their own imaginative play from the Bo bag of tricks. Bell took the handoff, swept outside, only to stop and loft a touchdown pass to a wide open Jim Smith.

Following a brief OSU possession, Michigan again drove downfield within scoring range. With five seconds left in the half, Gregg Willner missed a 36 yard field goal, preserving the halftime tie.

In the third quarter, the woeful performance of the OSU offense continued. Michigan continued to contain Griffin, and neither Johnson nor Greene was able to contribute much, either. The entire quarter passed with not a single first down by Ohio State. Only the brilliant punts of Skladany salvaged any advantageous field position. Michigan was able to piece together several brief drives, though Willner was short on a 43 yard field goal, so the score remained deadlocked.

Michigan again drove into OSU territory as the third quarter ended, but the embattled Buckeye defenders kept the home team out of field goal range. Michigan defensive end and punter John Anderson uncorked his finest punt of the day, to open the final quarter, as UM was temporarily repelled. The kick bounced 33 yards downfield, finally being downed on the OSU five.

With the running backs lined up in the end zone, OSU failed to generate any gains. Two running plays yielded a loss of one yard, so Skladany was brought in to punt on third down. Unfortunately, Skladany suffered his one disappointing kick of the day, with his floater tailing out of bounds at the Buckeye 43.

Finally taking advantage of the worn down OSU defenders, Bell and Lytle ripped through the fatigued visitor line. A short pass to Smith helped the UM cause, as did a rare penalty on OSU. Leach threw incomplete on a third and nine situation, and OSU was ruled offsides. Given another chance, Leach hung on to the ball and ran in for the score on the ensuing play. With 7:11 remaining, UM led 14-7.

This go-ahead score jolted the lethargic OSU offense from their long stupor. Ohio State started on the 20, after a Bob Wood kickoff sailed out of the end zone. The rallying effort began in characteristically lackluster fashion, as Greene threw incomplete on each of the first two downs. On third down, with this game and any realistic chance at a national title slipping away, the leadership of the seniors came to the surface. Baschnagal freed himself for a 17 yard reception, being leveled and knocked senseless in the process. This display of fortitude, the first inkling of offensive success in almost 40 minutes of game time, inspired OSU.

Instantly, the Bucks seemed unstoppable. Greene connected with Willis for two consecutive passes of 14 yards each, then Griffin came through in the clutch. He rattled off his longest run of the day, 11 yards, to give Ohio State another first down. Seemingly rattled and disoriented by this series of OSU first downs, UM yielded a 12 yard option keeper by Greene and a six yard burst up the middle by Johnson, putting the ball at the two. The Wolverines tightened, although Johnson finally cracked the goal line on his third thunderous attempt. With 3:48 remaining, following the Klaban conversion, the score was tied. A national television audience could not help but recall a similar situation in the '73 game.

After Skladany jacked the ensuing kickoff over the end zone, Bo revealed his strategy, devised prior to the game. Michigan would play for the win, disdaining any chance of not going to the Rose Bowl if the contest was a tie, since that subsequent decision rested with the Big 10 council. After all, the decisions of that council had not been favorable to Michigan in the recent past.

Thus emboldened, Leach came out firing. Following a nine yard sack at the hands of Brown and Brudzinski, Leach tossed an ill-advised pass down the middle. Ray Griffin stepped in, grabbed the misfire, and demonstrated his running back roots by twisting, cutting, and breaking tackles all the way to the three yard line.

This was the very first interception of Ray's life; few interceptions in the history of Big 10 football have been as pivotal. On the first play following the return, Johnson crashed in for his second touchdown within a 59 second span. When Klaban tacked on the extra point, OSU was joltingly up 21-14.

Now struggling just to salvage a despised tie, Michigan got the ball back with less than two minutes remaining. On a desperation fourth down play, Cassady made his second theft of the day, turning possession over to OSU. Johnson carried three times for 19 yards, each carry followed by an UM timeout, as the home team frustratingly saw the clock tick inexorably to 0:00. Johnson ended the day with 52 yards on 18 rushes, and his three scores put him at a prodigious 25 for the year (Lydell Mitchell of Penn State held the NCAA record at that time, with 29 TD's in '71).

After the final carry, an exasperated Michigan crowd filed out, aware they had just witnessed one of the most improbable comebacks in the history of the rivalry. The loss was just the fourth in the last 70 games for UM, and each loss came at the hands of Ohio State. Woody immediately christened the miraculous comeback as, "...the greatest game I've ever coached." Greene was named the offensive player of the game by the television sportscasters, and revealed that as OSU fell behind, he took it upon himself to intone a prayer in the huddle. Such a divine request was, "...not to win... but to give us strength."

Apparently, this behest worked better than expected. Greene ended up seven of 16 passing for 84 yards, suffering two interceptions; his MVP award derived as much from his leadership role as from his performance. His UM counterpart Leach suffered through a predictably miserable passing day, connecting on only eight of 20 tosses, though he did gain 102 yards through these attempts. Three of his passes regretfully ended up in the wrong receiving hands.

With this win, OSU emerged, for the first time ever, from a regular season owning 11 victories (perhaps partly because, as Woody jestfully acknowledged, this was only the second time that many games were scheduled). In the tumultuous post-game locker room, Dannelly proposed over the celebratory din that game balls be presented to Hayes and defensive architect George Hill. This request was met with loud approval. Disappointingly, Bell (21-124) and Lytle (18-104), had each powered for over 100 yards, while the Griffin string of such efforts came to a crashing halt.

Griffin was battered, abused, and treated very roughly by an aggressive Wolverine defense, yet the affable Archie was perhaps the happiest Buckeye in the post-game locker room. Ray was basking in the glow of the predominate media crush, and Archie could not have been happier. Following the presentation of game balls, Hayes, Hill, and very popular equipment men John Bozick and Phil Bennett were playfully dunked, fully clothed, in the shower.

Hayes dried off somewhat and addressed his team briefly, then he ventured to a small, cramped, storage room beneath the stadium to face the media. In a speech as improbable to victory celebrations as the OSU comeback win seemed midway through the final quarter, Hayes mesmerized all assembled.

Woody began his monologue by reminding those present that 12 years previously, to the very day, President John Fitzgerald Kennedy was shot and killed. "I have to believe that this nation, from that day forward, we've been on the skids. I think we started doubting one another and doubting our own abilities," Hayes claimed.

By this time in the speech, the newsmen had absolutely no idea what was coming next, as Hayes ceased his understated manner. "But I'll tell you something. That Michigan team didn't doubt one another and this great Ohio State team didn't doubt one another, or we couldn't have won." Hayes agreed with former UM head coach Bennie Oosterbaan, who informed, "The place for doubt is in the dictionary."

This impromptu speech of Hayes went on to draw an analogy between the OSU comeback and the capability of the USA to right itself from a decade of misfortune. Football brought out ideals and paths of action which, if applied to life, could benefit all of mankind. Knute Rockne and Hayes each thought, "Football brings out the best in everyone."

Hayes went on to express concern over the actions of himself, just four years before, in Ann Arbor. Hayes recalled that he protested a call during a tense game, went berserk, shredded a sideline marker and nearly precipitated a riot. In a very rare expression of remorse, Hayes admitted he would ponder long and heavily before acting in a similar fashion again, particularly in front of an already hostile crowd. Hayes was concerned that a repeat of such demonstrative behavior by himself might tilt a large crowd from normal, enthusiastic fandom into uncivil, uncontainable hooliganism. Hayes promised to temper his outbursts in the future.

Woody casually turned and left, leaving a sense of awe and amazement in his wake. The magnanimously calm intellectual musings of the Coach welled up from a source of joy Woody never before exhibited to such an extent in public. Woody always traveled his own path, even in victory.

The celebration did not last long for Hayes, who plunged right back into his work of preparing for the Rose Bowl. One week after the win up north, the Buckeyes' opponent in the January clash was decided. The familiar Bruins of UCLA beat the Trojans of USC to win the Pacific Athletic Conference title and the right to face OSU, again.

That battle of bitter archrivals was the last game of Trojan coach John McKay's collegiate career. McCay was departing to the NFL as the first head coach of the expansion Tampa Bay Buccaneers, and stumblingly lost the final four games of his SoCal reign. The Bruins triumphed in spite of fumbling 11 times, as the superb UCLA defense shut down the leading rusher in the nation, Rickey Bell, inside the 20.

Finishing the year with a solid 8-2-1 record, the Bruins hoped to avenge their early-season blowout loss to Ohio State. The Bruin defense was much improved, maturely supporting the ever-explosive UCLA offense. Amazingly, in the last Bruin trip to the Rose Bowl, back in '65, UCLA avenged a 13-3 regular season loss to the MSU Spartans, besting the Big 10 rep 14-12 in the second meeting. The '75 Bruins took comfort in and derived incentive from that precedent.

Hayes gave his squad some well deserved time off after the barbaric UM war, to allow the students time to cram for final exams, as the coaching staff prepared for the next meeting with the upstarts from Westwood. Hayes did take off some brief time for celebration, accepting the key to the city at a lavish banquet put on by the Cleveland (Ohio) Athletic Club. Woody thanked the members of this organization by delivering a typically empowering speech.

"You win with people who are trained and highly motivated," explained Woody, further stating that leadership is the single greatest factor in winning at any task. Woody forged leaders the way Lombardi did: "...they are made through effort and hard work."

To Hayes, nothing better explained the success of '75 than great leadership, especially the leadership which emanated from the players themselves. Legendary coach Tom Landry taught, "A lot of winning is tradition," and Hayes likewise believed fine leadership was handed down from the upperclassmen to the younger players. Griffin and Baschnagel, in particular, took their roles as leaders quite seriously, often instructing by example, and willingly taught the other players perhaps as much as the coaching staff did.

Hayes utilized his former players, too, in the teaching process. Tim Burke recalls, during his time ('75-'79) at OSU, that on more than one occasion, 12-15 members strong of the '68 national championship team addressed the undergrad Buckeyes on what it took to achieve such an honor. A rich history of winning, and awesome leadership lineage, were not qualities to waste or take lightly, taught Hayes.

Rewards, beyond winning a coveted conference crown, went to All-Conference designates Ward, Greene, Griffin, Johnson, Brudzinski, Buonamici, Fox, Smith, Skladany, Dannelly, Curto, Brown, Thompson, and Cassady. Curto topped the list of All-Conference academes, joined by Ward and Fox, with repeaters Ruhl, Lukens, Kuhn, and Baschnagel. Smith, Griffin, Fox, and Skladany each made one or more All-America listing.

The greatest honor, accorded prior to the bowl game, went to Griffin, as Archie edged out Pitt junior Dorsett for an unprecedented second Heisman. Interestingly, Dorsett almost matriculated to OSU in '73, after being chaperoned by Griffin himself on a weekend recruiting visit. Dorsett eventually declined because Archie was already so entrenched in Columbus, not only on the football field, but in the community.

The stupendous ceremony at which Archie was honored with his repeat Heisman, was merely a step toward the ultimate goal: The long-elusive national championship, coveted especially by the '75 seniors, and Hayes himself. In his acceptance speech, Griffin allowed, "Football prepared me to do whatever comes later in life," though he acknowledged his sole remaining agenda as an undergrad, outside of early graduation, was to win the Rose Bowl and maintain the coveted number one national ranking OSU had now held for the past nine weeks.

Hayes, who was selected "National Coach of the Year" by a multitude of organizations, brushed aside all congratulations with, "I'd rather be coach of the team of the year."

Traveling to New York for the prestigious Heisman presentation, Woody presented his most accomplished athlete to the assembled throng, packed with newsmen; fellow Buckeyes; honored guests, including former OSU Heisman awardees Vic Janowicz and Hop Cassady; and the proud Griffin family. Speaking of that especially close-knit clan, Hayes opined, "There are too many people who can too easily identify with defeat" - then, pointing to the Griffin's, Woody emphatically offered, "This family doesn't identify with defeat." Archie, in representing his teammates, did not even consider the spectre of a loss in the upcoming rematch with the Bruins.

The morning after the gala, the Buckeyes were back at work for the first time in exactly three weeks. Based on the unusually warm mid-December Columbus weather, Woody felt the conditioning and timing of his squad would recoup quickly. Corny Greene was basking in the glow of recently being named the team "Most Valuable Player" in a vote of his peers, and followed that honor with his selection as the "Conference Player of the Year".

Ever the team player, the flamboyant one credited much of his blossoming passing success to the brilliance of his hometown Washington, D.C., pal Lenny Willis, who latched onto 16 receptions on the year, good for 329 yards and two scores.

Most ominously, though, some cracks appeared in the dynasty as the intense workouts resumed. Although Mark Lang struggled back from the sore knee which had hampered him during the Michigan contest, Craig Cassady incurred a bad case of whiplash when his car was struck from behind. He lost valuable practice time in recuperating, and the peaking defensive unit sorely missed the speedster whose eight '75 interceptions just missed the school-record of nine, set by Mike Sensibaugh in '69.

Terry Vogler was felled with a nasty concussion, caused by an accidental fall in the shower. Former Buckeye powerhouse Bob Ferguson was still slowly on the mend from a recent cerebral hemorrhage, and the fragile health of the once-sturdy fullback weighed heavily on the minds of all Buckeye boosters.

In the midst of these hardships, the weather in Columbus turned exceptionally nasty, prompting an outburst of the flu among the team, probably striking Ted Smith and Pete Johnson most harshly, among the many affected. Then, a bizarre report surfaced out of Dallas, Texas.

According to investigative reports from several area newspapers, it was alleged that Rod Gerald illegally accepted a sum of money from a University of Tennessee alumnus, in the year of Rod's graduation from high school. Gerald and his father denied the acceptance of the money was illegal, for they had treated the deal as a loan and promptly paid off the debt. Following this, Rod originally signed a letter of intent to attend Arkansas, yet never mailed the letter agreeing to matriculate as a Razorback.

Based on the tone of certain investigative articles printed in Southwestern newspapers, Gerald then decided to instead attend OSU, primarily because Hayes visited the senior Gerald's church, and presented large offerings of cash as the Sunday services collection plate was offered. Hayes and the Reverend Gerald each conceded that Hayes had indeed visited his congregation, though Hayes denied his modest, voluntary tithes had anything to do with Rod's decision to attend Ohio State.

The entire matter was initially discovered during an NCAA investigation into the Southern Methodist recruiting program. A Mustang assistant coach, upon hearing that the highly coveted Rod had signed with OSU, apparently waved a wad of money in front of the high school senior's face, stating, "This could have been yours." The indictment of wrongdoing against both Woody and his young quarterback never materialized, though the situation did disrupt preparations for the approaching bowl game.

The Bruins of UCLA were not without their troubles at this time, either. Leading rusher Wendell Tyler, who ended the year with 1216 yards, was adjusting to a cracked left wrist, which continued to pain him even after the cast was removed. Star offensive lineman Randy Cross was hobbled by a sprained ankle, and the Bruins were accorded underdog status for the rematch, usually by a spread of at least two touchdowns.

Despite the underdog role, Vermeil and staff actually thought the Bruins possessed the advantage in the second go-round of the season. Due to his professional experience, Vermeil realized that the advantage usually rested with the vanquished side for the second meeting, and believed that the vastly-improved Bruin defense could hold the esteemed OSU offensive juggernaut in check. The OSU players and coaches admitted that the Bruin offense was dangerously lethal, capable of lighting up the brand-new computer graphics scoreboard recently installed in the Rose Bowl.

The Bruins looked at this bowl as a catalyst in springing their program into the ranks of the nation's elite, for Vermeil stated, "Opportunity to you is what you allow your preparation to make it." Due to his workaholic ways, the blue and yellow clad Bruins would definitely be prepared.

As OSU embarked for the sunny environs of California just a few days before Christmas, several Buckeyes slugged it out for the right to travel with the team, though if truth be told, sometimes the honor of dressing at a bowl game paled in relation to the status of those players who did not travel with the team.

As the squad of 60 was pared down, those players on the bubble often did not mind being left off the travel squad, for this reason: Instead of practicing in hot weather and enduring the curfews imposed on those dressing, the players left off joined the entourage at a later date, and were under virtually no restrictions during their stay in California. In essence, they received a stress-free vacation, without the rigors of daily workouts, while their teammates, who admittedly got to dress yet often did not appear in the contest, were under the usual harsh team restrictions.

Senior fullback Lou Williot earned the right to travel, as he was elected to back up Pete Johnson. Frosh Tim Vogler, who just barely lost out in that backfield battle, was listed at tight end, and also made the traveling roster. Tony Ross was selected as a fifth quarterback, solely because he imitated deceptively speedy Bruin signalcaller John Sciarra so expertly. Frosh Byron Cato earned the right to travel with the team, despite the surplus of fine defensive lineman, for he had become an essential cog in the goal line defensive unit.

Fellow frosh Joe Garcia, a native of California, was somewhat surprisingly selected to travel back home, though a virus afflicted him once back in his home state and prevented him from practicing with the squad. Classmate Richard Brown filled in during his absence.

Woody was fairly pleased with the readiness of his boys as gameday approached, conceding, "I've never seen a team nuttier." Hayes felt the '75 unit had avoided the dreaded "senioritis" malaise for the team remained focused in their concentration on the national championship, and did not seem at all content to rest on their considerable laurels. The closeness and unity of the squad was cited by coaches and players alike as the impetus and reason for the phenomenal '75 success. Woody remained mostly relaxed and accommodating, even as he vowed, "I didn't come out here to enjoy myself."

The team did have some high-profile fun, including a big Christmas Eve celebration at which several players imitated the coaching staff. Most notably, Ken Kuhn performed impeccably as George Hill, Eddie Beamon parodied Chuck Clausen, and Ted Smith sent up Hayes, though Ted admitted he was concerned because Woody did not laugh throughout the merriment. So-called "brain coach," or academic tutor (among his many other duties, including the handling of on-campus recruiting), Jeff Kaplan escaped imitation, though he hilariously entertained with a version of the "Buckeye Battle Cry," performed with a comb.

The holiday celebration ended with each player kissing honorary surrogate mother Mrs. Anne Hayes, since their own mothers could not be present. By Christmas Day, Hayes had relaxed to the point that he ate dinner at a potential recruits house, finding time to wow yet another set of parents.

Curiously, it was the UCLA team which seemed to be having slight dissension problems in coping with the demands of their driven head coach. Even as the UCLA players were allowed to reside in their normal living quarters and faced no curfews or other intrusions on their normal activities, since they practiced on their same field and Pasadena was a mere twenty minutes from Westwood, Vermeil drove his players much harder than normal during these pre-Rose sessions.

A team meeting, convened by the Bruin players, addressed their concerns at being driven too hard, and Vermeil conveyed his sentiment: It was not acceptable to be content with playing in the bowl game, UCLA was actually going to win! As the Bruin players altered their objective upward, a mood of optimism enveloped the now-more strongly inspired home team.

Through all the hoopla, Hayes was on his best and most mellow behavior. During a special Rose party featuring various Hollywood celebrities, Hayes generously accepted the good-natured ribbing of his compadre Bob Hope, who called Woody, "...the [George] Patton of the pigskin." Hayes was very pleased at the comparison.

Later, Hayes likened the outstanding Tournament of Roses committee, which handled all pre-game logistical concerns, to the exemplary leadership detailed in Plato's *Republic*. None could recall Hayes ever being as gracious, accommodating, or downright pleasant as he was on this venture to the West Coast.

Hayes even let some of the players go deep-sea fishing, on the condition they return in time for the team meal. Dinnertime approached and passed, with no sign of the fishermen. Finally, as the meal was in progress, the sun-burned players burst in, carrying their prizes: Several miniature sharks! Even Hayes was so shocked he remained calm and relatively unangered, as the menacing creatures of the deep were placed on the serving trays, next to the other, simpler fare, much to the uproarious delight of the Buckeye players.

Finally, the day before the eagerly awaited return matchup, Woody finally relaxed in his self-control and exposed that side of his personality the paparazzi long anticipated. During an innocuous press conference involving Hayes and the Buckeye co-captains, Woody suddenly grew irate at a question directed toward Greene. A member of the press asked Cornelius if he thought himself the equal of Sciarra, who had been named on several All-American squads, and before the Buckeye quarterback could respond, Woody verbally barged in to vent his anger.

Yelling at Greene not to answer such a leading question, Hayes retorted, "...we're not going to give them anything that will fire them up!" Woody explained, "Right there is the difference between coaching and writing," and steered the conversation more towards what he termed "positive reinforcement." Disdaining the assembled journalists, Hayes took over the process of questioning his players, and asked more banal questions, in a most civil manner, for the remainder of the interview session.

The brief flare-up was widely reported by a resounding, critically judgmental press, who castigated Hayes for his total dominance and control of his players, in direct contrast to Vermeil, who let his Bruins speak freely to any and all inquirers. To the press, it appeared as if Vermeil was as intense as Woody, yet understood better the changing nature of the game: College football, particularly as applied to the bowl picture, was increasingly a media circus, and the days of tight control by a central figure, like Hayes, were receding in favor of a more socially pleasing, laid-back (in terms of allowing his players greater personal liberties), style of a Vermeil.

As the Bruin coach himself explained, Woody was "...the type of man I was raised by, my dad," and Dick combined the finer organizational qualities of Hayes, along with a more lenient, "let the players be themselves," mentality which was equally indicative of his own adaptation of the Hayes-type coaching style. Try as he might, Woody could not totally bring himself to relinquish control over any aspect of his team; rightly or wrongly, he was therefore portrayed as a harsh dictator, while Vermeil came off as a more benevolent leader.

CHAPTER THIRTEEN: ROSE BOWL

The following afternoon, at two p.m. Pacific Standard time, in the first official event of the American Bicentennial celebration, and in front of 105,464 mostly-UCLA fans, the Vermeil coaching method was proven more beneficial, at least on this one day. Hayes himself flatly admitted, "We got outcoached," as he and his Buckeyes were rudely denied their coveted national championship, falling bitterly to the upstart Bruins by a 23-10 margin.

Strangely enough, former OSU coach Paul Brown, the only head coach in the history of the Cincinnati Bengals, shockingly announced on this day his intention to step down from the coaching ranks. It was not a pleasant day for then-Buckeye coaches, either.

Halftime adjustments, made by UCLA and never effectively countered by OSU, proved the difference in this tale of two widely divergent halves. Ohio State dominated the opening half, completely clamping down the Veer rushing attack of the UCLAns, while the Buckeye offense moved the ball almost at will against a Bruin defense which did grow pesky and stingy near the goal line.

Despite the tremendous statistical offensive Buckeye display, OSU was only able to take a slim 3-0 lead in at the break. After the break, UCLA switched to a possession passing attack, solved the riddle of the Buckeye passing game, and capitalized on turnovers and gigantic offensive plays to overwhelm the opposition.

Ohio State began the game looking every bit the role of the top team in the nation. Taking the opening kick, the Buckeyes marched 58 yards down the field on the strength of a dominant rushing game, only to have UCLA stiffen deep in Bruin territory. Klaban came on and drilled a 42 yard field goal, providing an early three point margin. Besides not piercing the goal line, the only disappointment in this drive came on the third play from scrimmage. Establishing a pattern of untimely mistakes continued throughout this battle, Greene was errant on a pitch to Griffin.

Archie courageously dove into a pile of Bruin defenders, recovering the ball yet breaking his dominant (left) hand in the process. Expectedly, Archie guttily played on, not even missing a single play in spite of the tremendously painful break. Nothing, it seemed, could deter the nation's finest player in his quest for a national title.

Surprisingly opening with an eight man defensive front, the Buckeyes absolutely stifled the intended home rushing game, quickly forcing a Bruin punt. Vermeil and staff were shocked at the appearance of the overloaded OSU defensive line, and the vaunted UCLA rushing game was unable to circumvent the stack for the remainder of the half. After the ensuing punt, OSU again drove steadily downfield, only to come up short on a fourth down conversion attempt deep in Bruin territory. Once more, Greene was slightly off on the key play, and the Bruins assumed possession.

The rest of the half followed the same pattern of Ohio State moving the ball in between the twenties, while UCLA did not go anywhere at all. Near the end of the half, just as it appeared OSU would finally cross the goal line, linebacker Terry Tautolo, an acclaimed 6'1", 224 pound bundle of intensity, cracked Greene from the side, forcing a fumble, which huge defensive lineman Cliff Frazier pounced on. Another golden opportunity for OSU had fallen by the wayside, and the 3-0 lead sufficed at the half.

The second half was a completely different matter. The home team charged out of the locker room, took the second half kickoff, and marched virtually unimpeded to a 33 yard Brett White field goal. Sciarra came out firing, exploiting man-to-man matchups in the secondary and finding seams in the OSU zone defensive schemes. As OSU scrambled to defend against the suddenly clicking pass, avenues for Eddie Ayers and Wendell Tyler to run through opened wide.

The Bruins had altered their strategy at the half, while OSU stuck with their first-half plan. As UCLA proceeded to shred the once-ominous Buckeye defense, Ohio State failed to adjust and execute as they had for the previous eleven games.

Offensively, Ohio State was stuffed in three rude plays on their initial possession of the second half. Skladany came up with a rare short kick, and Sciarra immediately passed to an open Wally Henry for the go-ahead score. Henry, a lithe, speedy, flanker who entered this game with nine receptions on the year, finished with five receptions totaling 113 yards.

Quick developing and crisply run patterns kept him in the clear often in his magnificent game, as the ominous threat of a Sciarra run somewhat froze the Buckeye pass rushers and placed horrific pressure upon the pass coverage unit. Fortunately, the point after following this touchdown was wide, keeping OSU well within striking range.

Once more, the OSU offense was unable to muster much of a threat, and the Bruins again had the ball in decent field position. Senior Pat Curto soon after recovered a fumble, violently forced by Beamon, and it appeared OSU was right back in the game. However, Greene was pestered by hard-rushing end Dale Curry and outside linebacker Raymond Bell on several pass attempts, and this excellent opportunity fell to waste.

Curiously, OSU had seemingly abandoned the running game, so successful in the opening half, even as their passing game was stymied by the fierce rush of the Bruins. Consequently, UCLA took over at their 17.

The feared Bruin offense exploded to paydirt, as Sciarra and company took only four plays to traverse the 83 yards. Sciarra effected a marvelous second half rebound from a godawful beginning, finishing with 13 completions in 19 attempts, for 212 yards, and earned the game's Most Valuable Player award.

The monster play in the drive was a quick slant to Henry, who caught the ball in full stride at the OSU 40 and outran Cassady to the end zone. This time, the point after succeeded, making the score 16-3.

With their national title hopes crumbling, OSU responded with their finest drive of the day. Capably mixing the occasional pass with plentiful runs, Ohio State powered to a short Johnson score, cutting the margin to 16-10 with 11:46 remaining. On the ensuing Bruin possession, Cassady stepped in front of the intended Sciarra target to pilfer the ball. On the runback, Cassady was tackled, late, out of bounds at midfield, and the resulting penalty placed the ball at the UCLA 35. Craig dislocated his shoulder with the illegal stick, and never returned. Still, ominously, OSU seemed poised to seize the moment and forge a lead.

Looking over center, Greene spotted a coverage mismatch on Willis, and called for an audible. True to plan, Willis broke into the clear, and Greene fired the ball toward a wide-open target. However, the pass was slightly underthrown, and instead of going the distance for a touchdown, as it might have, the changed play resulted in a momentum-dashing interception. The Bruins had dodged another bullet, and their grateful, opportunistic offense chewed precious time off the clock with a short drive.

Eventually, the proud Buck defense forced a punt, and OSU finally got the ball back with a little over five minutes remaining. The pride of the fantastic senior class was on the line, and Hayes had no doubt his favorites would deliver. Unexpectedly, Greene was again intercepted, capping an unfortunate afternoon for the OSU field general. A few plays hence, Tyler blasted through the bunched Buckeye line, sprinting 54 yards to the touchdown which sealed the unlikely upset. Tyler, bouncing back from a disastrous start, ended with 172 yards on 21 carries.

The Bruins, held to two first downs and 48 total yards at the half, ignited for a shocking total of 366 yards in the second half. On the final OSU possession, a fourth and 17 desperation pass sailed incomplete, with 1:57 left, and the terrible fate was sealed. Vermeil was very gracious afterwards, stating, "OSU is a first class football team, and it's a real privilege to play against them."

Accordingly, in the wake of perhaps his most disappointing loss ever, Hayes was stolidly mum, refusing to acknowledge any reporter request for a comment. Woody snuck out a side door fairly undetected, a difficult feat in the cramped, dingy quarters which masquerade as locker rooms at the Rose Bowl.

According to his personal diary, never revealed until after his death in '87, Hayes had anticipated retiring after this bowl victory, able to leave on top, with perhaps his most beloved class at last crowned national champions, and with his especially close leader, Archie Griffin, adding to his trophy collection. With the absolutely crushing defeat, Hayes instead scuttled his plan to exit at the pinnacle of his profession, though his pervasive disappointment over this defeat never quite faded, even in the face of the many victories to follow.

One final piece of controversy remained to cap this bittersweet season. An unnamed OSU assistant coach uncharacteristically criticized Greene in the press during the following week, blaming the senior quarterback for faulty judgment in changing plays at the line of scrimmage. According to the perturbed assistant, Corny audibilized away from intended running plays, resulting in several pivotal turnovers. In the wake of the impossible defeat, more rumors and unlikely criticism was aimed at Greene. Without a doubt, the fabled unity, which had carried this OSU program to such lofty heights, was beginning to show the stressful cracks brought on by this painful loss.

Never again would an OSU team, particularly one coached by W.W. Hayes, be so close and so successful as the '75 squad. The period of unquestioned dominance by Ohio State, fueled by massive player leadership and blind devotion to a cause, was beginning an inexorable downhill path. Success remained, tradition continued, yet this was the summit to which Hayes had led his squad, and they had fallen just shy, never to regain their same rock-solid grasp on a national title.

CHAPTER ONE: PRE-SEASON '76

The Buckeyes began the '76 fall practice full of questions. Coming off the inconceivable, traumatic loss on New Year's Day, OSU was a little shaky in the self-confidence realm. Furthermore, the team was decimated by graduation, especially on the offensive side. Gone was the majority of the '75 offense: Corny Greene, a three year starter as an option quarterback, an astute, instinctive runner and greatly underestimated passer; Archie Griffin, the legendary two-time Heisman winner, missed as much for his inspirational leadership as for his prodigious blocking/receiving/rushing production; and Brian Baschnagel, the underpublicized, versatile, soft-spoken leader via example and a renowned big-play performer.

Also lost to graduation were offensive line stalwarts Ted Smith and Scott Dannelly, and the fantastic receiver and fine blocker at tight end, Larry Kain. Lenny Willis took his fantastic speed and deep route abilities to the NFL, and loyal backup tailback Woodrow Roach would also be sorely missed. Also departed, from the defensive side, was end Pat Curto; backfield general Tim Fox; turnover master Craig Cassady; and perhaps the soul of the ferocious '75 defense, the tough-as-Ike Kelley middle linebacker, Ken Kuhn.

As Hayes spoke before the first press crowd of the fall at the Grandview Inn outside Columbus, he conceded the '76 team would start off extremely green, lacking Greene, particularly at that quarterback slot and in the running back position. Hayes expressed no doubt that the '76 team would be a fine team, yet admitted a strong start amidst another taxing schedule was imperative.

In all, the Bucks returned only three starters on offense, with a somewhat more substantial seven returnees on the defensive side. Thirty-eight returning lettermen took the field in late August to prepare for the volatile opener against MSU. Stepping into the flamboyant shoes of the departed "Flam" at signalcaller was Rod Gerald. In a mere 21.5 minutes of action in '75, Gerald managed to manufacture a hellacious impact. He averaged 8.6 yards on 16 option keepers, including touchdown bursts of 45, 14, and 26 yards.

The consensus of the coaching staff was that Rod ran the option more smoothly than Greene, was probably even quicker than the mongoose-fast Greene, and gave every indication of being as fine a passer. Of course, Gerald still had to perform on the field, although his potential promised rousing success.

The backup quarterback again was little-used senior Jim Pacenta, whose extremely capable play in spring ball aroused great confidence among the coaches. The 6'3", 190 pound pre-med honor student possessed precious little game experience, yet seemed increasingly set if anything happened to the skinny Gerald.

Perhaps the greatest challenge of '76 was filling the vacated tailback spot of Archie. Griffin not only captured the overwhelming respect and love of the Columbus community as no one before, he most importantly occupied a very privileged place in the heart of his old Coach. Much of the source of Hayes' post-Rose Bowl anguish was the fact that the outstanding '75 senior class of leaders, exemplified by Archie, never won the national championship which always remained narrowly, painfully, just out of their reach.

Junior Jeff Logan was the heir apparent to the position, and he readily solidified his claim to the role by gaining 174 yards in the annual spring intrasquad game. The North Canton, Ohio, native was an exciting bundle of quickness, speed, and power eager to prove his mettle as a starter. Logan worked his tail off, and emerged slightly ahead of two perhaps more athletic competitors, who had each been expected to supplant Jeff.

Close on the heels of Logan was a freshman from Santa Maria, California, Ricky Johnson, who ended up missing most of this year with a broken hand. In turn, Johnson was supplanted by Coffeyville (Kansas) junior college transfer Ron Springs. Springs really impressed with his breakaway speed and surprising power, and showed marked improvement in his inside running capabilities.

Springs was a prize catch, and promised great things once he was acclimated to Ohio State. So prized was Ron, that UCLA head coach Vermeil spent the day following the shocking Rose Bowl win wooing the running back, trying to convince Springs to journey further west.

Also in the wings was freshman Chuck Hunter, from Newark, Delaware. Hunter was fresh from a prep career in which he amassed an apparent national-record total of 4997 rushing yards. The entire running back stable was deep and impressive, though bereft of intercollegiate experience. Also in contention for carries were frosh Tom Blinco, Jim Laughlin, Ricardo Volley, Paul Campbell, the quick Mike Schneider, and the large Bill Harmon.

Even bigger and faster was returning fullback Pete Johnson. The 6'1", 250 (give or take 25) pound pulverizer led the nation in scoring in '75, and found enough opportunities in the senior-laden backfield to accumulate 1059 yards rushing. Johnson was a crushing lead blocker, returned kickoffs, and generally was widely feared by anyone who got in the way of his plowhorse, wrecking-ball running style.

The '76 senior continued the well established Hayes tradition of punishing fullbacks, a la' White (who was also an outstanding punter), Ferguson, Otis, Brockington, and Henson. Virtually every OSU offensive lineman from these days recalls the hardest hit he ever took as being a blast in the back from Pete on the goal line.

On 74 short yardage or goal-line opportunities in '75, Pete converted 54 into either a first down or a touchdown. This was accomplished despite the fact every defender in America realized Pete was getting the ball in these situations.

Like Pete and new arrival Paul Ross, frosh wingback Matt Jackson hailed from Fort Valley, Georgia. Jackson was outstanding in the bid to assume the four year residence of Baschnagel.

Junior Jim Harrell carried the ball only once in '75, as he fought back from a knee injury which sidelined him the entire '74 campaign. Harrell was not quite fully recovered, yet showed traces of brilliance with each passing day. Also in competition for playing time at wingback was Bob Hyatt, a senior.

Offensive line coach Ralph Staub welcomed back accomplished junior tackle Chris Ward, along with the gutty, speedy, technician Bill Lukens, a 6'1", 233 pound senior. Jimmy Moore had shared the tight end slot with Kain in '75, and the 265 pound sophomore now had the position all to himself.

Moore was coming back nicely following the major knee surgery which cut short his frosh year, and by all accounts demonstrated the most potential of any Buckeye tight end ever. Not only was Moore a jarring blocker, he proved deceptively fast and possessed a pair of feathery hands big enough to haul in any pass within reach.

The newly-appointed starters were Jim Savoca, a recent conversion from linebacker, now at one guard; Mark Lang, a new convert from middle guard, now at center, and Lou Pietrini at the tackle slot opposite Ward. Ron Ayers enjoyed a fantastic spring and would rove between tackle and guard, providing solid backup at both positions. Sophomore Joe Robinson also would see plenty of minutes at tackle - he actually started in the spring, only to be supplanted later as the senior Pietrini made a resounding comeback from knee surgery to claim the starting nod. Herman Jones drew the start at split end.

George Hill directed a defense blessed with both game experience and leadership. Leading '74 tackler Ed Thompson returned to call the defensive signals from his inside linebacker spot, overseeing an accomplished line featuring tackles Eddie Beamon and Nick Buonamici. Hayes brusquely brushed off any discussion involving the off-season suspension of Buonamici. The reason behind the punishment was never publicly disclosed.

"He's a heckuva kid and on the field he's superb," was all Hayes would say regarding the matter, though Woody cringed each time Nick barreled into the Biggs practice facility parking lot on his rumbling Harley Davidson motorcycle.

The rapidly improving end Bob Brudzinski and impossibly quick middle guard Aaron Brown also retained starting berths. The backfield returned Bruce Ruhl and safety Ray Griffin. Ray remained on this side of the ball despite an invitation to return to the tailback slot he filled as a frosh, when he backed up older brother Archie.

Also expected to contribute defensively was sophomore inside linebacker Tom Cousineau. In near 90 degree heat during the first pre-season practices, Cousineau asserted himself as probably the best conditioned athlete on the steamy field. After starting or playing extensively with the first unit during five '75 games, Tom was put on a fast track to All-America honors. The Buckeye defense was geared to take full advantage of his tremendous lateral pursuit, and the widespread OSU publicity mill cranked out his praises at every turn. The outgoing, marketable, and personable Cousineau was on the road to stardom.

Other youngsters demonstrating considerable promise included sophomore defensive back Leonard Mills, who packed plenty of highly-graded feats into 76 minutes of action, including a couple starting assignments, in '75. Classmate Kelton Dansler was coming off 40 highly productive minutes of his own in '75, at the end position.

Joe Allegro was also assured of some quality time with his continually stellar play in the backfield. Allegro appeared in all 12 '75 contests, logging 44 minutes, even though continually nagged by back injuries. He underwent corrective surgery following the Rose Bowl, and seemed fully recovered. Newcomer Mike Guess drew fast attention for his natural ability to defend the pass, too.

According to secondary coach Dick Walker, probably the hardest hitter and most ferocious competitor of all the many defensive backs was hometown product Jeff Ferrelli. Largely unnoticed by major colleges coming out of Columbus West High, Jeff fulfilled a life-long dream by walking on to the stellar OSU program, and was soon offered a scholarship. Despite this status, Jeff was never able to exceed his tag as a one-time walk-on, for several reasons, none necessarily related to his playing ability.

From his first OSU practice ever, in which he blazed through his sprint tests in stunning late-summer '73 heat virtually unrecognized (since a scholarship player merited more attention with a hamstring twinge), Jeff realized that cracking the talented Buckeye lineup would be a fierce task.

Ohio State, long recognized for their extensive recruiting web, often was hindered by this dependence on the network. Boosters and other influential alumni helped single out a prospect from their geographic sphere of influence, and once that player made it to campus, bearing a scholarship, those helpful recruiters were rewarded as that player received every chance in the world to eventually start. Unlike walk-ons, or other lightly regarded recruits, these blue chip catches were obviously presented with greater, concentrated coaching, care, and concern, based on their own potential and future support perhaps generated by their (already helpful) booster benefactors.

Granted, the prized recruit did usually pan out, yet, their success was often achieved at the expense of unknowns like Ferrelli, who may have been every bit their equal, if only presented with the same spoon-fed teachings and numerous opportunities to correct shortcomings. It is a lament of extremely successful programs, personified by OSU in the '70's, that many such talented players did slip by practically unnoticed, mostly due to first impressions, from back in high school as the recruiting process began, and other necessary time constraints.

Once a player was assigned to the "gunga" or "toolie" platoons, reserved for players not in the two-deep lineup, they experienced a highly different lifestyle than their first and second string teammates. For one thing, taping and other trainer's room considerations were skewed in favor of the starters and top reserves, and space for the remainder of the squad was very limited.

The emphasis on prevention and treatment of injuries was dedicated to those players most in demand; no one was neglected, the gungas merely received less concentrated attention. Even the logistics of moving the team, either to practice or games, favored the better players, as the toolies were packed into cramped, massed traveling quarters, and even faced a long walk in from the practice fields, no matter how inclement the weather might be.

During the games themselves, the gungas actually customarily sat in a different area of the locker room, both in pre-game and halftime meetings, while the starters and top reserves were ministered to more personally by the assistants and Hayes himself. The neglected status of the lowly substitutes actually became a badge of honor, in the guise of martyrdom, as the upperclassmen leaders of the gungas often handed out Buckeye leaves for mistakes committed during rare game appearances. Sometimes, these mistakes were not necessarily that players fault.

Jeff Ferrelli recalls late in one game, the contest was long since decided, and the gunga defensive unit went in. At that point, they were given little specific direction from the coaching staff, were thus confused as to their assignments and responsibilities, and therefore yielded a quick touchdown.

The situation was a perfect catch-22: The toolies received fewer repetitions and patient teaching during practices and games, consequently committed errors not usually made by the starters, and therefore remained planted low in the lineup.

Admittedly, some players, who began their Buckeye careers with earnest intentions and always practiced to the utmost of their abilities, in time grew disappointed in the futility of their playing status and eased off, if only subconsciously, in their practice habits. For example, if a gunga made a spectacular play in practice, that particular play was run, again and again, until the gunga did not succeed and the starter did. Instead of risking injury on a great play which only increased his subsequent chances of invoking the ire of a starter and a coach, the gunga perhaps began to ease up a bit, becoming a worse football player and further cementing his status as a deep reserve.

The fate of a gunga was not all bad, however. By necessity, a reserve player sometimes matured more quickly than a starter, at least in terms of academic responsibilities and in concentrating on a future after college football. The better football player, with many notable exceptions, often concentrated more on the game of football to the exclusion of a career, and perhaps did not as adequately prepare for a life after his playing days were over, until it was too late to realize.

As Duncan Griffin recalls, the primary opportunity afforded by a football scholarship was the chance to pursue a great education, and that academic pursuit gradually took precedence over the sport. Like Archie, Duncan achieved so well, he graduated ahead of schedule.

In the process of this transition to various inexperienced hands, OSU prepared for another grueling schedule to start the year. In order, OSU faced Michigan State, Penn State, Missouri, and UCLA. Hayes was eager and willing to take on all comers. "I'm enthusiastic. The day I'm not, I'll quit," he practically bellowed. Woody quoted the *Papyrus*, a series of old Egyptian historical papers: "It is one's own fault if his enthusiasm is gone; he has failed to feed it."

One big reason for his enthusiasm was the return of two-time All-American punter Tom Skladany. As a junior, the enthusiastic Skladany outdistanced all other collegians to lead the nation in punting. With the graduation of '75 kicker Tom Klaban, the smiling senior now held down the placekicking chores as well. As a token of the respect accorded Skladany, he was chosen a tri-captain, along with Lukens and Thompson.

These three continued the fine tradition of outstanding leadership from the senior class. As an example of the tri-captains resolve, the '76 seniors entered fall practices in the best shape any class ever had, according to Hayes. In his first formal speech to the team after practices began, Hayes outlined "...how we win." The foremost two factors in this prescription were attitude and pre-season conditioning. Hayes felt confident each factor was in healthy condition this year.

Even in the midst of grueling two-a-day workouts in full pads under a scorching sun, the OSU players gave thanks they were not Indiana Hoosiers. Indiana coach Lee Corso was experimenting with a three-times-each-day conditioning program, and his team was really struggling in adapting.

Also struggling was Craig Cassady, on the mend with a broken hand and chafing at being sidelined from the New Orleans Saints training camp. Cassady did confirm that former Buck Kurt Schumacher had sewn up a starting berth at tackle with the Saints. The enthusiasm Hayes felt for former players' pro hopes was tempered slightly with a rush of minor injuries to his current Buckeyes. Bruce Ruhl, sophomore guard Tom Waugh, Pete Johnson, and Matt Jackson all were sidelined with various aches. Johnson had a very sore neck, and Jackson strained a knee on perhaps the finest catch of camp.

Until his injury, the 9.6 (100 yard) speed of Jackson really dazzled. Sadly, Jackson became so homesick for his smaller, more countrified hometown roots that his effectiveness gradually diminished, until his urge to return home overpowered his zest for the game. Jackson played only the one year with the Buckeyes.

Late in the initial week, Hayes met with the roving reporters of the Skywriters publicity team. Hayes was remarkably restrained and very low-key. With OSU placed as high as fourth nationally in the preseason polls, Hayes had good reason to feel confident, although recent allegations in certain Michigan and Michigan State student newspapers disturbed his sense of tranquility. Michigan State recently was levied a three year probationary sentence by the NCAA for 34 separate, mostly recruiting, violations. The sentence prohibited any lucrative television appearances or bowl appearances within the three year time.

In mid summer, Hayes openly and bluntly admitted, for the first time, that the NCAA investigation of the Spartan football program was initially begun at his request. Hayes discovered that MSU was blatantly utilizing unfair recruiting advantages and in effect bribing great athletes to attend their university. Consequently, Hayes purposely blew the whistle on their program.

A very controversial segment of the resultant penalty was the suspension of seven Spartan players (quarterback Ed Smith; defensive back Ted Bell; and defensive linemen Larry Bethea, Melvin Land, and Jim Epolito were each suspended for one game, which happened to be the opener at OSU. Tight end Mike Cobb was banished for five games, and defensive back Joe Hunt was barred for the entire season. After being notified of the suspension, prep star Bell quit the program, supposedly due to an unending spate of minor injuries).

Consequently, the MSU student newspaper quoted anonymous sources in providing supposed details of alleged recruiting violations by Hayes. In Ann Arbor, these allegations were seconded and widely publicized. Schembechler immediately and characteristically very vocally defended the recruiting methods of Woody and detailed the unflinching, unquestionable honesty of his former mentor. In turn, Hayes almost got carried away in praising Bo, particularly championing the speedy recovery of Schembechler following open heart by-pass surgery over the summer.

Prior to the season's start, and the consequent headlong rush toward the climatic showdown with UM, Hayes was normally charitable, courteous, and even downright loving towards Bo. After all, the two men were eerily similar, especially in their passion for excellence. Each recognized the great qualities of the other, although publicly, they were usually portrayed as merely one-dimensional rivals.

As preparations for the year began in earnest, Hayes emitted a glow of health and vitality even as he slaved through typical 19 hour days. Hayes was at his lightest weight in years, at a trim 200 pounds. If anything, the crushing loss to UCLA prompted Woody to work even more fervently towards his goal of a fourth national title; Woody's dad had instilled the philosophy of hero Theodore Roosevelt into his son. "I always believe in going hard at everything," said the 26th President of the United States. "My experience is that it pays never to let up or grow slack and fall behind."

Like this fellow advocate of the vigorous life, Hayes "...lived every moment with magnificent gusto... he lived inwardly and outwardly with the same zest." Captivatingly, Hayes and Roosevelt each literally worked themselves into such states of ill health, their once-sturdy bodies never recovered, though neither regretted the intensity of his prematurely shortened life.

Bringing more cheer to Woody's mood were the comments of New England Patriot rookie Tim Fox. Fox immediately landed a starting spot in the pros, and credited his quick assimilation to Hayes and the well-run OSU football organization. Fox considered his alma mater as an equal with the Patriots organization, and even thought some aspects of OSU superior in efficiency to his NFL team. Comments like these confirmed and re-inforced the concepts Hayes instilled in his players.

Also bringing joy to Hayes was Eddie Beamon, recently a scintillatingly perfect 4.0 student over the summer quarter. Beamon further filled his busy days working with underprivileged youngsters, devoting many hours to the (OSU assistant athletic director) Dick Delaney led, inner-city Columbus sports program.

As OSU practice time dwindled before the crucial MSU showdown, the emphasis increasingly shifted toward developing depth. The starters on both sides of the ball appeared set, while the intense battle for backup slots raged on. In a full-scale scrimmage one week prior to the opener, Springs really stood out. Brian Schwartz, a 6'1", 195 pound frosh from Simi Valley, California, also looked impressive from his defensive back spot.

First team secondary players Mills, Ruhl, and Allegro all were bothered by nagging injuries, so the backfield reserves drew plenty of practice repetitions. Duncan Griffin, Tom Roche, and Max Midlam all played considerably well and often.

Midlam was an All-State football and track star from Marion (Ohio) Pleasant, whose prep gridiron team had swept 38 consecutive contests during Maxs' years, capturing Class A state titles in both football and basketball in the same year. Incidentally, Max landed his football scholarship primarily because of his exploits during a prep basketball game, which Hayes attended and was impressed by the phenomenal leaping abilities of Midlam. Woody was also taken with the fact that Midlam's father was the school principal, and education administrators came just after lawyers and doctors in the Hayes pantheon of society. Shockingly fast afoot, Midlam faced a huge adjustment in hurdling from such a small high school to a major college program.

Marion was such an isolated community, that Woody forever after immortalized Max as, "The boy who went to the school with no locks [on the doors]...." Interestingly, Woody characteristically referred to one particular aspect, such as this, of a player, in order to keep track of his many "boys." For example, after Ferrelli graduated, Woody always addressed him as "...the man who played with a separated shoulder" (Jeff had once made a savage open-field tackle after sustaining the injury earlier in the same play).

When Savoca injured himself in a freak accident on a blocking sled, 6'4", 250 pound frosh Doug Mackie opened eyes with his intense style. The muscleman from Saugus, Massachusetts, took advantage of the extra work at right tackle, and improved considerably as time went on. Sophomore Farley Bell shared reps with classmate Kelton Dansler at the defensive end position, and the 6'4", 230 pounder from Toledo pushed Kelton to improve, or risk losing his job.

Several former OSU stars were in the news this week. Former Buckeye running back and safety Paul Warfield returned to his original NFL team, the Cleveland Browns, after five years of sensational exploits at wide receiver with the Miami Dolphins. The fleet, graceful Warfield epitomized class and style, even when he bucked conventional wisdom a few years previously and jumped ship to the fledgling World Football League. Pridefully back in the Browns uniform, Warfield remained one of the most feared gamebreakers in the history of the NFL.

Buckeye golfer Jack Nicklaus continued his own recordbreaking career, winning the revamped World Series of Golf in Akron, Ohio. Hayes had taken a special interest in Jack, stemming from the undergraduate days of the special duffer. While Nicklaus was competing as an amateur in the '60 U.S. Open, Hayes telephoned latebreaking tournament results across time lines, at his own expense, so that the winning exploits of a fellow Buckeye would be properly and timely reported in the Columbus morning newspaper. Hayes just happened to be in the West on a recruiting trip, and actually had never met Nicklaus at the time. The unfamiliarity with both the subject and the sport involved did not lessen the enthusiasm Hayes always exhibited for an Ohio Stater.

Also this week, former Buckeye baseball and basketball giant Frank Howard, managing in the Pacific Coast League for the Spokane minor league baseball team, earned a long suspension for his role in a fracas with an opposing team. Even the worst outburst imaginable from the tempestuous Hayes paled in comparison to this donnybrook involving the (thankfully) normally mild-mannered 6'7", 265 pound Howard.

Hayes showed a little fire in the belly himself at his initial Monday afternoon press conference at the Jai Lai restaurant, near the OSU campus. This tasteful restaurant was one of the few off-campus haunts of Hayes, and the proprietors of the establishment rejoiced over his presence. For years, a large billboard, bearing a portrait of Hayes, the Jai Lai logo, and the phrase "In all the world, there is only one," had been on prominent display along the main thoroughfare traveling past the OSU campus.

Hayes became agitated as he talked about a trick play which beat his alma mater (of his coaching experience), Miami, during the first weekend of the '76 season. North Carolina took advantage of the confusion brought on by a faked substitution, and edged the Redskins. This loss was only the second for Miami in almost a three year span, and really generated controversy on a Saturday in which few games were played.

According to Hayes, this benefit via deception was, "...not real football. Nothing beats good hard tackling and blocking...," allowed Woody.

Following this brief lecture, Hayes was bombarded with questions concerning his alleged recruiting violations. Hayes refused to entertain any thoughts on the matter, and when the media did not cease their queries, Woody abruptly ended the press conference. Several former MSU players, in the fall of '76, now insisted Hayes offered them cash, cars, free trips, and other illegal inducements in years previous, if they would attend OSU. Hayes bluntly said, "I've got more important things to do than sit around and answer charges that are ridiculous," and walked out of the meeting hall.

The maelstrom of controversy at MSU only compounded the many hurdles already facing new Spartan coach Darryl Rogers. Well known for his wide-open passing programs at San Jose State, Rogers was expected to shake up the comparably stodgy Big 10 by airing the ball out, and often.

Rogers faced the difficult task of replacing deposed head coach and athletic director Denny Stolz, who lost both his jobs as a result of the NCAA findings. Rogers stepped into a fishbowl of pressure and extra scrutiny at East Lansing, given the simultaneous tasks of cleaning up the program and continuing the recent winning ways.

Unfortunately, at least in the early part of '76, Rogers inherited a team considerably tainted from and weakened by the imposed sanctions. The Spartans also incurred an inordinate amount of severe knee injuries in the '76 camp. All told, six starters or top reserves were either currently sidelined prior to, or attempting a comeback from, major knee surgery. Additionally, starting defensive back Bill Broadway suddenly quit the team to become a minister, leaving Tom Hannon as the only experienced deep defender.

The brouhaha concerning the alleged OSU recruiting violations, and the bitterness in regards to the Hayes role in beginning the NCAA investigation into MSU violations, added spice to an already tumultuous rivalry.

In '51, the first year of the Hayes era, MSU coach Biggie Munn and his top-ranked Spartans barely won, with a thrilling comeback in the final minutes. The deciding score came on a rare "transcontinental" option pass to the quarterback, a play in which four Spartans handled the pigskin in the backfield.

In '66, Duffy Daugherty brought the number one team in the nation to Columbus. In a fiercely fought match, the Spartans barely prevailed 11-8. In '72, Daugherty inspired a seemingly overmatched Spartan team with a stirring talk concerning his impending retirement. The impassioned MSU players knocked off the heretofore undefeated Bucks 19-12, behind the kicking exploits of Dirk Krijt. Krijt, a native of the Netherlands, booted four field goals in his first American football game.

Not only was it his first game, it also was the first game he had ever even watched! Legend has it that prior to the game, Krijt asked Daugherty, "...do I kick it over or under the crossbar?" Duffy apparently translated the intent of a kick successfully, gaining a trip off the field on the backs of joyous fans, who also uprooted both goalposts.

These exciting battles were merely a prelude to the '74 meeting of the schools. This game contained the most confusing, hectic ending of any contest Hayes ever coached, save perhaps his last. In perhaps the most controversial game ever contested in storied OSU football, the home-field Spartans upended the unbeaten and top-ranked Buckeyes. Late in the final quarter, with MSU trailing 13-9, fullback Levi Jackson exploded 88 yards for the go-ahead score. Ohio State gallantly retaliated, driving 76 yards to the Spartan one-half yard line. Champ Henson bulled to a point right at the goal line, with one official desperately signaling touchdown. This lone official was tardily overruled, despite fierce Buckeye protests.

Much needless time ticked off the clock during the argument, and OSU hurriedly attempted one last snap as the game clock expired. Baschnagel somehow ended up with the fumbled ball in the end zone, and at first it appeared that the visitors had miraculously staved off the upset.

Each team hesitantly ran off the field claiming victory, as thousands of energetic fans scrambled onto the playing field and mass pandemonium ensued. The crowd was alternately jubilant and outraged in their uncertainty over who won, and both teams struggled tremendously in reaching the relative safety of their respective locker rooms.

Upon reaching that relative safety of the stadium, Hayes grew ever more livid. Feeling the pain of "his boys" being cheated on the last several plays, Hayes sought out an equally outraged Buonamici, for despite the differences between the two, Woody and Nick were perhaps the two most similar, feisty, brawling competitors in the Buckeye program. Hayes beseeched, "Let's go kick some butt!" Nick, being of kindred spirit, was right behind his Coach in a charge out of the locker room, just as the below-mentioned contingent of representatives, led by Wayne Duke, entered.

Thankfully, their entrance ended the intended assault mission, though the anger of the entire OSU team continued to rage. Still, no immediate, official statement of the outcome was issued; the decision pending upon a haphazard conference of Big 10 representatives, game officials, and a review of the game films. Finally, a full 46 minutes after that last mad scramble into the end zone, a 16-13 MSU victory was designated as the official outcome. Without question, the Ohio State players had been treated very unfairly and unjustly.

A much less controversial part of OSU history was slated for recognition on opening day '76. Former OSU band director Eugene Weigel would be honored in a special ceremony at halftime, in recognition of his noteworthy service to the university. Weigel was a renowned innovator who not only instituted the widely copied all-brass concept for marching bands, he also memorably developed the legendary script "Ohio." The very first script was performed

October 24th, 1936. Coincidentally, Weigel's grandson, Richard Underman, was now a bruising fullback for the visiting Spartans.

One other legendary figure in OSU annals, Archie Griffin, overcame a lingering groin injury to capture a starting nod for his Cincinnati Bengal regular season debut this week. Griffin was making the very difficult transition to the NFL in fine fashion. Though his statistics did not quite attain those of his Heisman days, Griffin already demonstrated a clutch ability to catch, run behind occasionally inconsistent lines, and provide heady leadership for the Bengals.

Griffin's former blocking back, Pete Johnson, was equally determined to start off his season in strong style. The senior desperately wanted to have a sparkling last year, particularly as a leader. "I'm not a holler guy, so I decided I could show leadership by going all out," Johnson declared. Pete was the ideal fullback in the estimation of his coach, Mickey Jackson. Johnson possessed power, speed, and blocking talents; it seemed that whatever Pete put his mind to, he could do, and do with excellence.

Amazingly, as a youngster Johnson did not follow college ball, and had virtually zero knowledge concerning the OSU dynasty. Chuck Clausen discovered the unpolished gem of physical abilities in an unrelated visit to Long Beach, New York. Johnson originally looked to attend West Virginia, but over time, the now-attractive allure of the OSU legacy enticed him to Columbus.

Upon arriving at OSU, Johnson endured painful, actual physical pangs of homesickness which eventually subsided in direct proportion to his increased playing time. As Johnson became more and more an integral part of the offense as a frosh, his anguish lessened. The more his homesickness diminished, the more improvement the amazing athlete showed. From his first day on campus, the unfathomable physical abilities of Pete demanded attention, despite his youth and inexperience.

Ed Thompson was another who led by example. Thompson was neither big nor fast, he was just a good football player with a nose for the ball. Ed came from Waverly, Ohio, as a quarterback, and used this offensive breeding, at his linebacker spot, to instinctively locate where the play was going.

The recent loss in the Rose Bowl served as a catalyst for improvement to the great defender, and Thompson's goal for his unit was to lead the nation in scoring defense. The aim was to never allow more than seven points during a contest. Hayes also thought this feat within reach, and was accordingly concise, yet confident, in his comments as the final week of pre-season practice wound down.

CHAPTER TWO: MICHIGAN STATE

This confidence proved legitimate, as OSU captured a resounding 49-21 victory in the home opener. Logan and Pete Johnson teamed with Gerald as the offense opened an insurmountable lead early, though this margin was assailed very late in the game by a successful MSU air attack. Logan accounted for three touchdowns, Gerald and Johnson contributed two each, and the halftime margin of 35-0 held up under three late Spartan scores, the last with one second remaining.

Spartan quarterback Marshall Lawson threw on virtually every down after halftime, as MSU accumulated a game total of 259 yards on 16 completions in 35 attempts. The estimable MSU ground game proved virtually non-existent, garnering just 54 yards in the battle with a stout Buckeye defense. Tailback Rich Baes had 30 yards on 13 carries, and nemesis Jackson was held to just 21 yards in 11 tries.

Ohio State was literally unstoppable in the early going. The Bucks scored a touchdown on each of their initial five possessions, hopelessly burying the Spartans. On the day, a multitude of OSU runners weaved and blasted for 463 yards. Ron Springs made a dramatic debut, netting 76 yards on 15 carries. Gerald led the option flawlessly, twisting and turning for 104 yards on ten runs, mostly option keepers. Pete Johnson sped his way to 99 yards in 12 attempts, including a 58 yard touchdown romp.

Even in light of these dominating statistics, Logan was especially eyecatching. Jeff exploded for 112 yards on only seven carries, including a 75 yard scoring sprint only 51 seconds into the second half. Logan also threw the only OSU completion of the day, a 36 yard option toss to Harrell early in the contest. Logan powered in from three yards out for another score, and also negotiated a 68 yard punt return for a touchdown, in the fourth quarter. The only time all day he was halted came via a penalty - an additional 72 yard touchdown gallop was negated on a holding call.

The comments of Jeff after the game capture his elation and thankfulness regarding his first opportunity to start: "You think you're pretty good, but every man here [at OSU] is tremendous. I just had fun out there today," as did the spectators who witnessed this incredible performance.

Despite Ray Griffin nursing a slight head bump suffered in a late-week practice and thereby participating in only part of the first half, the Buckeye defenders looked powerful until the waning minutes. Buonamici was a constant thorn in the Spartan backfield, as was Dansler. Each of these stalwarts recovered a fumble that led directly to an OSU touchdown.

Buonamici was subsequently named the Big 10 player of the week for his recovery, three passes batted down, and seven jarring tackles. Brudzinski also made his presence repeatedly known.

Only a late-game inability to throttle rampaging Spartan wide receiver Kirk Gibson, who battled for two long scores, spoiled an otherwise impressive defensive outing.

In an unprecedented move for Hayes following a home victory, he skipped the post-game interview, instead sending lieutenants Hill and Staub. Unlike the Hayes absence following the recent Rose Bowl defeat to UCLA, this absence was ostensibly an attempt to avoid a controversial interaction with reporters. Hayes did notify members of the press corps of his impending absence by the halftime break, plus sent out a mimeographed statement on his impressions of the opener.

Later, Hayes explained, "...if I think there are some people who will want to bait me and spoil the press conference...," he would continue the practice of not showing up after a game. Rather than avoid harsh questions himself, Hayes likely wished to spare others the bite of his sharp temper. Of course, since Hayes was a renowned fountain of perpetual quotes on just about any and every subject (a recent gem was, "The Russians can't beat us at anything - they can't even feed themselves!"), his absence created a void unfillable by any replacement.

Such was the way of Wayne Woodrow Hayes: He had created a persona which delighted the media and provided plenty of copy, yet this persona could become a nuisance to the creator if it was demanded or taken for granted.

With this convincing victory, OSU vaulted to number one in the UPI poll, while Michigan sat atop the Associated Press poll. Indiana basketball coach Knight recently had visited the Wolverine camp to study the Schembechler coaching technique, and came away very impressed by the discipline, concentration, and effort demanded by Bo. Only Bo or Woody at this time could make Knight appear mellow or fledgling; in '76, it was perhaps inconceivable that any basketball coach's intensity could approach that of these two football coaches, or even that of a bespectacled, cleat-wearing coach called Joe.

Next up for OSU was a nationally televised affair at University Park, Pennsylvania, against traditional power Penn State. In ten years at the helm of the Nittany Lions, venerable coach Paterno was working on a 95-18-1 record. His teams had been in the top 10 national rankings at the finish of the year on eight occasions, and the Lions had been to eight straight bowls, in an era before such trips were commonplace.

Despite a very strong frosh class, the Lions struggled to beat Stanford 15-12 in the '76 opener. This narrow victory did little to diminish the respect Hayes felt for his counterpart. Paterno was "...one of the great coaches of the game.

He does an awful lot of coaching. An intelligent man, his record speaks for itself," Hayes said.

Paterno seemingly made few mistakes, yet one error of judgment really benefitted OSU. When recruiting Skladany, Paterno told the Bethel Park, Pennsylvania, native that no matter how good Tom was as a frosh, he would not play, since upperclassmen were entrenched at the PSU kicking spots. Then, Penn State released a photo and enclosed statement which notified several Pennsylvania news publications that Tom was attending the State College university. The prep star Skladany was also under heavy pressure to attend nearby Pitt, for he had uncles who had starred there.

George Chaump first recruited the athletic Skladany for split end, though a plodding 4.9 40 (yard) time dashed that chance. Skladany averaged 40 yards a punt in rainy, muddy conditions his senior prep season, and Chaump caught the attention of Hayes by insisting, "Skladany will average 50 on artificial turf."

Hayes himself would not visit Tom in Bethel Park, for the previous year a teammate of Tom's gave Woody his word of honor he was going to OSU, then reneged to attend Michigan. In the view of Hayes, the entire high school campus was therefore suspect and not to be trusted. Still, Skladany impressed Hayes enough that Tom received the first scholarship ever given to a kicker at OSU. Of course, perhaps the only reason Hayes did tender that scholarship was due to the fact Michigan had first offered Tom a full ride. The popular "Ski" did not disappoint, though there was a lot of pressure on him as the first specialist scholarship recipient.

Even Tom admits, "I was not the best punter my first year," yet Hayes made an investment in the future and started the frosh anyway. Tom credits his broken left leg in the UM game his frosh year as the "...best break I ever got," for, as a result of the heavy cast and consequent favoring of his right kicking leg, Tom greatly improved his leg strength.

Due to his dual punting and placekicking chores in '76, Skladany cut way back on his practice time, in order to keep his leg fresh. As an example of his work load, against MSU, Tom kicked off eight times, punted six times, and converted seven extra points.

To fill the down time during the week's practices, Tom continually wreaked mischief, throwing passes, catching passes, and juggling footballs. Like many OSU players, football was a complete and absolute joy to Tom, and this joy was reflected in childlike enthusiasm. Skladany enjoyed intoning words and phrases backwards for comic effect, but had curtailed his magic performances in front of the squad.

Not attributable to magic, yet amazing nonetheless, was the continued avoidance of major injuries to OSU. The squad enjoyed marvelous health overall. This health was necessary, for the Nittany Lions presented formidable opposition. Penn State had a dominating offensive line, speedy receivers, and big, crushing backs who operated from a variety of sets.

Rampaging 209 pound fullback Matt Suhey was the first Lion frosh to ever start an opening game under Paterno. He erupted for 119 yards in 23 carries in that debut, in the squeaker over Stanford. Tailback Steve Giese blended speed and toughness, while wingback Jimmy Cefalo was arguably the most versatile back in the country. An extensive array of talents, mixed with pure speed and uncommon gutsiness, enabled Cefalo to repeatedly make clutch plays. Senior quarterback John Andress directed the offense in a steady, if rarely spectacular, fashion, much in the manner of his head coach.

On the other side of the ball, Kurt Allerman continued the fine tradition of intelligent Penn State linebackers, while defensive end Bill Banks performed at All-American levels. This fine Nittany Lion defense, in addition to the extremely slow natural grass field of Beaver Stadium, really concerned Hayes. If the powerful OSU running game could assert and dominate, the Buckeyes should win, Hayes reasoned.

On the eve of the showdown, Eastmoor (Columbus) High School renamed their football stadium in honor of distinguished graduate Archie Griffin. The NFL rookie was overwhelmed at this rare accord. "Winning two Heismans is nice," said Griffin in a world-class understatement, adding,"but how many are lucky enough to have something like this happen to them?"

CHAPTER THREE: PENN STATE

The next day, OSU triumphed before a Beaver Stadium then-record crowd of 62,503, although not before a rocky flight into State College. The airport in this small Pennsylvania hamlet was not large enough to handle the customary jet aircraft which OSU normally traveled by, so the team divided in half and took two older, propeller-driven planes. As the aircraft approached the tiny landing strip, turbulence increased to a point where passenger concern became evident. The landing strip was carved out of a forest, so trees were seemingly everywhere, and uncomfortably close.

Legend has it that Hayes, concerned about a safe landing, sent the plane containing the "gungas," or third and fourth stringers, in first, to ensure that his plane, containing the first and second string units, would not crash. After all, there was a game to be played!

In this hard fought contest, OSU won not because of luck, but due to pluck. The game was essentially a straightforward, stolid, conservative matchup pitting two effective offenses and two equally stingy defenses. Granted, PSU connected on 16 of 31 passes, yet most of these came late in the game as the Lions trailed by two touchdowns. Big name talent and lesser-known heroes combined to win this game for the Bucks.

Following a scoreless first quarter filled with traded punts, the home team threatened first. Taking advantage of a 15 yard penalty called against Herman Jones following an OSU punt, the Lions marched from their 35 to the OSU five. Andress was picked off by Ray Griffin deep in the end zone, and the rash return by Ray was bolstered by a 15 yard penalty charged against PSU. Logan quickly dashed 48 yards, well into Lion territory. Logan again proved impossible to contain the entire day, rambling for 160 yards on 25 rushes.

Johnson was bothered by a slight ankle sprain, and did not carry the ball until 8:57 remained in the half. Pete made his first four attempts count, powering all the way to the PSU eight. From there, Gerald produced some amazing sleight-of-hand fakes, allowing him to scoot around end for the initial score. On the ensuing PAT, Skladany picked up the bobbled snap, only to be trampled under short of the goal.

Penn State threatened once more before the half, only to again be turned away with nothing to show when Brudzinski recovered a fumbled pitch on the OSU four. The halftime speech of this year paled a bit in comparison to the '75 rallying cry.

During that halftime, Hayes related to his squad the conversation he held with Paterno prior to the kickoff. Paterno jogged across the field, welcoming Hayes and his team, then ever-so-innocently added, "How's your heart?" to the greeting, in reference to the well-publicized ticker troubles of Woody. Hayes was deep in the throes of his combat mood, and took great offense to this, as he imagined, underhanded attempt on the part of Paterno to establish a seed of doubt as to the fitness of Hayes. To the astonishment and great delight of his players, Hayes related how he responded with a snarled, "Screw you, and screw my heart," to this query of Paterno.

Woody went on to say to his players that he could drop dead of a heart attack in the middle of this game, yet didn't care, because OSU was still going to win! The OSU team emerged from the locker room unbelievably pumped, exhibiting every bit the tenacity and reckless abandon of their beloved Coach.

The above example points out several of the immense leadership skills as practiced by Woody. The following quotes were descriptions of German World War Two tank commander Erwin Rommel, one of the men whom Woody respected most; each quote also applied to the Hayes methodology on football. The initial epitome of a special leader was "...to be physically more robust than the troops he led, and to always show them an example."

Until the last few years of his coaching span, Woody prided himself on his physical toughness, most evident in his penchant for disdaining long sleeves, regardless of how low the mercury dipped, and his custom of bellying up to the line and demonstrating correct blocking procedures. Never mind that Woody was in short sleeves, blocking someone half his age who was equipped in full gridiron regalia. When Woody engaged you in a block, strap it on, because Woody did not mollycoddle. Rockne once said, "Love to block and let them know you love it"; that was the essence of Woody as a lineman.

Secondly, another "...great aspect of military leadership is the dual quality of moral strength and verbal articulateness." Allowing for his sailor roots in the art of swearing, Woody was otherwise as prudish as a dowager; his honesty and character were most often considered beyond question, especially by those who knew him well.

As for his articulateness, Woody could (and often did) hold court on any subject from the British royalty ("...like [Winston] Churchill, the Duke of Marlboro was most master of himself amid the den of battle.") to German sociology ("...the charismatic leader [according to Max Weber] draws his power from people who share his values and trust that leader to act on them."). The breadth, scope, and depth of the Hayes intellect seldom failed to astonish, particularly if the audience expected a cut-and-dried discussion solely about football.

The third facet of the Rommel leadership ethos which applied to Hayes is most eloquently captured in this description: "The Afrika Corps followed Rommel wherever he led, however hard he drove them... the men knew that Rommel was the last man to spare Rommel." Woody never required anything from someone, other than that which he demanded first from himself. Sure, Woody drove his assistants and players long and hard; then, as they bedded down, totally exhausted, he continued to work. Like another historical figure much admired by Woody, Alexander the Great, Hayes forever "...aspired to perfection." Quite simply, Woody never gave in to the urge to relax.

Similarly inspired this year after halftime, Ohio State put on an overpowering display in the third quarter, everywhere but the scoreboard. In this quarter, OSU held the ball for 12:43 of the allotted 15 minutes, yet failed to put the ball in the end zone as the Nittany Lion defense tightened close to the goal. Skladany fell just short on a 45 yard field goal opportunity, and early in the final quarter had another long kick partially blocked. Neil Hutton returned this tipped ball to the Penn State three, whereupon Ohio State clamped down and forced a short punt which Ray Griffin fair caught on the Penn State 35. Gerald, Logan, and Pete Johnson dragged the ball to the seven with short runs.

At this spot, Gerald artfully faked a plunge into the line, and pitched to the trailing wingback, Bob Hyatt. The seldom-used senior darted to paydirt through the stunned PSU defenders. Hyatt entered the game when Harrell was unexpectedly forced to leave with an eye injury, as Hayes seemingly opted to go with the age of Hyatt over the athleticism of the more gifted frosh Jackson.

Actually, Hyatt took it upon himself to enter the game, as he saw Harrell exit. In fact, the playcall was already made by the time most of the offensive unit and coaching staff realized the starter was not on the field, yet Gerald disdained a timeout and ran the play anyway. Hyatt responded to this confidence by scoring his very first touchdown since graduating from high school. For a former walk-on only recently granted a full scholarship, this score was the stuff of dreams. Gerald tried for two on the conversion, only to be felled short of the goal.

On the ensuing PSU possession, the Lions boldly marched 87 yards in a marathon 15 play drive bolstered by five complete passes. Key strikes were to Cefalo, halfback Rich Milot, and split end Rich Mauti. Suhey continued his workhorse ways, powering in from the one to keep PSU victory hopes flickering.

The Bucks managed to chew out a few precious first downs following the kickoff, including a crucial fourth down conversion on a short Johnson run. The clock whittled away, and time was extremely limited as PSU finally got the ball back.

On that critical fourth down play, Pete powered for two yards when an inch was required, from the OSU 39. "I thought if we couldn't get that one inch, we didn't deserve to win," explained Hayes afterwards.

The final was 12-7, in favor of the visitors, only the sixth home defeat on the Paterno career ledger. Dansler picked off a pass in the closing seconds, sealing the win.

In the aftermath of this big win, Hayes spent over an hour entertaining and enlightening the press, because "You're all such nice fellows." Dansler, Buonamici, and Brudzinski again spearheaded the superb defensive effort. The staunch D thwarted two Nittany Lion drives inside the OSU five, denying necessary points and providing the margin of victory. Johnson limped and blasted his way to 60 yards on 19 carries, many on essential short-yardage situations. Despite connecting on only one of three passes for a piddling ten yards, the OSU offense was in control almost the entire game.

Cousineau, Griffin, and Logan amassed rewards for their fine play, and Jimmy Moore led the way with five Buckeye leaves, three of those for devastating blocks. Ward and center Doug Porter also received high marks for their blocking, while Paul Ross and Roche played sterling games. In addition to the sprained ankle of Johnson, Beamon and Ross also suffered slight ankle twists.

The exultation over the big victory rapidly dissolved in the very first practice of the next week. Upset over a sluggish offensive practice performance, Hayes erupted in a startling outburst, in one of his so-called megaton rages. Hayes kept the offense on the field for an extra 15 minutes of bonecrunching repetitions, all the while berating himself. "You're the All-Americans, it must be my fault you make mistakes," Hayes would say.

The outbursts of Woody would proceed from stomping on his glasses, jumping on his watch, and shredding his trademark black "O" cap, to actually biting and punching himself to the point he drew blood and severely blackened eyes.

In this manner, Hayes utilized reverse psychology on his youngsters, who were disgusted to the point of nausea when Hayes would batter himself. If Woody wanted to punish himself for their mistakes, then they would force improvement upon themselves in order to halt such battering.

Although Woody was known to have a ready supply of cheap wristwatches and inexpensive eyeglasses ready in anticipation of destroying them, and even occasionally had head equipment men Phil Bennett in the early years or John Bozick in the latter years, loosen the stitches on hats to make rending easier, the episodes in which he physically punished himself were usually neither premeditated nor construed. It is a tremendous sign of the Hayes quest for perfection that even his own physical comfort and well-being was often sacrificed to elicit greater effort from his boys.

Perhaps the eruption by Hayes was in response to the impressive offensive onslaught by Michigan on Saturday. In a 51-0 victory, the top five Wolverine backs accumulated 516 rushing yards on 51 impressive carries.

This week, *Columbus Dispatch* reporter Wil Kilburger captured the essence of the Penn State game, and many of the other past victories of Hayes, in a superb article. According to Kilburger, the winning Hayes formula boiled down to this: "Hayes, like the military generals he quotes, has a simple order of the day. His teams are totally dedicated to the cause of hard work and preparation; they build a massive defense and then let the enemy die in its own mistakes."

In addition to this, Hayes always felt the Bucks were in better shape than any team they faced. Not surprisingly, this philosophy on football was not only widely duplicated (see Schembechler, Knight, etc.) but patently successful for virtually all its practitioners, if taught correctly.

As was often the case with his good pal Lombardi, the duplicators and detractors of the Hayes coaching style often overlooked the true compassion and love each of these two consistently harsh disciplinarians felt for their players. The cheap duplications and press releases which were based solely on the aggressive, driving side of Woody and Vince completely missed the point; that this strict style was countered, "...with a heart as big as Ohio Stadium," to quote central Ohio sportscaster Jimmy Crum. The tempestuous outbursts Lombardi and Hayes grew famous for were done expressly for the sake of eliciting improvement; not to draw attention or praise to that particular facet of their complex personalities.

Unfortunately, the underlying reason for the frequent tantrums was usually lost in the relaying, though former players of Woody and Vince readily admit that a punch from their Coach was, to borrow from OSU defensive back Jeff Ferrelli, "...like getting a spanking from your father."

Also attempting to match the winning ways of Hayes was Wittenberg grad and new OSU basketball coach Eldon Miller. Miller came from a successful program at Western Michigan, and looked to lift roundball fortunes of the once-rich scarlet and gray court program. Predecessor Fred Taylor retired following a number of halcyon years, although fortunes had recently ebbed somewhat. Miller intended to counteract the slight slide with a renewed emphasis on recruiting, using the vaunted football program as a guide.

Hayes gave Eldon a hearty stamp of approval, promising to help in any manner possible. Hayes never felt in direct competition with other OSU athletic programs; he was the patriarch and benevolent dictator of all OSU fortunes, forever seeking to improve every aspect of the university.

With upset-minded Missouri marching into Columbus, the Buckeyes really buckled down after the Hayes outburst of Monday in hopes of continuing their fine season. The Tigers had developed a penchant for the unexpected win, witness Alabama in the '75 opener and USC in the '76 opener. Each win came on the road in front of a hostile crowd. After this emotionally draining triumph over the Trojans, Missouri unexpectedly lost to Illinois. Head coach Al Onofrio and his squad hoped to bounce back to form versus the Bucks.

Ohio State defensive back coach Dick Walker lauded the talents of Tiger offensive stalwarts running back Curt Brown and quarterback Steve Pisarkiewicz. Running behind a powerful offensive line, Brown was a quick, shifty, darting runner whom Walker praised as "...truly great".

Pisarkiewicz, or "Zark", possessed one of the strongest and most accurate arms in all of college ball. He was the emotional leader of the Tigers, and Walker described him as, "...the best passer in the country." Zark severely jammed his shoulder against the Illini, and was listed as very doubtful for the Ohio State contest.

If Zark was unable to go in the horseshoe, the backup was Pete Woods, a husky 6'4" and 210 pounds. Woods eagerly looked forward to assuming the mantle of leadership, for he was an equally strong runner and competitor. If the Tiger defense, despite a proclivity to yield lots of yards through the air, could hold the OSU advance in check, Woods was confident he could engineer an upset.

CHAPTER FOUR: MISSOURI

The Buckeye's tenth clash with Missouri, and their first since '49, became just the upset Woods predicted. In front of a stunned Columbus crowd of 87,936, the Missouri offense at times manhandled the vaunted OSU defense, to provide a shocking 22-21 win. The inexperienced sophomore Woods capped a brilliant rushing performance with a dramatic two point conversion carry with just 12 seconds remaining in regulation. Woods, also a featured hurler on the Tiger baseball team, snapped a phenomenal 25 game home winning streak of the Buckeyes.

In a portent of a season-long inability to launch an effective passing game, OSU began on their first possession with three straight incompletions. On the day, OSU managed just one completion in nine attempts, with one critical interception. The opening quarter finished scoreless, with the sole threat being a missed Missouri field goal of 31 yards.

Two plays into the second period, Pete Johnson finished off an 80 yard, 13 play drive with the first score of the day. Undaunted, Missouri fired right back, scoring on a 31 yard strike to flanker Joe Stewart. Continuing the flurry of scoring, OSU soon retaliated, as Johnson scored with 9:47 left in the half. This scoring drive featured a 19 yard Johnson streak and a 31 yard Logan dash.

Despite being hobbled by his recurrent ankle injury throughout most of the game, Pete totaled 119 yards in 23 carries. Logan enjoyed another stellar day, compiling 110 yards on only 13 attempts.

On the ensuing Missouri possession, Buonamici grabbed a tipped pass and rumbled to the Tiger 26. A personal foul on the visitors pushed the ball to the 11, and Johnson bulled in for his third score of the half, with 7:54 remaining. The last Missouri possession of the half ended in the closing seconds with a Brudzinski interception. Ahead 21-7, the Bucks appeared well on their way to another convincing victory.

However, OSU failed to mount any sort of sustained offensive threat in the closing half, and their normally airtight defense was victimized both by the Tiger running game and timely Woods passes. The Tigers narrowed the margin in the third, thanks to a Gerald interception which gave the visitors great field position at the Ohio State 37. From there, Missouri pounded the ball in, cutting the gap to a touchdown.

The third quarter came to a close with a Skladany field goal miss, as the ball was partially blocked and just failed to clear the crossbar. This was the last time OSU even came close to scoring.

The two teams traded mostly ineffectual possessions throughout the final quarter, as each defense held the opposing offense well in check. With only five minutes remaining, the Tigers got the ball 80 yards away from the end zone. Largely on the powerful runs of Brown, Missouri pushed the ball to the OSU 42. Brown had a phenomenal day, ending with 20 carries for 108 yards against a defense primed to halt him, and his best was yet to come. With a scant 1:58 left, Woods scrambled desperately, only to be dumped for a 17 yard loss.

In an unexpected, huge reversal of that sack, OSU was penalized for illegal use of hands on the play, negating the loss and putting the new line of scrimmage at the OSU 44. Brown miraculously broke three separate tackles in a dazzling 30 yard run a few plays hence, eventually being dragged down at the nine. Sixteen seconds remained.

The ball was snapped, and Woods located an open Leo Lewis just inside the end line in the back corner of the end zone. Lewis hung on to the ball as he tightroped down the end line, somehow contorting his body enough to stay in bounds. The stunning catch put the score at 21-20, with OSU still in the lead.

Eschewing the tie, Missouri played for the win and went for a two point conversion. Ohio State denied the bid, and appeared to have escaped with a win. Alas, a penalty against the defense gave the Tigers one more shot at a victory. Woods kept the ball, ran slowly down the line of scrimmage, found a small opening, and snuck over from one and one-half yards away to clinch the thrilling comeback victory.

A shocked Hayes was extremely calm during the postgame interview. His patience finally wore thin after close to an hour, following a barrage of sharp questions concerning the officiating. Hayes kept refusing to put any blame for the loss on the officiating crew, despite a myriad of opportunities, as presented via leading questions of the expectant journalists.

Woody did eventually end the long press session with an angry outburst, after plenty of prodding. "You just want me to make an alibi. Well, nuts! Nuts! (or something comparable)," he yelled, and stormed out, much to the delight of many journalists, who now had colorful copy for their Sunday edition.

The Missouri backfield amassed 211 rushing yards in the game, with Woods and Brown eluding most of the tackles to accrue these significant yards. Woods connected on nine of his 20 passes for 113 clutch yards, with the two touchdown tosses. Despite their best efforts, the OSU defense just could not stop the Tiger offense when necessary. Byron Cato paved the tackling parade with an astounding 15 hits from his tackle slot, followed by Buonamici, Ross, Cousineau, and Brudzinski.

Conversely, the OSU offense could neither retain possession nor score, except during the second quarter outburst. Gerald was really held in check by the swarming Missouri defense, netting just 42 yards on 21 carries. The Tigers forced Gerald into keeping the ball on numerous busted option plays, usually for small or negative gains. Due to the ineffectiveness of the option, OSU was unable to mount a sustained drive following halftime. Springs carried just twice, for eight yards.

Bouncing back from this shocking setback was no easy task. In a captivating rematch of the most recent Rose Bowl, the UCLA Bruins traveled to the Midwest in an attempt to topple the Bucks again, this time in a more hostile environment.

Following that awesome victory on New Year's Day, head man Dick Vermeil sought new challenges in the NFL, becoming the head coach of the Philadelphia Eagles. Young (32), passionate, and knowledgeable, former defensive line coach Terry Donohue was the new head man.

Currently ranked number two in the nation, the high-powered Bruins looked exceedingly strong in winning their first three games of the '76 season. Each win was a convincing, lopsided affair. Due to its placement early in the season, this game was considered by Hayes to be even more critical than the Rose Bowl matchup. Accordingly, Buckeye practices were noticeably more intense than in previous weeks, and the players seemed to respond at a level of performance untapped earlier.

For the first time all year, injuries markedly hampered this OSU improvement. Both Cato and Johnson were ailing, with neither being close to healthy status. Johnson in particular was struggling, with nagging ankle injuries to each leg. Ruhl and Midlam were each banged-up in an especially hard-hitting Monday practice, and team doctors declared their status for the Bruin game extremely doubtful.

On the cheery side, Ray Griffin was fully recovered from his early-season head mishap, and a stringent review of Missouri game films revealed that Ray made two touchdown-saving tackles. According to the coaches, Griffin was operating at peak efficiency.

Also coming into his own was Brudzinski. "Bob played the finest game [of anyone] in the six years I've been here," asserted Hill following the Missouri tilt. The esteemed scout and football historian Esko Sarkinnen always claimed that Jim Houston was the best end he had ever coached. Houston was an All-American for OSU in '58 and '59, then enjoyed a distinguished 12 year career with the Cleveland Browns. Sarkinnen placed the 6'4", 228 pound Brudzinski right up there with Houston.

"[Bob] has a great attitude, great consistency, and intelligence. Also great character, great intensity," Esko admitted. According to Sarkinnen, "If you had 200 Brudzinski's, you would have been in Berlin long before Patton."

Showing vast improvement each time out, the unobtrusive senior from Fremont, Ohio, quietly, though not unnoticeably, did his job with real disdain for life and limb. Bob defended equally well against both the run and the pass, and was well respected for his toughness and willingness to mix it up come Saturday.

Originally, Bob contemplated attending either MSU or playing at Michigan with hometown pal Rob Lytle; his ultimate decision to attend OSU was gratefully acknowledged by coaches and his fellow players. Interestingly, Bob was an All-State tight end at Findlay High School, though he seemed a natural at crashing into people.

Quarterback Jeff Dankworth piloted the Bruin offense, hoping to avoid Brudzinski and company. The Reno, Nevada, native was a strong rusher in the ground-oriented UCLA scheme. Although neither was 100% healthy, still-feared backs Wendell Tyler and Theotis Brown were expected to play. Each quick runner successfully burst explosively behind the brutal blocking inherent in the vicious Donohue split-back veer set. Right tackle Manu Tuiasosopa led the way in both pass blocking and on numerous runs.

In spite of a groin pull, Tyler recently had passed former great Kermit Washington as the all-time Bruin rushing leader, with 2519 yards.

On defense, the roving inside linebacker Jerry Robinson had made a successful switch from his '75 position, tight end. The extraordinary athlete was fresh off a 28 tackle performance against Air Force, and was beginning to dominate. Although the Bruins respected the Buckeye duo of Logan and Johnson, their tenacious "firefighter" defensive unit was confident of their ability to throttle any opposition. Outside linebacker Raymond Burks displayed great speed, coupled with superb instincts, providing another standout presence. The Bruins had allowed a meager total of 26 points in their three wins.

Hard to believe, and even more remarkable than the dominating defense, was the fact that football now exceeded basketball in terms of success and popularity on the campus of Westwood. With the retirement of legendary basketball coach John Wooden, the gridiron UCLAns now outperformed, and supplanted by vociferous student support, drew more attention than, their once untouchable hardcourt contemporaries.

This ascendance came very rapidly. The school itself was a relatively young 57 years old, and football fortunes did not reach national title levels until the '60's. Donohue played on the defensive line in the historic '66 Rose Bowl upset of top-ranked MSU, and in fact was the first Bruin to play in and coach in a Rose Bowl.

Donohue so loved the Westwood school, he fondly remarked, "I'd hate to leave this place, even for heaven." As an offensive line coach under Pepper Rodgers and Vermeil, Donohue built a reputation for churning out fast, big, heady technicians - most notably '75 standout Randy Cross.

Equally outstanding was the very brief history of Bruin/Buckeye confrontations. In '61, the initial meeting produced a 13-3 victory for OSU, largely behind the offensive exploits of backfield mates Paul Warfield and Matt Snell. Hayes called that '61 team the hardest working team he had ever coached.

In '62, OSU was ranked number one going into the contest, only to be edged 9-7 when their famed powerhouse offense was shut down. The Bruins held the running game of OSU well in check, as the Buckeyes sorely missed the injured Bob Ferguson.

The next matchup was not until '75, and of course OSU dominated in the regular season tilt and were subsequently upended in the Rose Bowl. Equal excitement was anticipated in this '76 contest.

Rare, yet well-deserved, attention was focused this week on the OSU equipment department. This usually overlooked department was responsible for everything from laundering jerseys, to sizing shoes, to keeping Woody outfitted in all his traditional sideline garb. Presiding over this monolithic task was the brash, outspoken John Bozick. The self-confessed "...harshest critic, yet biggest fan," of Hayes, Bozick probably spent more time with Hayes than even the Coach's wife Anne did. As such, Bozick offered his knowledgeable opinion on why Woody was so successful. "The greatest thing about the old man is he knows how to handle people," said Bozick glowingly.

Behind-the-scenes, also, and equally indispensable was the OSU training staff and the assemblage of student managers. In addition to treating all sorts of injuries, both major and minor, head trainer Billy Hill estimated he and his comrades wrapped approximately 3000 miles of tape around ankles, wrists, and knees every season. Hill parlayed a high school sideline as a trainer into a Tennessee State collegiate foray into the field, augmented by extensive time in Vietnam as a corpsman in the Army.

Hill started at OSU in '71 as an assistant to the icon Ernie Biggs, and had graduated from the university in '73. After years of expert tutelage under Biggs and then Alan Hart, Hill had become the head trainer. Hill constantly expanded his job parameters, making it a priority to be in-the-know concerning advancements in everything from circuit weight training to hydrotherapy, and had recently served as the head trainer at the Pan Am Games in Mexico City.

The unheralded and unpaid managers handled an equally overwhelming load of tasks, everything from editing game films, to chasing down errant balls in practice, to coordinating press box and onfield communications during games. Each manager in '76 resoundingly agreed that the toughest of their wide-ranging duties was serving as the official timekeeper in practice. Hayes demanded a rigidly regimented timetable, yet hated to leave any facet of that regimen until he was satisfied. It fell to the student manager to interrupt the Coach, with all due temerity, to keep the practice on schedule.

Equally alone, and under increasing fire from the public, was the new quarterback Gerald. Rod was suffering through an extremely fiery indoctrination of running an offense, and his baptism was coming against very good teams. The passing game for OSU was severely lacking at this stage. The Gerald completion percentage stood at an abysmal 23% (3-13), though offensive coordinator Staub defended the youngster.

Staub praised the option decisions of Gerald, his avoidance of many turnovers and wrong decisions, and believed Gerald should throw more, not less. Gerald had run for 196 yards on 55 carries, and Staub felt this threat of a run could open up the passing lanes if exploited properly.

Staub felt that as Geralds' fortunes went, so did the teams' as a whole. The slender whippet was stepping up as a leader, assuming the burden of running an offense and rallying his teammates around him, and Staub could see the youngster increasing in both wisdom and confidence. Hayes backed the somewhat embattled field general totally, realizing that some severe growing pains were necessary for long-range stardom to occur.

Preparations continued apace in the last few days before the game. Beamon, who only got in for a couple of plays versus Missouri, was back near full health. Acclaimed frosh Mike Guess stepped into the starting spot of Ruhl, as it became apparent Ruhl could not return from his knee sprain. Mills returned to action after sitting out the Tiger game, further strengthening the secondary.

In another of his prophetic strokes, Hayes devoted much extra time and concentration to the kicking game. Ironically, this was the one area OSU fell short in on Saturday; at least in comparison to the exceptional special teams effort put forth by the Bruins. Painfully aware that OSU had not suffered two consecutive losses at home since '71, Hayes vowed, "We will be ready".

CHAPTER FIVE: UCLA

A near-record crowd of 87,969 gratefully enjoyed mid-summer skies and temperatures on Saturday. The game was a taut tug-of-war which unfortunately did not end on that same enjoyable note. The first quarter was a defensive struggle featuring a punting battle between Skladany and Frank Corral. Each alternated booming kicks in a masterful fight for field position.

The first break of the game occurred when Ray Griffin returned one such long punt 17 yards, into Bruin territory, with 11:41 left in the half. Starting at the visitor 46, Gerald continued the pattern begun on the second play of the game, tossing the ball deep downfield. Greg Storer, filling in quite handily for the injured Moore, caught this Gerald attempt for a spectacular 19 yard gain. Johnson and Logan carried the ball to the four, from which spot Johnson punched in to break the scoreless tie.

For the remainder of the half, each defense dominated the other offense. Ohio State managed to subdue the explosive Bruin backfield even as Buonamici missed all but a few plays of the half with a toe sprain. The deepest penetration for UCLA carried only to the OSU 44.

The Bruins finally broke loose early in the third quarter. Corral nailed a 47 yard field goal, after Dankworth found flanker Wally Henry for a critical third down completion which prolonged the drive. Several minutes after the successful kick, Griffin recovered a Bruin fumble. The Bucks marched down to the Bruin 17, when Logan returned the favor with a fumble of his own. The Bruins capitalized on this unfortunate turnover by marching 83 yards in 14 plays.

The big play in this mammoth drive, and perhaps the key play of the game, came on a 25 yard Theotis Brown dash through a mostly unsuspecting OSU specialty unit on a fourth down fake from punt formation. This was the longest Bruin run of the day.

Dankworth came through with another key play moments later, finding a well-covered Rick Walker for a 15 yard pickup. Other than these two plays, the yards came slowly and arduously against the determined home defense. Nevertheless, UCLA finally managed to pound the ball across the goal, Dankworth going the final foot on a sneak with 13:08 remaining.

Jeff Ferrelli recalls how closely he came to snuffing this fake to Brown before it got underway. Ferrelli was in a backfield position, ideally designated to watch the UCLA tight end or other up-back and assume coverage if either peeled off for a pass out of punt formation. In the seconds leading to the snap of the ball, Jeff noticed that Brown, the up- and blocking-back, was staring nervously in the direction of the OSU backfield, his eyes wide with a combination of fear and anticipation. Since Brown normally was not concerned with the backfield of the defending punt team, it dawned on Ferrelli that a fake was imminent. Jeff excitedly began yelling to the down lineman directly in front of him, Joe Dixon, "It's a fake, Joe, it's a fake."

Dixon, so intent on performing his assigned role of briefly engaging the blocker, then rapidly peeling off to set up a return wall, did not acknowledge the repeated plea. Ferrelli himself was momentarily frozen at the snap of the ball, for he still had to determine if the fake was a pass into his assigned area. This brief, unavoidable delay was enough to spring Brown for the big pickup, though Ferrelli did burst in, upend two blockers, and get his arm in the way of the hard-charging Brown. The immense thighs of Theotis powered through the attempted arm tackle and the huge Bruin rampaged downfield. Of such microscopic turns of fortune are games won or lost (or in this case tied), and Ferrelli's shot at stardom had so very fleetingly slipped by.

Ohio State received the ensuing kickoff and mounted a drive of their own. Johnson, Logan, and Gerald hammered into stiff Bruin resistance, eventually reaching the eight yard line. The visitors toughened, and Gerald was nailed in the backfield for a pivotal one yard loss on a third and three call. Plenty of time (about five minutes) remained, so Hayes went the logical route, and opted for a 25 yard Skladany field goal, which was good. The game was tied up, and Hayes felt OSU would receive one final chance at a win.

The Bucks counted on their defense to get the ball back, and true to the foreseen script, UCLA was soon forced to punt. The Buckeye offense mounted a short drive, yet then came to a fourth down situation at the UCLA 48. Fifteen seconds remained, and Hayes did not want to risk failing to convert a fourth down try, which would give UCLA excellent field position. Much to the dismay of many in the crowd, Hayes elected to punt.

After receiving the ball, the Bruins were pinned deep in their own territory and likewise did not want to risk turning the ball over. As the Bruins rattled off two conservative runs to wind out the clock, a chorus of boos began to emanate from the stands. As the final gun sounded, ending the contest in a 10-10 stalemate, thunderously loud boos rained down on both teams as they ran off the field.

Hayes was very critical of the booing later. In his estimation, shared by Donohue, this game was so hotly yet evenly contested that, "Our kids didn't deserve to lose." Hayes and Donohue both agreed that each defense demanded so much respect, that the offenses essentially were forced to play for field position, and not points. Neither coach was willing to take too many chances of throwing conservatism to the winds, especially late, for a miscue at any time in the last several minutes on offense probably meant defeat.

Ohio State fans were not used to seeing this philosophy until the Michigan game, and the Columbus crowd did not respond kindly. This was a prototypical button-down offense, close-to-the-vest strategically, count-on-the-defense-to-acquire-field-position, wait-for-the-other-team-to-make-a-mistake, style of play which did not appeal to anyone but defensive purists. With nothing personally at stake but pride, the majority of fans vehemently disagreed with this conservative approach; hence, the boos.

To Hayes, this disapproval served nothing but harm to his players, who expended all they had in the effort to win, and were guided within the parameters of the Hayes decisions. Woody did not mind the fans booing him; he did not appreciate the team being included in that animosity.

Donohue classified the game as "...an intense struggle, a classic struggle...." The novice coach butted heads with an acknowledged master of the craft, and did not lose. Donohue revealed he was a gigantic fan of Woody, although his first meeting with the Coach was a necessarily brief post-game handshake.

Donohue religiously read every book written about or by Hayes, and this fantastic struggle was now fodder for future books.

The courageous return of Buonamici in the second half really buoyed the Buckeye defense, which allowed only the one extended drive all afternoon. Brown played heroically through a painfully sprained ankle, leading the way with an outrageous 17 tackles, despite being double-teamed all game.

Cousineau, Cato, Thompson, Beamon, and Brudzinski each enjoyed spectacular games, and UCLA very pointedly avoided the zone of Griffin, deliberately throwing and running away from the superb safety. UCLA ground out 205 yards rushing, Dankworth hit eight of 14 passes for 83 yards, and Corral punted for a bodacious average of 47.1 yards on his six kicks.

The OSU offense was equally thwarted by an aggressive Bruin defense, which was spectacularly headed by Robinson's 21 tackles. The Buckeyes managed only 180 yards rushing, with Logan totaling 81 on 20 attempts, Johnson reaching 50 in 14 runs, and Gerald adding 46 on 13 chances. Gerald connected on three of his eight throws for 41 yards, though the offense sputtered and bogged down at many critical junctures.

Logan played despite a badly bruised shoulder, and both he and Hayes brusquely denied that this disability had anything to do with the crucial fumble late in the third quarter. "Coach, I just dropped the ball," Logan said truthfully.

Skladany was barely overshadowed by the astounding performance of Corral, though Tom still averaged 42.3 yards on his six punts, many of which bailed OSU out of terrible field position.

Early the following week, a mini-controversy erupted after each head coach had occasion to peruse the game films. Each man offered totally disparate views on the officiating, with each head coach claiming the other received several advantageous (mis)calls. Donohue piped in from the West Coast with the classic line: "Some of those officials have to be related to Woody by marriage." Woody, for his part, argued in vain that Brown was illegally in motion prior to his backbreaking 25 yard run. Fortunately, the furor died down quickly, as OSU prepared for an enigmatic Iowa team.

Two weeks previously, Iowa beat OSU common opponent Penn State (currently saddled with a woebegone 1-3 mark) 7-6, in a game eerily similar to the narrow Buckeye win against the Nittany Lions. The very next week, Iowa got in an early hole against USC and ended up being trounced 55-0. That shellacking did not cause OSU to downgrade the Hawkeyes, however. As Hayes saw it, the only decisive advantage the Buckeyes enjoyed was in the arena of overall team speed.

Hayes praised his defense this week, and contrastably expressed great concern for his inconsistent offense. Johnson declared himself healed from his two sprained ankles, so Hayes had reason to feel somewhat upbeat heading into the hostile environment of Iowa City.

Iowa head coach Bob Commings welcomed the invasion with more than a little trepidation. The Hawkeye offense was directed by the able-running quarterback Butch Caldwell, though the run-heavy Iowa attack was dominated by the exploits of fine tailback Ernie Sheeler. A young, rough defense featured linebackers Tom Rusk and Dean Moore.

Overall, Iowa was blessed with fine talent, though the program featured little depth and few marquee players. Hawkeye confidence was present, if not prevalent. Commings hoped that the traditionally hostile environs of Kinnick Stadium could provide additional impetus to his upset-minded club.

Late in this week, Schembechler made national news as he vocally disdained the negative angle in reporting football news. Bo preferred sportswriters to be more supportive of their home programs, especially, though not exclusively, at the collegiate level. Bo railed against the strident detractors of his alma mater, Miami of Ohio. The Redskins of Dick Crum had unexpectedly stumbled to a horrendous 0-5 start, and critics were outspokenly attacking the coach and his program.

Schembechler argued that more attention should be focused on the past successes of the Crum regime, and the current season should merely be judged an uncommon aberration. Despite the well-reasoned argument by Bo, the majority of the media continued to harp on the Redskins and the equally-unfortunate Detroit Lions, in lieu of overlooking the misfortunes of these regressing organizations.

Later in the week, Hayes himself was publicly angered by an avoidable late hit in a practice which needlessly injured the freshman Ron Barwig. Barwig dislocated his knee and was lost for the year.

CHAPTER SIX: IOWA

The Buckeye offense bounced back to enjoy a fine first half in powering OSU to a 34-14 victory come Saturday. Pete Johnson stormed into the end zone three times, in the process becoming the all-time conference touchdown scorer with 48. Ohio State scored on each of their first three possessions, while the defense shut down the Hawkeye offense, allowing a piddling 30 total yards in the opening half.

The Buckeyes began the scoring on an 82 yard drive, culminating in a 17 yard Gerald sprint to paydirt. The next possession was a shorter 57 yard drive, featuring a spectacular 39 yard pass and subsequent run, to Jones. Johnson rammed the ball in from the two, tying Billy Marek of Wisconsin for the most touchdowns in conference annals.

Iowa promptly fumbled following the kickoff, with Brown diving on the loose ball at the Hawkeye 20. Shortly thereafter, Johnson broke the record with a short touchdown jaunt.

Ohio State again got the ball back, and Johnson quickly broke free on a 45 yard romp, finally being dragged down from behind by Chuck Sodergren at the 11. The offense sputtered a bit at this point, and Skladany was brought in, converting a short field goal.

Iowa responded to this mild defensive stand with their only scoring threat in the half, which was abruptly stopped when Guess picked off a Caldwell pass in the OSU end zone. A late hit by Iowa after Guess downed the ball gave OSU fortuitous field position at their 35, though the offense could not take advantage. The half ended with OSU comfortably ahead 24-0.

In the second half, Iowa made several adjustments which severely foiled the OSU option attack. Still, State opened the half with a short drive capped by a 46 yard Skladany field goal. The scoring for OSU concluded when Cousineau intercepted a Hawkeye pass, weaving and powering his way to the visitor's six. Johnson obliged, taking the ball in from the three.

Following this score, Jim Pacenta entered in relief of Gerald, and Ohio State lost all consistency on offense. A Pacenta fumble was converted into the first Iowa touchdown, on a 17 yard drive after the recovery. Iowa scored another touchdown late in the fourth, behind the impressive runs of Sheeler and Caldwell. Sheeler ended with 94 of the Hawkeye total of 188 yards rushing, and Caldwell broke loose to dominate the last two Hawkeye drives of the game, at least with clutch plays and a defiant leadership style.

The resilient signalcaller ended with 37 yards on 18 carries, while hitting five of 13 passes for just 39 yards against a very rugged OSU defense. Gerald fared slightly better, accumulating 31 rushing yards on 16 attempts, while passing for a more-impressive 73 yards on four of eight accuracy. Unfortunately, Gerald also threw two interceptions and lost a fumble.

This game highlighted a continuing '76 pattern of the Buckeyes: Get off to a fast start offensively, then suffer a second half steep decline in production and points. The after-intermission letdowns were condemned by Hayes - too many mistakes, too many turnovers, and too many lost opportunities. Included in the rash of mistakes was a disturbing trend of missed assignments and a plethora of penalties.

Hayes was pleased with the squad's propensity in busting out of the gate strong, though this pleasure was more than offset by his concern over offensive inconsistency. "We won, and that's the big thing," was his final comment on the matter.

Skladany, in particular, was not pleased with his performance against UCLA, vowing to, "Start the season over," against Iowa. Indeed, the senior came out and reaffirmed his stature as probably the pre-eminent specialist in the country. His kickoffs repeatedly boomed into and often out of the end zone.

Kickers were still allowed at this time to tie their shoe tips to their ankles, creating a mallet-type striking surface which was extremely telling. The instant Skladany connected with the ball on a kickoff, he could tell if the boot was long and true, or if a slightly mis-hit ball had a possibility of being returned. When Tom really laid into a kickoff, he made it a point to sprint directly to the sideline and try to take a seat on the bench before an official could signal the touchback. Thus, on film days, kicking coach Staub was often heard yelling at the screen, "Where is Skladany?" as a kick sailed over the end zone.

The magnificent play of Griffin in the Iowa contest prompted Commings to state, "Ray Griffin may be the best player in the nation." The talented safetyman completely stifled any attempt to throw into his area, and provided fierce run support as well. Brudzinski and Buonamici were also complimented very highly by Hayes, especially considering Nick was unable to practice in the week leading to the game.

Unbeknownst to many, Hayes spent much time and effort during the early '76 schedule assisting a young high school coach afflicted with cancer. Hayes first heard of a Dave Pavlansky, the head coach of Poland High, near Youngstown, Ohio, on one of many OSU recruiting sprees into this area. Hayes discovered that Pavlansky required delicate surgery to remove a dangerous brain tumor.

Despite the fact Hayes had never met the young coach, Woody arranged for the surgery to be performed at the world-renowned OSU University Hospital. As the ailing prep coach checked into the hospital, Hayes was on hand to introduce himself and lend moral support. Before the scheduled surgery, Pavlansky and his wife attended a Buckeye practice. Hayes interrupted the tough workout to greet the couple and had his entire team wish them a hearty good luck.

Following that difficult operation, both Woody and Anne Hayes stayed with the couple for extended periods of time. Just a few short hours after the bitter loss to Missouri, Hayes visited with Pavlansky for over an hour. This is just one glowing example of the mercurial tendency of Hayes to confound and delight his observers, usually going well out of his way to help those most in need. This incident was unusual only because it generated publicity, while most of the many humanitarian deeds of the Coach went unreported.

Amazingly, Woody had no desire to see any of his many, many, good deeds publicized or even acknowledged. The man was perhaps the most caring, thoughtful, considerate person ever encountered by many who met him, yet his reputation as a fierce football warrior necessitated the squelching of his good Samaritan side. Woody did not ever want an opponent or even his own team to think he was at all mellow or kind-hearted, so he himself made sure most of his plentiful good deeds went unobserved.

Sportscaster Jimmy Crum recalls entering the office of Hayes, and discovering an elaborate erector set assembled on the Coach's desk. Woody explained the toy was a gift for an ill youngster, whom Woody did not know, yet had been informed was an Ohio State fan. After this explanation, Hayes leaned across his desk, forcefully grabbed the front of Crum's shirt, and snarled, "...dammit, you better not tell anybody." Woody unselfishly gave so much of his time and spirit to causes, yet he felt compelled to preserve his cultivated image as a tyrannical barbarian of sorts.

In another incident, Hayes encountered a very ill little child, who was a gigantic OSU football fan, during a hospital visit with Crum. As Woody was leaving the boy's hospital room, the child expressed a desire to meet then-Buckeye Archie Griffin. The gracious child muttered, "But if Archie can't make it, I'll understand." Woody left without saying a word to the youngster, then hurriedly turned to Jimmy, demanding, "Get Archie in here tomorrow." To his credit, Griffin made a well-received visit the following day, and Crum's crowded desk still holds a photo of that memorable encounter.

Later this week Baschnagel spoke very highly of his former Coach. As a devout Catholic, the heavily recruited high school-age Brian desperately wanted to attend Notre Dame. His decision to instead enroll at OSU came about solely because of Woody. Hayes made such an impression on Baschnagel, that Brian redirected his deep-set lifelong goal and became a Buckeye.

In direct response to the alleged recruiting violations supposedly committed by Hayes, Brian stated, "He's the most honest person I know... Woody does not cheat." Baschnagel was drafted by the Chicago Bears as a flanker, and was originally tried in camp at defensive back. Soon realizing their mistake, Chicago inserted Baschnagel into their special teams and passing-set offensive schemes. Baschnagel responded fantastically, becoming the team's third leading receiver, playing hell-bent-for-contact on all coverage squads, and averaging an amazing 36 yards per kickoff return.

Asked about the recent Hayes penchant for skipping press conferences, Baschnagel quipped, somewhat revealingly, "I think he now trusts the players more than he trusts himself."

Next to Archie, Woody perhaps admired the leadership traits of Baschnagel more than any of his players. Brian was the epitome of the scholar/athlete, good citizen/fierce competitor, naturally gifted athlete/exceedingly hard worker, and an inspiring, flat-out motivator of others, which Hayes admired and aspired in all his players. Brian came from a fantastically supportive family, which added to the admiration Woody felt for Brian.

Yet, in spite of their immense closeness and high regard for each other, at one point, after Brian graduated from Ohio State, Woody actually stopped speaking with one of his most cherished leaders. The reason? Hayes felt very strongly that each person, if blessed with the opportunity, should attend law school.

To Hayes, a law degree was the absolute pinnacle of achievement, and Woody felt Brian was not living up to his potential brilliance, as Baschnagel decided to forego law school after attaining his undergrad degree. The Coach believed, "If we bring a young man to our university and don't make sure he gets an education, we've cheated him." In the case of Baschnagel, Brian was cheating himself by not pursuing the path of law school. Fortunately, Woody and Brian did eventually resolve their difference of opinion concerning higher education, and resumed communication.

Mrs. Mary Ellen Guess, mother of the fantastic frosh Mike, responded angrily in both print and voice to those fans who loudly voiced their disapproval at the UCLA game. Her son made at least one touchdown-saving tackle in that game, graded out to a scintillating 91% efficiency, yet the fans who booed removed all vestiges of pride Mrs. Guess held towards her son's performance. The loud denigration of the Hayes policy to not take unnecessary risks actually damaged the players, she felt, since their all-out efforts were not appreciated. Motivationally, this lack of support would serve to inhibit future player performance, Mrs. Guess reasoned.

Her unhappiness at this lack of support, though certainly not the most outspoken, was perhaps the most understandable. If anything, now that she had the opportunity to vent her feelings, Mrs. Guess' pride in her son and his teammates was doubly resolved. Booing was certainly a rare spectacle in Columbus at this time, and the outrage over its occurrence may seem surprising if viewed in the context of the Earle Bruce and John Cooper years, when booing unfortunately became more prevalent.

A disturbing injury had occurred late in the Iowa game, further depleting the tight end position. Greg Storer, doing a remarkable job in place of the sidelined Moore, separated his shoulder and was expected to miss at least two weeks. Storer was rapidly becoming a top performer, and had in fact graded out as the top lineman in the UCLA contest.

Scrambling to find another replacement, Hayes tabbed sophomores Joe Robinson and Bill Jaco as co-fill-ins. Each was now at a tackle slot, after beginning their Buckeye career at the tight end position, and the switch was not surprising in the least.

Tim Vogler was new to the center spot, and had become a jack-of-all-trades up and down the offensive line. Vogler, remembered for his attacking style as a '75 fullback, was also given practice reps at the vacated tight end spot.

Good fortune came in the improved condition of Johnson, who sat out virtually the entire second half of the Iowa game following a flare-up of his ankle woes. The big man seemed healthy, though he was held out of practice to prevent further damage to his fragile ankles.

In the interim, Springs impressed all with his increased exposure in practice, and in his limited appearances in games. The transfer's startling speed and overall athleticism translated into some stunning practice sessions, which greatly increased the confidence of Hayes as a road trip to Wisconsin loomed large. "We simply have to buckle down and get to work," became the oft-repeated Hayes refrain, and his prescription for all problems.

Wisconsin was a truly explosive offensive team. The Badgers stood second in the conference in total yards, fourth nationally in the same area, and led the Big 10 in passing scores. The Badgers gave Michigan a tussle before barely succumbing 40-27. That impressive effort demonstrated they could score regardless of the level of competition. Quarterback Mike Carroll powered the dynamite offense, often tossing to the elusive split end Dave Charles, who topped all conference receiving lists. With all his success in throwing touchdowns, Carroll also threw interceptions by the bundle.

When the Badgers stayed on the ground, stout senior fullback Larry Canada bore the brunt of the load. An equally talented blocker, Canada averaged 4.6 yards on each of his 98 attempts. A torn knee ligament in the latest game, an 18-16 defeat to Purdue, shelved the premier Badger breakaway threat, halfback Mike Morgan. The shifty junior was averaging a spectacular 6.4 yards a carry. Morgan underwent surgery, and a gaggle of replacements auditioned for his spot. Foremost among the candidates was Ron Pollard.

Badger punter Dick Milaeger boasted lofty credentials, averaging 45 yards per kick, just a shade better than the more renowned Skladany. On defense, Buckeye assistant coach Mummey singled out senior end Pat Collins and sophomore linebacker Tim Halleran as the obvious strength of a somewhat suspect Badger unit.

Platitudes for the Iowa clash went to Brudzinski for his continuing dominance; the steady Pietrini, who fended off Mackie and Robinson to retain his starting spot; and the prolific pointmaker Johnson. As game day approached, Moore continued his painful recovery while Storer was on an amazingly fast mend, planning on making the trip north to dairyland.

Badger head coach John Jardine pointed out the significance of this game, offering, "If we beat the Bucks, it would make our season."

A Wisconsin victory was more likely than Ray Griffin enduring an off performance. The ever-improving junior continued to draw great respect and attention from opposing offenses, who paid tribute to his blossoming talents by avoiding him as often as possible, both in the secondary and on kick returns.

Ray entertained thoughts of transferring as a frosh, for he played the same position as older brother Archie. Comparisons were inevitable, and it was difficult for a first-year newcomer to top a certified All-American, even though Raymond was a better athlete, as all the Griffin family attested. To take nothing away from Archie, brother Duncan still contends that Ray was a better running back. Impress as he might, though, Ray could not escape the belittling sobriquet of "Archie's little brother."

Nonetheless, Ray pluckily endured, playing for 52 minutes and piling up 223 yards in a backup role to his Heisman-winning sibling. Just as importantly, Ray excelled in and enjoyed participating on kick coverage teams. When '74 graduation opened up three spots in the secondary, Ray asked Woody for a tryout at defensive back.

The amazingly fast youngster just wanted to play, even at a strange position. He learned on the job in '75, relying on his amazing physical gifts, with hours spent working on foreign techniques and diagnosing offensive tendencies outside of practice. The promising year peaked with his phenomenal performance at Michigan, while in '76 he soon surpassed even that skillful level.

At long last free from the estimable shadow of Archie, Ray professed nothing but pride in the many achievements of his famous brother. The hard-hitting safety displayed great talent as a painter in his free time, and aspired to join his brother in the NFL (Coincidentally, this dream came true, and by some accounts, Ray had the more successful professional career).

CHAPTER SEVEN: WISCONSIN

On Saturday, a then-record Camp Randall Stadium crowd of 79,759 nearly saw the underdog home team surpass a wilting Buckeye squad. Ohio State continued the distressing pattern of scoring early and often, then barely withstanding a furious barrage to narrowly emerge victorious. The Wisconsin faithful vociferously roared until the final seconds, as a last-gasp Badger scoring attempt barely went awry.

As expected, at least according to Jardine, the Wisconsin offense pounded and dented the OSU defense to the tune of 416 yards, mostly on the ground. Badger turnovers proved most damaging in the final analysis.

Wisconsin leaped into the scoring column first. Scott Erdmann (he of the late-hit fame) picked off an overthrown Gerald pass, and the Badgers opportunistically drove 47 yards in eight plays, with Pollard plunging in from the one. The Badgers drove into scoring position on their next possession, although a fumbled snap on a Vince Lamia field goal attempt was recovered by OSU on the Wisconsin 33.

The visitors seized this opportunity and drove to the tying score early in the second quarter, as Gerald kept on an option fake from 12 yards away. Logan busted free for a 23 yard gain in this short drive, continuing his remarkable season with a 19 carry, 113 yard day.

On their next possession, following a nifty Griffin punt return to the Buckeye 43, OSU pounded down the field on the legs of Logan, Johnson, and Gerald. Ohio State seemed to befuddle the Badgers by switching predominately to the I formation. In the first five games of '76, the Bucks had operated mostly from the pro set and the veer. This switch on this day was made to accommodate the brilliant ability Logan had of running toward daylight behind his blocking. The I formation allowed the tailback much greater freedom in reading defenses and in choosing the open hole to run through, and Logan proved extremely adept at picking the best spot to run toward.

The blocking assignments for this style were reminiscent of the Green Bay Packers and their unstoppable "Run to daylight" offense. Often, the defender's own momentum carried him out of the play, and the elusive Logan needed just the briefest window of opportunity from his blockers to break clear. Johnson performed his usual finishing duty, busting over the goal on a short run to forge a 14-7 OSU lead.

The proclivity of Carroll for interceptions manifested on the ensuing drive, as Guess stepped in front of Charles to pluck the underthrown ball. Guess roared 22 yards before being pushed out of bounds at the Badger 30.

Shortly thereafter, Johnson thundered in for another score and, although Skladany pulled the conversion wide left, it seemed as if the rout was on.

Lamia unsuccessfully attempted a 48 yard field goal for Wisconsin as the half ended, with OSU comfortably up 20-7.

As the second half began, Dansler continued his excellent pass defending abilities, picking off a short Carroll pitch and rumbling to the Wisconsin 49. The Buckeyes again converted a turnover into points, albeit on a very fortuitous break. Gerald and Logan began the weird play by botching a handoff exchange at the 29. Unexpectedly, the ball bounced crazily and perfectly back into the hands of Gerald and he sprinted past a dazed, confused Badger defense for the touchdown.

This was among the last tastes of glory for OSU, however, as the Badgers fairly dominated the remainder of play. The momentum shifted almost totally to the home team, as the Badgers outperformed the faltering Bucks from this point on. Wisconsin began the comeback after receiving the kickoff following the touchdown. The Badgers blithely marched to a fast score, utilizing the darting, speedy tailback tandem of Ira Matthews and Terry Breuscher, in combination with the bullish Canada. The touchdown with 2:30 left in the third narrowed the margin to 27-14.

The Buckeyes did summon enough wherewithal at this time to drive all the way to the Badger 12. After stalling in close, OSU elected to have Skladany boot a chip-shot field goal. This attempt was foiled as Wisconsin busted through the line to knock the kick down. The underdogs could not capitalize with a turnaround score, as the OSU defense forced a punt, which traveled a surprisingly short distance.

Ohio State began the drive at midfield, and backup fullback Paul Campbell burst through the line for a startling 33 yard pickup. Skladany followed this dash with a short, 25 yard field goal after the drive sputtered. These three points seemingly placed OSU out of harm's way, for it was late in the final quarter.

Without resorting to an alibi, much of the offensive woes of OSU, particularly down in scoring position, were attributable to injuries. Both Johnson and Logan were forced to exit as the hitting became very ferocious in the closing half. Johnson suffered a recurrence of his ankle problem, denying him any power or leverage with which to run, while Logan was inadvertently injured when one of his own lineman accidentally kicked him in the calf. The muscle became severely knotted, and Logan was forced to exit.

The kicking game suffered tremendously when regular snapper Doug Porter, an excellent placement man, tore knee ligaments and was replaced by guard Tom Waugh, who was unused to the tricky snapping chores. Since Logan was the usual holder, the absence of both the snapper and the placement man negatively impacted the normally precise timing of Skladany.

Wisconsin fired right back after yielding the short field goal. Carroll briskly marched his troops down the field, ultimately firing a 13 yard scoring strike to fullback Joe Rodriguez. On the essential try for two, OSU came up with a huge stop. This defensive stand was made even more critical as Tim McConnel swiped the ball away for Wisconsin on the ensuing on-sides kick.

Although only 37 seconds remained, Carroll was not through. He continued his courageous, yet futile, comeback effort by nailing flanker Randy Rose with two intermediate gains. As the game clock expired, a Carroll pass just bounded off the outstretched hands of Charles in the middle of the end zone. Ohio State had survived, 30-20.

Wisconsin again proved with this effort they could play with the elite and barely flinch. Though Carroll was not exactly accurate in his throwing, hitting just 11 of 25 passes, his brave demeanor and repeated clutch conversions never allowed OSU to put the comeback threat of Wisconsin completely away. Despite the absence of Morgan, a slew of Badger backs, led by Canada with 94 yards, bravely pounded into and around the fatigued OSU defense. Irregardless of the second half letdown, Buck defenders Brudzinski, Cousineau, Dansler, and Thompson continued in their high standard of play.

Hayes was especially happy about one particular play which occurred early in the second quarter, with the score knotted at seven. During a Skladany field goal attempt, the center snap was botched. Logan scooped up the loose ball and broke into the clear for a surprising first down. Just a few plays later, Johnson ran in for the go-ahead touchdown.

Hayes was basically upbeat and enthusiastic in addressing newsmen following the game, reserving special praise for this effort by Logan. Hayes was outspokenly empowering in his other comments, too.

Rather than dwell on the pattern of second half troubles or disturbing lapses in the kicking and defensive areas, Hayes preferred to look at the fact that his team was improving, and that they had won a tough road game. "I'm so sick and tired of negative thinkers," was the Hayes reply to questions concerning the OSU inability to deliver a knockout blow. "...I put myself in the positive category," concentrating on what went right, regardless of the numerous backfield injuries, the Coach insisted.

Woody claimed, "Anyone who will tear down sports will tear down America," and he wanted solely upbeat press releases concerning his team. Ara Parseghian agreed, theorizing, "Athletics... may very well be the last bastion of discipline left in the United States;" this was a belief he inherited from his former coach, Hayes.

This positive thinking spiel seemed a successful effort on the part of Hayes to re-gather momentum in what many regarded as a disappointing season. The team was in a position where nothing could be held in check for Michigan, as was usually the case. If maximum use of all strategical, tactical, and emotional weapons was not utilized immediately, the end-of-the-year matchup would prove somewhat meaningless, at least in terms of Rose Bowl and national title implications.

Even Hayes confirmed that yes, the proverbial OSU backs were against the wall, and the team could afford no further lapses. He honestly had thought his troops would be undefeated at this point in the year. The glitches on the schedule were mostly due to a pronounced lack of late-game productivity, on both sides of the ball, for OSU had most uncharacteristically been outscored 56-19 in all fourth quarters (combined) in '76.

Good fortune appeared to be arriving as a date with Purdue loomed large. Johnson had basically been physically unable to practice for almost a month; this week he finally bounced back enough to participate during the week.

Head trainer Hill was largely responsible for the rehabilitation of the injury-plagued Pete, actually driving the student from his apartment to the training facilities and back virtually every day. On one occasion, Pete, who loved to linger in the whirlpool and training area prior to practice, procrastinated so long that he missed the team bus which transported players to and from the practice field. Predictably, Hayes was incensed, though not necessarily at Johnson.

From that instance forward, Woody held Hill personally liable for the timely appearances of Johnson, and the matter became a running joke, though not always a laughing matter, between the player and the trainer. If Pete was tardy, Hill's job was in jeopardy, a fact which Johnson never failed to kiddingly hold over his healer's head. Despite the pain and loss of mobility in both his ankles, it is a testament to the OSU training staff and Pete's competitiveness that come Saturday, Johnson always suited up.

Roche, Logan, and Paul Ross were also nursing injuries, and they too would be able to go on gameday. Ailing linemen Buonamici and Beamon were inching back to full strength with every passing day as well. Amazingly, Johnson, Beamon, and Buonamici scarcely suffered a drop-off in game performance despite their disabilities, although each was logically a better player when healthy.

Following his cheerful mood at the conclusion of the Wisconsin game, Hayes quickly turned irascible and short-tempered. That very night, Hayes engaged in a bitter series of exchanges with the co-host of his locally produced television program, "The Woody Hayes Show," televised on Columbus station WBNS.

In front of a live studio audience and with the cameras rolling, Hayes grew increasingly aggravated with the comments of Lee Vlisides. Vlisides, a large, burly sort who briefly played in the CFL, began this particular show by questioning the veracity and efficiency of the Buckeye defense alignment, especially the so-called "prevent" formation frequently used in the latter stages of a game.

Hayes instantly became bitingly sarcastic and almost overwhelmingly patronizing as he started questioning Vlisides. Hayes grilled Lee endlessly about the latter's knowledge regarding football principles. After this extended, charged exchange, Vlisides slightly shifted gears. Lee questioned the validity in allowing Gerald to predominately attempt long, slow-developing bombs with low chances for completion. Hayes again bore down hard on the chastened commentator, who now appeared to regret the inadvertently untoward sting of his questions which prompted the calculated, downgrading responses.

Neither Hayes nor Vlisides really came off as boors in the heated discussion, while the defensive stance of the Coach regarding said topics did lend more credence to the queries of Vlisides. Evidently these types of questions fell into the realm of negative influences Hayes wished to avoid, hence the anger.

Another subject of interest at this time was the mandatory retirement policy maintained by the state of Ohio. Any employee of the state was forced to retire upon reaching the age of 70, and Hayes of course was employed by a state-run university. Speculation began to arise during this time that Hayes, who would not turn 70 until '83, was in the process of grooming his successor from the ranks of his assistants. As Woody said, "The first thing I was interested in was the man's character," so each assistant was the kind of man Hayes felt capable of entrusting the Buckeyes to, at least on a moral level.

Each assistant possessed an interesting playing and coaching background, and a rundown of their own collegiate experiences proves enlightening. The elder statesman of the Big 10 in terms of experience, Esko Sarkinnen was an All-American end on the '39 OSU national championship team. George Hill lettered at both tackle and fullback in his days as a Denison undergrad. Dick Walker was a '58 graduate of John Carrol. Ralph Staub was a standout end on the strong Cincinnati teams of '49-'51. George Chaump played center and guard at tiny Bloomsburg State. Alex Gibbs was a '63 graduate of Davidson and had an MA from North Carolina. Mickey Jackson was a track and football star at Marshall, finishing fourth in the nation in (football) scoring in '65, and was one of the finest players in the history of the distinguished Thundering Herd. John Mummey played both quarterback and fullback at OSU from '60-'62, demonstrating incredible rushing talents.

It should be emphasized that neither Hayes nor any assistant put much stock in this mandatory retirement rule being invoked for Woody. Though some people assumed Woody would voluntarily step down upon reaching age 70, most knew otherwise; for Hayes forever insisted that he would be the sole judge of when he should step down.

Of course, Hayes did wish to go out on top, so if a national championship opportunity existed, his leaving was expected. Still, Hayes resented any such public speculation, wishing to choose the time and place of his retirement. Sadly, this choice effectively eluded his grasp.

For this week at least, any such retirement talk was scuttled in favor of preparing for the Purdue contest. Boilermaker head coach Alex Agase had been an All-American guard at both Illinois and Purdue, and was renowned for his rugged intensity. He had interrupted his three seasons of national honors at these universities, to capture a Bronze Star and a Purple Heart on Okinawa during World War Two. After pacing the Illini to a Rose Bowl rout in his final collegiate game upon getting out of the service, Agase became a well-respected, hard-nosed lineman for the Browns and Baltimore Colts.

His current Boilermaker team was a typically well balanced one on offense, effectively blending the pass and run. Reflecting the lineage of Agase, the offensive line showed great technique amidst awesome size. With the defense returning ten of 11 starters from '75, that unit exhibited experience and skill in copious quantities. The sole weakness appeared to be the secondary, which was playing most porously.

Boilermaker quarterback Mark Vitali demonstrated a vastly improved ability to run, and in the tradition of great Purdue quarterbacks, could also throw a little. Although Cecil Isbell starred from '32-'35, going on to great success with the Green Bay Packers, the magnificent line of Purdue arms began in earnest in '45. Freshman Bob DeMoss, in just his fifth game, engineered a stunning 35-13 Boilermaker victory over top-ranked OSU.

The long line of phenomenal passers went on to include Dale Samuels, Len Dawson, Bob Griese, Mike Phipps, and Gary Danielson. A tall, '76 high school senior named Mark Herrmann waited for his chance to join that distinguished list.

Scott Dierking, a bruising, slashing tailback, was the Riveters top rusher with 634 yards, despite missing the upset loss to Illinois with an aggravating ankle sprain. Dierking had wedged his way behind the fabulous Otis Armstrong as the number two all-time rusher at Purdue. Dierking grew up idolizing Kent, Ohio, native and Northwestern record-setting tailback Mike Adamle, though Dierking now displayed much more power than the diminutive Adamle.

Agase had Mike Northington tabbed to fill in at the tailback slot should Dierking go out again. In position changes which paralleled those of Ray Griffin, Northington began his Purdue career as a tailback, moved to defensive back when Dierking emerged as a star, and was now called upon to perform yeoman work with the pigskin. Northington had shocked the league with a five touchdown game against Iowa as a frosh, so he was no slouch in the backfield.

Rough and tumble fullback John Skibinski, 6'2" and 222 pounds, paved the way for the other backs with jarring blocks. Skibinski was a fine runner, and his father Joe had played for the Browns and Packers, so the Skibinski heritage was proven.

Also proven was the all-around play of former Niles McKinley (Ohio) standout Bob Mannella, the linebacker extraordinaire and psyching expert. The Mannella desire to beat his home state school proved nearly maniacal.

Just as desperate in his quest to improve was Mr. Olympia-like specimen Tom Cousineau. As Tom believed, "A winner strives constantly to reach higher ground." The youngster arrived at OSU with a career plan of becoming a dentist - his high level of play and physical attributes virtually guaranteed any such medical hopes would be preceded with a stop at the pro football level.

Among the many great athletes at Ohio State, Tom's combination of good looks, a flair for the dramatic, and a fine public presence propelled him into the national spotlight. The Buckeye defense was designed to funnel the ballcarrier toward Tom, and the grinning gridiron wildman enthusiastically complied. The intense, excitable sophomore's father, Tom Sr., was a former Indiana guard who briefly played for the Oakland Raiders of the AFL. Tom Sr. later went on to great renown as the player/coach of the Indianapolis entry in the old Continental Football League.

Jeff Logan also grew up hoping to follow in the footsteps of his father, former Buckeye Dick Logan. Dick coached Jeff in midget ball for four fruitful years, instilling in Jeff many of those qualities which prompted Hayes to offer the youngster, whom he had known since infancy, a scholarship out of high school.

As Tim Burke recalls, most of the OSU players in those days possessed at least a modicum of Buckeye pride upon their arrival in Columbus: The realization that as a wearer of the scarlet and gray, one represented not only an intangible quality such as school spirit, but, more importantly, each individual reflected upon all those similarly-believing players who preceded and all those such-minded players who would follow in the program.

This seed of Buckeye pride was then further cultivated and nurtured by Hayes, who acted as the fertilizer in the growth of this evolving, expanding tradition. As a result, the whole of the Buckeye experience was of necessity greater than any single sum of its parts. Logan personified this tradition.

A shoulder separation slowed down Jeff's progress in his frosh season, and as a sophomore he carried only 23 times, for an eye-popping 7.3 yard average in a backup role to Archie. Logan respected Archie, "...more than anyone," and reminded many observers of the multiple Heisman winner with his quickness, balance, drive, and overriding belief in the Lord as a focal part in any success (Logan was the modest president of the OSU Fellowship of Christian Athletes, which included many fellow footballers). The phenomenal success of Jeff in this '76 season was the culmination of a life-long dream for the entire Logan family.

The long history of the OSU-Purdue encounters included the controversial '40 game. The Buckeyes won on a last second field goal, repelling a Purdue comeback from a two touchdown deficit. Charlie Maag, a tackle for OSU, entered the last minute of the game illegally (substitution rules then in effect prohibited his return following an earlier exit) and kicked the winning field goal. Purdue noticed the violation and protested violently, yet the winning points remained on the board and the victory was allowed to stand. Interestingly, Maag kicked just one more field goal that year, providing the only points in a 6-3 loss to Northwestern.

After that contest, the potential All-American lineman was curiously benched by coach Francis Schmidt. This seemingly inexplicable move, among many others, precipitated the dissension and internal bickering which eventually contributed to the dismissal of Schmidt. A 40-0 pasting at the hands of Michigan was not beneficial to job security, either. Maag transferred to Bowling Green, where he resumed his stellar play.

In '69, Woody's self-proclaimed "Best defensive team ever," manhandled a fine Purdue team 42-14. This OSU team featured Jack Tatum and Jim Stillwagon on defense, among a unit of standouts. Perhaps the most notable occurrence in this OSU blowout was the attire of Woody.

On this wintry, wind-swept, snowy day, Hayes went contrary to form and donned a scarlet warm-up jacket. This marked the first time in roughly 15 years that anyone could recall Hayes wearing anything on the sideline other than his traditional white short-sleeved shirt.

The next year, '70, the Bucks edged Purdue 10-7 behind a late Fred Schram field goal kicked into the teeth of a very stiff wind. Schram was from Massillon, Ohio, and was participating in just his second year of football. After this stirring win, President Nixon telephoned the OSU locker room to pass his heart-felt congratulations on to Hayes and Schram. Ever the politician, just a few minutes later, Nixon placed a sympathy call to Purdue coach Bob DeMoss.

Agase hoped to repeat his past successes against OSU. In '71, the Agase-led Northwestern team became the last conference squad to win in Ohio Stadium. For the '76 game, defensive end Blaine Smith was certainly in an upset mood, sporting a freshly shaven dome a la' popular television fixture Telly Savalas, and an equally intimidating manner.

On the OSU side, Johnson soaked his sore ankles; Skladany entertained the Quarterback Club with an impromptu Hayes-ordered display of his accordion skills; while Tim Vogler broke his thumb practicing at tight end and was moved to guard, awash in praise from the coaching staff for his aggressive style. The Buckeyes approached Saturday in anticipation of a huge, supportive homecoming crowd.

CHAPTER EIGHT: PURDUE

Saturday dawned very gusty, and the heavens poured forth cold rain all afternoon. Many of the 87,890 fans present who initially braved the elements exited extremely early, just after halftime Also on this day, Pitt star Dorsett eclipsed the Griffin standard of 5177 rushing yards on his final carry of the Panther game versus Navy.

Even more depressingly, Gerald suffered a hairline fracture of his lumbar (back) vertebra on a first quarter carry, and was expected to be out of commission at least five weeks. The departure of Gerald forced little-used senior Pacenta to enter. Jim struggled early, improved throughout, and actually looked very good late in the contest. As the fortunes of the new quarterback rose, so did the overall Buckeye performance.

Purdue lost their tailback Northington to a shoulder separation on only his second carry of the game. His fill-in, since Dierking was unable to go, was third stringer Rickey Smith. Smith hurt his shoulder, yet had to continue despite the pain.

The play of the first quarter was overshadowed by the exit of Gerald, who left the hushed stadium on a golf cart, surrounded by Dr. Murphy and a host of other physicians. Ohio State could move the ball only inconsistently, and amidst atrocious kicking conditions Skladany was errant on field goal attempts from 38 and 55 yards.

On the second play of the second quarter, Skladany found the range on a 27 yarder, staking OSU to a tenuous 3-0 lead. On their ensuing possession, Purdue achieved their farthest penetration of the half, to the OSU 23. Kicker Rock Supan was wide left on a field goal effort, preserving the three point margin. The half ended as Skladany missed a 50 yarder after nine hurried Buckeye plays.

The second half began miserably for OSU, prompting the mass exodus of bone-chilled partisans. Springs bobbled and then fumbled the opening kickoff. Purdue recovered, the Bucks resolutely held, and Supan connected on a short field goal just two minutes into the half. Undaunted, OSU came right back with a good drive, ending in disappointment as Skladany was errant on a 37 yarder. The abysmal weather conditions really wreaked havoc with both kickers on this day, proving too miserable to overcome.

Ohio State continued the offensive tailspin, botching a pitch on the next possession. Cleveland Crosby grabbed the loose ball on the home 11, yet Supan missed a 27 yarder after the Bucks again denied the touchdown. Logan almost singlehandedly carried OSU to their initial touchdown on the ensuing drive. He toted the ball seven times in the trek, on the last carry propelling into the end zone from 13 yards out. This dominating drive also featured a well-executed third down pass of 13 yards to Harrell, yielding a first down.

Once more, following the kickoff, the Buckeye defense stopped Purdue in their tracks, and Griffin nearly busted loose with a thrilling 20 yard return on the resulting punt. Starting at the Boilermaker 45, OSU powered into the end zone again, with Johnson careening the final yard.

Upon next receiving the ball, courtesy of a Brudzinski interception, OSU began their final touchdown drive beginning at the Riveter 31. Logan took a sweep play way outside, outran the pursuit, and scored from 29 yards out to make the final score 24-3. Logan ended with a whopping 175 yards on 28 carries, providing the bulk of the Ohio State offense.

Purdue responded to this score with a marathon drive, pushing all the way to the OSU nine. The wet and weary Buckeyes accepted the challenge and kept the visitor's from putting six points on the board. On fourth down, newly-inserted Boilermaker back Keena Turner could not find the handle on a pitch play, and OSU took over on downs.

The Buckeye offense was unable to run out the last few minutes of the contest, and Purdue received one last chance to find the end zone. Roche denied the touchdown, squelching the last Riveter rally with a timely interception.

Hayes emerged from this contest in fine spirits, despite the severe injury to Gerald. The Bucks had played their finest second half of the season, reversing at long last the trend of poor finishes. Pacenta garnered glowing praise, particularly for his somewhat surprising success in the passing department. His performance in this game exceeded his usual performance in practice sessions. Pacenta connected on five of nine attempts for 65 yards, including two pivotal third down conversions on two respective touchdown drives. Storer made an early, triumphant return to tight end, snaring three balls for 37 yards, each reception occurring at a critical juncture.

Defensively, OSU held the thin Purdue running game to a mere 114 yards, with Skibinski ramming his way to 97 of those, on 20 bullish carries. The defensive heroes were the usual: Cousineau, Dansler, Brown, Brudzinski; and the unusual: Duncan Griffin made a big stick and recovered a fumble in a rare flurry of playing time.

Sunday and Monday brought further details of the Gerald injury. The official diagnosis was three fractures of the top transverse processes in the lumbar vertebra, or in layman's terms, three breaks in the small bones located in the lower back at about belt level. Rod was resting comfortably in Columbus Riverside Hospital, and was expecting to be released by the end of the week. At the time of release he was to be fitted with a brace and would be able to resume classes. The outlook was a full recovery by approximately the time OSU would perhaps participate in a bowl game.

The new offensive leader, Pacenta, played just 17 minutes in '75, and had only 19 minutes in '76 prior to the back break. Pacenta came out of Akron (Ohio)-St.Vincent as an All-Ohio selection at quarterback, only to virtually disappear behind a very talented and deep OSU corps at that spot.

As a frosh, Pacenta competed with Greg Hare, Dave Purdy, Steve Morrison, and Corny Greene - each extremely talented and most likely better natural athletes than Pacenta. A separated right (throwing) shoulder put the youngster even further behind. His sophomore season was spent behind Greene, Purdy, and Morrison, and again Jim separated the same shoulder. In '75 Pacenta was given more practice time, though he was still listed behind Greene and the dazzling newcomer Gerald. His '76 confidence increased markedly with a bit more playing time and a subsequent improvement in performance.

Pacenta credited Hayes with persuading him to aim for entrance to medical school. With a 3.71 grade point average in pre-med, the senior's chances for acceptance, buoyed by the backing of Woody, seemed extremely solid. Jim's older sister had already graduated from the OSU College of Medicine, so the Hippocratic oath was no stranger to this starting quarterback.

The sudden ascendance of Pacenta presented upcoming opponent Indiana with some complications. Head coach Lee Corso lamented the fact there was so little film to view of Pacenta, since his game action was so sparse. Corso had what he considered his finest Hoosier team in his four year reign, despite a 3-4 record. In spite of having a very low-scoring offense, Corso thought that if the Hoosiers played above their heads and OSU beneath expectations, IU would win.

Indiana quarterback Scott Arnett hailed from Columbus Walnut Ridge, and behind him was the talented backfield duo of Ric Enis and the speedy frosh sensation Mike Harkrader. Harkrader replaced the injured Courtney Snyder, who was gone for the year.

Corso had recently implemented the insertion of an innovative, so-called "elephant" backfield in most short-yardage and goal-line situations. Corso brought in tackles Bill Jones, a 6'2", 270 pound specimen, and Jeff Phipps, 6'2", 240 pounds, either singly or in tandem, at fullback to provide extra line thrust. The formation was all the rage, with scores of imitators popping up in high schools and colleges across the land.

Ohio State freshmen Greg Castignola and Mike Strahine saw plenty of practice time this week in the battle for playing time behind Pacenta. Castignola in particular caught the eye of Woody with his quick grasp of the offense. Greg was coached at his Trenton, Michigan, high school by his father, Jack Castignola, who played for Woody at New Philadelphia (Ohio) high school. Fellow Buckeye Joe Dixon was also a prep teammate of Greg's.

It was confirmed in mid-week that almost 13,000 OSU supporters would make the short journey to Bloomington to cheer on the Bucks. Ruhl was back at full go, while Johnson and guard Ron Ayers caught a light touch of the flu, somewhat weakening them.

Spirits were lifted on a surprise motivational visit to practice, by the legendary Jim Parker. Parker made his first return to his alma mater since graduation in '56, and left after promising to return more often. Recently named a starter on the prestigious "First 100 Years of College Football" All-Star squad, Parker was equally respected for his exploits as a member of the Baltimore Colts.

In response to the allegations that Hayes cheated during recruiting, the genial giant emphatically denied any such possibility. Parker knew that unlike many other schools, Woody offered no inducements to attend OSU; nothing, that is, except the privilege of attaining an education and playing in an outstanding program. Parker told Chris Ward, among others, about Woody: "The greatest thing that ever happened to me was meeting this man."

Despite his prolonged absence from campus, Parker still supported his old Coach in any way possible. His latest discovery was the frosh Ricardo Volley, whom Parker discovered in Virginia and convincingly sold Ric on the merits of Hayes and OSU.

CHAPTER NINE: INDIANA

The Bucks encountered another chilly, wind-swept, rainy day on Saturday, which limited the game crowd to a disappointing 39,663. In a virtual repeat of the Purdue clash, OSU endured a trying first 30 minutes.

Ohio State was never able to get fully untracked in the first half, uncharacteristically losing two fumbles; fumbled a punt through their end zone for a touchback; drew two costly clipping penalties; and fumbled a snap on an extra point attempt. Ward badly sprained his ankle, and was forced to hobble out of the contest to be outfitted with crutches. The visitors accumulated the paltry sum of 84 yards total offense in the first half, yet somehow still led 12-7.

Indiana started the ballgame most impressively, driving down to the OSU five in 14 plays prior to being halted shy of the goal line. Arnett hit Mark Fishel on an 18 yard pass in the drive, as the Hoosiers seemed to slightly confuse the Bucks with their diverse playcalling. Arnett looked for Fischell again from the five, and a jumping Buonamici tipped the ball and came down with it in the clear.

As the big lineman lumbered toward the nearest 30, he grew weary, and began looking for someone, anyone, to pass the ball to. At first Brudzinski looked to be the recipient of a handoff, when Ray Griffin ran over and took the ball from a grateful Nick. Griffin darted the final 65 yards with little pursuit, charging into the end zone untouched.

The 95 yard combined run was protested by IU, who contended the exchange of the ball was facilitated by an illegal forward lateral. The protest did not hold up. On the point after, Skladany nabbed the errant snap and was rudely slammed to the turf shy of the goal.

Logan fumbled on the next OSU possession, with IU recovering, though the peaking defense again held the Hoosiers out of the end zone. On the resulting Buckeye possession, Pacenta fumbled, with IU again gaining control. This time, the home team was able to capitalize. On the first play of the second quarter, Arnett found George Edgar alone in the end zone for the score, putting IU ahead 7-6.

The next time IU had the ball, Cousineau fell on a loose ball at the Indiana 42. Ohio State put their only sustained drive of the half together, with Johnson rumbling in for the second Buckeye touchdown of the day. A try for two was halted by an anticipatory Hoosier defense. Taking into account all their blunders, poor execution, and missing-in-action-offense, OSU was happy to take the five point lead in at halftime.

In the closing half, the rain finally slacked off somewhat. Dryer hands and far superior reserves finally wore down the Hoosiers, as OSU eventually gained a 390-155 edge in total offense.

On the initial IU possession of the closing half, Brudzinski burst in to force a bad handoff exchange. Mike Guess pounced on the bouncing ball, giving the Bucks excellent field position at the IU 24. Johnson obliged the defensive favor by ramming the ball in from the two, providing every bit of offense on this short drive. The next chance OSU had with the pigskin, Pacenta connected with the big-play receiver Harrell on a stirring 59 yard touchdown bomb.

Stopping the Hoosiers cold after the kickoff, OSU embarked on an 11 play, 60 yard drive culminating in a ten yard Logan scoring dash. With the IU offense moving absolutely nowhere, Hayes inserted Castignola into the fray, to provide the youngster with some much-needed game experience.

Also inserted for some unaccustomed extended action were Springs, Campbell, and Matt Jackson. Springs in particular looked extremely impressive, proving impossible to contain. He did stop himself on one occasion, turning the ball over via a fumble as he was on the precipice of the goal line.

The Hoosiers assumed control on their two, yet the turnover was negated as Duncan Griffin came up with possession of a Harkrader fumble a few plays later on the IU 19. Springs vaulted 13 yards to paydirt, then with 1:09 left topped his outstanding afternoon with a brilliant 62 yard touchdown run. The run was replete with the cutbacks, breakaway speed, and elusiveness OSU fans soon grew so accustomed to seeing. Springs ended with an amazing 107 yards on only six carries. Logan was held to 57 yards on 14 rushes, while Harrell hauled in three balls for 78 yards.

The supreme defensive effort was championed by Beamon, with Buonamici, Cousineau, and Brown providing solid support.

Due to the mishap to Ward, the aggressive, speedy frosh Doug Mackie moved into the starting lineup. Lou Pietrini, in the midst of a shockingly fine season, was shifted from right to left tackle, to lend that all-important protector of the quarterbacks blind side a bit more experience. Hayes counted heavily on Joe Robinson to provide solid backup, with Washington Courthouse, Ohio, native Garth Cox filling in at both tackles. As the week progressed, the reports for the recovery of Ward were increasingly optimistic.

Cox was bouncing back nicely from a sophomore year, '75, in which he was injured and sat out practically the entire season. During his period of inactivity, Cox realized his best chance to remain at least on second-string status lay in accentuating his versatility. Thereafter, Cox played up and down the offensive line, even centering on placements occasionally.

As a high school senior, the highly-coveted prep star from the small southern Ohio farming town actually signed a letter of intent to attend Notre Dame, yet never mailed in the agreement. Cox grew up with visions of being a Buckeye, though it was not until Hayes personally visited his school that the dreams of Garth were realized. Woody met the large lineman in the middle of a school day, completely taking the youth by surprise. The first statement out of Woody's mouth was a challenge: "I understand you want to be a lawyer. You can't study to be a lawyer and play football at Ohio State." Garth stood his ground, retorting that if this was the case, then he did not wish to attend such a university.

This was exactly the fortitude the Coach wanted to see, and for the next two hours, Hayes and the now-sealed recruit spoke of everything but football. Of course, during that two hour time, during breaks between classes, the salesman facet of Hayes took Garth into the hall and walked the building, engendering all kinds of commotion in the tiny facility.

The addition of muscular bodyweight in the off-season pushed Tom Roche into the special category in '76. Fifteen extra pounds of bulk on his heretofore skinny frame enabled Roche to succeed all expectations. His slight frame had previously limited him to substitute roles behind the likes of future NFL hitting virtuosos Steve Luke and Doug Plank.

Roche stepped into the starting lineup after the opening game in '76, when Mills developed extremely painful tendinitis in his knees and was unable to play to his previously high levels. Roche was playing at a select level; his performance against IU graded out to a most remarkable 90%, which Dick Walker insisted was the highest grade he'd ever seen for a defensive back. For his splendid effort, Roche was awarded nine Buckeye leaves, which tied the record set only the week before by Beamon.

Interestingly, the now-sturdy 6'2", 195 pound Roche grew up in Staten Island dreaming of playing for the Fighting Irish of Notre Dame. His father, a leading New York City administrator, and mother both fell in love with Hayes as the Coach came calling on a recruiting visit. A decision was immediately made for Tom to attend OSU, based on the charm and integrity of Woody. The astounding play of Roche was even more remarkable, given that he missed all of '75 due to a severely sprained ankle.

Cousineau was really hitting his stride too. Not only was he a participant in 15 stops against IU, he recovered a fumble, broke up two passes, and pressured Arnett into two more incompletions. Despite being desperately affected by their ankle hurts, Ward and Johnson each received six Buckeye leaves for their IU efforts. Springs carried off "Back of the Week" honors.

In contrast to these accolades, the Buckeyes underwent an unusually rigorous Wednesday practice in preparation for the Fighting Illini, coached by Bob Blackmon. Illinois was an unpredictable 4-4 on the season, and OSU hoped to maintain the fever pitch which the defense was now performing at. That sizzling unit now led the conference in virtually every statistical category, and was playing near the peak of expectations.

This statistical domination came with a price, however. Coordinator George Hill often, perhaps unwittingly, became so consumed with preserving the impressive statistical record, that he left his starters and top reserves in the game for the duration of a not-in-doubt contest. Many of the reserves who sweated and toiled throughout the week remained sidelined on Saturday, as Hill sought to keep the high national ranking of his fine unit.

Contrast this with the offense, which Woody was essentially in charge of: Once the outcome seemed assured, the bench was essentially cleared, as the subs received a reward for their normal obscurity. Of course, exceptions to each units' substitution patterns did occasionally occur; generally, though, the underlings on offense were given playing time while the defensive backups were usually not.

The night of this rough Wednesday workout, Hayes was in an unusually verbose mood. He spoke at length on several widely disparate topics, ranging from the disappointing dearth of quality movies available for his team to view on Friday nights before the game, to the interesting, innovative training methods of long distance runners.

First off, since Hayes refused to let his team watch any movie which could even remotely be judged racy, controversial, excessively violent, or immoral, the pickings were rather thin indeed. The players sometimes snookered Mickey Jackson, who was in charge of selecting the film, however.

Jackson essentially had no idea, because of his packed coaching schedule, what a new release entailed and contained. Some mischevious players would delude him as to the merits and contents of a film, and Hayes would agree to the selection, since Jackson supposedly insured the quality of the film. Then, safely in the theater, the players derived much good-humored mirth at the expense of Jackson and Hayes, who quickly realized said movie was not as they thought. Hayes would only take so much, cursing all the while, before he physically left the room. As the grumbling of Woody increased, the chagrined Jackson would sink lower and lower into his seat.

One such example was on the eve of the '76 Penn State clash, as OSU viewed "The Longest Yard." Woody became extremely incensed as he realized that a band of convicts, led on screen by (real-life) former Florida State football participant Burt Reynolds, were the heroes in this film concerning penitentiary gridiron shenanigans. The players howled at the ribald humor of the movie, as Woody seethed.

On another memorable occasion, the selected film was the foul-mouthed takeoff on minor league hockey, "Slap Shot," starring Paul Newman. Woody was aghast at the excessive profanity in this movie, and afterwards, threatened to personally apologize to each player's parents for subjecting their son to such blue humor.

Meanwhile, as Hayes worked himself into a frenzy concerning the extravagant amount of four-letter words in the cinematic farce, he himself used language far worse than that used on screen. This irony was not lost on the players, who of course enjoyed such despised movies far more than the usual fare of cheesy black-and-white newsreel documentaries they were forced to endure.

Due to this limited selection of what he considered quality programming, Woody related that the night before the IU clash he administered a quiz to his team, in lieu of a film. The twenty question educational quiz was administered to players and assistant coaches alike, with on-the-spot grading and performance review performed by Hayes.

Secondly, Hayes went on to speak, on Wednesday, of the hidden powers of the human spirit, and the limitless achievements possible to great, daring men. Hayes related how Roger Bannister and John Landy, the first men to crack the four minute barrier in the mile run, were shining examples of mankind's capacity to perform the seemingly impossible. According to these men, overtraining was a myth and the human body could be trained to endure much more than previously thought.

On the lighter side, this night marked the debut of the 30 member OSU all-female brass band, under the astute direction of marching band director Paul Droste. Hayes attended the debut gig, and as was his custom at all university functions, led the crowd in a rousing ovation.

Hayes had more reason to applaud as the week concluded. Ward was recuperating so rapidly, it was virtually assured that he would start against the Illini. Johnson struggled through his first complete week of practices since his ankles began bothering him, too.

Hayes also admired the courageous effort of co-captain Lukens, whose horribly painful shoulder prevented any contact during the week, except for one brief day. On each and every Saturday, Lukens persevered through the battle, and his blocking consistently graded out near the top of all linemen.

The Fighting Illini arrived at Ohio Stadium boasting an explosive offense, capable of voluminous outbursts of yards and points. The Illini averaged 22.6 points a game, largely due to the number four all-time passer in school history, Kurt Steger. The 6'3", 220 pound flinger enjoyed fine success throwing the ball to 9.8 (100 yard) sprinter Eric Rouse, and the more possession-type receiver, Frank Johnson. The running game was solid if not spectacular, based on the efforts of Jim Coleman, and the inappropriately-named scatback Chubby Phillips.

The defense funnelled plays towards their fine middle linebacker Scott Studwell. This appropriately monikered 6'3", 235 pound ox was on pace to exceed the school tackling records established by Dick Butkus. Studwell demonstrated great range, a tremendous nose for the ball, and a rabid Mike Curtis-like propensity for roughhousing and very hard hitting. His play was all the more remarkable, since fellow linebacker standout John Sullivan was injured and gone for the year.

Potentially strong pro prospects, end Dean March and end John DeFeliciantonio, cleared the way for the sinus clearing blasts of Studwell. Another outstanding kick specialist in a conference loaded with them, kicker

Dan Beaver was poised to surpass Red Grange as the all-time leading Illini scorer.

CHAPTER TEN: ILLINOIS

Come Saturday, the Illinois team failed to live up to the expectations of their coach. Blackmon honestly thought Illinois was set to upset Ohio State. Instead, OSU steamrolled to a 42-10 victory, behind the four touchdowns scored by Johnson. In front of 87,654 screaming horseshoe occupants, OSU held the visitors to a solitary field goal , until the last three seconds.

On a day on which Purdue stunned top-ranked Michigan 16-14, the Buckeye win was magnified in importance. Just as anticipated, the annual matchup with the Wolverines loomed larger and increasingly more significant.

Incidentally, the winning points for Purdue were scored via the foot of premier sophomore safety/placekicker Rock Supan. Supan suffered through a miserable kicking day against OSU, although he contributed 16 tackles in that disappointing loss. Against Michigan, the versatile youngster enjoyed fine kicking and tackling days, greatly contributing to the huge Boilermaker upset.

Johnson carried the Bucks on his prodigious back this day, providing more short-range offense than the Illini could handle. The OSU pass defense continued their recent mastery with five interceptions, three of which either set up or resulted in touchdowns. Logan ended the contest just ten yards shy of the magical 1,000 yard standard, ending the day with 94 yards on 16 carries.

The Bucks eased into their scoring fest, with Ed Thompson finally breaking the scoreless ice late in the first quarter with a spectacular 81 yard interception return for a touchdown. After holding Illinois motionless, OSU regained possession, with Johnson capping a 12 play, 41 yard thrust by blasting in over right tackle.

Ohio State increased the lead on their next chance, with a nice sustained drive of 70 yards featuring a well-conceived 16 yard pass to Jones. Johnson again plunged over the goal line, this time from one yard out.

Illinois finally got on the board on their ensuing possession. On the first play of the drive, Steger hit streaking tight end John Peach for a slam-bang 44 yard pickup. The Buckeyes resolutely kept the visitors out of the end zone, and Beaver kicked a short field goal to cut the lead to 21-3 at the half.

The rousing halftime show featured a raucous tribute to the disparate figures of Vic Janowicz and trumpeter extraordinaire Maynard Ferguson, to the wild cheers of the crowd.

Any momentum set in motion by the late, first-half Illini score was reversed at the start of the second half. The staunch OSU defense forced a punt from deep in Illinois territory, and the offense took over in great field position at midfield. The resulting 50 yard march ended with a very familiar Johnson touchdown, on this occasion from four yards away.

The next Illinois possession was thwarted by a Bruce Ruhl interception. Ruhl had recovered from his earlier knee injury, and was pressed into duty when Roche went down with a strained leg muscle and was unable to dress. Ruhl performed admirably.

Following this intercept, Pacenta found Storer open for an 18 yard pickup, Springs darted for 11, and Johnson powered in for his fourth score of the day. Later in the third, the Illini defense finally lived up to their hype, stopping the OSU power T offensive set short of the goal on four downs, giving Illinois possession at their one foot line.

Shortly after this heroic goal line stand, the procession of backup quarterback insertions by both teams began. Mike McCray took over for the Illini, while both Strahine and Castignola saw extended action for Ohio State.

In the final quarter, Illinois again turned away the home team deep inside scoring territory. A fourth down pass by Castignola was broken up, and Illinois promptly embarked on a long drive to the OSU 19. Allegro ended this threat prematurely, recovering an Illinois fumble at that spot, yet the sub-studded offense could not penetrate the rejuvenated Illinois defense.

McCray once again led the Illini deep into the OSU side of the field, though no points resulted. Finally, after a series of defensive stands and exchanged punts, David Adkins picked off an errant McCray pass and zoomed into the end zone from 19 yards away, exhibiting his fine promise in a rare piece of extended playing time

The Illini quarterback struck back, undeterred, eventually hitting Marty Friel with a touchdown toss with just a few ticks left on the clock.

The vastly-improved OSU defense yielded just 81 yards on the ground this day, and despite being pierced for 246 passing yards, limited the two Illini quarterbacks to only 12 completions in 33 attempts, with those five crucial thefts. Hayes always figured an interception cost the offending team 40 yards each occurrence, so he was not overly concerned with the amount of yardage the visitors otherwise compiled. Much of this Illini yardage was gained late, after the contest was decided, and much of it came on virtually-desperate second and third down heaves.

Offensively, the Bucks generated 271 yards rushing, while Pacenta struck on seven of ten passes for 101 yards. Despite the seeming dominance on this day, Hayes vowed his improving team would not take upcoming opponent Minnesota lightly, going so far as to again paraphrase the laments of Napoleon on overconfidence, after the crushing defeat of his army at Moscow. "From the sublime to the ridiculous is but a step...," and OSU had no intention of stepping down.

Hayes spoke of his happiness over the success of Pacenta, while Blackmon graciously acknowledged that "[Pacenta is] a guy who could've had a great career at other places." Pacenta did take a helmet under the chin in the early going, opening a wound which required seven stitches. Despite the loss of blood, his performance did not suffer.

With no serious new injuries to report from the Illinois tiff, trainer Hill pronounced the team in fine physical shape for this last part of the season. Hill could not recall a year when the Bucks approached the final two games with such a lack of injuries.

One such healthy body was Ward, who despite zero practice time in the week leading up to the Illini scrape, played up to his usual excellent standards, grading out to a fine 86%. Hayes sarcastically joked that the performance of Ward, sans practice, "...showed the benefits of coaching."

Johnson received rave notices this week, not only for his propensity to put points on the board, but for his soft hands and the ability to catch the (rare) pass thrown his way. With two receptions against Illinois, Johnson had now caught each of the six passes lofted his direction in his senior year.

On Monday, Hayes entertained the usual press crowd, not with discussions of football; instead, he selected various passages from the Emerson writing *Essays on Compensation*, to share with the journalists. The passages included: "...I hate to be defended in a newspaper. As long as all that is said, is said against me, I feel a certain assurance of success." Apparently, Hayes often felt assured of success, for media sentiment was often against him. Most times, Hayes reveled in this criticism; after all, the winner laughs last.

Following that lesson on Ralph Waldo, Hayes continued his fine literary bent, touching extensively on several Henry David Thoreau writings, including this passage from *Walden*: "I learned this, at least, by my experience; that if one advances confidently in the direction of his dreams and endeavors to live... he will meet with success unexpected...." Hayes expected success, though his career achievements definitely surpassed his own youthful anticipations.

Practice that afternoon presented a fair replica of the expected Minnesota weather conditions - wet, rainy, and very slippery on the icy astroturf. Bad weather conditions were exactly what was needed on this practice day, for the Minnesota outdoor field was typically iced over and took a fair amount of getting used to.

As the week continued, the harsh weather subsided, only to see a rash of injuries develop. Hayes even halted an unusually rough practice early, on Tuesday, after Ruhl hurt his knee and Logan was shaken up on a vicious hit. For Ruhl, the injury was especially disappointing, coming in the wake of his valiant comeback effort just a few days prior. Although this injury was to the same knee, this latest setback was of a different, seemingly more serious nature, and was not just a flare-up of the previous condition.

Later in the week, Farley Bell got loads of practice time as Dansler was hampered with a bursitis condition in his elbow. Farley capably demonstrated his prowess and fine physical gifts during this increased time; as was often the case, the second-string Buckeye, if presented with the opportunity, often equalled the accomplishments of the starter. The practice time of Johnson was again curtailed due to a flaming toe infection, although Billy Hill and Pete vowed he would play come Saturday.

On the encouraging side, Moore was able to practice for the very first time since going down against Missouri. Although the huge tight end predictably was quite rusty, Jimmy showed enough flashes of talent to prime expectations for some playing time against, perhaps, Michigan.

The seniors on the Gopher squad were extremely fired up for this battle, for it was their final home game. Tony Dungy, the team leader behind center and holder of ten school records, desperately wanted to exit a winner. In '75, the 6'0", 192 pound effervescent bundle of talent, brains, and leadership led the conference in passing and total offense, while also earning a spot on the all-Big 10 academic squad. Despite less glowing statistics in '76, Dungy was still very feared, for both his passing and running abilities.

His favorite target, wide receiver Ron Kullas, was injured in their contest with Michigan and was not expected to play, despite practicing all week with the first team. Fullback Kent Kitzmann was the backfield workhorse, and appropriately led the Gophers in rushing.

Carrying the brunt of the load in short yardage and goal line situations was third string fullback Jim Perkins, whose ability to locate the end zone on his few carries earned him the nickname Mr. Touchdown. In '76, Perkins had just 59 rushing attempts (Kitzmann once ran 57 times in one game), yet had crossed the goal line an astonishing 13 times.

The '76 team of head coach Cal Stoll was a rock-solid 6-3; yet Stoll was discouraged since he had preseason visions of being 8-1 at this juncture. Much of the reason for the two additional losses was the absence, for a six game stretch, of outstanding middle guard George Washington. When Washington went down early in the year with a damaged knee, much of the Gopher defensive sting went with him. The accomplished Washington led all conference defenders in '75 tackles, and was widely regarded as one of the premier defensemen in the nation. He was now back and at full strength, and would require quite a bit of attention from OSU.

Thursday afternoon, following the last practice of the week in Ohio Stadium, Hayes delivered a stirring, motivating pep talk. A win Saturday would be the 17th straight conference victory, matching the remarkable record set by the '54-'56 Buckeyes and later equalled by the fabulous scarlet and gray teams of '67-'69.

On the individual level, Johnson was within reach of the NCAA record for touchdowns, 59, held by the famous "Mr. Outside" of Army lore, Glenn Davis. With these standards on the line, Hayes was even more determined to win than usual.

Extremely disturbing news surfaced out of Michigan late in the week. Former standout OSU fullback Champ Henson was quoted extensively in the

MSU student newspaper, concerning the practice of OSU players illegally selling complimentary game tickets for cash profit. Tim Fox, with the Patriots, and Rick Middleton, a former Buckeye linebacker then with the San Diego Chargers, were listed in the investigative article as corroborating sources. Perhaps more damagingly, the article implied, Hayes was attributed as admitting that this scenario may indeed have infrequently occurred.

The article also implied that this practice of scalping did not meet with the disapproval of Hayes, who, according to these three former players, did nothing to prevent it from happening. Fox claimed that some of the assistant coaches during his years at OSU also sold their complimentary tickets, receiving in return lease-free automobiles for their private use. *The State News* printed a purported receipt from '73, which allegedly documented how an OSU assistant drove a car, totally gratis, throughout the year.

Hayes refused comment, though the accusations seemed daunting in their detail and informants. Both NCAA and OSU officials remained silent for the time being.

Further controversy hung over Hayes even as OSU barely eclipsed the Gophers 9-3 in a rollicking defensive struggle. During the televised contest between Alabama and Notre Dame that same day, ABC television commentators announced that Hayes was planning to resign on the Friday before the Michigan game. This timing, as reported on ABC, would spark a terrific effort versus the archrival Wolverines and hopefully propel OSU to their unprecedented fifth straight Rose Bowl. This report was explicitly denied by Hayes following his own game.

When questioned directly about the report, Hayes really made his feelings known. "I'll tell you one other thing - if I ever do retire, before ABC knows it, [long-time confidant and *Columbus Dispatch* columnist] Paul Hornung will know it."

Sadly, this Hayes intention to first inform his fine friend Hornung of his retirement plans, although it technically came to fruition (since Paul was supposedly the first to hear directly from Hayes), was effectively put in motion first in front of a Friday night national television audience just a little over two years later.

CHAPTER ELEVEN: MINNESOTA

Before 53,190 frozen fans in Memorial Stadium, the Buckeyes captured a most unimpressive (at least offensively) victory. The defense did their part, keeping Minnesota out of the end zone on both of the Gopher's threatening drives. On the other hand, OSU could mount just one sustained scoring drive in its own behalf.

The game began on a high note for OSU. After halting the opening Gopher drive, OSU fielded the ensuing punt and quickly drove 27 yards to the home 22, aided by a 16 yard pass to Storer. Greg was slightly shaken up on the catch, although he later returned to action. When this short drive stalled, Skladany drilled a 39 yard field goal to put OSU up 3-0 less than five minutes into the game. Unfortunately, this was essentially the extent of the Buckeye offense for the rest of the first quarter and most of the second.

On their second possession of the second quarter, Minnesota marched from their 36 to the Ohio State 32. The big pickup in this drive was a 17 yard Dungy completion to tight end Ken Wypyszynski (this is not a typo). Kicker Paul Rogind was summoned as the drive petered out, and his 39 yard field goal barely made it over the crossbar to knot up the game with 6:34 remaining in the half.

This tie seemed to jolt the OSU offense out of its temporary lethargic rut, for Pacenta immediately led OSU on a 14 play, 73 yard touchdown drive. Short passes to Logan and Harrell sustained the drive deep in Gopher territory, and following a pass that barely missed connecting with Storer, Pacenta kept on a sweep right and slipped two tacklers to tally the only touchdown of the game.

In a continuation of recent kicking woes, the extra point snap was mangled and the kick subsequently blocked by the extraordinary Washington. The score came with just over a minute left in the half, putting the visiting team up 9-3.

Minnesota made some waves on their first drive upon re-emerging from the locker room. Following a short-lived Buckeye possession and a Skladany punt which was almost blocked, Minnesota took over on the home 38. Dungy heated up, hitting three passes and carrying once for short yardage. At the OSU 25, Dungy twice misfired long. Rogind entered, only to miss the 42 yard attempt.

Ohio State failed to move on their next two opportunities, and after the second failure, Minnesota took control near midfield. Dungy called two consecutive quarterback draws, temporarily baffling the hard-charging Buckeye defenders. When Dungy drifted back into the pocket on the next play, Brudzinski broke through and knocked down the intended pass.

On the very next play, Dansler popped Dungy and the ball as the quarterback brought his arm forward in a passing motion. The ever-alert Buonamici snatched the ball out of the air, lumbering and stumbling 42 yards to the Gopher 23. It was the burly defensive tackle's third pick of the season, and afterwards he willingly admitted he was looking for Guess, Griffin, or anyone faster than himself to lateral the ball to.

In keeping with the ineptness of the OSU offense on this day, the Bucks lost yardage following this return and Skladany could not find the range on a 47 yard effort. Despite the opportunity to forge ahead on a score and extra point, the final two desperation Gopher drives ended futilely on the OSU 27 and 35 yard lines, respectively. Though Dungy connected on 16 of 38 pass attempts for 201 yards, he was unable to pierce the point-stingy defense from inside the red zone.

On the last Minnesota chance to surpass the visitors, Brudzinski broke through on fourth down and hammered Dungy exactly as he delivered a pass to a wide-open Gopher. The altered toss instead hit a defender in the back to fall incomplete and end any shot at an upset. As both players peeled themselves off the cold turf, Dungy exasperatedly asked the everpresent Brudzinski, "Where did you come from?"

In his postgame comments, Hayes pointed to a play which happened with just over five minutes remaining as being essential to the win. On a third and 13 situation deep in their own territory, OSU converted for a first down. Logan bolted straight over center for 14 yards, preserving the drive which chewed up critical minutes off the clock. Those minutes assumed greater importance as Minnesota drove deep into Buckeye territory in the closing seconds.

Hayes was of the opinion, "I never saw a better defense," than the OSU display today. Individually, Brudzinski and Buonamici were glowingly extoled. Almost lost in the wake of their heroics from the outside was the fantastic pressure exerted by the middle guard Brown. Included in his ten tackles were four hits behind the line of scrimmage, totaling 42 yards in lost yardage. In addition to the fierce pass rush exerted all day, the Buckeyes permitted the Gophers just 46 yards rushing on 35 attempts (sack yardage figured in).

George Hill always considered the greatest defensive display he'd ever witnessed to be a 24-0 blanking of Wisconsin in '73. In that display, the Badgers never crossed the OSU 34 yard line. Hill admitted "...this has to be very close to that," particularly in light of the fact that the offense lent little support. Even Stoll claimed that the Buckeye defensive unit was, in his learned opinion, superior to the Wolverine unit which blanked his squad 45-0.

One bright spot in the otherwise bleak offensive day was Logan, who surpassed the elite 1,000 yard mark. Jeff finished the day with 116 yards in a 30 carry performance. Pacenta completed half of his twelve pass attempts, for 79 yards, leaving Hayes somewhat pleased with the way the passing game was shaping up.

For the Gophers, in just his second stint since returning from his injury layoff, Washington was everything advertised, and more. He participated in 16 tackles, plus had the PAT block, which could have been instrumental in a Gopher comeback, had Minnesota subsequently reached the end zone

On this same afternoon, Rob Lytle of Michigan became the all-time leading ground gainer in the history of his school, surpassing Billy Taylor in a 38-7 stampede over Illinois.

The week before the Michigan matchup began with encouraging medical news. The back break of Gerald was healing nicely, though he was not quite ready to resume workouts. It was anticipated that he would be at full go by bowl time, however. Moore was essentially back to 100%, and his practice performance was especially remarkable in light of his extended absence. Ruhl was expected to be back at full strength by kickoff time, while Cousineau continued practicing in spite of shattering eight tiny bones in his left pinky early in the Minnesota game.

The OSU coaching staff spent scant time in reviewing the Gopher films, for Wolverine preparations were foremost. As usual, all OSU players and coaches were deemed off limits to the press, per the instructions of Hayes, until after the conference war was decided. Hayes allowed himself the task of conversing with the media, repeatedly declaring the OSU-Michigan rivalry, "...the greatest in all of football, pro or amateur."

In terms of importance, few could argue with this assertion. For the eighth time in nine years, this game would decide the conference champion, and therefore the right to represent the conference in the granddaddy of all bowl games.

Hayes explained the close, low-scoring nature of recent games in the series, stating, "...the element of surprise is usually not there." Defensive preparations on either side were such that neither opponent could necessarily shock or surprise the other. Extensive scouting and continual, year-long awareness of their rival allowed each defense the luxury of essentially becoming an expert on the other side.

This game was the first since Bo began coaching UM in '69 that each team entered the finale with a loss. Michigan had not won against OSU since '71, yet Bo scoffed at any mention of a jinx. Schembechler was in a jocular mood on Monday, jesting, "Hayes stands tall among coaches everywhere... and wide, too." Schembechler gravely, though humorously, said of Woody: "Under no circumstances do I talk to him in the winter."

The Bucks started to taper off after an especially heavy Tuesday practice. Hayes became annoyed when, despite mild November temperatures, the practice field froze solid on both Monday and Tuesday nights. Because of the already treacherous footing, Hayes rescinded his customary order to water the turf before practice.

Despite this mild annoyance, Hayes felt quite comfortable heading into this battle. According to Bo, "I believe this is as strong as I've ever seen an Ohio State defense," and Hayes obviously felt likewise.

The Michigan forte in '76 was a high-powered running attack, fueled by the speedy and powerful Lytle. The Wolverines led the conference in both rushing and total offense, augmented by the considerable improvement of sophomore signalcaller Rick Leach. Leach operated behind a big, mobile, aggressive line, which enabled him to complete 47 of his 87 passes, for a sparkling 13 touchdowns.

His favorite big-play receiver was versatile senior wingback Jim Smith. Bo called Smith "...the greatest receiver in Michigan history," feeling that Jim surpassed Tom Fears, Ron Kramer, and all other fabled predecessors. Smith had hauled in 24 passes for an incredible 662 yards, and was a definite threat to score each and every time he touched the ball, be it on a pass, a return, or a carry.

On the year, Michigan had run on 590 occasions, with just 93 passes. The numbers stacked up quite similarly for OSU (606 rushes, 76 passes). The maize and blue tandem of Lytle and Harlan Huckleby combined for almost 2100 yards rushing and scored 23 times. The yards per attempt for each Wolverine back were even more eye-catching: Lytle 7.1, Leach 6.8, Smith 5.9, and Huckleby 5.8.

Lytle was closing out his collegiate career to the same acclaim his hometown buddy Brudzinski was. The business/finance major aspired to take over the Lytle-family clothing store in native Fremont, Ohio. This business had been operated continuously through five generations of Lytles, and Rob wished to prolong the tradition. Considering his speed (9.6 in the 100 yard dash), which earned him a fifth place finish in the 60 meter conference finals as a sophomore, NFL scouts were really hoping to put the clothing career on hold for at least a few years.

The Wolverine defense was not as heralded as their Buckeye counterparts. Nonetheless, they were very accomplished. Michigan defensive philosophy had not changed since the '40's, when then-head coach Fritz Crisler stated, "Offense is poise; defense is frenzy." The line was led by the very quick and persistent Greg Morton, who had really stepped up a notch to intensify the '76 pass rush. Speedy Dwight Hicks provided both explosive run support and fine pass coverage from his defensive backfield spot, while Calvin O'Neal was the latest in a long line of phenomenal Wolverine linebackers.

Perhaps this was not surprising, as Adolph (German) Schultz, a lineman at Michigan in the early 1900's, had ostensibly invented the position, much to the perplexed amazement and subsequent pleasure of his coach Fielding Yost. One day in practice, Schultz grew tired of kneeling on the line, stood up, stepped back, and the position was invented.

Since that essentially accidental beginning, Bob Brown, Mike Taylor, Roger Zatkoff, and Dick Kempthorn had all left their mark on the Wolverine position, tattooing opposing ballcarriers with equally reckless abandon.

Placekicker Bob Wood was the conference leader, with greater accuracy, though not as great a range, as Skladany.

It was a tradition at Ohio State for a scrimmage to be held on Thursday, between the substitute squads and after the starting units had been dismissed. This year, the talent level of the underclassmen was such that the curiously coined "weenie bowl" was conducted on both Wednesday and Thursday nights.

The "weenie" often determined which fringe players would enjoy the luxury of dressing in the upcoming game, and was also an environment in which to test players coming off disabilities. Once a Buckeye moved into a starting or top reserve role, the "weenie" was something to avoid at all costs, for participation was inherently scoffed at by the regulars.

Imagine ending an already rigorous Hayes workout, then have to endure a full-contact scrimmage with Woody and the assistants poring over every move, while the regulars got to leave and run to the buses traveling to the locker room, all the while laughing at the misfortune of the substitutes.

Speaking of hardships, it is a little-known fact that not every athlete on the team was allowed to eat at the luscious training table. The team banquet hall had accommodations for only about 65-70 players, so the remaining 30-40 scrambled after practice, and if they were fortunate, made it back to the dormitory in time to eat whatever the general student body was offered. On nights when they were kept especially long, such as on the "weenie" night, the scout teamers and other lesser known Buckeyes were really in a bind, and had to fend for themselves when it came to dining.

Participants in the "weenie" had a love/hate relationship with the ritual. On the one hand, participation was dreaded, for the teasing by teammates was merciless and the play of often-desperate young men was brutal. On the other hand, this was a shot to move up in the depth chart, and was secretly welcomed as a chance to catch the eye of Woody. Consequently, effort was total and the competition spirited and ferocious. Through it all, Hayes stood vigil as the taskmaster, with dozens of youngsters flying recklessly around him in an attempt to shine.

As was his policy, Hayes refused much specific comment on his underclassmen this week, although he was genuinely pleased at their overall level of talent and desire. Hayes did speak freely on the success of fifth-year senior Lou Pietrini.

The roundabout path to success for Pietrini began his freshman year. After briefly appearing in five games that '72 fall, his season abruptly ended due to a severe case of mononucleosis. Sent back home to recuperate in Milford, Connecticut, Pietrini had plenty of time to think of his competition for playing time - Hicks, Schumacher, Dannelly - and began to doubt his own ability. He decided to hang up his cleats.

Upon being notified of the retirement plans of his close friend, Ken Kuhn went AWOL from the OSU campus, drove all the way to Connecticut, and forcibly brought Lou back into the scarlet and gray fold. Ken slipped a note under the office door of Woody before he left, vowing not to return until he convinced Pietrini to renege on his decision to quit. This mission escaped the wrath of Hayes only because it was for a good cause, and because it succeeded.

Pietrini redshirted the '73 season, taking the year off to fully recover from the mono. Lou played sparingly as a backup to Schumacher in '74, and in '75 injured his knee on the very last day of spring practice. Pietrini never quite recovered from this setback, played little during the season, and decided to undergo surgery over the winter. Sufficiently rehabilitated to only lightly jog during spring drills in '76, strenuous workouts and no missed practice time vaulted him into a starting spot during fall camp.

"He hangs in there and gets better and better," Staub proudly said of the surprising improvement out of the battered senior. In several '76 games, Pietrini actually graded higher than Ward, and many critical plays were run to his right-side position, a sure-fire sign of confidence from Hayes.

The success of the Michigan program was indirectly a result of the Hayes influence, coupled with the training received by Wolverine coaches at the breeding ground of innumerable coaches, Miami of Ohio. Besides Schembechler, those Michigan assistants with decided Hayes and/or Miami connections included Gary Moeller, former OSU captain, the Wolverine defensive coordinator who had never, in his life, been associated with a losing football team; Paul Schudel, who played for Bo at the Oxford campus of Miami; Tom Reed, a standout offensive back on two Redskin Mid-America Conference championship teams; Jerry Hanlon, a star halfback for Ara Parseghian at Miami; and Tirrel Burton, a native of Oxford who became a star halfback and hurdler at his hometown university. Additionally, assistant Jack Harbaugh starred at Bowling Green, and Chuck Stobart was a standout quarterback at Ohio University.

As often happened, the Hayes influence, so prevalent among Ohio coaches, had extensively branched out across the land. Some of the innumerable Hayes proteges learned their lessons so well, their own exploits occasionally eclipsed those of the master. Hayes felt, "...my expertise as a teacher is on the line each Saturday"; that was never more true than on Michigan gameday.

Bo summed up the education process with, "Oh, how I learned from [Woody]." Schembechler was the prodigal son, and like Hayes, his fierce will to win and dominant force of personality matched the legendary excesses of Woody. Like Hayes, Schembechler "...coached from the heart and throat." The two great coaches were amazingly similar, yet Bo understandably had a fervent desire to emerge from the shadow of his mentor. A victory Saturday would place him further along that path.

Equally as legendary as the two coaches were some of the games in the storied rivalry between OSU and "the school up north." In '46, the Wolverine team of Fritz Crisler led by an invincible margin of 55-0, when Crisler elected to kick a field goal, a move widely derided by the press of the day. The final ended up 58-6, with the sole OSU score coming on the soon-to-be-outlawed "sleeper" play. Billy Doolittle passed to Rod Swinehart, who had stood unobtrusively on the far sideline as the huddle broke. Swinehart raced in for the touchdown virtually unseen.

Two years prior to this, in '44, OSU won 18-14, capturing a Big 10 title by coming from behind in the final minutes. Les Horvath led OSU on a last-ditch drive to the Wolverine two, whereupon the charitable Horvath called plays designed to let a freshman score the winning touchdown. After several failures, captain Bill Hackett forcibly ordered Horvath to run the ball in himself. Les complied, possibly as much to avoid the wrath of Hackett as to clinch the game!

In '63, the showdown was tragically postponed at the last minute due to the JFK assassination. The game was played the following weekend in Ann Arbor, and OSU anticlimactically won 14-10. The '65 Buckeyes won another comeback thriller, 9-7, behind the rushing heroics of fullback Will Sanders and wingback Bo Rein, whose late, mad dashes fueled the winning drive. The clinching points came on the third game-winning field goal of the year by kicker Bob Funk.

In '72, the Buckeyes upset the number three ranked Wolverines 14-11, dealing Michigan their first loss in 21 regular season games. The game featured three amazing goal line stands by the home Buckeyes, whipping the frenzied crowd into unrestrained hysteria. On twelve attempts spread over those three occasions, with each attempt originating inside the five yard line, Michigan was unable to cross the goal line.

The play of OSU linebackers Middleton, Gradishar, and Arnie Jones was exemplary on each of the denials. These three men personified the adage, "If you're ever in a barroom brawl, you'd want him covering your back." For all the recognized magnificence of Gradishar, Middleton and Jones were just as ruggedly fierce. Covered in blood and mud, these men would, and did, do anything possible to make a tackle.

Just before the last thwarted play of these dozen, Hayes led police into a mob of fans who had stampeded onto the field. Order was briefly restored, only to have hundreds of overanxious fans charge into the south end zone in a mad dash to tear down the goal post. Hayes again led the way in restoring order, although he badly wrenched his leg in the process.

On the final play of the nailbiter, George Hasenohrl nailed Wolverine quarterback Dennis Franklin in the backfield, preserving the win. Of course, the thrilling victory in '75 was included in the pantheon of these great games, and Hayes hoped to duplicate that success in '76.

CHAPTER TWELVE: MICHIGAN

Most unexpectedly, OSU was instead shut out for the first time in 123 games, dating back to a '64 10-0 pasting by the same Wolverines. Michigan dominated the second half this year, to convincingly emerge victorious by a 22-0 count. The dominating tenor of the win was such that Hayes called Bo the "...coach of the year," in making such a strong return from his pre-season heart attack. Hayes also said, "Any team that can beat us this badly has to be #1."

Woody was not entirely chastened by the defeat, adding, "...defeats are the things that make men out of you," although he was of course sadly disheartened at the lackluster showing in front of the then-largest OSU home crowd ever, 88,250. Michigan simply overran the fabled OSU defense with quick-hitting, outside runs, and the OSU offense could not keep pace.

The first half was a strong defensive battle until the final four minutes, when OSU embarked on their only extended drive of the game. On long runs by Logan and Pacenta, OSU reached the Michigan eight just before halftime. Hayes felt that Pacenta could exploit the matchup Storer had in the secondary, and expressly called for a pass to the tight end. Wolverine defensive back Jim Pickens instead stepped in front of Storer, and the only OSU scoring chance of the day fell by the wayside.

At the half, the daredevil exploits of three stunt parachutists provided perhaps as much excitement as the two offenses had.

After that lively break, Michigan busted out of the malaise, charging 80 yards in 12 plays, with Lytle, Leach, and Russell Davis providing the fireworks. Davis pounded in from three yards out, and Michigan had their insurmountable lead.

Ohio State continued to muster little on offense, and Skladany boomed a long, high punt which Smith made a dazzling return of, to the visitor 48. The Wolverines scrapped for 52 yards in ten plays, with Davis again running the final three yards.

At the start of the final quarter, Logan fumbled, with Michigan recovering. Leach was picked off on the first Wolverine play, and OSU went for a big play via a pass to get back into the contest. Alas, Pacenta's pass was pilfered on the opening play, and the maize and blue took over at the OSU 15. When Lytle scored soon thereafter, with 8:13 left, the game was effectively over.

The remainder of the game was a show of offensive ineptitude by an out-of-sync OSU offense, while their Michigan counterparts essentially played just to run out the clock. After hearing "Hail to the Victors," the Michigan fight song, one too many times, most of the record crowd sullenly trudged out prior to the end of regulation.

Perhaps the brightest spot of the gloomy day for OSU was the punting of Skladany, who blistered eight kicks for an eye-popping 52.2 yard average. His driving kicks repeatedly kept Michigan out of good field position, and most likely these strong kicks kept the score from being even more one-sided. Both Ray Griffin and Skladany made touchdown saving tackles on returns by the slippery Smith, who continually threatened to bust loose.

The anemic OSU offense could scratch for only 173 total yards, including just 104 on the ground. Logan was held to 63 on 17 carries, Johnson was limited to just eight runs for 21 yards, while Pacenta netted a mere 20 yards on 12 attempts. Michigan gained 366 yards on the day, with every single yard coming on the ground. Leach went zero for six on his pass attempts, but it did not matter. Lytle asserted his brilliance, bursting for 165 yards on 29 punishing runs.

Brudzinski often led the way in corralling his hometown comrade, as the proud OSU never relented, in spite of the futility of their effort. Davis was a continual thorn in the Ohio State side, picking up many necessary short gains to conclude with 83 yards in 24 carries. Thompson, Cousineau, Brown, and Beamon courageously kept the plentiful Wolverine backs from further mayhem.

Afterwards, a shell-shocked Hayes seemed practically emotionless, except when he reasserted his claim (subsequently confirmed by television replay) that the UM left tackle jumped offsides prior to the first touchdown. During the game, when this occurred, Hayes went berserk, charging onto the field and protesting in vain.

Most of the sentiment displayed in the Buckeye locker room, afterwards, was merely utter disbelief that the Rose Bowl was now out of reach. Many players had never known anything but Pasadena to exist after the rough UM game, and in truth had almost come to expect the Rose trip as a given.

Indeed, that following Monday, at the traditional concluding team banquet, most Buckeye players overlooked the Orange Bowl bid which had been tendered, and accepted, late Saturday night. The speakers during that banquet repeatedly slipped and said "Rose" when discussing the upcoming bowl game. The team seemed as downtrodden as it had ever been, as did Hayes, whose extensive review of the game films had dropped him into a deep funk.

Brudzinski took home team MVP honors that Monday, and the hard-core, team player saluted his teammates for working together to enable his personal success. Springs and Guess captured the top newcomer awards for offense and defense, respectively. Springs led the team with nine kickoff returns for 158 yards, and contributed 291 yards rushing in his limited appearances. Buonamici was selected the outstanding defensive lineman, as Hayes proclaimed him the top tackle in the country.

Nick was perhaps the most misunderstood player of the Hayes era. He was a fascinating, complex individual. On the one hand, Nick was a legitimate hell-raiser and brawler, personifying the tough, overachieving, undersized player who succeeded against (seemingly) more talented opposition. Hayes loved the sort of player Nick was: No matter the circumstance, no matter the odds, Nick could punish himself the most, and demonstrate more guts than any opponent. As Woody said: "The tough will make it." Nick was nuts about the game, and unbelievably fierce.

Yet as much as he pleased Woody with his attitude on the field, Nick rebelled against authority and occasionally chafed under (what Nick thought to be) the stringent off-field restrictions of Hayes. Still, much like Woody and equally unknown to the public, Buonamici customarily made many unannounced junkets to area hospitals and schools, cheering up and aiding adoring children of all ages. Nick was like putty around kids, and even willingly signed home-made drawings children sent to him. As with many other OSU players, and reflecting the style of their Coach, this charitable, philanthropic side was kept mostly anonymous.

Lukens was likewise chosen the top lineman on offense. As Bill accepted the trophy, he prophetically razzed his presenter and coach, Ralph Staub. "I've had five coaches since I've been here," said Lukens, "...so you can see I've been kind of rough on them." Lukens maintained a staggering 3.6 grade point average in his major, veterinary medicine, and soon after this banquet received a post-graduate scholarship from the NCAA.

Logan won the fraternity award for the premier homecoming game performance. While accepting the trophy, it fell and broke apart, tragi-comically symbolizing the crashing halt to the '76 Buckeye season.

Hayes avoided any mention of the dreaded loss to Michigan on this Monday night, saying only, "In theater, they have an axiom where an actor is only as good as his last performance... leave it at that." Perhaps the most emotion he displayed the entire evening came as he took a parting shot at recent NCAA legislation which limited coaching staffs to a maximum of eight full-time assistants. When Chuck Clausen departed from the staff before the season to accept a position with the Philadelphia Eagles, he left a void which Hayes never felt was adequately filled.

Hayes also touched upon the amount of money and prestige which OSU brought to the conference, acerbically stating that such lofty contributions went largely unappreciated by fellow conference members.

Later in the month, Ward, Lukens, Brudzinski, Brown, Buonamici, Griffin, Cousineau, and Skladany each made various All-Conference teams. Brudzinski was subsequently named on most first team All-American squads, earning the privilege of being a guest on the prestigious Bob Hope Christmas show. Johnson, Buonamici, Griffin, and Ward were also selected as UPI second team All-Americans.

As the new year approached, this distinguished group of honored players prepared for a face-off with Big 8 co-champion Colorado. The Buffalos stampeded their way to an 8-3 regular season record, defeating co-champs

Oklahoma and Oklahoma State along the way, thereby earning the lofty Orange Bowl invitation. The Colorado coach was another with deep ties to Hayes.

Bill Mallory was in his third year at the school in the Rockies. He served as the defensive line coach at OSU from '66-'68, leaving to become the top man at his alma mater, Miami of Ohio. He directed an extremely young team in '76, with absolutely no pre-season indication of impending greatness, to an astounding conference championship. Mallory considered Hayes to be one of his closest friends and, "I consider him one of the truly great coaches."

Colorado was an explosive offensive team, capable of piling up multitudes of both points and yards. The Buffalo quarterback was a sophomore transfer from UCLA, the 6'2", 195 pound Jeff Knapple, who expertly led a speedy option attack. The featured back in the Colorado scheme was fast, 191 pound tailback Tony Reed, who reminded many observers of Jeff Logan.

Reed played his prep ball in armed services schools in Japan, and was so unknown coming out of high school that he went to a junior college so he could immediately play. Now well-known by NFL scouts, Reed accounted for 1210 rushing yards in '76.

The biggest weapon for the Buffalos was 6'7", 241 pound tight end Don Hasselbeck, a product of Cincinnati (Ohio) Lasalle High. The huge, mean receiver was on the mend from a broken hand incurred at midseason. The injury did little to slow his brilliant blocks, which sprung Reed for much of his yardage.

Ohio State began Orange Bowl preparations in a slight dilemma. Gerald was again practicing with the team, in relatively good shape, although he still endured periods of great pain and discomfort. He was able to participate in running and fundamentals drills, and was expected to be cleared for contact about a week before the game itself. Hayes made it clear that Rod would play, if cleared by the medical staff, though he would not commit to starting Gerald.

Sadly, Jimmy Moore was done for the season. Renewed swelling in his damaged knee necessitated surgery on the third day of the new year, and the disappointed tight end was relegated to a convalescence at his Arizona home. Mark Sullivan badly twisted his knee, and also went under the scalpel of the surgeon.

While still in Columbus, the squad did an extreme amount of running to stay in shape, though mild December weather allowed a couple of outdoor practices. With all the cardiovascular work, Johnson supposedly was down to a svelte, shadowy 236 pounds, the lowest of his OSU career. Both of his damaged ankles continued to bother him, despite the weight loss.

In a freak accident, Max Midlam suffered a broken hand, courtesy of an ill-timed slammed door. Newly-converted to guard, Bill Harmon had surgery on his gallbladder and also would not dress.

Just prior to the departure for Miami, the principle architect of the recent run of formidable OSU offensive lines, Staub, was hired as the new head coach at Cincinnati. Staub was a record-setting wide receiver under Sid Gillman during the Bearcat glory years of the early '60's, and the lure of coaching his alma mater proved irresistible.

Only 48 years of age, Staub had recently surfaced as the most likely heir apparent should Hayes step down at OSU (assuming Woody ever left). In addition to his offensive line duties, Staub helped coordinate the OSU offense, supervised the kickers, and headed up the phenomenally complex network of high school and junior college recruiting. He offered to stay on at OSU through the bowl game, yet his departure sent shock waves cascading through the Buckeye program.

Woody had lost another right hand man, ostensibly to a better job. It was to the misfortune of Hayes, and the glory of his departed assistants, that Woody launched so many into head coaching positions.

Staub became the 17th former Hayes assistant to rise to a head coaching position at either the professional or collegiate level. Some of the others (with their '76 billets listed) included Bill Hess, Ohio University; Doyt Perry, formerly of Bowling Green; Ara Parseghian, formerly of Notre Dame; Bill Arnsparger, N.Y. Giants; Gene Slaughter, Capital (Ohio) University; and Lou Holtz, N.Y. Jets (within days of the Staub announcement, Holtz was named head coach at Arkansas).

Dave Adolph, for the previous four years the defensive coordinator at Illinois, was the leading candidate to replace Staub. Three days before the new year, Adolph officially was hired by Ohio State. Eventually, several Buckeyes transferred to the UC campus, foremost among them the gifted Farley Bell.

Along with the refreshing sunshine found in Florida, came a reinvigorated attitude, emanating as always from the top of the coaching hierarchy. Hayes emerged from the wreckage of the disastrous UM loss even more consumed by his passion to win, and accordingly his outbursts of raging frustration became more frequent. As Woody often remarked, "Never forget, the whole pleasure is in winning...[for] winning is the epitome of group effort." Even George Hill bristled at suggestions by some media types that the Orange was a second rate bowl contended by two very so-so teams.

On the contrary, as evidenced by their excitable demeanors, both participating schools seemed pleasantly overwhelmed with everything concerning the bowl game, from the comfortable 70 degree practice weather to the excellent accommodations for the entire traveling parties. Even more so than the more-entrenched Rose Bowl, the organizers of the Orange went all out in assuring everything about their operation was strictly first-class, and enjoyable. Even the Purdue University-developed natural grass of the stadium was deemed outstanding.

The Bucks were determined to prove they were a vastly superior team than the one last on display against Michigan. The goals were to reclaim their totally dominant defensive prowess, and to reestablish their offensive eminence, particularly on the ground. With practices conducted in the cool of the day, at nine a.m., followed by relaxing days on the sunny beaches, the Buckeye players saw most negativity present after the UM debacle dissipate.

This bowl presented Ohio State with the opportunity to proclaim their true greatness. As Hayes felt, "The Orange Bowl is a matter of integrity." Hayes repeatedly hammered into his players the notion that true greatness is achieved only by overcoming great obstacles and great tests of adversity.

One player who had battled adversity all year was Johnson, who, by his standards, had a disappointing year. Johnson finished with 698 yards rushing and 18 touchdowns; although better than most, certainly far from the scintillating marks of his junior year. The year was disappointing principally because his right foot, although fine when cutting or moving, pained him considerably whenever he stopped. As Paul Campbell alternated with him in practice, Johnson hoped to conclude his career with a bang.

It is likely that had Johnson stayed healthy all year, the outcome of the blemishes on the OSU record may well have turned out differently, and Pete felt that anguish. Professional scouts drooled over Johnson, bad feet or not. A fullback with that size, acceleration, and wondrous ability had not been seen since the days of Marion Motley, if at all.

Unfortunately for Pete, Hayes became so enamored of Campbell, and intentions of developing the backfield for the '77 season, that Johnson neither started nor played a significant role in his final collegiate contest.

Fellow senior Thompson also had aspirations of a pro career. Ed grew up in a basketball-crazed family, and the young Thompson dreamed of playing hoops at the college level. Amidst this dream came Marshall University, who recruited the Waverly (Ohio) High product as a quarterback. When his childhood love OSU entered the recruiting scene, the lanky Ed gladly matriculated. He was soon switched to the defensive side of the ball.

After ballooning up with 40 pounds of hard-earned muscular bodyweight since the conclusion of his prep days, Thompson began a gradual improvement that never slowed, as he familiarized himself with linebacking duties. His senior season went so well that Hill compared Thompson to former OSU standout and Baltimore Colt tackling dynamo Stan White.

Perhaps the only Buckeye to exhibit more improvement than the rugged Thompson was Aaron Brown. Brown had always been able to explode with the big play, and this year he still produced the big hit, while also consistently controlling the line of scrimmage.

As gameday approached, both Gerald and Pacenta were ready for action. Although Hayes insinuated that the senior would probably start, he refused to absolutely commit, barking, "Let Mallory worry about that."

Since Colorado featured a constantly shifting defensive front, forever changing from a five man up to an eight man line, in reality the outstanding attributes of each quarterback could be utilized. Gerald could freeze the smaller pass rushers with the threat of the option run, while Pacenta could bedazzle with play-action fakes and intermediate passes if the Buffalos stacked to prevent the run.

Colorado featured Brian Crabrab at linebacker and Mike L. Davis at strong safety. These two players hoped to continue the winning tradition of their school: In the past ten years, Colorado had split their six bowl appearances, a fine percentage for post-season games. Mallory traditionally had strong defensive teams. As the head man at Miami, four of his six teams finished among the top six in the nation in total defense, including his 11-0 '73 Redskins, who whipped Florida in the Tangerine Bowl.

In the last meeting between Colorado and OSU, in '71, the Buffalos prevailed 20-14. That victory extended the Big 8 winning streak over Big 10 teams to an otherworldly 20 games, despite an uncharacteristic aerial display by OSU. Buckeye quarterback Don Lamka threw often and long to Dick Wakefield, but the exploits of Colorado wide receiver Cliff Branch and Buffalo running back Charles Davis were too much to overcome.

This week revealed two contradictory stances taken by families with OSU ties. Jim Hackett, a senior reserve center for Michigan, ignored the Buckeye tradition established by his family to attend the school up north. Jim's father, the aforementioned Dr. Bill Hackett, was an All-American guard at OSU in '44, while Jim's brother Bill was a backup linebacker on the '69 OSU Rose Bowl champions. Despite the apparent conflict of allegiances, the Hacketts stood as one in support of their son.

On a totally different level, the parents of the Vogler twins, sophomores at OSU, vowed to never attend a game while their sons played for the Buckeyes. Bob and Edna Vogler desperately wanted their talented twosome to attend Dayton University. The Covington, Ohio, athletes defied the wishes of their parents, and the rebellion created a sizable rift which still separated the family. Tim claimed that the twins selected Ohio State primarily for the strong opportunity to achieve the industrial arts degree they each craved, as Dayton did not offer this same favored curriculum.

Another set of player parents, Dick and Gloria Logan, in Florida to see their son Jeff, were excitedly reliving their '53 honeymoon trip to the Orange Bowl. On that romantic interlude, Dick, on break from his second season with the Green Bay Packers, watched Alabama decimate Syracuse 61-6 in the New Year's contest.

In other news, Guess was announced as the first OSU frosh defensive starter in a bowl since Tim Fox in the '73 Rose Bowl. Buonamici was expected to play, although he was being pestered with an ankle sprain. As Billy Hill stated, "Pain does not bother him."

CHAPTER THIRTEEN: ORANGE BOWL

On the day of the game, Gerald did not seem troubled by his extensive layoff. Rod entered the clash with OSU reeling both on offense and defense, and the sophomore completely changed the tide of the contest. With 3:54 left in the first quarter, the Bucks trailed 10-0 and were going absolutely nowhere on offense.

Colorado snagged a fumble by Pacenta on the opening drive of the game, beginning an 11 play scoring drive from their 43. The Buck defense held in close at the tail end of this drive, forcing a short Mark Zetterberg field goal. Ohio State responded with a short drive, and Colorado took over on their 20 when Skladany fell far shy of a 56 yarder.

In just eight slam-bang plays, the Buffalos traversed the 80 yard distance, chiefly on a 20 yard catch by wingback Emory Moorehead, followed by a brilliantly executed 40 yard reverse by the talented Emory. Moorehead ultimately scored the touchdown on a short snare of a Knapple toss, putting Colorado quickly in front by ten.

The Buckeyes rebounded quickly. After Harrell returned the short kickoff to the OSU 47, Gerald entered and the team immediately perked up. On his first play, Rod darted 17 yards through the overwhelmed defense. Logan followed that fast gain with a 36 yard touchdown stomp, and just like that the momentum shifted completely to Ohio State.

Late in the second quarter, a 19 play, 56 yard drive ended in a 28 yard Skladany field goal, tying the score at ten. The Buffalos had rallied to hold OSU in check this time near the end zone, though there was a feeling in the huge crowd that it was only a matter of time until OSU blew this game wide open. The OSU defense held Colorado on the ensuing possession, but Joe Allegro fumbled the punt, with Stan Brock recovering at the OSU 36.

Again the Buckeyes held, and the field goal attempt by Zetterberg was partially blocked by the gutsy Buonamici. The bouncing ball was finally downed at the OSU one yard line, putting Gerald and company in a tight spot.

Unfazed, OSU unleashed a 99 yard march, with Johnson scoring the final touchdown of his illustrious college career from three yards away, with 24 seconds left in the half. The marathon drive vaulted Buckeye spirits to new heights, and following the requisite long halftime show, the OSU defense was impenetrable.

Colorado amassed 134 rushing yards on the day, with just 37 of those gained in the second half. The majority of their 137 passing yards were also accrued early on.

This game featured a brand new "quick-back" offensive look for the OSU offense, with the 218 pound fullback Campbell spelling Logan, who actually moved to the fullback position on occasion to allow Ron Springs a chance to display his considerable talents at tailback. With a speedier array of backs in place, including Gerald, the offense turned to fast option reads and quick-hitting sprints by the fullback, in an approximation of the UCLA veer offense. Colorado never really adjusted to this influx of raw speed.

Although OSU was denied points on two occasions after venturing deep into Colorado territory, the Bucks were able to tack on a 20 yard Skladany three-pointer in the third. This kick followed a Griffin punt return to the CU 49 and a fantastic catch by Harrell, good for 24 yards. Continually pinned deep in their own part of the field by booming Skladany punts, Colorado lost most of the fourth quarter battles for field position.

In the waning moments of the game, with only 45 seconds left, Gerald capped his amazing comeback with a four yard scoring dash. The resounding final was 27-10.

Hayes could not speak highly enough of his defense in the loud aftermath. The spirited defenders held an explosive offense completely in check after enduring a rough acquaintance period for the first 15 minutes. Reed was limited to 58 yards in 22 carries, and was repeatedly pummeled by Cousineau, who accumulated 17 tackles and grabbed an interception, and the hard-hitting Thompson.

On the other side, some of the late Buffalo defensive woes were attributable to the first quarter collision which caused middle guard Charlie Johnson to break his leg. Mostly, the Buckeye carnage derived from motivated athletes executing in superior fashion, with tremendously greater speed.

After the final whistle, Mallory attempted to congratulate Hayes, who was already exiting under a squadron of police protection. Mallory quipped, "The day I need a police escort I'll retire," and then added seriously, "[Hayes] can coach until he's 90. I have a lot of respect for the man."

The day following this uplifting victory, the Orange Bowl reception committee threw a party, for both the Colorado and Ohio State players. The soiree was held at the posh Cross Creek Country Club, one of the most exclusive and extravagant golf courses in all of the wealthy Miami area. Still amazingly disappointed by the previous day's loss, the Colorado players were accordingly morose and not in a celebratory mood.

Hayes seemed to recognize his players deserved an outlet for all their hard work and accomplishments, so he soon vanished from the outdoor area his team was dining in. The Orange committee sprinkled the gathering with a bountiful supply of nubile young hostesses, and the courtesy drinks were flowing freely. Before long, the Buffalo players had exited and the Buckeyes reveled in their triumph.

Among the many legendary feats of that insane evening of partying, Ernie Andria recalls that, while elaborately bedecked in suits and ties, several exuberant Buckeyes climbed into palm trees and playfully dove out to crash land on unsuspecting bystanders. Later, more than one golf cart was driven at full speed into an outlying body of water, and Tim Sawicki creatively added to the appeal of an ornate, decorative, ceramic fountain of water as the alcoholic consumption peaked.

At times such as these, Woody distanced himself from his players. Though he obviously knew what was transpiring, the Coach sensed these wild eruptions were part of a maturing process. He did not condone such mischief, though contrary to his image as a constant control freak, he entrusted the players with the ultimate responsibility for their own actions, and selectively allowed them some leeway from his otherwise stringent rule. As Hayes pointed out, "We control by attitudes, and not rules."

CHAPTER ONE: PRE-SEASON '77

Ohio State emerged from their resounding Orange Bowl rebound win with extremely high hopes for the '77 season, and even more hungry for continuing success. Gerald had a certain, solid grip on the signalcaller slot, having fully recovered from his painful back injury. There were no signs of any lingering effects from the breaks which caused him to miss the final four regular season games in '76.

Mindful of the fearless play which seemed to make Rod susceptible to further injuries, Hayes ensured that backup Greg Castignola received plenty of spring and fall practice action. Chaump, and others, did not want a rehash of the '76 scenario, when a terribly unseasoned Jim Pacenta was forced to learn by doing. It is to the credit of Pacenta that OSU did not completely falter, though the offense did miss the terrific athleticism of Rod.

Not only was Castignola "...heady, reliable, and a quick learner," according to Chaump, his development might also keep Gerald fresh and strong the whole season. Castignola was a 6'2", 180 pound sophomore from Trenton, Michigan, and he was understandably pleased with the vigorous interest in his role. Fellow sophomore Mike Strahine was also improving, though the snaps were not quite as plentiful for him in practice.

As partially demonstrated by their success with the speed-oriented, underclassmen-led offensive attack in the victory over Colorado, OSU was undeniably quicker in '77, both in the backfield and at the receiving corps. Gerald was undeniably quicker than Pacenta, Springs was a complete thoroughbred, and Campbell was very fast for such a strong runner.

Although the top two returning receivers, Herman Jones and Jim Harrell, were both hobbled by slight injuries and were not full-go early in the fall, their temporary absence looked to be advantageous. Extra attention was thereby focused on a host of freshmen flankers, including Doug Donley and Doug Pauley, while sophomore Chuck Hunter impressed the coaching staff with his extra chances. Even frosh fullback Joel Payton drew notice in preseason workouts, for his blend of deceptive speed with typical plowhorse power.

The offensive line was again anchored by gargantuan Chris Ward. Ward was very confident in his linemates, assured that their collective performance would measure up to his lofty expectations. Not only was the line in better condition than in '76, according to Chris, partly due to the savagely hot, humid weather conditions summer workouts and fall practice were conducted in, he felt the line also benefitted from several altered blocking schemes which better utilized their specific talents.

On a personal level, Ward had dropped around ten pounds, to put his weight close to 270. The weight loss aided his foot speed in backpedaling during pass blocking, and his explosiveness off the line at the snap during running plays.

Up and down the line, there were no glaring weaknesses. The likely starters early in the fall appeared to be Ward at left tackle, Doug Mackie at right tackle, Ken Fritz and Mark Lang at guard, and Tim Vogler at center. The tight end slot was to be shared by Greg Storer and Bill Jaco, with Jimmy Moore at the other tight end, still not completely back from his bad knee.

Ward could not speak enough about how the unusually high heat and humidity had aided the conditioning process, thus reducing injuries. "I think it has put us in better shape than ever before," he asserted. The hot weather was of additional benefit, for OSU played three typically-tropically conditioned teams early in the year (Miami of Florida, Oklahoma, and Southern Methodist). Adaptation to high heat was essential in order to lessen the advantage these teams usually derived when the temperatures skyrocketed.

Hayes thought very highly of the hard-working Ward. With another standout year under his belt, Hayes felt he would be able to compare Chris to the all-time greats like Parker, Rufus Mayes, and John Hicks, whom Woody still considered his most inspirational, emotional leader. The philosophy of Ward was simple. "I like to improve every time out - that's my personal goal," he steadfastly declared.

With the quicker backfield and experienced offensive and defensive lines, Ward thought the '77 outlook very rosy. "I'm one of the few who can say we've had a shot at winning the national championship four times... and I think that this year it's going to be ours, too."

In direct contrast to the relatively easy-going Ward was the other tackle, Mackie. Even newly-hired tackle coach Bill Myles admitted that Mackie was exceptionally, almost unnervingly, intense. Coming off an April operation to repair torn knee ligaments, Mackie was pushing himself even harder than Myles or Hayes cared him to. They did not wish to see him suffer a setback in rushing his recovery, though Mackie refused to slow down.

Doug was not an outstanding football player, though his physical condition and inhuman strength allowed him to hold his own on the field. Mackie was perhaps the strictest adherent to weight training of all the players on the team, and definitely used strength training to his benefit.

A big boost to the recovery of other injured OSU players was the addition of new strength advisor Kevin Rodgers, who greatly expanded the existing weight training program. This intensified program was conducted in a newly remodeled weight room, designed after the fashion of the Miami training facility which OSU used during Orange Bowl preparations. Hayes felt imitation was the most sincere form of flattery, and he had been greatly impressed by that modern set-up. Perhaps more importantly, archrival

Michigan was already wowing recruits with the size and extent of their weight program. Hayes had to keep pace.

Hayes was never really an advocate of all out strength training for football, and for most of his career actually thought that bulking up via a resistance program ran counterproductive, to all positions but those on the line, to improving play on the field. According to an earlier Hayes belief, "Weightlifters are too egocentric, unable to subjugate themselves to a team principle."

Typically, until '74 or so, Hayes believed running and running only was the most important training a player needed to stay in shape, and the OSU staff rarely required much beyond sprints and timed-mile runs. Along with this philosophy, off-season conditioning was practically unheard of, outside of running and some occasional light lifting, and the usual Hayes barometer to tell if a player reported to fall camp in good shape was a prescribed time in the mile run. After years of this practice, Woody realized that football was a game containing short, intense bursts of running, and changed his fall good-shape determinater to a series of timed sprints.

Archie Griffin recalls being overjoyed when the mile run was dropped in favor of the dashes, and on the surface the sprint test seemed simple enough: Each player was assigned a 40 yard and 30 yard dash time, based on his fastest clocking at each distance. The player then had to run eight or ten sprints at each distance, staying within a certain range of his fastest clocking, with only 25-30 seconds rest in between each sprint.

Of course, those seconds elapsed quickly, since the count began as soon as the finish line was crossed, and the player still had to jog back to the starting line, for his next timed sprint. Archie remembers people vomiting in between runs, and even the best conditioned studs struggled to pass this deceptively masochistic exam. Hayes believed in the old Green Bay Packer coach Curly Lambeau credo, being simply, "Run them to death."

Duncan Griffin recalls running his initial sprint test, on a gray, overcast, summery day prior to his frosh year. Duncan passed his test, then collapsed on the grass, all the while thinking the gloomy sky was going to come crashing down on him. He was so exhausted, he simply didn't have enough energy to move.

Accordingly, if an OSU player ran onto the field prior to the first game of the year with a Buckeye leaf on his helmet, one knew that this player had passed his sprint tests, a rare honor indeed.

One summer, lineman Garth Cox had done a little imbibing of adult beverages until late in the previous evening, and dragged himself to an unsupervised weight room workout early the following morning. It was all Garth could do to concentrate on the task at hand, when, out of seemingly thin air, Hayes materialized. Standing over the queasy Cox, and wearing an out-of-character rumpled fishing hat, Hayes suggested (read: demanded) that Garth perform his sprint test for his Coach.

Grudgingly, Garth began his timed runs, with Woody clocking each dash. About half way through the series, Hayes disappeared from sight. Cox contemplated quitting before he performed all 16 sprints, though he resolutely, painfully, kept on running. Good thing, for as soon as the last sprint was completed, Woody again mysteriously appeared as if from nowhere, and somehow knew the times from all of the sprints.

Prior to this hiring of Rodgers, John Mummey and Billy Hill ran a somewhat loose weight training regimen, based on the Hayes guidelines. In fact, the original OSU weight room was actually a primitive Universal machine and some basic benches and barbells which were contained in a cramped garage. Billy Hill really began to urge Hayes to update the lifting facet of the OSU program after spending a month in DeLand, Florida, at the home/laboratory of eccentric Nautilus inventor Arthur Jones. Hayes balked, although lifting continued to become more and more prevalent among the players, and conditioning started to become a year round process.

Archie was an early exponent of weight training, and his frame rapidly put on lots of mass, especially when Mummey forced Archie through a summertime program concentrated with negative repetitions. The tailback's arms bulked out to an impressive 17.5 inches, yet Hayes exploded when he saw the muscular Griffin. "You look like a guard!" Hayes bellowed, and, concerned that Archie would lose his quickness, forced him to ease off the weights.

One player who was not at ease yet, though he was growing more comfortable at his new position, was guard Ken Fritz. The 6'3", 232 pound sophomore had started off his OSU career on the defensive line, and his natural instincts and great strength, in addition to the discipline involved in what he considered a less "haphazard" offensive role in the structure of a game plan, led to a switch to the blocking side.

The prep star from Ironton, Ohio, looked to be a future collegiate star, too. Already vying for plenty of playing time, the unassuming Fritz was pushed into the actual starting role when senior Jim Savoca was forced to undergo back surgery to correct a debilitating ruptured disk. The usual lack of recognition for offensive lineman did not concern the rugged redhead, for Fritz preferred to let his improving play stand on its own merits, and he was content to labor in relative anonymity.

Fritz also was one of the few players to ever short-circuit a dreaded, tempestuous Hayes lecture. Ken flubbed an assignment during one practice; immediately, Hayes was in his facemask, demanding an explanation for the flub. Ken, acting entirely discombobulated, began mumbling and sputtering incoherences. The more he jabbered nonsensically, the more flabbergasted and uncertain Woody became. Finally, with his thoughts thrown completely off-track, Hayes just walked away to a different part of the practice session.

One worrisome facet of the squad, for the otherwise confident Hayes, was the kicking game, which had an extreme lack of experience. In the Hayes view of a well-rounded team, the offense, defense, and specialty teams formed an equilateral triangle, with each corner assuming equal importance. He strongly felt that the kicking game should be a catalyst for both the offense and the defense, providing them with great field position and providing the crucial difference in close games.

Prior to his selection of '76 graduate and four year starter Tom Skladany as a scholarship athlete, Hayes was primarily of the opinion that the kicking game existed only as the weakest contributing member of a game plan, and that a kicker's responsibility was to not lose momentum achieved by the offense or defense. With the success of Skladany and Tom Klaban, coupled with an increased concentration on coverage teams and the field goal as an offensive weapon, Hayes now felt that the kicking game could actually provide the winning difference. Consequently, he concentrated much more extensively on this facet than ever before.

The current crop of kickers was headed up by junior punter Dave McKee, a walk-on from Upper Arlington (Ohio); sophomore placekicker Vlade Janakievski from Whitehall (Ohio); freshman Doug McEldowney of Centerville, Ohio, who seemed the most consistent, though he was prone to great nervousness when Hayes stood close by; and fellow frosh Tom Orosz, who particularly pleased Hayes with his long, high kickoffs.

Janakievski walked onto the squad in mid-season '76, confounding many since at the time he was a starting forward on the OSU soccer team. The 5'7", 145 pound placekicker was not devoid of experience, for he had kicked quite successfully during his prep days.

In this, the year that Hayes was considered to be somewhat de-emphasizing his accustomed brand of power football, his emphasis on learning via the power of words intensified. Each year for most of his coaching career, Hayes sent every recruit a copy of the book *Word Power Made Easy*, with typically emphatic directions to study its contents exhaustively. Hayes had eased up on this regimen in recent years. The incoming '77 class received no such relaxation.

Hayes fervently believed in the philosophy espoused by former Buckeye basketball legend Jerry Lucas, now a renowned learning expert, who felt "...thought begets thought." "Anything we can do legitimately to help youngsters get a better education, a firmer grip on what they are doing and learning, we're willing to take the time to do," Hayes stated. Appropriately, classes concerning the book were formed, and ably instructed by the already overbooked coach.

Woody welcomed an opportunity to actively participate in the education of his team. On one occasion, somewhere around 16 Buckeyes were enrolled in a certain astronomy class. Hayes decided that if his players could learn something new, then so should he. Correspondingly, Woody began attending classes, ensuring that his enrolled team members payed fervent attention. If Hayes could not attend a particular class section, he instructed an assistant to attend; consequently, those players probably learned more astronomy than any other students in the class! Garth Cox recalls that Hayes even took the course quizzes and tests right alongside the students.

One week prior to the season opener, OSU conducted a simulation scrimmage of that upcoming Miami game. Afterwards, the lone drawback seemed to be the hobbled condition of Herman Jones, still bothered by his sore heel. The offense looked particularly sharp, whether directed by Gerald or Castignola. Based on the talented crop of frosh recruits, Hayes hoped that several of them would demand playing time based on their scrimmage excellence.

Many of these outstanding first year players manned the secondary. Vince Skillings, Ray Ellis, Bob Murphy, and Todd Bell all drew attention for their blend of skill and athleticism. Combined with a standout veteran starting unit, the defensive backfield looked to be a strength of the squad. Spearheaded by perhaps the pre-eminent safety in the land, Ray Griffin, the unit also featured Joe Allegro, Mike Guess, and Lenny Mills.

The able linebacking corps boasted Tom Cousineau, and the rough and tumble David Adkins, a senior in his first starting nod. The defensive line was as experienced as the secondary. Byron Cato, Eddie Beamon, Aaron Brown, and Kelton Dansler were all returning starters, with the sole new starter being Paul Ross.

Ross played phenomenally at middle linebacker in the fall '76 camp, yet was somewhat inexplicably switched to an outside lineman position at the start of the season. He was beaten out by Farley Bell for playing time, primarily because he was not entirely familiar with his new role. This time around, Ross looked settled in and was ready to bust some heads. Overall, the defense was quick, powerful, aggressive, knowledgeable, and plentifully deep.

The captains of the '77 team were also a balanced mix of offensive and defensive talent, leadership, and attitude. Named in a vote of their peers to assume the mantle of leadership were Ward, Jeff Logan, Griffin, and Brown. These four seniors had proven with their previous play and off-the-field contributions that they were worthy of this great honor. Each looked forward to the opening game with Miami as a springboard to a national championship run.

New Miami head coach Lou Saban entered his latest job not having coached collegiately since '66. The intervening years saw Saban achieve success with the Buffalo Bills, predominately because his teams featured the remarkable running talents of O.J. Simpson (Orenthal James Simpson, the incomparable 2,000 yard (in one season) gainer, affectionately termed the "Juice," who was barely contained by the Buckeyes in the New Year's Day '69 Rose Bowl).

Saban was now coming to a college program featuring another O.J., the splendid Ottis Anderson. Anderson was coming off a spectacular '76 year in which he narrowly missed eclipsing most of the seasonal school records held by Chuck Foreman.

Because it had been over a decade since Saban had coached in the undergraduate ranks ("I always look for more difficult challenges," Saban said in explaining his return to the collegiate ranks), OSU had little specifics to base their game preparations on. Consequently, OSU prepared for a little of every possible contingency - providing valuable experience they otherwise might never have received.

Around this time, Woody made a shocking concession. Based on his respect for the patriotism and bravery of the British people during the Second World War, Hayes granted a film crew from the British Broadcasting Corporation complete, total access to the Buckeye football program. The BBC was planning a documentary on various facets of Americanism, and chose Hayes as an icon representing sporting leadership.

The film crews followed the OSU players and coaches into team meetings, taping sessions, and even into practice huddles, for most of the fall practices and the first few weeks of the season. Woody explained his unaccustomed generosity by suggesting that perhaps the British could succeed where the U.S. journalists had fallen short.

Disappointingly, Woody perhaps was somewhat chagrined by the end result, which was later televised widely on public broadcasting channels in the States. In the hour-long final cut, the Brits portrayed the Buckeyes somewhat as barbarians, and perhaps made light of the seriousness with which the American brand of football was accorded.

For Mills and Jones, this Hurricane confrontation took on added importance. Each hailed from the city of Miami, and was eager to play his hometown college. Mills was a 6'3", 187 pound blend of hitting power and speed from Killian High, who originally was wooed by Miami and Tennessee, among many others. Mills and his family were good friends with newly appointed Volunteer head coach Doug Dickey, since Leonard had attended football camps run by Dickey since junior high school.

Although the state of Florida featured phenomenal prep talent (Mills captained a '74 state All-Star team which also starred Reggie Kinlaw, attending Oklahoma, and, in '73, Elliot Walker, attending Pittsburgh), the colleges in the state were not yet very successful. Mills was a hard-nosed prep middle linebacker, whose hero was fellow Miamian and NFL star Ted "Mad Stork" Hendricks, and the recruiting needs of OSU in '75 demanded linebackers.

So, Hayes made a patented, influential visit to the Mills household. Woody shook hands with the young athlete, then the Coach cornered Leonard's parents and talked with them alone for several hours while Mills actually left the house. Because Miami and Tennessee fortunes were then at low tide, Mills was already leaning towards a legitimate, immediate bowl contender. His parents were smitten with Woody, so the decision was made to attend OSU.

In fact, Woody made such a typically close bond with Leonard's parents that, prior to the January 1, '77 Orange Bowl contest, Woody personally traveled to the stadium in a limo with Mr. and Mrs. Mills.

Leonard's friends Anderson and Bryan Ferguson chose Miami, and had not been to a bowl game, while Mills had been to a Rose and an Orange Bowl. Upon arriving at Ohio State, Mills was judged slightly small for a linebacker role, and his speed fit well with the needs of the secondary, so he moved to the halfback spot. Despite a long run of nagging injuries, he retained his nose for the ball and the ability to really explode into the ballcarrier.

Jones also had leaned toward Miami, yet was similarly swayed by the impact of Woody and the colorful OSU tradition. Jones eagerly awaited the renewal of his ferocious competition with the Hurricane defensive back Ferguson, who had teamed with Mills in high school to give Herman fits. Jones also was bothered by injuries throughout his Buckeye career, though his potential as a game-breaker seemed unlimited.

Other standouts for the Saban-led 'Canes were fleet quarterback E.J. Baker, who reminded many of a slightly skinnier (if that is possible) Gerald, and the schools best athlete and physical specimen, 6'3", 245 pound middle guard Don Latimer. Though Saban had undergone open heart surgery over the summer, he felt healthy and confident that his new team could contend for national recognition. Saban won championships as a player for the Cleveland Browns, and could always recognize talent.

This game was also a homecoming of sorts for Hurricane defensive backfield coach Len Fontes, who played in the secondary for Hayes on the '57 OSU national championship team.

Interestingly, Hayes deserved a lot of credit for the resurgence of the Miami program. During the December/January stay in the city, while practicing for the Orange Bowl, Woody lent his name and considerable reputation to various fundraising efforts for the struggling Hurricane gridiron program. Coupled with the hiring of the well-regarded and experienced Saban, the efforts of Hayes did much to legitimize the sport at Miami.

Woody also got the word out among his plentiful contacts about the fantastic infrastructure, in terms of facilities and philosophies, which the school was developing. Because of recent low fortunes, contemplation had even been given by Miami administrators to shutting down the sport, much as cross-state Tampa University did. In reflection, based on the national dominance of the Hurricanes from the early '80's on, this was a sound decision not to do so.

CHAPTER TWO: MIAMI

The sleek, fleet, high-powered OSU offense got off to a slow start in the home opener; then was disturbingly derailed by injuries. Senior Jeff Logan, on a quest for another banner 1,000 yard season, was felled early in the contest with an extremely severe ankle sprain.

In spite of the injury to Logan, OSU got on the board first. A stiff Buckeye defense absolutely curtailed the Miami rushing attack throughout the first quarter and gave increasingly improved field position to the home team. Finally, into the second quarter, OSU managed a short drive which led to a 31 yard Janakievski field goal. Vlade was given the job just days before the opener after a fierce competition with the other candidates.

The replacement for Logan was sophomore Ricky Johnson, whose entrance ignited the sluggish Buckeye offense. As Johnson entered the game, OSU was pinned on their own seven yard line, compliments of a fine Robert Rajsich punt. Johnson immediately exploded for gains of 32, eight, and four yards during the drive, which culminated in a 21 yard pitchout sweep to Springs for the only touchdown of the game.

The remainder of the half passed with few offensive fireworks. Following the halftime pause, Johnson sustained a deep thigh bruise and also sprained his knee. Both injuries occurred on the same play. Ricky left the contest having accrued 64 yards on seven carries; most of the yards accumulated with tremendous second effort following the initial hit. The fine backup tandem of sophomores, the excitable Ricardo Volley and Campbell, was pressed into action.

Due to the various injuries and his own blossoming talent, Springs thus became the featured highlight of the Buckeye offense. Ron finished with a powerful 114 yards rushing, despite running into Latimer and company, who were specifically keying on him. With Springs as the only consistent offensive threat, OSU managed just one drive, during this half, that reached scoring territory. That solitary chance went past, as Janakievski had a 45 yard field goal attempt blocked in the third quarter.

Miami abandoned the running game altogether in the second half. Every consequent pass attempt by Baker was thrown into a fierce OSU rush; the elusive Baker was dropped five times for losses. Nevertheless, he somehow managed to evade the constant harassment enough to lead the Hurricanes into scoring position late in the third quarter. His short passes were grudgingly conceded by OSU, in lieu of longer gains, although the plethora of short completions allowed Miami to march downfield.

On the final play of the period, as a visitor score seemed imminent, Cousineau stepped in front of another short pass and made the theft. Saban considered this to be the play which clinched the OSU victory, for the fourth period was essentially a defensive struggle, with OSU expediently running out the clock when on offense.

For the afternoon, the harried Baker somehow managed to complete 15 of 30 passes for 210 yards, with two critical interceptions. The self-destructing Hurricane offense also fumbled on four occasions, although they lost just one. Several drives were disrupted by the miscues, however. Anderson was limited to 36 yards on 12 carries, receiving vicious treatment from his hosts every time he touched the ball.

On the OSU side, Gerald connected on six of nine passes, for 60 yards, throwing one interception. Added to the injury list was Ray Griffin, who incurred a nasty hip pointer early in the game. In the teeth of horrendous pain, he continued playing, contributing an interception which he brought back 38 exciting yards. Ray also nearly busted the second half kickoff for a score, finally being tripped up after dashing 47 yards.

Following the 10-0 victory, Hayes was very happy with the defensive outing. The Buckeyes held Miami to a miniscule net of 13 yards on the ground, and according to new defensive line coach Dave Adolph, achieved nine of their ten appointed goals. Dansler fronted the fierce forward wall, earning 8.5 Buckeye leaves for his efforts, as the linebacker and secondary units also repelled the few trespasses into their regions.

Ominously, Hayes said that OSU must play better to even have a chance to win their next game, Minnesota, particularly without Logan or Johnson in the lineup. Hayes also admitted that the offense must pass more in order to propel the running game into high gear.

At his weekly Monday press luncheon, Hayes flabbergasted everyone present by hinting that Ray Griffin was perhaps being moved to tailback to shore up that weakened position. Griffin had not played on offense since switching to the safety spot in the spring of his sophomore year. Throughout the week, Griffin indeed did take some repetitions at his old spot, as he and the assistant coaches joked about and took a lighthearted approach to the move.

In a particularly strange twist, the pre-game press packet for the upcoming game featured Ray and focused on his pleasure at switching to the defensive side of the field. Although Logan insisted his ankle felt considerably better, Dr. Murphy reported that Jeff was out of commission at least ten days and Johnson would most likely miss a week or so.

Meanwhile, Minnesota head coach Cal Stoll was more concerned with his own squad. With the departure of the phenomenally talented quarterback Tony Dungy to the NFL (coincidentally, he was immediately switched to a safety position), the Gophers had implemented the tricky wing T offense as the basis of their attack. In their opening game, a 10-7 win over Western Michigan, only six turnovers and ten penalties by the Gophers kept the victorious margin so low. New signalcaller Wendell Avery directed the run-oriented offense which included sophomore back Jeff Thompson and the promising frosh halfback, Marion Barber.

On the defensive ledger, nine of the eleven '76 Gopher starters returned, prompting many to think that this could be the best team in the Stoll reign. Since OSU barely escaped with a 9-3 win in the '76 confrontation, hope was high for a Minnesota victory.

Saturday was also induction day for the charter members of the newly christened Ohio State Sports Hall of Fame. The star-studded list of inductees included, among the 23 great names, such football legends as: L.W. St. John, the first OSU athletic director, who served in that capacity from '12-'47; John Wilce, the head coach who guided OSU to their first Rose Bowl appearance in '21; Ernie Godfrey, a fixture as an assistant coach from '29-'61; Wes Fesler, star player, and later successful head coach from '47-'50; Bill Willis, legendary two-way performer from '42-'44; and Jim Parker, universally conceded as perhaps the greatest offensive lineman in college football history. Also inducted were Heisman winners Les Horvath, Vic Janowicz, and Howard "Hop" Cassady.

The weekend also played host to a memorable reunion for the '17 Buckeye football team. The several remaining survivors of that bygone era gathered and praised the man who, almost singlehandedly, put the OSU football program in the national eye. This fantastic athlete, Chic Harley, was also being posthumously inducted into the school Hall of Fame this Saturday. Each '17 squad member remembered the three-time All-American Harley as at least the equal of, if not slightly better than, the legendary Illinois back Red Grange. The '17 Bucks, guided by Wilce, went 8-0-1 in capturing their second straight conference crown.

Continuing in this reminiscent vein, this Saturday was also the first matchup between in-state rivals Iowa and Iowa State since '34. A standout participant in that long-ago game was Ike Hayes, older brother to Woody. Ike starred at guard in that Cyclone victory. Although Ike was undersized at 5'6" and 158 fighting pounds, Woody knew him to be "...strong as an ox." Adoringly, Woody recalled one of his favorite people, a man who influenced his younger brother in ways perhaps Woody could not even acknowledge.

Ike was considered too small to play for Ohio State, so he took his feisty talents and became a little college All-American for the Cyclones. "He was some football player," recalled Woody. "...Captain of his team his senior year... and what a character. The first time you met him, you'd feel as though he was your best friend."

Sadly, Ike passed away shortly after OSU won the national title with a victory in the '55 Rose Bowl. Ike was a much-too-young 43 when he went to meet his maker, and the successful veterinarian was still very much missed by his younger brother.

CHAPTER THREE: MINNESOTA

In this, a weekend of remembrances, the Buckeyes played a game to remember. The expected offensive juggernaut at last made an appearance, sparked by Gerald and Springs. These two fronted an attack which erupted for 30 first downs, accumulating 385 rushing and 518 total yards.

Perhaps the sole Gopher highlight was the third quarter kickoff return by Bobby Weber, who fielded the kick several yards deep in the end zone, then weaved and sprinted the entire length of the field for the only Minnesota score. In spite of the unseasonable 85 degree temperature, the Buckeyes never relented, as their supreme conditioning overpowered both the elements and the opposition.

True to the Miami post-game comments of Hayes, OSU came out firing. The home team moved crisply down the field as Jones grabbed a 29 yard toss to open the afternoon scoring. Jones finished with three clutch receptions for 87 yards.

A marathon 16 play, 78 yard drive was undertaken on the next OSU possession, which Janakievski capped with a short field goal.

Ohio State soon got the ball back, and Springs scampered 33 yards, putting Volley into position for a two yard bullish touchdown run. Springs was a workhorse on this muggy day, ending with 27 grueling carries for 147 yards. At the half, OSU was well in command, leading 17-0.

Weber inched the Gophers a bit closer with his spectacular return, only to see the extra point flubbed, yet even that score was neutralized when OSU drove 87 yards in 12 plays, which included an outstanding delivery to Jones for 35 yards. Gerald exited following this touchdown drive, departing with 63 rushing yards and five of seven passing accuracy for an additional 95 yards.

Castignola entered for a slight taste of game experience, and acquitted himself very handily, nailing newly-appointed wide receiver Doug Donley with a beautiful 38 yard scoring toss.

For the final scoring drive of the day, Strahine came in and handed off to the frosh backfield of Joel Payton and Calvin Murray, as OSU marched right down the field to make the final score 38-6.

Throughout the scorching day, the OSU defense was relentless, holding the Gophers to 123 rushing yards on 37 attempts. Avery was pressured endlessly by Ross in particular, and the front line pass rush harassed Wendell enough to allow just one completion in seven tries. Cousineau contributed 15 tackles from his middle slot.

Ray Griffin did indeed play tailback on this day, starting tentatively and warming up as he reacquainted himself at finding holes to run through. Ray finished with a flourish, to total 58 yards on 14 carries. A relaxed Hayes held his enthusiasm in check after the game, joking that due to the success of Ray, Chris Ward would move to fullback.

Hayes contended that a harsh rain on Friday night made the playing surface perfect to run on, and he commented that the excessive heat had gradually worn down the Gophers and not the deeper Buckeye squad. Woody complimented Volley on his fiery performance, and praised Beamon, Brown, Ross, Adkins, Dansler, Cato, and Mills for their intense level of play. Gerald received 8.5 Buckeye leaves for his strong leadership, Ward was awarded 6.5, and Cousineau plastered four leaves on his helmet. Cato and Orosz were accorded three leaves each.

Woody also acknowledged with great pride the halftime ovation accorded Hall of Fame inductee John Havlicek. Hayes always referred to this Boston Celtic star as the "...greatest athlete I've ever seen." In the ceremony, which featured long and continuous applause for the celebrated inductees, Havlicek received by far the most stupendous ovation, as the screaming throng of 87,799 rose as one to drown out the cheers accorded to the other honorees.

It is enlightening to point out that Hayes recruited Havlicek as a quarterback when the prep star first entered Ohio State, yet agreed to abide with the wishes of Fred Taylor and Havlicek himself, in advising the talented Hondo to remain on the hardwood, hopefully for the greater good of the university. As seen in this light, the resulting success of Havlicek meant all the more to Hayes.

With two important victories under their belts, OSU could now look undistracted toward one of the most ballyhooed and anticipated games of any Ohio State season. The third ranked Buckeyes now faced the fourth ranked Sooners of Oklahoma in a tremendously even matchup of explosive offenses, historically successful programs, and stupendously successful coaches.

This game was the brainchild of former Buckeye All-American Gomer Jones, who had scheduled this contest way back in the '60's. Jones was the athletic director of Oklahoma at that time, and fervently wanted to play his alma mater. Over a decade later, he had his wish.

The '77 Sooner offense was, in the estimation of Hayes, the fastest and most volatile system in the entire country. Oklahoma was coming off a 62-24 crushing win against Utah. Starting quarterback Thomas Lott had not played in that game because of a nerve injury to his knee, and the Sooners still did not skip a beat. Lott, regarded by many observers as the best wishbone operator ever at a school long noted for such talent, was again practicing with the first team and appeared healthy.

The remainder of the Sooner backfield included the tremendous breakaway threats Elvis Peacock, Billy Sims, and rampaging fullback Kenny King. It seemed the only way OU was ever halted on offense was by their own mistakes. The complicated wishbone was noted for producing many fumbles and resulting in plenty of penalties, though these drawbacks were usually more than offset by a wave of scoring the attack also spawned. The Sooners had fumbled an incredible 17 times in the first two games of '77, though some of these were attributed to the absence of Lott.

Senior Dean Blevins stepped in for Lott this year, temporarily reclaiming the starting role he held the previous year. Blevins lost his starting spot when a groin infection sidelined him, and Lott played so well that Blevins remained on the bench. Blevins was a fine athlete who also lettered in basketball for the Sooners, yet even he was being pressed for playing time by the shifty frosh Jay Jimerson.

On defense, the Sooners were an improving lot, spearheaded by a big hitter, linebacker Daryl Hunt, and the ailing middle guard Reggie Kinlaw. Kinlaw was far below par health-wise, and his status for the game was heavily in doubt. In his absence, the Sooners would be hard-pressed to stop the powerful OSU running game.

Safety Zac Henderson was among the finest in the country, comparing very favorably to Griffin and holding an edge in experience. It is ironic that perhaps the top two safeties in collegiate ball would have a chance to compete directly against each other, if Ray remained on offense.

The injury situation for OSU was not looking too bad. Logan was recuperating nicely, although the knee injury to Johnson was proving more severe than originally thought. Center Tim Vogler strained his knee during practice and was expected to miss about two weeks; the starting OU center, Jody Farthing, was also out of commission with an injury. Doug Porter, who handled all long snapping chores for the Buckeyes, had stepped into the Vogler void quite nicely.

On a similarly pleasant note, Tom Roche, whose eligibility status had been in doubt due to some academic troubles, was declared eligible and would be available for reserve duty.

Pressed for a prediction on the upcoming clash of titans, on Monday Hayes stated, "It will be a relatively high scoring" affair. The very next day, Hayes admitted that games like these, "...usually don't turn out to be high scoring" affairs. Admittedly, this outcome was very tough to gauge, for either of the Hayes predictions seemed equally likely. Interestingly, Hayes turned out to be correct with each of his theories, with one right assumption per each half of play.

Oklahoma coach Barry Switzer was in his fifth year at the helm. He contended that this game should vault the victor onto a national championship level. Emanating from a man who had not lost until his 31st game as a head coach, and had won back-to-back mythical national championships in '74 and '75 (OU was on probation for part of this time and thus ineligible for a legitimate national title), this contention was not taken lightly.

Overall, Switzer had compiled a 43-3-2 record at OU, had captured four consecutive Big 8 titles (or shares thereof), and had won both bowl games the Sooners were invited to. Switzer was proving to be the latest, and to some the greatest, in a legacy of fine Sooner coaches, including his successors Chuck Fairbanks and Bud Wilkinson.

Switzer was particularly enamored with and fearful of Gerald, whom he called "...as quick as a hiccup." Gerald, much like his counterpart Lott, had a seeming knack to disappear right before a tackler could grasp him. Buckeye quarterback coach Chaump agreed that this lightning-like quickness indeed seemed magical. "I wouldn't trade him for any other quarterback in the country in terms of quickness," Chaump related. A junior, Gerald had immeasurably improved from his sophomoric play in '76, when his inexperience was occasionally made painfully obvious.

Rod admitted: "I have a better understanding of our offense and I am much more relaxed... this year I hope to play more on instinct... I want to play on a much more consistent level."

Despite the tone of despair, his sophomore year had not been all depression, however. He finished as the third leading Buckeye rusher, despite the four game layoff, with a very respectable 465 yards. His meager completion percentage (35%) was a factor not only of inexperience, but was also due to a slight case of bursitis in his (right) throwing shoulder and a painfully dislocated finger on his throwing hand.

In '77, Gerald was much stronger physically, thanks to a stepped-up conditioning program, and was much better at reading the myriad of defensive coverages thrown his way. With the experience provided by the year of partial failures, Gerald also was not as likely to force the ball into ill-advised coverages, although his confidence in his arm remained intact.

Switzer also spoke very highly of Hayes. "I don't think Woody Hayes' true image has been presented in the press," Barry emphatically stated. Switzer humorously recounted the story of his first meeting with Hayes. In the early '70's, during Title IX hearings in Washington, D.C., the two ate dinner and had breakfast together. The elder Hayes treated the young Sooner like a son, as the two discussed the issues and nuances of their shared passion, football.

After the series of enjoyable conversations, Hayes, without warning, proceeded to sternly lecture Switzer on the hazards of putting too much sauce on his food, warning that the practice would result in a severe hardening of the arteries. The psuedo-diatribe was of course delivered in the full throttle, typically confrontational Hayes style, and Switzer could not help but be amused at its recanting.

The key for the OSU defense seemed to rest in the continuing success of the line in funnelling plays and ballcarriers to the middle. The OSU defense was designed to allow the middle linebackers, Adkins and Cousineau, to proceed unobstructed to the path of the play, relying on the down linemen to tie up available blockers. Adkins was especially adept at head-on collisions, while Cousineau roamed sideline to sideline, meting out fiercer punishment via lateral pursuit.

George Hill glowingly said, "Wherever the ball is, is where Tom will be." Cousineau derived considerably more pleasure in delivering hits than in taking a hit on one of his frequent interceptions, as pass coverage was a forte of the nimble linebacker. Many compared Cousineau to former Buckeye Gradishar, for like Randy, Tom was never satisfied with his play. "I feel there is always room for improvement," said Tom, and the chiseled junior also claimed he was the first player Woody ever saw who smiled as he made a tackle.

CHAPTER FOUR: OKLAHOMA

On the day of the big game, Cousineau was not smiling much, unfortunately. In front of an intent national TV audience, 88,119 feverish Ohio Stadium occupants, and the largest press contingent ever seen on the banks of the Olentangy, OSU and OU played a game for the ages. Ohio State first appeared doomed to a crushing defeat, in the face of an insanely fast OU scoring burst, then battled resolutely back to take a late lead, only to finally be vanquished by the visitors on a last second field goal.

The loss was among the most bitter, disappointing outcomes in the long history of OSU football, for the '77 team poured every last ounce of emotion towards winning the contest, only to emerge just one point shy. As their triumph was astoundingly snatched from them, the tears flowed freely and unashamedly.

At the outset, it never appeared that OSU would even be in contention to win this contest. Oklahoma burst out of the blocks and completely dominated the first period of play. The Sooners took the opening kickoff and charged 61 yards in six plays for the initial touchdown. The scoring play came on a peculiar happenstance, as Peacock picked up a Lott fumble, which bounced unexpectedly and perfectly into his hands, and dashed 33 yards to paydirt without breaking stride.

Just seconds after the ensuing kickoff, a dazed OSU crowd became virtually paralyzed when Gerald fumbled the first OSU snap from center and Oklahoma's George Cumby recovered. On the very next play, Cousineau was leveled by a wall of OU blockers, separated his shoulder, and was done for the day. The stunned, shell-shocked OSU defense watched almost hopelessly as Sims burst 15 yards for a second Sooner touchdown.

The reeling Buckeyes were unable to gain a first down on either of their next two possessions. Oklahoma furthered the rout by putting together respective drives of eleven plays for 43 yards and nine plays for 33 yards, each short drive culminating in successful Uwe von Schamann field goals. The OU lead appeared insurmountable at 20-0, with time still remaining in the first quarter.

Just as quickly as OU built their commanding lead, the tempo shifted urgently to the home team. Gerald began dropping back into the pocket and displaying the threat of a pass, which froze the OU linebackers and did not allow the Sooner secondary to rush up and help contain the run. The OSU running backs began to run wild, and their confidence grew as large as the holes they ran to daylight through. The Buckeyes ground out an exquisite 80 yard drive, finishing with a 30 yard dart by Springs for the initial OSU score.

On the second play following this score, Lott again fumbled, with OSU making the recovery deep in Sooner territory. Immediately, Gerald broke loose for a 19 yard scoring run.

After the OSU defense repeatedly repulsed the Sooner attack late in the second quarter, OSU twice drove deep into Oklahoma territory. On these two occasions late in the half, once at the 12 yard line and the other at the 25, Hayes spurned field goal attempts. "We were behind in the game and had to score TD's," he reasoned afterwards, but in both instances, OSU was stopped on downs and came away with zero points. The decisions to make it into the end zone, seemingly wise at the time, were widely criticized by viewers after the fact.

This perfect hindsight, however, is not a luxury afforded to head coaches in the heat of a nationally televised game of the ages. Hayes believed that if OSU expected or deserved to win this or any game, they must be able to convert short yardage and high percentage fourth down opportunities. In this game, they failed to convert and paid the price. The Bucks did go in at the half somewhat buoyed by their second score, trailing just 20-14, and their late offensive and defensive prowess renewed the hope to scratch and claw ahead of the slumping Sooners.

Coming out of the halftime break, the Buckeyes, on their second opportunity, moved 52 yards in nine plays. Payton bulled over from the one, Janakievski nailed the extra point, and incredibly, OSU led 21-20. On the ensuing Sooner drive, Lott injured his left knee and was forced to exit the brutal theater of combat. Blevins entered, only to have his pass picked off by Dansler at the OU 33.

Already missing one marquee quarterback, the game lost another when Gerald was belted in the head and suffered a twisted neck on only the third play of the ensuing drive. Castignola came on and blithely fired a 16 yard bullet which Jimmy Moore made a spectacular catch of in the end zone, furthering the score to 28-20, with 4:44 left in the third quarter.

For the remainder of the third and most of the fourth quarter, the two teams traded punts and short drives, as both defenses really put the clamps on the backup quarterbacks. With time running down to 6:24 remaining, the OU wishbone offense really began clicking for the first time since they built their long-since-disappeared 20 point lead.

The Sooners achieved possession through a Castignola fumble, and drove 57 yards in 13 tough plays. On a fourth down and four situation from the OSU 12, OU was denied the first down on an inspired defensive stand. This outstanding play was negated, however, by an offsides call on the Buckeyes, prolonging the Sooner drive. Four plays after this fresh life was granted, Peacock took a pitch and dove over from the one.

Needing a two point conversion to tie the game, the Sooners tried the same exact pitch play to Peacock. Tom Blinco, filling in admirably for Cousineau, along with Ross and Mike Guess, read the play correctly, breaking through to dump Elvis for no gain.

Everyone in the audience knew that an on-sides kick was forthcoming, and OSU sent in the so-called "hands" team to thwart the kick of von Schamann. Amazingly, the bounding kick was bobbled and Mike Baab of Oklahoma recovered. With 1:21 left on the clock, OU had the ball just past midfield. In four quick plays, including a clutch flip from Blevins to Steve Rhodes for a gain of 18, OU got the ball to the OSU 23 yard line. Von Schamann trotted into the teeth of a hostile crowd, awaiting the opportunity to try a 41 yard field goal which would either snatch victory from the grasp of defeat or fall gallantly short in a comeback effort.

In a wonderfully ironic moment prolonged by a time-out taken to magnify the pressure, the German born von Schamann led the OSU Block O student section in rousing chants of "Block that kick, block that kick!" With just three seconds left on the clock, Uwe lifted his kick straight through the uprights, giving OU the dramatic 29-28 victory.

The initial post-game comment of Hayes was completely apropos. "To hell with the most exciting game," Woody cried in response to a reporter's comment that the game was the most exciting he'd ever witnessed. "I'd rather have them drab as hell and win," Woody curtly explained. Hayes also dealt with many questions regarding an altercation with an Oklahoma student manager immediately following the game.

Captured on live television, the isolated film clip seemed to show Hayes rudely rebuke the student's consoling handshake with a sharp left jab. As Hayes explained, and as complete coverage of game films later corroborated, the handshake of the student manager was extended only after the student had rashly tried to grab the hat off of Woody's head. Later, the OU student admitted he had tried to take the trademark hat as a souvenir.

As it was widely and incorrectly reported, this incident served to further the Hayes reputation as a sore loser, which of course he admittedly was, though not in the sense that this story was portraying. Hayes firmly believed the adage "Show me a good loser and I'll show you a loser."

Despite the crushing loss, Hayes took solace in the effort of his squad in this dramatically intense confrontation. Even after the loss of Cousineau, the OSU defense had really picked up after the flat start, especially in the face of a wonderfully talented opponent. "It was an extremely hard-hitting game," Hayes proudly recalled, and there was no shame or disgrace in losing to such a fine team as Oklahoma.

On the Sooner side of the statistical ledger, Lott gained 43 rushing yards in 12 carries prior to his injury, and was pounded on virtually each play by the aggressively pursuing Buck defense. Peacock ran for 58 yards in 11 carries, as he was pretty much contained after his fortunate fumble romp. Sims contributed 60 yards on his 11 rushes, confounding the stacked OSU defenders with the same moves which carried him to the '78 Heisman, and future fame with the Detroit Lions. King, whom OSU coaches possibly feared the most heading into the game, was held to nine rushes for 29 yards, while dangerous David Overstreet was similarly contained, garnering 25 yards on 12 carries. The backup pivot men in the 'bone, Blevins and Jimerson, were held in check, with Jimerson gaining just four yards on ten rushing attempts and Blevins seven on his three tries.

Oklahoma capitalized on critical Buckeye turnovers and broke free for several big plays, yet could rarely muster a sustained drive. Isolated instances of greatness won this game, rather than consistency.

The OSU defense was keyed by the formidable presence of Adkins, who was seemingly involved in every play. He finished with 24 tackles, and was usually the first Buck to stick his nose into a Sooner. There were no statistic-padding pile-ons for Adkins, just plain hard hits, even as he played with a bad shoulder bruise incurred during the game.

Brown had an equally amazing 17 tackles from his interior spot, Ross and Dansler participated in 15 stops each, and Mills added 13 stops from his backfield spot. Mills also came up with two pivotal fumble recoveries, while Beamon added 11 tackles and Blinco ten fierce stops in the violent game.

Although Gerald did not complete a pass in his four attempts, he did gain 37 tough yards on 16 option runs and scrambles. Springs led the way with 64 yards in 14 carries, Griffin made a difficult catch for a 13 yard gain and picked up 16 yards in seven rushes, and Logan carried once in brief appearances. Jeff was limited to blocking and decoy purposes, due to his injury, yet volunteered to enter the contest as the Bucks got off to the disastrous start.

With Springs and Griffin playing unfamiliar roles, Hayes agreed that the presence of his senior leader might help. Sure enough, the insertion of Jeff did seem to stabilize the heretofore bumbling offense, and with Springs back at his accustomed tailback spot, the ground game picked up. Payton contributed 25 yards on nine tough, short-yardage attempts, as he did an adequate job in some stressful situations, especially for a freshman.

Still, the Bucks were inconsistent at best from the robust T, and all in all, the rugged OU defense proved almost impenetrable, especially after Gerald went down. With the exception of their two second quarter scoring drives, the home team also could muster little sustained offensive success. This great game was essentially a defensive battle, punctuated by momentum shifting turnovers and the occasional offensive breakthrough past two intensely driven masses of defenders. Except for the outcome, this was just the sort of game which the war historian Hayes loved.

Perhaps the most joyous moment of this weekend was the reunion of the '42 Buckeye national championship team. Paul Brown was the architect of that team's phenomenal success, and had recently stepped down from his head spot with the Cincinnati Bengals, the second professional team Brown founded and brought to prominence. The first team, of course, bore his name, and much of the glorious achievements of the Browns came via members of this '42 Buckeye team.

Brown was effusive in his thanks to the surviving members of this close group, who included Bill Willis, Lin Houston, Chuck Csuri, Jack Dugger, Bill Hackett, and Les Horvath. Brown was a gigantic influence on the younger Hayes; witness the Brown philosophy on leadership by a head coach: "Complete control. There is no other way for a team to operate and be a winner."

Even in the midst of the heartbreaking loss to Oklahoma, the delight and wonderful reminiscences of this fantastic '42 team were not dampened. Like the legacy of former players often demonstrated by Hayes' teams, this '42 group boasted of far-reaching successes not only in football, but in business, teaching, and service to country. A marvelously in-depth profile of this team may be found in *Expanding Your Horizons*, written and compiled by a member of that squad, Dr. Donald Steinberg.

Bouncing back from the one point loss was a tough task, yet Hayes believed his team had the fortitude to do so. As he often said: "Football players are pretty resilient people - they have to be." Rebounding was made somewhat easier by the comforting news that Cousineau might only miss one week, and that the deep shoulder bruise suffered by Adkins was not as severe as originally believed. Alex Gibbs reiterated the Hayes assertion that the hitting in the OU game, exemplified by the pugnacious Adkins, was the most savage and brutal he'd ever seen.

Review of game films brought honors to Adkins and Ross as the top defenders, while Moore was praised not only for his touchdown catch but more so for his sterling block which sprang Springs to his long touchdown run. Ray Griffin was also moved exclusively back to the safety spot this week, in light of pass-happy Southern Methodist being next on the schedule.

The game was to be played in Dallas, so native son Gerald (who missed several days in recuperating from the wrenching high tackle which drove him from the OU contest) was exuberantly looking forward to his collegiate homecoming. Not only would many classmates and admirers from his South Oak Cliff High days be in attendance, his father had also arranged for over 2,000 of his congregation's parishioners to attend as well. Interest in the Buckeye-Mustang matchup was so great that Hayes himself had made a pre-season promotional trek to the Southwest to further publicize the affair.

The teams had met only seven times previously, with the lone SMU win occurring way back in '50. That was the final year of the Wes Fesler reign at OSU, and the game kicked off that season. Mustang quarterback Fred Benners threw for an extraordinary 415 yards in the second half alone, keying a 32-27 comeback win.

In '77, SMU was led by another hotshot passer, Mike Ford, who loved to throw as often as possible. The Mustang offense, masterminded by head coach and Westerville (Ohio) High '59 grad Ron Meyer, featured a plenitude of formations with many shifts. Emmanuel Tolbert was the go-to receiver in the pass-conscious attack.

Interestingly, Meyer credited Hayes and star back Hop Cassady as spurring his lifelong interest in the game of football. Meyer grew up a devoted OSU fan in the early '50's, and imitated the moves of Cassady in many a suburban sandlot game. Meyer felt, "...most people just don't realize the greatness...," of Woody Hayes, and had based many of his own coaching principles on the tenets of Woody.

Certainly an individual who did not court the favor of Hayes, at least this week, was fledgling central Ohio WCMH-TV sports reporter Marty Reid. Primarily because of the incident with the OU student manager, Reid delivered a stinging on-air commentary which bashed Hayes for his decided lack of sportsmanship. This diatribe was among the first in what became a running series of Reid criticisms seemingly directed at Hayes, sowing the seeds for numerous future confrontations.

Curiously, the newsman mentor to Reid, Jimmy Crum, had also gone through his battles with Hayes. Several years previously, Hayes had lashed into a young sideline photographer during a surprisingly tight ball game, severely intimidating and frightening the novice cameraman, whose only transgression was to capture on celluloid the sideline antics of a disturbed Woody. After that game, and following the obligatory press conference, Crum chastened Woody for his actions, expressly calling them "horsebleep."

For six full months following that leveling, Woody treated Crum as a leper, as a complete persona non grata. Eventually, Crum ran into Hayes at an eatery, and inquired if Woody was still sore at him. Ultimately, in the course of their conversation, Hayes revealed he did not bear a grudge against Crum, and actually respected Jimmy for speaking his mind and standing his ground. Neither of the proud men ever apologized, yet each gained renewed respect for the other after this period.

From that time on, Woody was outrageously accommodating toward Crum, especially in regards to charitable and promotional requests.

Although his actions may have occasionally strayed from his ideals, deep inside Woody respected those who spoke their mind, intelligently articulated their opinion, and resolutely maintained that opinion in the face of all opposition. After all, that was exactly how he acted, and Woody steadfastly admired unflinching honesty and determination. As contemporary Grambling coach Eddie Robinson stated, "If a man doesn't stand up for what he believes in, he isn't worth a damn." Hayes was always standing in support of his beliefs.

Hayes was not the lone member of the coaching fraternity on controversial ground this week. Schembechler had been feverish in his criticism of the officiating both during and after his Wolverines' matchup with Navy. His comments were deemed so public and fiery that conference commissioner Duke was compelled to censure any future dialogues by the pugnacious Bo. The reprimand from Duke did not deter Schembechler, though. Following the next UM game, with Texas A&M, Bo ripped into the officials again in a post-game press conference. Strangely, Duke offered no further rebuttals after the latest Bo tiff, perhaps wisely deciding to let (relatively) sleeping wolverines alone.

CHAPTER FIVE: SOUTHERN METHODIST

Gerald could not have asked for a better homecoming come Saturday. The junior triumphantly paved the way in a 35-7 OSU romp. In the first Buckeye scoring drive alone, Gerald popped for three long gainers, all through the air. The home team had stopped OSU cold on the visitor's two opening possessions, so a scrambling Gerald took over on the third opportunity.

Rod drilled a pass to Campbell for 20 yards, connected with Moore on a thrilling 31 yard pickup, then flipped the ball on a dead run to Harrell for a gain of 13. A momentarily healthy Logan topped off the mammoth 88 yard scoring drive with a 16 yard sweep into the end zone.

On the ensuing SMU possession, a jumping Beamon picked off a deflected Ford pass on the Mustang 33. On the very first OSU play after that turnover, Gerald somehow salvaged a busted play to dash in for a second score. Just two plays later, Dansler intercepted a Ford pass. In just six plays, OSU traveled 34 yards, with Payton hurdling over the goal line from two yards out. Suddenly, OSU led 21-0.

From that point on, the Mustangs futilely attempted to catch up, predominately through the air. In the second quarter alone, the freshman flinger Ford suffered three interceptions, each coming in the Buckeye end zone, just as it appeared the Mustangs might score. Ford ended the day with 19 completions in 36 attempts for 273 yards, yet tossed an ungodly seven interceptions.

Southern Methodist was able to drive into scoring position on repeated occasions, only to be thwarted each time by an interception. Sophomore Guess tied a school record (held jointly by Arnold Chonko, Bruce Ruhl, Fred Bruney, and Craig Cassady) with three pickoffs of Ford passes.

The disappointed Dallas crowd saw SMU score their lone touchdown with 10:37 remaining in the game; the only home highlight after that was a block of a Janakievski field goal attempt with 3:48 left on the clock. Coupled with an earlier block of an OSU punt, Meyer could at least take pride in the play of the Mustang specialty teams.

Gerald ended with five completions in eight attempts, for a total of 88 timely yards. Payton received rave reviews for his play, which included a 44 yard touchdown gallop in the second half. Joel finished with 91 yards on 12 carries. Campbell was the workhorse on this day, accumulating 92 yards on 20 time-consuming carries.

Disappointingly, Logan reinjured his ankle shortly after his nifty scoring run. Beamon was also stricken with a bad ankle sprain, while Mills suffered a severe concussion.

The center spot proved especially vulnerable to injuries. Vogler re-injured his damaged knee right before game time, and Porter later sustained a knee injury of his own on the first play of the game. Mark Lang assumed the snapping responsibilities after that, and somehow emerged unscathed.

Despite their injuries, a very pleased Hayes praised the defensive effort, particularly in defending the airwaves, as "...the best it ever has been." Meyer acknowledged the Buckeye excellence as well, ruing the OSU secondary schemes which tripped up his young, inexperienced quarterback. Meyer was proud of the effort put forth by his team, although the Bucks were simply too much on this evening.

Ohio State completely shut down the hitherto strong Mustang running game, as backs Art Whittington and Paul Rice could muster a mere 31 yards on 17 combined carries. Forced into passing almost exclusively on each down, a harried Ford was manipulated into attempts against camouflaged coverages, which OSU capitalized on by grabbing many ill-advised tosses.

The Buckeye mastery of the airwaves continued even following this game. A mutual friend of Storer and Garth Cox somehow materialized on the sidelines of the Cotton Bowl after the game, yet did not have a way home, so the zany pair decided to smuggle their pal back to Columbus. Shielded by the immense frames of Mark Sullivan and Tim Burke, and wearing an official scarlet team blazer, the castaway made it onto the flight. Once the plane was off the ground, Billy Hill discovered the additional passenger, yet was harriedly convinced to keep the secret. Somehow, the flight landed and the guest escaped, undetected.

Storer was a refreshing, creative, free spirit who defied pigeonholing. An extremely talented painter and art major, Storer was also a very accomplished performer on the gridiron. After one outstanding game, Storer was selected to appear on the local Hayes television program. This appearance interrupted a typically wild post-game bash at the home Greg shared with Cox and Tim Vogler, the domain which should have served as the model for the soon-popular Delta House in the movie "Animal House."

Typically, Woody skewed his questions for the players on the show so they could be answered quite simply. Unexpectedly, Hayes asked a somewhat-inebriated Storer a rare question requiring more than the traditional monosyllabic response, and Greg took off on an indecipherable tangent. Amazingly, since Greg was such an independent thinker normally, this answer was not considered all that extraordinary.

As a further example of the fluid tight end's eccentric behavior, Storer elected to have a swirling mass of butterflies tattooed on his calf (the popular tattoo craze among the Buckeyes, along with the adoption of a pierced ear, was apparently begun by the irrepressible, big-city native Nick Buonamici).

This success against the pass-prevalent Mustangs boded well for the upcoming Purdue game. The Boilermakers also boasted a standout freshman passer, in Mark Herrmann. Herrmann was a 6'5", 190 pound stringbean with a whippet frame and an appropriately golden manner in his throwing arm. He led the nation in total passing yards, with 1224 through the first four games, though he also displayed a penchant for throwing interceptions (three versus Wake Forest, four against Notre Dame).

The former All-State basketball player from the hoop town of Carmel, Indiana, had favorite targets in wide receivers Ray Smith and Reggie Arnold. Fullback John Skibinski and tight end Dave Young also were worthy recipients of many Herrmann tosses.

The tall stature of Herrmann afforded him a great view of opposing defenses. As long-time former OSU assistant Ernie Godfrey felt, the value inherent in the vision of a tall man behind center must never be underestimated. According to Godfrey, the ability of a pocket passer to read and manipulate defensive coverages was immeasurably aided by great height. Thus far, this principle had indeed worked in favor of Herrmann.

Purdue head coach Jim Young was in his first year at Lafayette, freshly arrived from Arizona. He spoke very highly of the OSU defense, claiming they were the best unit he had ever seen at batting down and tipping pass attempts. Young previously had visited Ohio Stadium as the defensive coordinator of Michigan, yet had not won in those three trips. He was confident this invasion would end differently.

Hayes continued to be in a remarkably pleasant mood, even while in the grip of an irritating cold. He was especially pleased with the customary Wednesday running workout, plus Cousineau seemed practically healed and was ready to return with his usual thoroughgoing exuberance. Hayes lavished praise on Lang, for stepping into a testy situation and performing remarkably well. The adaptability of Lang, between a variety of line positions on either side of the ball, was truly commendable.

Tackle Joe Robinson received his highest grades thus far for the SMU game, and Fritz also assumed increased responsibilities in the absence of Porter and Vogler.

On the defensive side, Esco Sarkinnen stated that Ross and Dansler were the linchpins in the pad-crunching success of the defensive line, especially against the pass. This week, Griffin again practiced solely at his defensive slot. As Hayes commented: "Against a team like this, we need Ray at safety. We don't even consider a switch...," not even with the renewed inactive status of Logan.

Because of the disappointing injuries to the senior tailback/more often fullback, the expected "blur" offense was being supplanted by more traditional fullback power, for the continued maturations of Campbell and Payton lessened somewhat the absence of Logan. Logan, so schooled by his ex-Buckeye father, was the consummate team player and was really struggling to cope with his frustrating run of bad luck.

Strangely, Jeff's unfortunate senior year continued a skein of unlikely last seasons, started the previous year in the case of Pete Johnson, for OSU running backs. In the future, virtually every backfield star seemed cursed with either an injury or some bizarre misfortune: Springs, Keith Byars, Vince Workman, Carlos Snow, Scottie Graham, and Robert Smith each had success dashed or severely undermined by incredibly bad circumstances.

Smitten with misfortune, yet still smiling, was the irrepressible former Buckeye, Skladany. Embroiled in a controversial season-long holdout from the Cleveland Browns, Tom still found a myriad of ways to enjoy life.

One former Buckeye leading a charmed life was ex-halfback Frank Howe, who learned many unique offensive ways from his college coach, Francis Schmidt. Howe parlayed this special knowledge into a skein of fantastic years at the helm of Columbus (Ohio) Northland High. Howe was renowned for his razzle-dazzle assortment of plays, including the forgotten arts: Statue-of-liberty passes from punt formation, reverses from any part of the field, quick kicks, and multitudinous forms of the single-wing were all commonplace attractions for a Howe squad. There was never a dull moment at a Viking game, and Howe also did not neglect the defensive arts, as his mentor sometimes chose to do.

CHAPTER SIX: PURDUE

Becoming nearly as commonplace as a Howe victory was the domination of OSU over another dangerous passing team. The vaunted Purdue offense never seemed to recover from a setback on the very first possession of the game, and the rout was on. Herrmann aimed a pass into the flat to open the contest, and Guess came out of nowhere to catch the ball on a dead run and sprint unimpeded for a shocking 65 yard touchdown. The Boilermakers were so demoralized by this stunning turn of events, they never really threatened to score from that point on.

Ohio State burst out of the gate quickly on offense as well. Gerald launched a beautiful 45 yard pass to Jones on the initial Buckeye play - then the awesome running game took over. Behind the long distance dashes of Springs and the goal line charges of Payton, the Bucks led 29-0 after just one quarter. The last score of the quarter was set up by a Dansler interception, and sent Purdue into virtually a run-only approach for the remainder of the half.

Following the short halftime break, Purdue turned to the pass almost entirely, in a futile effort to catch up. The Boilermakers could manage to get close to scoring just one time, marching 47 yards to the OSU 20, where the drive petered out. This solitary drive was about the extent of the Purdue offense on the day. The clamps were applied defensively by a healthy Cousineau and the steady Adkins. Gary Dulin filled in brilliantly for the injured Beamon, while Dansler and Cato were exquisite.

Hayes credited his defensive backfield coach, Gary Tranquill, with a brilliant scheme that limited Herrmann to 11 completions in 21 attempts for a measly 117 yards. Griffin, Guess, Allegro, Mills (who also had a magnificent punt return), and the much-welcomed Roche blanketed the Purdue receivers, neutralizing the amazing talents of Herrmann in the process.

Prior to the contest, Hayes felt a high score necessary, for Purdue could light up the scoreboard in a hurry. In response, hard-charging Joel Payton proved he could provide scoring theatrics worthy of an entire team by his lonesome. The frosh from Mentor, Ohio, fell just short of the Pete Johnson single game school scoring record, 30, by scoring four touchdowns and providing a two point conversion.

Springs gobbled up huge chunks of real estate each time he touched the ball, leaving with a whopping 151 yards on only ten carries. Included in that total was a third quarter touchdown dash of 66 yards. Campbell tacked on an additional 83 yards on his 13 runs.

A healthy dose of rain began right before kickoff, though the wet conditions did little to deter the increasingly fancy passing of Gerald. Rod struck on three of his six throws for 90 yards, including a 36 yard rainbow to Harrell. The newly discovered long-range success of Gerald obscured a re-injury to the knee of Johnson. Also injured were the seemingly snakebit Ron Barwig and the vastly-improving Robinson, each lost to an ankle injury.

Hayes conceded after the 46-0 shellacking, "Yes. This was about as perfect a game as we could play against a team as good as Purdue." The estimable offense of Purdue never saw the shadow of the goal line, while a runaway squirrel contrastingly amused the crowd early on by dashing onto the field and eluding capture as it sprinted into the end zone. Since that score did not count against OSU, Hayes had sufficient reason to feel good about the overpowering win.

Especially singled out for stellar performances were Ward and Payton, as each achiever added ten leaves to their helmets. Springs tacked on eight, Fritz and Lang received five, while Dansler led the defenders with 7.5 and Guess garnered five. Hayes could not gush enough about the positive impact of Lang, whose hustle and gritty determination fired up both players and the coaching staff.

The feistiness of Lang evidenced itself in practice occasionally, too. In one instance, Storer made a mistake during a play, and Woody charged into the offensive huddle to vent his wrath. The Bucks were aligned in a semi-circular formation, and Hayes began at one end and forcibly articulated his anger with physical jabs to each player's padded body. That is, until he reached Storer, when Woody inexplicably drew back and ordered the play rehearsed again.

This was too much for Lang, who refused to run another play until Hayes punished the initial offender, Storer. Taken aback by the temporary mutiny, and perhaps realizing the authenticity of Lang's argument, Woody laughed, playfully jabbed the tight end, and practice continued in a more lighthearted manner.

Logan was almost running at full speed as the new week began, although he still stiffened up and had trouble getting limber. Hayes was unusually excited this week about an upcoming game other than his own, the compelling clash between Michigan and Wisconsin. Michigan, over the strident protestations of Bo, was the top-ranked team in the land, while Wisconsin was a surprising 5-0 and ranked in the twelfth spot in the latest polls.

The euphoria over the Purdue game faded as the talk turned to upcoming Buckeye opponent Iowa, and the unusually strong Hawkeye defense. "We have to be ready for it, or it could give us a lot of trouble," cautioned the Coach.

The Hawkeyes were 3-2, and had regained their early-season confidence in a hard-fought 18-6 victory over Minnesota. That win effectively removed the onus of loser from the Iowa team, for the Hawkeyes had been beaten consecutively by UCLA and Arizona after a 2-0 start. That conference win boosted Bob Commings' hopes of eclipsing OSU, as Ohio State had a 12 game win streak going against the Iowa program, and Commings believed the odds were ripe to end that string.

Commings emerged from the high school ranks of Struthers and Massillon Washington (where Steve Luke, former Buckeye defensive back, starred for the Tigers), both deep in the heartland of Ohio gridiron fever, the Northeast, and still exerted tremendous influence in the recruitment of great athletes from that area. Indeed, his influence was such that twelve Ohio prep players made the journey to Iowa to become Hawkeyes, a statistic which galled Hayes.

The rugged Iowa defense was led by one of these transplanted Ohioans, Akron East product Dean Moore, a fine linebacker. Tom Rusk was another crucial fixture of the outstanding defense, also at linebacker, in a Hawkeye set that was quite comparable to the schemes employed by OSU.

On offense, Iowa ran the wing T, a wingback set featuring constant men-in-motion, also much like the similar setup employed by Ohio State. Iowa played a simplistic brand of football, designed to quickly find out who the better man was, they or the opponent.

The leading rushers for the Hawkeyes were Jon Lazar and Rod Martin, and overall, the Iowa offense was very solid and played conservative, power football. Once more, the Hayes influence among Ohio high school coaches had spread into the college game. Iowa looked to be an ascending team, due for greater feats and possibly a national ranking if such improvement continued.

Certainly one OSU player continuing to stake his claim for national stardom was sophomore Mike Guess. The man who had started the final nine games of his frosh year was now forcing teams to contend with both him and Ray Griffin each time the quarterback dropped back in the pocket. Guess' playing style bordered on cocky, for there was a certain congruence to his play, an almost contemptuous manner in his game, which made him seem experienced beyond his years.

Guess had been a prep teammate of Ray at Columbus Eastmoor, and the younger Mike idolized Griffin even as Ray played on offense and Mike remained on defense. "He's sort of a big brother to me here," Guess claimed, and indeed, Guess enrolled at OSU chiefly so he could perform alongside his mentor. "I've got as much respect for him as anybody in the world," Mike said of Ray, crediting the brilliance of his idol as forcing teams to challenge the other members of the secondary. Guess was now being similarly avoided in upcoming game plans, for he had proven himself the master of the interception. There was little margin for error where the Eastmoor products patrolled the airways, and few runners likewise emerged unruffled.

An extremely successful former NFL star delivered a special message to the Ohio State team during this week. Ex-Cleveland Brown and ex-Washington Redskin running back/kick returner nonpareil Bobby Mitchell, director of pro scouting for the 'Skins, passed on a little of his profound knowledge in a sincere message which warned the players that football was but a steppingstone in the journey of life. Success in sports should lead to bigger and better things outside the playing field, and a professional sports career was not an end in itself, warned Mitchell.

This enthusiastic pep talk mirrored the message that Hayes continually tried to instill, and was perhaps more effective to some, since Mitchell was a bona-fide professional Hall-of-Famer. Hayes was duly impressed, particularly since he remembered Mitchell as the most clever of any back his teams ever faced, although Mitchell never scored against OSU while competing for Illinois.

CHAPTER SEVEN: IOWA

On this Saturday, Iowa could not contain Gerald. For the third straight game, Rod was the catalyst for a dominant OSU offense. Gerald enjoyed perhaps his finest game as a Buckeye, both at passing and running. In more good news, Logan was able to suit up, and his old style was evident as he darted for 64 yards on ten carries.

In front of the then-fourth largest crowd in Nile Kinnick stadium history, the OSU offense chewed up much yardage and time on the ground, punctuated with pinpoint passing from Gerald. The OSU defense harassed and shut down a thoroughly outmanned, overmatched Iowa offense.

Gerald ran 13 times for an even 100 yards, including two scintillating touchdown runs. One scoring dash covered 44 yards; on the other he dodged numerous Hawkeye defensemen to score from the two. His passing prowess reached an apex on this day. Rod completed nine of 12 passes, for 91 yards, displaying remarkable accuracy and skill at locating open targets.

Springs added 45 yards on just ten rushes, and Johnson came back from his knee-injury layoff to salvage a 34 yard gain from what looked like a sure loss. The Buckeyes ground out 373 rushing yards, and finished with 464 total yards against the highly respected Iowa defense.

Perhaps the only glaring sore spot in the 27-6 OSU romp came in the first half. Joel Payton, the leading scorer in the nation with 50 points, was stuffed on four consecutive tries beginning from the Hawkeye one yard line. Unfortunately for the home team, this heroic goal line stand was about the only defensive highlight in an otherwise disappointing performance.

After the game, Hayes bristled when asked about this inability to crack the line of defense. "Good blocking would have enabled... [Payton to score]", Hayes snapped sorely. Yet Woody did admit that except for this disturbing breakdown, and a few lesser others, OSU was practically unstoppable.

In the lopsided first half, Iowa generated just enough offense to make the visitor 43 their deepest penetration. In the third quarter, they scraped out even less yardage, making it to only their own 35 yard line. Only a Gerald fumble, recovered by Iowa at the Buckeye 45 late in the game, allowed Iowa to threaten for the first time. The Hawkeyes subsequently advanced to a fourth and two situation at the OSU 18, whereupon Guess flew in and drilled tailback Ernie Sheeler for a stunning five yard loss.

The only Iowa score resulted from another OSU turnover later in the game. Castignola, inserted into the blowout, fumbled and lost possession at his own 39. Hawkeye quarterback Tom McLaughlin capitalized on this turnover by hitting three of five passes in a drive to the OSU two. Lazar ran it in from there, with only 1:11 remaining, though the outcome had long since been decided.

Overall, the frustrated Hawkeye offense totaled just 69 anemic yards rushing on 40 attempts. McLaughlin did connect on 11 of 24 passes, though most went for minimal gains, and he had two passes pilfered by Cousineau and one snagged by Roche. Hayes spoke highly of the dogged Iowa effort, and especially respected the tenacity, guts, and fiery leadership displayed by McLaughlin in the losing battle.

"We completely throttled a good Iowa team," was the succinct Hayes game description. Campbell, Gerald, and Logan drew raves for their strong play.

In a continuation of a rapidly escalating problem, the baseball hat was stolen right from the head of Woody immediately following the game. A daring Hawkeye fan eluded both security, and more frighteningly, the grasp of gigantic Chris Ward, and escaped undetected.

Also escaping that afternoon, though not as narrowly, was the Michigan football team. The Wolverines buried the upstart Badgers by the score of 58-0, outgaining the hopelessly overmatched Wisconsin team 546 total yards to 126 in the process. It was a blockbuster showing for the nationally top-ranked maize and blue, marred only by several injuries to an already depleted offensive line.

That Monday, after a weekend of intensive film critiques, Hayes altered his favorable impression of the Buckeye offense. Too many fumbles and missed assignments to be considered a satisfying performance, Hayes grumbled at a press luncheon. Woody insisted that his charges must continue to improve if they wished to finish out the year in typically strong fashion. He did grudgingly concede that it was tough to keep a team at fever pitch for every game, especially as the less-than-formidable Northwestern was next on the schedule.

A few seasons before, in '73, as a kickoff with the Wildcats loomed just ahead, Hayes sensed in the locker room that his team was not emotionally prepared to go to war. Conspiratorially, Hayes whispered in the ear of defensive tackle Pete Cusick, telling him that NU ran all their offensive plays off-tackle during the pre-game warmups. This told Hayes that there must be a weakness in the OSU defensive line, and the Wildcats were poised to exploit whatever they had uncovered in their scouting report.

Of course, a pre-game offensive run-through always centered on off-tackle plays, yet Hayes knew that by insinuating that the OSU tackles were weak, the intensely proud Cusick would become angry.

Angry is not the word. The incensed Cusick would have nothing to do with being a weak link, and the emotional heart of the defense which allowed just 64 points in 11 games proceeded to fire up the entire Buckeye team. How dare Northwestern find a weakness in an OSU team! The Bucks charged onto the field and dismantled the Wildcats 60-0.

On another occasion later in that same year, Hayes again used his knowledge of human psychology to empower his squad. It was the pre-game meal before the long anticipated Rose Bowl matchup with the Trojans of USC, and OSU was extremely tense during the traditional team feast. There was an air of uncertainty, nervousness, and even timidity hanging over the team. Coming off an emotionally draining 10-10 tie with Michigan, some sportswriters contended that OSU backed into the Rose Bowl, claiming the Buckeye bowl appearance was due solely to an advantageous vote of the conference council and not the merits of their play in the final regular season game.

Hayes sensed this tentative mood, and responded with typical wit and aplomb. The main course that day was steak, and immediately after the portions were served, Hayes began yelling for the chefs. The startled OSU team watched in awe as Hayes ordered four ounces trimmed from every single portion.

As the harried chefs repaired each individual slab, Hayes explained himself. He had ordered a certain serving size of the meat, and somehow the Southern California coaching staff, masterminded by the diabolical John McKay, enlarged that intended serving, in order to slow the Buckeyes down. Hayes was on to their antics, however, he gleefully announced, and ensured that Ohio State would be leaner and meaner than anticipated on gameday. Instantly, the mood of the team shifted from one of some self-doubt to one of a team with a secret advantage. The sufficiently inspired Buckeyes went on to win 42-21, displaying fantastic team speed in the process.

During this same Monday news conference, Hayes became demonstrably upset when asked if Ohio State was a great team in '76. Hayes fairly exploded. The season was not over yet, and with one loss already, the Buckeyes could not possibly be great. Hayes roared his disagreement to anyone even hinting that OSU was a great team, perhaps in an attempt to fire up his players. Woody sensed even at this early date that the team was a little too mentally relaxed in their approach to the Wildcats. Woody knew better than to take anything, especially a precious win, for granted. As Woody taught Ara Parseghian, "There's no greater game than the one you're playing today."

Continuing this animated press conference, Hayes insisted that film replays of the Iowa game confirmed that Payton had indeed scored on at least one of his four attempts from the one, although game officials failed to recognize this fact. Hayes judged this crucial miscall in the heat of battle a perfect example of the need for instant replay. There was absolutely no compelling reason for the NCAA not to adopt a replay rule, thought Hayes; such faulty preservation of the status quo of incorrect calls through a fear of change were not healthy for the game. Crazily enough, these same criticisms used by Hayes were the very same accusations often leveled at the Coach, throughout his long career.

Based on evidence such as his forward thinking regarding rules changes, training methods, speed as a formidable weapon, and psychological underpinnings to the process of teaching, perhaps Hayes was more static and forward thinking than (at least) many of his contemporaries and critics were ever willing to admit. As with clothing, old ideas always came back into fashion among football coaches, and Woody had been around long enough to pretty much see it all, although he might not have originated said implementation.

Still in the confrontational mode, Hayes was readily incensed by a certain OSU professor's stinging criticism of the emphasis placed on the OSU football program. Hayes, certainly as outspoken a proponent of academics as there was, readily agreed that more emphasis should be placed on scholarship, though not to the detriment of the football program.

Hayes always felt that books and sports went hand in hand; the Greek notion that a stronger body allowed a stronger mind, and vice versa, was always a Hayes credo. Woody felt that the discipline and self-sacrifice applied on the football field translated into the same workaholic application in the classroom, and was always particularly proud that his teams had among the best graduation rates in the conference.

As a matter of pride, Hayes also pointed out that the graduation rate of the football team was routinely greater than that of the university proper. Woody also gleefully noted the revenue generated by the football program was the hub around which the large number of university intramural and intercollegiate programs revolved and were funded from.

"We have taken in $45-50 million in the last 20 years, and the money is put to good use," Hayes contended. If "...sport and religion made America," as Hayes was fond of saying, then college football should make better institutions of higher learning.

Hayes felt that criticism of football per se would be more properly directed at the professional ranks, instead. "What do the pros do with their money? They use it to pay a lot of spoiled athletes," snapped Hayes. Even in '77, that seemed a valid argument; in the present day, it is even more of a truism.

One OSU athlete admitted during this week that he was injured at least partly because he did not report to fall camp in desired condition. Eddie Beamon blamed his severe ankle injury on his own lack of conditioning over the summer, a rare admission from an athlete. In the struggle to whip himself into shape during regular practice sessions, his ankle underwent undue strain and ultimately gave out. As Hayes forever contended, "...you can't learn football and get in condition at the same time." One, or more likely both, facet was doomed to suffer, and Beamon paid the price with his health.

The 256 pound senior had started every game in '75 and '76, and his play was expected to reach its peak during his final year. The first missed road trip of his career was for the Iowa contest, and Beamon was fed up with missed games and missed practices, waiting for his ankle to mend. As much as Beamon missed the game, his teammates missed his considerable presence. Beamon possessed an infectious blend of humor and childlike enthusiasm which endeared him to players and coaches alike, and the entire OSU program counted the days to his return.

Tackle and tight end coach Bill Myles spoke very highly of Gerald this week, especially in regard to his fantastic Iowa performance. The signalcaller added 8.5 Buckeye leaves to his rapidly expanding assemblage, while Ward graded out to a team-high 77% on the offensive line, which, as the coaches did not hesitate to illustrate, left a lot of room for improvement. Cato and Adkins were also singled out for their exemplary efforts in the Iowa game.

This week, even more than most, was a time of tremendous physicality during practices. "There isn't a team hitting harder than we are...," in preparation for the Dyche Stadium trip, Hayes insisted.

The practices were that intense because the coaching staff was all too aware that facing NU, boasting an 0-6 record, overconfidence was always a threat. Granted, much of the ferocious practice time was taken up on preparations for Michigan; this was customary during the week of a game against an apparently overmatched opponent. Duncan Griffin recalls that OSU actually devoted only the brief Friday run-through to Wildcat concerns.

On paper, this overconfidence seemed justified. Ohio State was playing at a fever pitch defensively, and the Wildcats entered this contest with just three touchdowns for the entire year. Northwestern was dead last in the conference in total offense, primarily since they were using their fourth quarterback of the tender season. This revolving door was created by a wealth of injuries, and an additional five more Wildcat starters would also miss the OSU contest. Head coach John Pont, who starred under Woody at Miami, was making do with a patchwork quilt constructed of backups, and lightly regarded substitutes.

The injury status for Ohio State was somewhat more acceptable. Ric Volley was troubled by a sore back, Beamon remained doubtful, and Barwig continued to be hobbled by his ankle sprain. Castignola began the week with a sore and swollen right throwing arm, which continually got worse.

His injury was eventually diagnosed as a partial obstruction of the main blood vein in his arm. This clot would apparently put the sophomore out of commission for the remainder of the year. This unique predicament was probably due to an abnormal enlargement in a small muscle resting under the collarbone, which was possibly prompted by a collision during the Iowa game.

Whatever the cause, the resulting pressure caused a clot to form, and Castignola gradually lost the use of his arm. Doctors were perplexed by the bizarre injury, yet thought that rest would provide a complete cure.

Another previous severe injury was the increasing tightness in the back of Jim Savoca, which resulted in season-ending surgery earlier in the year. Originally, when notified of the impending surgery, the senior lineman was going to quit the team. Jim believed he had no shot at a professional berth in the sport, and thought he should switch concentration to his prospective business career. Because of an unresolved class scheduling snag, Savoca was forced to delay his graduation plans by a full quarter, prompting him to reconsider resuming his football activities.

By sitting out the remainder of the '77 season, Jim would be granted an extra season of medical red-shirt eligibility, which he decided to utilize in '78. Savoca was taking the extra time afforded by his absence from football to really get into his books, and was mentally gearing up to resume the sport he realized he could not yet live without. "I'd love to play [this season], but I can wait," Jim said.

CHAPTER EIGHT: NORTHWESTERN

Not content to wait for a win were 30,000 Northwestern homecoming fans, who braved rainy, cold, and blustery weather to exhort their troops. The fan's enthusiasm communicated a possibility of victory, and the inspired Wildcats very nearly delivered. An extremely unhappy Hayes declared that OSU did indeed perform at a sub-par level, as the 'Cats played to unforeseen heights, and Woody truly felt that his Buckeyes were fortunate to escape with a 35-15 victory.

Ironically, the Minnesota Gophers upset Michigan on this very same day, and OSU assumed sole ownership of first place in the Big 10.

The Buckeyes did not necessarily perform like a first place team, regardless. Ohio State fumbled the ball eight times, and lost possession on four of those occasions. Gerald threw two interceptions, though he did complete nine of 14 attempts for 148 yards. Ohio State again relied on somewhat isolated big plays by the offense, in order to come out ahead.

Springs set up the first OSU touchdown by romping 72 yards through the wet field to the Wildcat eight. Payton subsequently rammed in for the first of his two scores. Two other Buckeye scores were set up by fumble recoveries of Wildcat miscues, both occurring deep in NU territory. Ohio State fortuitously capitalized on both takeaways, first on a five yard Logan run and then on a one yard Payton plunge, both runs for touchdowns.

The only two sustained drives for the Buckeyes on the day came in the second half. On the first possession following the intermission, OSU held the ball long enough to march 71 yards in eight plays. Gerald sprinted in on a draw from 24 yards out.

Another flash of greatness came during the final quarter, when a ten play, 80 yard drive carried them into the end zone. This drive featured a 63 yard Logan jaunt, which set up a one yard Campbell run. In all, these infrequent flashes of superb OSU play were dimmed by overall inconsistency.

The Buckeye defense was even more inconsistent than the offense. Northwestern scored twice as many points in this contest as they previously had in any single '77 game. The Wildcats played emotional, all-out ball, and their line manipulated the terrific defensive line of the Bucks, quite handily at times. Fullback Harold Gilmore found enough openings to amass 123 rushing yards, including a 14 yard touchdown blast late in the game.

Ohio State yielded their first passing touchdown of the year, a surprising 33 yard strike from the freshman Dana Hemphill to an open Mike Taylor. Northwestern ran up 279 yards on the ground, by far the most against the Bucks thus far in '77. Only the impassioned play of Cato and Dansler, who each made thrilling tackles near the goal line, kept NU from scoring more.

Springs led the way for OSU, continuing his spectacular season with a 14 carry, 132 yard game. A multitude of atypical OSU mistakes, and the surprisingly tough play of the Wildcats in pressure situations, kept this contest from being the expected Buckeye rout, although the game was actually closer than the score appears. The Wildcats actually had a chance to pull off an upset, until they were stopped on downs, deep in Buckeye territory, for no score; shortly thereafter, Logan responded with the sizeable jaunt which led to the final OSU score.

On this day, OSU breathed a sigh of relief and took the win as a blessing. As Minnesota proved, the conference was steadily growing tougher from top to bottom, and the bygone days, of virtually guaranteed weekly blowouts by the Wolverines and Buckeyes, were rapidly receding.

As a further safeguard against a disruption of their winning ways in the face of this growing opposition, and due to the mysterious Castignola clot, Hayes made sure that Strahine was behind center for part of this game, even as the outcome was in doubt.

Also receiving infrequent action was wingback Jim Harrell. Harrell was extremely disappointed that he was not more involved in the offense in '76, especially since he had the option of casting his name into the NFL draft prior to the start of the year. This option was available because Harrell tore up his knee and missed all of '74. The fifth-year senior finally decided to come back into the Buckeye program, and was leading the '77 team in receptions (actually, he was tied with Jaco) with seven.

Despite his own perceived lack of activity, Harrell's remarkable abilities were well-respected by the Buckeye coaching staff. According to Hayes, "He made the best catches we had last year, and he's doing the same again." Harrell had learned the art of the big play from another infrequent, yet deadly, OSU weapon, Brian Baschnagel. Jim enjoyed a fine game at Northwestern, catching passes of 25 and 37 yards, as Gerald was really starting to find his passing range. At least Harrell was able to make the most of his limited chances, and further proved his worth by becoming the holder on all conversion attempts when Logan went down.

Yet Harrell strongly felt, even if he was only presented with the chance to block in the season finale, if the Buckeyes could beat Michigan, his final season would be well worth the price of inactivity. "If we win on November 19th, it will all be worth it," stated the prep tailback out of Oregon (Ohio) Clay. Harrell passionately wanted to avenge the two losses suffered to UM since his arrival in Columbus, particularly since Michigan spurned Jim out of high school in favor of Rob Lytle. That recruiting slight further fanned his competitive flames.

Hayes remained an individual who needed no further motivation. At the Monday practice, Hayes went ballistic, even in the presence of special guest Jack Nicklaus, because there were too many fumbles. He calmed down much later, in time to proclaim Lang as "Lineman of the Week" and Harrell "Back of the Week."

Hayes tried to always vent his anger completely when he did lose his temper, and once the anger subsided, did his utmost not to continue in that tempestuous mind-set. "If you clench your fist, the longer you keep it clenched, the weaker your arm becomes," was a favorite Hayes saying. Woody harbored a grudge very infrequently, and if he did, as sometimes seemed the case toward journalists, that ill will was built up over time, and was not usually based on one incident.

The mood of Hayes brightened somewhat as he learned that Beamon was expected to be back at full strength against upcoming opponent Wisconsin, and that the continuing emergence of Campbell partially offset a re-injury to Logan.

As mentioned above, sophomore Strahine, from Lakewood (Ohio) High School, had moved into the number two quarterback spot. Incidentally, Mike's prep coach was Tom Cousineau, Sr., so the 6'0", 186 pound Strahine was well-schooled in the nuances of the game and was fundamentally sound.

On Monday Mike suffered some slight elbow pain, probably brought on by the increased workload, though the discomfort turned out to be inconsequential. By Wednesday, Strahine had an exceptionally sharp session, both in passing drills and in running the complex option.

The athletic Mike played tailback as a senior at Lakewood, and in fact had missed the '77 spring practice to play shortstop on the OSU baseball team. Ohio State quarterbacks were not usually afforded that chance to pass up spring ball, but extra cram sessions following baseball and his above-average breeding in high school grudgingly let Hayes release him from those few weeks. Both Chaump and Hayes lauded the Strahine work ethic. "He gives it the complete effort," the two said in unison.

Also on Wednesday, Hayes received a most unexpected and apologetic letter, along with a $5 check, from University of Iowa '73 graduate Mike Gatens. This repentant young man was the one who had snatched the cap from the head of Hayes "...in exuberance over homecoming and that last-minute Iowa touchdown." On the heels of this belated honesty, Hayes related an even more exemplary tale of righteousness.

After the last Northwestern contest, a Wildcat student manager requested the hat Woody wore during the game. Hayes politely declined the request as he walked to the showers and dressing area, then deliberately placed said hat in full view of the student. Following a lengthy hot shower which absorbed the chill of the day, Woody noticed that the hat still remained in that very same conspicuous spot.

Woody went out of his way to locate the honest manager, who had passed up an easy opportunity to steal the desired object, and gave him the hat and a gracious handshake. Both of these young men, in varying degrees, lived up to the Hayes belief in, "...the basic honesty of most people."

Wisconsin was bringing their finest personnel in years into Ohio Stadium. The Badgers started '77 with five straight wins, before losing decisively to Michigan and Michigan State. Head coach John Jardine was hoping for a pattern interrupt this week in Columbus: He was winless in seven tries against OSU, with three of those losses coming in Ohio.

Wisconsin hung in to only lose 30-20 in '76, and Jardine thought this squad could pull off the upset. The Badgers utilized a wing T, short-motion offensive set, with a fair balance between the pass and run. Their running game featured fullback Mike Morgan, with tailbacks Ira Matthews and Terry Breuscher, along with backup fullback Tim Halleran, who contributed nicely to the mix. Quarterback Anthony Dudley supervised this explosive offense, and was a fair runner himself. His passes were hauled in most often by split end David Charles and the versatile Breuscher.

On the defensive side, the Badgers employed a seven man front, blitzing on almost every single down.

This solid Wisconsin defense was hoping to capitalize on a disturbingly unusual Buckeye tendency - a sudden spate of fumbles. The eight fumbles incurred against Northwestern were the most ever for a Woody Hayes team, topping the seven drops against Illinois in '73. "Fumbles have to be psychological," and tend to come in bunches, suggested Hayes. The thirteen fumbles thus far on the year matched the total for all of '76, and were exceeded in the Hayes reign only twice previously (17 in '51, and 16 in '74).

Perhaps the evolution of a better conditioned player, in much finer armor, and an increasingly encouraged tendency for a defender to strip the ball when tackling, contributed to this escalation in fumbling, although Hayes would tolerate no rationalization. According to the fierce commandment of Woody, the fumbles would stop when proper concentration was applied.

As a trivial aside, the Wisconsin athletic director was Elroy "Crazylegs" Hirsch, so named for his numerous mad dashes after frequent receptions as a Hall-of-Fame performer for the Los Angeles Rams. Prior to his arrival in the pros, Hirsch had been a star as a sophomore on the number three-ranked '42 Badger team.

Then the second World War struck, and like so many players, Hirsch was forced to transfer, to a school with a military training unit. Hirsch was assigned to a Marine Corps training unit in Michigan, and in between his duty to country, found time to letter in four different sports in '43 for the Michigan Wolverines. He remains the only person to accomplish this feat in the long, glorious history of Wolverine athletics.

The '77 OSU squad featured some illustrious, albeit lesser-known, performers at this stage in the season. Herman Jones capitalized on his limited opportunities, and was second on the squad in receptions with six, for a remarkable total of 160 yards. Castignola had been positively brilliant in relief, succeeding on five of six passes, including two touchdown heaves. Lang was as consistent and workmanlike as possible, both in games and practices, and Jaco was rapidly becoming a glue-fingered favorite of the Buckeye quarterbacks.

Jaco was another imaginative character, who stood out, even on a team of many such fascinating individuals. A favorite ploy, employed by Jaco and Storer alike during games, was to momentarily confuse a tightly-wound opponent with off-the-wall comments. One such distraction was a phrase such as, "We're going to systematically destroy your morale;" delivered just before a snap, the phrase often puzzled hyper defenders.

Jaco was unused to extended game action, and on one occasion, when Storer was injured, was in for twice the amount of plays as normal. Late in the contest, Bill caught a pass, then physically, visibly, hit the proverbial wall of exhaustion. Afterwards, the exhausted Jaco humorously stated he did not wish to start again, if this was how fatigued a starter became.

The conservation of his energy also extended into the Jaco off-season. Bill secured a job with a local construction firm over one summer, and anticipated a cushy, laid-back process of essentially worthless "busy" work. However, disproving the myth that football players received easy, high-paying employ from benefacting alumni, Jaco soon discovered this job entailed brutal, difficult, manual labor. His disappointed foreman responded, "This is the laziest boy I've ever seen." Regardless, Jaco expended plenty of energy on the necessary pursuits, sometimes including football.

Though the pair was not underrated, Griffin and Ward were sometimes taken for granted, for their level of performance rarely fell beneath excellent. Hayes was especially proud that Ward seldom sat out a play in practice, and ran every innocuous practice repetition as if it were fourth-and-goal at the Michigan one.

Griffin was outstanding on kickoff returns, having brought back five for 130 exciting yards. His open-field maneuverability and supersonic speed also came into play after his three intercepts, and as seen, he was always a candidate to take a lateral from a thieving teammate all the way.

An exceptionally inspirational leader for OSU this season was Aaron Brown. The strong middle guard promised the lapses displayed against NU would be temporary, and ultimately the lessons absorbed in the underachieving victory would result in a better team. "We'll be emotional this week," the Warren, Ohio, native guaranteed. The experienced senior did not hesitate in proclaiming this '77 defense the finest he had ever been a part of.

The notoriously quick Brown had been continuously double-teamed since settling into a starting role three games through his sophomore season; consequently, a lesser man may have rued the loss of personal glory and glowing statistics. Not Brown, who contended, "Individual stats aren't important to me." Brown recognized that by drawing the constant attentions of two or more offensive opponents, he freed up a lineman or linebacker to make an easier stop.

By the end of the week, Badger quarterback Dudley was out of the lineup with a disabling knee injury. He was replaced by the duo of Charles Green and Mike Kalasmiki. Perhaps feeling this strain of losing his field general on the eve of an essential confrontation, Jardine's usual calm exploded during a Friday afternoon run-through in Ohio Stadium.

In front of mostly partisan Wisconsin fans personally extended an invitation to attend this practice, Jardine abruptly pulled his team from the field after only 15 minutes. A (Columbus) local television cameraman did not heed Jardine's repeated demands to stop filming, so the Badger head smartly marched his troops to the sanctuary of the locker room, yelling all the while.

CHAPTER NINE: WISCONSIN

Unfortunately, that was the extent of the excitement for the Wisconsin faithful during the weekend, for the next afternoon Ohio State reclaimed their defensive dominance and ignited offensively for an overpowering 42-0 victory. On the very first play from scrimmage, Gerald narrowly missed a completion to a streaking Jones. Undaunted, Gerald came right back on the next play to hit Harrell in perfect stride for a 79 yard touchdown bomb.

Wisconsin seemed to never recover from this opening strike. The visitors threatened to score only once on this day, but Cato blocked this 46 yard field goal attempt in the opening quarter, and Wisconsin managed no further threats.

On the next two OSU drives after the quick opening score, the Buckeyes stopped themselves. A fumbled pitch and an illegal procedure penalty put an end to each drive, respectively, yet the Badgers themselves showed little ability to slow the OSU offense. In the second quarter, Ohio State hammered down the field via the run, marching 80 yards in 17 surges of the line. Payton powered in from the one, making the score 14-0 at the half.

Following the break, the Badgers could sustain nothing on offense and garnered only 88 total yards. By late in the third quarter, Badger middle guard Dan Relich was out with a knee injury, and OSU found plenty of running room right up the gut of the delapidated visitors (remember this injury, for it would ignite a controversy one year later). With their defensive stalwart gone, the Badgers were virtually helpless in the face of the Buckeye running onslaught.

Logan darted 33 yards for a third quarter touchdown under the bright, sunny skies; Dansler picked off a pass on the ensuing Badger possession, and the Bucks quickly scored again. An 11 play, 29 yard drive was capped by a Gerald sneak from the one. On this drive, Wisconsin was able to slow the Buckeye backfield, keeping the yardage per play at a minimum, yet OSU inched downfield to paydirt regardless.

The final quarter began with a Roche interception. Springs obliged that favor by rambling 31 yards for a touchdown, which sent the OSU regulars to the sidelines for some well-deserved rest. Strahine came on after the Badger offense was stymied once more, and led the Buckeyes on a mammoth 18 play, 80 yard drive featuring the running of Volley and Johnson. Volley twisted in from the two, putting an exclamation point on the dominating day.

Strahine played refreshingly well, adding confidence in regards to the depth at the playcalling slot, although now there were three capable quarterbacks: In an unexpected piece of miraculous news, the inexplicable clot of Castignola just as mysteriously faded. He was scheduled to begin light throwing on Monday, and was showing few indications he was ever disabled.

Ohio State came onto their field on this Saturday determined to prove a point: Gerald was a dangerous, accurate passer whose skills would not only be utilized, but would become an integral part of the attack. He hammered this point resoundingly home by hitting on five of 11 passes (all prior to halftime) for 139 yards. Coupled with the one for one effort, worth 22 yards, by Strahine, OSU surprisingly compiled 161 yards through the air.

The lone negative brought on by this new passing priority was a rash Gerald interception, thrown just 17 seconds before halftime. This particular pass was forced into fine coverage, and Wisconsin nabbed the poorly thrown ball in the end zone, preventing an OSU score. A stiff lecture, delivered by Woody at the half, reduced the possibility of repeating this mistake.

Springs once more was the leader of a strong rushing game, totaling 104 yards on 17 early carries. Logan also looked extremely impressive, piling up 81 yards in just ten carries. Volley provided some late excitement, amassing 49 yards on ten second half carries. Overall, OSU chewed up 304 yards on the ground, as the line simply overwhelmed the outgunned Badgers.

After the contest, Hayes joshingly revealed, "The number one team [Texas] called this week, wanting to know how to run block [from the robust T]." Ohio State definitely put on a clinic on this glorious afternoon. Just as impressive were the long receptions hauled in by Hunter, Storer, and Moore. Moore also made a typically devastating block on the long touchdown run by Springs.

The defense absolutely shut down the Badger offense, rendering it virtually impotent. Dansler, Ross, and Brown repeatedly overwhelmed the Wisconsin line as they effectively stuffed the run throughout. Cato made some big hits, and also recovered a Dansler fumble after the interception by Kelton. When Green or Mike Kalasmiki dropped back to pass, the pressure applied on the collapsing pocket was unceasing and unbearable.

Interceptions were consequently racked up by Dansler, Roche, Mills, and Guess. These ran the OSU intercept total to the year to an amazing 21, well within reach of the school record, 25, achieved both in '68 and '76.

Perhaps the sole down note of the day came when Vince Skillings blew out his knee covering on a kick return. The lithe frosh had become a real force to deal with on special teams, what with his blazing speed and a nose for the ball. Skillings was out for the remainder of the year.

Hayes began the next week in a tremendously upbeat mood. "The more I see of the tremendous attitude that our kids have, the more I think this is going to be a pretty darn good football team," he intoned on Monday. His optimism stemmed from many factors, not the least of which was Logan coming back to his All-American form as he haltingly regained his health.

Castignola was back on the playing field, which did immeasurable good in raising the optimism of the team. Anytime a player made a quick or unexpected recovery from an injury, the morale of the squad just naturally went up a notch.

The offensive line was really coming together as a unit, especially with the vocal leader Vogler back in action. The development of the run blocking performance was the key to the suddenly potent passing threat, for opposing defenses were unable to force the pass, in undesirable situations, since they could not halt the rushing game. Therefore, OSU dictated where, how, and when the pass was used, with predictably advantageous results.

Hayes predicated his offensive stratagems around the principles of ancient Chinese war historian Sun Tzu, whose *Ping Fa* described the key to any offensive attack as making the defense move. When the defense shifted, the offense struck the weakened, or vacated, area.

Beamon and Cousineau were also back near full strength, lending their prodigious talents to a jelling defense. The only other significant injury at this time was to reserve defensive tackle Marty Cusick, who underwent knee surgery and was lost for the year.

Upcoming opponent Illinois was not nearly as healthy. The first-year Illini coach was '62 Buckeye co-captain Gary Moeller, fresh off a four year hitch as the defensive coordinator at Michigan, and he was really struggling in his new post, particularly in dealing with the unaccustomed losses. For this Illini homecoming matchup, Moeller was hoping to reclaim some of his Wolverine success. Indeed, during his '69-'76 assistant tenure at UM, the Wolverines never lost a home game.

The hopes of the Illini dimmed with the crucial loss of their leading defender, middle guard Stanley Ralphs, to an injury. Original starting quarterback Kurt Steger was still recovering from a variety of injuries, while his backup, Mike McCray, was reeling from a recent head injury. McCray had revived a dormant offense, yet by the end of this week, it was apparent that a still-ailing Steger would have to start.

Illinois was an extremely young squad, and proved especially prone to self-destructive mistakes during critical times in a game. Without the presence of the run-plugging Ralphs, the Illini did not seem likely to improve their status as the worst rushing defense in the conference.

One Buckeye who seemed fighting mad all season was Kelton Dansler. The junior carried intense emotions over from the '76 season, when he played extensively and was, in his own harsh opinion, given a trial-by-fire indoctrination into the rigors of Big 10 football. This indoctrination was made more severe since the other end for OSU was team MVP Bob Brudzinski, and Dansler felt his play did not match that of Bob's. Of course, possibly no one's in the nation did, yet that was the level Dansler felt he should reach. Dansler had also played a considerable amount as a frosh, although his own expectations for his performance were not as exacting back in '75.

His goal for '77 was to showcase his amazing improvement on a game to game basis; accordingly, the smallish 205 pounder from football breeding ground Warren, Ohio, was in the midst of a spectacular year. His position coach, Dave Adolph, insisted that there wasn't a better end in the whole conference at this juncture in the year.

With little prodding, Dansler himself admitted: "Overall, I'd have to say it's been a much better season than I figured on." Dansler used the anger he felt about his sophomore season, to continuously propel himself towards increasingly better performances, and the quick, heady junior also used these surges of emotion to circumvent any drawbacks pertaining to his lack of mass. Intense desire and fierce will overcame size in the heat of combat, according to Hayes, and there was no better example than Dansler.

Hayes also used anger to motivate. After a period of relaxation in which he felt he was too complimentary to his players, Hayes made a conscious decision to return to his more accustomed role of the taskmaster. "Whenever I start to ease up on them, I'm the worst coach there is," he honestly felt, so there would be no further relaxation. "I can't be nice and win," declared Hayes. "It's not my way." Woody recalled the advice of John Heisman, who warned, "At times, [a coach] must be severe, arbitrary, little short of a tzar."

Accordingly, Hayes really began to crack the whip. His anger spilled over at a lackluster Tuesday practice. The terrible practice was made worse by a slight ankle injury to Ward, which forced the huge tackle to limp off early. Hayes felt so highly of Ward and the respect and effort the senior engendered in players and coaches alike, that Woody actually compared him to the usually incomparable Archie Griffin, in terms of leadership and motivation.

As stated previously, Hayes used his anger to focus attention on a problem, which was then corrected with massive effort. Woody never ignored any mistake, even a seemingly trivial one, and always overwhelmed such miscues with endless repetition. Perhaps his most famous phrase was, "Paralyze their resistance with your persistence," and by this he meant any opposition, especially self-defeating errors. Hayes traditionally made it a point "...to spend extra time on a player who makes mistakes...;" often, if Woody got that player mad at his Coach, that player's effort increased enough that the problem dissipated in the process.

"I've never seen a football player who isn't a better player than he thinks he is," thought Hayes. "And as a coach, it's my job to make a kid realize his potential." Hayes told players, "The only reason I'm mad at you is because I know you can do better, you can do more. The implication is always positive, no matter how I deliver it." Woody "...believe[d] I can recognize talent, then use it," and picked on people because he cared.

If this supreme goal could be accomplished with anger as a prime motivator, then so be it. Football was an intensely emotional pursuit, and Woody did not feel the game should be reduced to a cold, calculating, clinician's experiment with X's and O's. Knute Rockne believed, "In the proper emotional state, a team will do extraordinary things," and Hayes forever strove to keep his team at that peak.

As fellow Hayes soulmate Vince Lombardi believed, "Football is still just a blocking and tackling game," and it was the Hayes way to reduce things to their simplest essence. Hence, the repetition and the warlike mentality, for as Schembechler stated, "We're at war out there...[it's] combat without weapons."

One final negative item intruded during this week. Tailback/split end Tyrone Hicks, who could "...run like no one you have ever seen," according to several teammates, was sentenced to a period of strict probation after pleading guilty to a reduced charge of marijuana possession. The matter, which had been pending since May of '77, was finally resolved, and Hayes reluctantly gave Hicks permission to come back out for the team in '78. Hicks, another stellar prep All-American from Warren, Ohio, also had plans to rejoin the scarlet and gray track team.

CHAPTER TEN: ILLINOIS

The harsh discipline which Hayes meted out this week certainly worked, as an especially brutalistic Buckeye offensive line ravaged a poor-playing Illinois team for 402 rushing yards, 28 first downs, and a 42-0 final score.

This game began in a fashion which portended much greater success for the Illini. Taking the opening kickoff, Illinois chewed 8:06 off the clock in a 14 play march. At the OSU 24, Ross batted down a pass attempt on a third and four attempt, bringing on the field goal squad. When David Finzer missed the 41 yarder, OSU dodged a bullet and the Illinois spirits were crushed.

Putting themselves right back under the gun, OSU almost immediately turned the ball over. Linebacker John Meyer nabbed a tipped Gerald pass at the OSU 46, and the Illini exhausted the remainder of the first quarter with a drive of ten plays.

At the start of the second quarter, Ross came up with his second big play, as he sacked Steger for a seven yard loss on a third down pass. Finzer trotted out for the second time, yet again missed the field goal, this time from 49 yards away. The Bucks took over and drove 51 yards in ten plays, until Logan fumbled deep in Illinois territory. The Illini ran three plays and punted; OSU embarked on a 72 yard scoring drive for the only points of the half.

Campbell got the final call in a string of 13 straight Buckeye rushes, powering in from the two, as the OSU line fired out very aggressively throughout the impressive trek. At the break, the visiting team seemed fortunate to be up 7-0.

In direct contrast to the first half, the third quarter was all Ohio State. Fielding the kickoff, OSU marched 75 yards in 11 plays, ending with a one yard Payton score. Guess recovered a fumble on the first ensuing Illinois play from scrimmage, and Springs speedily charged 15 yards for the second Buckeye touchdown in the last 13 seconds. As Cousineau and Adkins terrorized the line of scrimmage, the Illini were again halted.

Ohio State responded with a 65 yard march, with a five yard scoring run by Harrell sending the starters to the sidelines with 3:17 remaining in the third. Strahine came on, and in the final quarter led OSU on an impressive 87 yard touchdown march. A 15 yard Johnson run ended the scoring.

The only scoring opportunity for Illinois occurred late in the contest. Alas, newly-inserted quarterback Tim McAvoy fumbled on a fourth and one run from the Ohio State five, and defensive back Todd Bell recovered to keep the shutout intact.

Although he had no single run longer than 15 yards, Springs ended with 132 yards in 24 carries. This familiarly consistent performance put the elusive runner a scant 69 yards away from the special 1,000 yard mark. Logan (eleven-48), Campbell (nine-46), Johnson (four-24), and Volley (seven-45) each chewed up further yardage, mostly in short, consistent chunks. Payton (seven-52), of all people, broke loose for the longest run of the game, a 34 yard burst.

Another standout play in a repetitive day of off-tackle power slants came in the second quarter. Gerald pitched the ball to Jones on a reverse end-around for a dazzling 11 yard gain which threatened to go all the way. Woody was almost childlike in his excitement over the success of this tricky maneuver. Incidentally, Jones had never even practiced this particular play prior to the game. Three yards and a cloud of dust, stand aside!

Hayes was in an upbeat mood all day. Even before the game, as the Buckeyes were undergoing warm-ups, Hayes took it upon himself to whip the several hundred OSU fans present into the appropriate frenzy. Seeing that the OSU cheerleading squad had not yet arrived, Hayes jogged over to the visitors' southwest stand section and initiated an enthusiastic round of cheers. The sight of the legendary Head Coach leading chants and yells was something those present never forgot. Hayes himself thought nothing of the feat. "I'll sweep out the gym if it will help us to win," thought Woody.

Practically the only bad news of the day came as Gerald briefly left in the first half after being nailed, hard, in the back. After a quick check by the training and medical staff, Gerald was pronounced healthy and came out for the second half at 100%. Lang also twisted an ankle slightly.

On the positive side, Castignola continued his incredible recovery by appearing for a few snaps at the tail end of the game. "Just getting back onto the field means a lot to me," said the grateful Greg.

Cousineau and Adkins led the stifling defense with 17 and 12 tackles, respectively.

The shutout pitched by this peaking defense tied the modern (since '40) school season record of four. Almost unbelievably, the pre-'40 school record was nine shutouts, set by the 1899 Ohio State squad, in just a ten game season! The following year's team, also coached by John Eckstorm, compiled seven more shutouts. At one point, the '99-'00 Buckeye team racked up 13 straight shutouts, albeit against smaller schools such as Otterbein, Oberlin, Marietta, and Case Western. The '77 squad had a ways to go in terms of that record, though they were playing admirably, against seemingly stiffer competition.

Indiana came into Ohio Stadium looking to go over the goal line often enough to ensure their first winning season since '68. The Hoosiers were 4-4-1, with victories including Iowa, Minnesota, and Louisiana State University, and their offense seemed capable of striking against anyone. The Hoosier quarterback was the much-improved Columbus prep product Scott Arnett, who was slightly injured the week before and replaced in the starting lineup by the strong-armed Tim Clifford.

The Hoosier offense was clicking despite the missing presence of diminutive tailback Mike Harkrader, a Barberton, Ohio, native whose father Jerry played on the '54 national championship Buckeye team. In '76, the frosh Harkrader scrapped his way to a 1,000 yard season, only the fourth freshman in the history of college football to reach that mark. In the '77 preseason, Mike tore up his knee in early drills. The cast he had worn since then had just been sawed off, and the rigorous process of rebuilding had begun.

His backfield replacement, the former starter Ric Enis, had been brilliant in relief, coming into the game with 918 yards. Additionally, the Hoosiers were without the services of nine other starters, because of injuries, and their four wins were far more than anyone could realistically expect with such obstacles.

Hayes admitted the tendency to look past Indiana, toward the annual showdown with the Wolverines, yet overcame that temptation. "We don't believe that will happen this year... We prepare for each contest as we get to it," he somewhat facetiously said.

One facet of the OSU team lacking somewhat in execution, if not preparation, was the punting game. Never a strong point, the '77 punting game was increasingly growing weaker as the season wore on. The dwindling production hopefully was to be shored up with the return to punting of a healthier Orosz, who until now had handled only the kickoff chores, being limited by a series of nagging injuries. In the quest for an unprecedented sixth straight conference crown, Hayes realized OSU needed all facets of the team operating in maximum overdrive.

As part of the quest for this crown, Hayes declared all players and assistants off-limits to the press until the Michigan game. Interestingly, Hayes imposed this gag rule on the eve of a brief trip to Kansas City, where he was set to replace the President of the United States, Jimmy Carter, as the keynote speaker at a Future Farmers of America convention. The gag rule traditionally imposed around Michigan week of course never included Hayes. The Coach could never be perfectly silent.

Indeed, he was very loud in his praise of Robinson and Fritz, who each received six leaves for the excellence of their execution against the Fighting Illini. Springs, Ross, and Brown also drew high praise from the Coach at a later Agonis Club luncheon.

It had become a Buckeye tradition to blow off some steam on Thursday nights, particularly if the game on Saturday was at home, by ending up at the neighborhood pub, the Crest Tavern. Relaxedly run by the Bill Dupler family, this casual establishment was billed as "Columbus' original dart bar," and the players loved the small tavern for its casual homeyness and equally friendly atmosphere.

The players spent an incredible amount of time together, both in and out of season, and experienced so many trials and tribulations, they eventually developed a bond which sometimes surpassed that of their families. In this local hang-out, the players were able to comfortably shoot pool, throw darts, and disperse the tension built up throughout a strenuous week of practice.

The majority of the players felt no need to join popular Greek fraternities, for the team was a fraternity of a different sort. The guys on the team grew from teenagers into men together, and the rites of passage allowed no racial or class boundaries to exist. A popular Hayes expression was, "Like the way Duke Ellington makes great music, it takes both black and white keys to make a great football team;" accordingly, the Buckeyes generally had few exclusive cliques or factions on their roster.

On Friday of this week, Wisconsin head coach John Jardine handed in his resignation, effective at the end of the year. The likeable Jardine was hospitalized twice this year for treatment of nervous tension, exacerbated by four straight losses after a scintillating start. After the latest loss, Jardine and his team were pelted with trash, and taunted and jeered unmercifully as they left the field. The truly shocking part of this disgraceful treatment is that it was perpetrated at home, by supposedly partisan Camp Randall homecoming fans. Wisconsin fans were notoriously uncouth, known to launch stinging pennies, with slingshots, from the stands.

Jardine was a decent, honest man, who could neither fathom nor cope with this despicable behavior. This sad incident kindled a sick rage among the Badger players, throwing a divisive wedge between the team and their supposed supporters. Rather than be subjected to any more similar displays, Jardine chose to preserve his health, dignity, and honor by departing.

CHAPTER ELEVEN: INDIANA

The Buckeyes thankfully faced no such hostilities from their fans on Saturday, even though OSU got off to their now-accustomed sluggish start. From the beginning of the game, IU coach Lee Corso's sideline antics and his hell-bent attitude propelled the Hoosier squad into a frenzy, and this surge of emotions kept them very much in this game.

Indiana began the contest by charging out of the locker room, immediately determined to assert a claim as a dominant member of the evolving conference order. The Hoosiers controlled the ball for 15 plays on their opening drive, marching from their 20 to a fourth and goal situation at the OSU two. In a typically bold stroke, Corso went for the touchdown. Arnett found Keith Calvin just open in the front corner of the end zone, and following the conversion, the upstart, confident Hoosiers led 7-0.

Ohio State came right back, as Harrell nearly busted the kickoff return, finally being halted at the Buckeye 47. The 53 yards were traversed in ten quick plays, as Payton blasted over from three yards away. The game was tied.

On the next IU possession, Corso could sense the chance for an upset, and again elected to daringly try for a first down in a fourth-and-short situation. With one yard to go from their own 24, the Hoosiers succeeded. Fullback Tony D'Orazio gained four yards, and once more it seemed the Hoosiers were on their way to another score. Several minutes later, they were again confronted with a fourth-down situation, although this time the yardage was such that Corso decided to punt.

The remainder of the first half was a shifting battle of punts and poor field position on the behalf of each team. At the half, the opponents remained deadlocked.

Ohio State emerged from the locker room stoked with emotion. Led by the charging Hayes, the entire Buckeye team ran to the closed end of the stadium and circled the goalposts before heading to their side of the field. The home crowd, jammed to the 56th straight sellout capacity, went momentarily wild, only to be stunned into amazed silence as Corso led his team in a route around the same goalposts, just seconds later. A resounding chorus of boos rained over the field. An impish Corso later said: "I figured it was a good idea if Woody did it." This was the final dose of fun for the Hoosiers on this day, however.

Harrell took the kickoff all the way to the Hoosier 32, barely being contained by the final man he had to beat. On a third and eight situation several plays later from the 30, Harrell continued his heroics. Jim made an extraordinary touchdown catch, grabbing the ball off the helmet of safety Tim McVay, giving OSU the lead which they never relinquished. According to Hayes, "His TD catch was the turning point of the game. He's had more great catches than any athlete we've ever had."

The stunned Hoosiers were quickly forced to punt, and Jeff Logan soon reminded spectators what he could provide when healthy. Jeff keyed an 84 yard scoring drive with a nifty 34 yard jaunt, looking as good as ever. The 11 play drive culminated with a seven yard Gerald keeper for the score. With the loss of leading linebacker Doug Sybert to an injury in this drive, IU pretty much lost the ability to stop the heated OSU offense.

Later in the third quarter, Cato recovered an Enis fumble deep in IU territory. The Buckeyes soon capitalized by pounding in for a touchdown; the honor accorded to Ron Springs from one yard away. Enis was kept in check the entire day - by the end of the game he was used exclusively as a decoy, as IU desperately passed long and often in a futile attempt to catch the streaking Buckeyes. Enis ended with only eight carries for 25 yards.

Ohio State extinguished any possible IU comeback hope by grinding out an 81 yard fourth quarter scoring journey. As Campbell terminated the march with a one yard touchdown plunge, the Buckeyes assured themselves of a least a share of their sixth straight Big 10 title, based on the 35-7 final.

As in most seasons, the outright title and consequent Rose Bowl appearance would be decided in the regular season finale with Michigan. The Wolverines had also started this day in slow fashion, once trailing 7-0, only to dominate the later stages of their game with Purdue. Michigan eventually won 40-7.

The Buckeyes gradually fashioned this particular victory via a steadily rising crescendo which climaxed in a rousing victory. Hayes liked the strong finishes the Buckeyes made, although the troublesome starts still irked him. A strong finish in the UM game most likely would determine the winner, and Hayes felt confident this '77 team possessed such resolve. According to the coaching and training staff, no OSU team had ever been this healthy so late in the year. Perhaps the only glaring sore spot in the entire IU game was the failure of the offense to take advantage of a late opportunity to score.

With just a few minutes to play, the Buckeye specialty squad forced and recovered a fumble at the Indiana nine. Despite the proximity to the end zone, the offense could not push the ball in, and Hayes was disturbed by this shortcoming. Woody truly felt, "You will find the extent of a man's devotion on the goal line," as Lombardi passionately said, and took every such failure personally.

The pain of this failure was readily eclipsed by the strong performance of Logan, who seemed all the way back in his recovery. In his first real extended chance to shine since going down early in the year, Logan seized the moment, gaining 148 yards on 20 attempts. Springs cracked the 1,000 yard barrier with 18 rushes for 72 yards, before being banged up a bit. He received a long, well-deserved rest throughout the second half. Campbell emerged in this absence to rack up 52 yards in nine tries. Harrell finished with 63 yards from the two long kick returns, and Cousineau and Adkins once again took advantage of their opportunities to record 17 and 16 tackles, respectively.

In the post game press conference, Corso's first comment was, "OSU is just an onside kick away from the national championship." He then went on to laud Hayes, saying: "You people don't realize he is an amazing human being. You guys are seeing something you may never see again;" by which Corso meant a man able to handle the rigors and unbelievable stresses involved in coaching at such a high level for so long. In light of the recent resignment of Jardine, the statements of Corso assumed added weight.

Hayes captured a few laughs during his own press conference. He saw no need for "...special preparations for Michigan, except to lock the gates a little tighter and say a little less about it all." This type of self-deprecating humor was mostly unexpected coming from Hayes, and the usual ring of truth to his pronouncements made them even more funny. Skladany swears that Hayes would have made a master comedian, for his sense of timing and delivery, running so counter to character, was impeccable.

Schembechler evoked similar laughs at his own press conference following his game, as he deadpanned that Michigan would not think about Ohio State until Monday, and in fact had not thought of OSU all year. Anyone even remotely involved with the rivalry knew this statement to be as far from the truth as possible.

By Monday, Hayes was especially direct and succinct on the importance of the Michigan game. This was the game the entire season built up to, and little else was important by comparison. Bo, first at OSU and then crossing over to UM, had long been steeped in the overriding importance of the rivalry. "You can't match this in anything you do," he stated. "This is a rivalry that pro football can't begin to touch," he intoned.

By the same token, Bo did not care for the extreme amount of hoopla which now surrounded the game, for he much preferred to stick with his comfortable weekly routine. Still, Bo was lighthearted enough to quip, when asked if any new stringent security measures would be implemented for practices in Ann Arbor, "Not any more than [ex-President] Jerry Ford has when he comes to practice."

Especially in these Michigan games, Hayes believed in the Lombardi credo, "Man can be as great as he wants to be." In a similar sentiment, Goethe, the German novelist, poet and playwright which Hayes was fond of invoking, wrote, "If I accept you as you are, I will make you worse; however, if I treat you as though you are what you are capable of becoming, I help you become that."

Hayes was a certified genius at reaching into a player's hidden potential and extracting the greatness which Woody believed existed to some extent in everyone. Numerous former players speak of performing feats which they physically should not have been able to, if Hayes had not demanded they exceed their pre-conceived limits. Many of the fond memories of the OSU football experience touch on this ability of Hayes to elicit great feats.

Barry Posner, author of *Leadership Challenge*, offers some insight into this fondness. "Answering the summons of adventure lifts our spirits. There is something about being invited to do better than we ever have done before that compels us to reach down deep inside and bring forth the warrior within."

Max Midlam recalls hearing Hayes talk to a young Dave Adkins on the eve of an earlier game. Hayes told the special teamer he was going to make two solo tackles the next day on kick coverages, and Midlam inwardly chuckled, for Woody had once told a younger Max the same thing. Sure enough, just as happened in Midlam's case, in the ensuing game, Adkins played like a man possessed and made several impressive solo shots. As Woody demanded by sheer dint of will, the player invariably delivered.

Several warriors were rewarded for their efforts in the IU clash, foremost among them being Dansler and Brown. Ward received six leaves for his usual fine game, and Logan racked up five of the helmet decals for his inspiring performance. Janakievski was also awarded two leaves for his successful kicking efforts. Coming off seven straight wins, the Buckeyes were upbeat and fairly emotional.

Hayes could not yet tell, at this early time in the week, if his team was absolutely psychologically prepared for the ultimate confrontation with UM, yet Woody never really gauged his team's readiness until right near game time. At that point, Hayes was a master at employing any number of a myriad of motivational measures to enhance any deficit in the proper emotion.

Hayes himself admired immensely the speech Winston Churchill delivered in preparation for the invasion of Britain, by far superior German forces, in World War Two. The speech, which never failed to elicit a fiery response from Woody, goes in part: "...we shall fight with growing confidence and growing strength... we shall defend our island, whatever the cost may be... we shall never surrender... we shall never give in!"

This week, Hayes was somewhat saddened by the retirement of John Pont, head man at Northwestern. Pont also had coached successfully at Miami of Ohio, Yale, and Indiana, and had led the Hoosiers to a '68 New Year's Rose Bowl berth. Pont was especially close to Woody, yet even closer to Bo, and his announcement gave each man pause in this hectic week, although John was merely stepping up to a position as athletic director of the Wildcats.

Nevertheless, Woody was especially jovial and good-natured by Tuesday. He was made even more pleased as the weather conformed to his wishes, ceasing to rain in time for the Buckeyes to hold their Tuesday evening practice outside.

Earlier that afternoon, speaking in front of the Chicago (Illinois) Football Writers Club, Hayes declared, "This is fun week. If you enjoy coaching, it's fun," albeit intense. When asked if his game plans might be affected if it rained on Saturday, Hayes jokingly allowed, "...it might hurt our passing attack."

For a Michigan week, there was an unnatural, unusual air of good humor and looseness in the Buckeye camp. The players did not seem upset in the least; at the increasingly upbeat practices, it was revealed through the play of the Buckeyes that, though the team was relaxed, they seemed to be building to a peak for Saturday, as their demeanor became increasingly more intense. The Buckeyes were extremely confident they could reverse the disappointing loss the previous year to the Wolverines.

Commenting on this hoped-for improvement in comparison to the '76 squad, Hayes made a startlingly prophetic statement. "The only meaningful statistic is number of games won." In the game soon to come, this adage would all too truthfully be hammered home, as OSU dominated every statistic but the final score.

Michigan came into the contest with as fine a team as any Bo had coached; this opinion offered by no less an expert than the premier Big 10 scout, Esco Sarkinnen. Hayes honestly felt (again, quite correctly) that the better defense around the goal line would determine the outcome.

A mere sophomore in class standing, yet a spectacular player regardless, Ron Simpkins led the maize and blue defense. John Anderson was a defensive end of high repute, and the secondary was deep, talented, and experienced. This veteran backfield defended very well against the pass, rarely giving up a big play, and contributed greatly to the rough run defense, too. As always, UM was a swarming, attacking group in which the sum of the whole was greater than any individual parts.

The UM option offense was directed by the junior flinger Leach. The ever-improving leader was the only quarterback in the entire conference to have more touchdown tosses than interceptions this year. The rapidly expanding Wolverine air attack was masterminded by ex-Bowling Green (Ohio) coach Don Nehlen, who had really worked wonders with Leach and the receiving corps.

The offensive line was top-notch, even without '76 standout Bill Dufek, who had missed the whole year with knee injuries. Guard Mark Donohue, center Walt Downing, and humongous tackle Mike Kenn were surprisingly quick and disarmingly powerful, expert at opening holes for the backs and keeping the rush from Leach.

Michigan had their own deep stable of runners, as usual. The only question remained, who would be healthy enough among the many to carry the ball against the keyed-up Bucks? The top three spots in the tailback depth chart were all nursing injuries; the starter would depend on who healed the quickest. The usual starter, speedster Harlan Huckleby, missed the previous game and was back at less than full readiness. Roosevelt Smith was also dinged up, and frosh standout Stanley Edwards was waiting in the wings, albeit with slight nagging injuries. Russell Davis was the rampaging fullback, and he was healthy. One other offensive stalwart, tight end Gene Johnson, was also hurt and would miss this game.

Earlier in the week it was confirmed that the loser of this all-important contest would journey to the Sugar Bowl in New Orleans to play Paul "Bear" Bryant's number two rated Alabama team. Neither OSU nor UM cared to acknowledge the possibility of a loss, however. It was not in the makeup of either Woody or Bo to admit there was even a possibility of defeat, particularly in this annual game.

As a further example of the magnitude of this matchup, UM athletic director Don Canham predicted Michigan would clear in excess of a half a million dollars, just for hosting this game. This figure was derived from anticipated gate receipts, television rights, parking, concession, and program fees. As the visiting team, Ohio State could still expect to make around a third of a million dollars.

In other news of this week, former Buckeye favorites Archie Griffin and Brian Baschnagel were experiencing diametrically opposite years in the NFL. Griffin was suffering through a disappointing second campaign with the Bengals, and had been occasionally benched in favor of the supposedly better receiver, Lenvil Elliot.

Rookie fullback Pete Johnson, necessarily overshadowed by Griffin in college, was again Archies' teammate. On this go-around, Pete was casting his own bid for stardom, and had bowled over all opposition in becoming the most feared Bengal ground gainer. Likewise, as a special teams/pass receiving standout with the Bears, Baschnagel was among the finest in the league.

On the college basketball scene, Miami (Ohio) Redskin tri-captain Randy Ayers and his capable teammates were touted as the Mid-American Conference pre-season title favorites. The steady 6'6" forward was coming off a junior season which netted him honorable mention conference merit, and the hard worker was seeking to improve in his final collegiate campaign.

As a final nail in the wall of preparation for the big game, Hayes outfitted his entire squad in special-order turf shoes. Woody was not comfortable with the playing surface in Ann Arbor, and was hopeful these new shoes would give greater traction and better results. This was merely the latest in a seeming series of atypical behaviors for Woody, going against the grain of his public persona, which was that of a grim, unyielding, crusty curmudgeon who failed to ever progress in his thinking.

Indeed, many pre-game articles, published prior to this game, centered around an updated opinion of Woody: He was a highly adaptable coach more than willing to forego his expected stubbornness and progress instead with any innovation that benefitted his team. Along with the newer image, expectations and emotions still ran high for a Buckeye victory. Disabled senior Marty

Cusick personified this emotion as he used his crutches to participate in the traditional senior tackle on Friday.

CHAPTER TWELVE: MICHIGAN

Sadly, Saturday was an occasion which Woody summed up as, "This is by far the best game we ever played and lost." On a gloomy day before an NCAA record-setting crowd of 106,024 exhilarated fans, the Buckeyes dominated every category but the important one, the scoring column. On seven separate occasions the Buckeyes had the ball deep within Michigan territory; five of these times they penetrated beyond the UM 15. The result of all this penetration was two measly field goals.

The OSU offense alternated between striking periods of excellence and then sudden ineptitude. As much as Ohio State self-destructed, credit should also be given to a Michigan defense which somehow prevented the Buckeyes time after interminable time from crossing the goal line. The Buckeyes stood atop all statistical categories: First downs (23-10), rushing yards (208-141), passing yards (144-55), and total yards (352-196). Yet UM came out ahead in the final analysis, by a 14-6 score.

The game began in a highly combative manner. Entering the playing field first, Hayes led his OSU squad toward the center of the field for their pre-game prayer. A group of Michigan supporters happened to already be gathered at the same midfield spot, holding a gigantic UM banner. A scuffle broke out amongst the conflicting forces, and in the escalating melee, several players and fans alike tangled and were knocked to the turf. Of course, Hayes was in the middle of this brief scrap.

Garth Cox swears that in the midst of this melee, as both teams brawled and other coaches attempted to dissipate the fisticuffs, Hayes was more interested in protecting the honor of his players, willing to brawl right alongside them. Incidents like this endeared the Coach even more to his "boys," who realized their leader would go toe-to-toe against any opposition to the OSU cause.

After some semblance of order was restored, Schembechler greeted the feisty Hayes, who promptly corrected Bo's grammar, in a never-ending display of gamesmanship. Particularly in an opposing stadium, Hayes thought every competitive edge should be seized.

Thereby sufficiently empowered, OSU grabbed the opening kick and bulled downfield to the Wolverine 12. The UM defense tightened, so Janakievski put the ball through the uprights for the early 3-0 advantage. Viewers at home, tuned in to ABC television, joined the contest in progress just prior to this field goal. Coverage of the game was pre-empted and delayed due to massive world-wide interest in the Egyptian president, Anwar Sadat, and his historic arrival in Israel for peace summit talks. A full seven minutes into this game, ABC began delayed live coverage, so the nation, including Columbus, missed the spectacular brawl before the opening whistle.

Michigan received the ball on the ensuing kickoff and punted after attaining a net of three yards on three plays. Ohio State promptly drove all the way to the Michigan eight, at which point the Wolverine defense again tightened, and in fact began pushing OSU backwards. On third down from the 16, Curtis Greer broke through the line and tossed Gerald for another loss, this time for nine big yards. Due to this added distance, Janakievski missed the resulting 42 yard field goal opportunity.

After this miss, the OSU offense sputtered slightly. Following a series of punt exchanges in which Michigan steadily got better field position, the Wolverines were able to start a drive from the OSU 46. The UM offense took nine plays to punch the ball in the end zone, with the big play being a 22 yard third down pass to Roosevelt Smith, expertly delivered by Leach. Leach subsequently dove in from the one, and the home team took a 7-3 lead.

Getting the ball back with 1:20 remaining before the half, OSU charged downfield behind the efforts of Logan and Gerald. They got just close enough to attempt another Janakievski field goal, and a Vlade miss from 49 yards ended the first half.

The Wolverines received the second half kick, were unable to generate much movement, and were soon forced to punt. The Bucks began a drive from their 16, and Springs fumbled on the very first snap. The everpresent Simpkins snagged the loose ball on the OSU 20, whereupon Leach led a short drive which was capped by his second touchdown. The slim 14-3 margin proved insurmountable, though Ohio State did not lack for effort. "Our kids never tried harder - they never quit," Hayes later remembered.

The Buckeyes did come right back after the UM score. Gerald, who connected on a remarkable 13 of his 16 passes, drove Ohio State from their 15 all the way down to the UM 11. Once again, the Wolverines stopped the Bucks shy of the end zone, although this time Janakievski converted a short field goal effort.

On the ensuing Michigan possession, a fierce hit by Adkins caused a fumble at the UM 27. Allegro leaped on the loose ball, and OSU had another golden scoring opportunity. The tenacious Michigan defense sidestepped another scoring threat by swarming over Campbell for a two yard loss on a third and one call inside the 20. Somehow, Janakievski missed his third field goal.

The Michigan offense still could not penetrate the Buckeye defense, and OSU again took rapid possession, driving down the field. Eschewing another short field goal as time was dwindling, the Buckeyes went for a touchdown on a fourth and one from the Wolverine ten. Once more, the first down, and points, were denied.

With just a little over three minutes remaining, in the teeth of fierce Wolverine resistance and the exhortations of nearly 100,000 rabid UM fans, Ohio State got the ball back. Gerald heroically led Ohio State down the field on an 82 yard drive, to the Michigan eight. On first and goal, just as a touchdown finally seemed inevitable, John Anderson flew in from his end position and separated Gerald from the ball. When the pile was cleared, Wolverine Derek Howard was holding the pigskin.

At the exact moment that Anderson collided with Gerald, ABC cameraman Mike Freedman shot an extreme closeup of Hayes expressing his anguish and frustration. When Woody realized his disappointment was being caught on camera, he flew into a sudden rage. Hayes charged the cameraman, who had ventured outside his designated filming area, and knocked the camera away. In the process of ridding Freedman of his camera, Woody also struck the man in the head and shoulder. Then Hayes resumed his coaching, for amazingly, OSU still had a glimmer of hope for a miraculous comeback.

The unbelievable Buckeye defense stopped Michigan in three quick plays, forcing a punt. Ohio State fielded the kick and resumed the comeback with just over two minutes left. On the UM 47, facing a do-or-die fourth down situation, Springs fielded a pitch and was promptly nailed in the backfield. Another chance had slipped away, and this time, there was no reprieve. Michigan ran out the remaining seconds, taking the win despite all odds.

Gerald enjoyed a phenomenal day against a defense set up specifically to slow him. Rod was hounded each and every down, yet somehow threw for 144 yards and netted 52 additional yards on the ground. Forced by the intense UM pressure into throwing short or intermediate patterns which were quick to develop, Gerald dumped the ball to Springs eight times for 58 yards. Harrell was able to free himself on three occasions for medium and longish gains, also totaling 58 yards through the air. Springs also led the way on the ground, carrying 14 punishing times for 89 yards. Logan contributed 50 yards on 16 tries, while Campbell was stuffed on his ten short-range carries, totaling only 17 yards.

Only the puzzling inability of the Ohio State offense to put up points kept this game from being a rout in their advantage, for the Buckeye defenders completely stifled the UM offense, except on the two short scoring drives.

A very weary and depressed Hayes barely raised his voice above a whisper after this game. He walked out of his post-game press conference prematurely, then sat desolately and dejectedly in a metal folding chair, in isolation, until the team bus was cleared to depart. On his way to the bus, Hayes stoically endured the vociferous taunts of many loud Michigan supporters.

From the very moment the incident with Freedman occurred, television commentary on the matter was decidedly anti-Hayes. Those fans in the stadium who had witnessed the incident of course did not hesitate in lambasting Woody. Possibly never had Hayes been so roundly criticized for an act, whether committed in the heat of battle or outside the stadium gates. The pillorying, even from Columbus, was sharp, pointed, and extremely vocal.

Monday night was the traditional year-end appreciation banquet. Prior to this banquet, Hayes brashly stated that he had done no wrong during the game, and would never apologize for the sideline incident. However, at the tail end of his speech that night, Hayes launched into a slight tirade concerning the matter. His comments concluded with the phrase, "I'm sorry for what happened," and Woody expressed his hope that the matter would now be dropped. His tone throughout his comments was most decisive, and not exactly remorseful or conciliatory by conventional standards.

In a theory much expanded on in *Bo*, the '89 autobiography of Schembechler, it was stated that part of the reason Coach Hayes lost his temper so completely during times of undue pressure, on this occasion and in the future, was attributable to some vengeful side effects of diabetes and extremely low blood sugar levels. The resulting imbalance brought on by these medical conditions contributed to the Hayes mind-set, to the point that Woody did not completely realize the extent of his behaviors, solely during these imbalanced, stressful moments.

Consequently, in Hayes' own thoughts and recollections, his actions were not nearly as severe as they appeared to others; therefore, Woody never felt the need to truly apologize. Throw utter exhaustion and deep despair on top of these worsening medical conditions, and it becomes quite understandable how, in extreme moments of stress and disappointment, Hayes could momentarily lose the rational hold on his (even in perfect times) boiling emotions. Soon after this night, Hayes did personally call Freedman to express his chagrin and regret.

Trying to rebound from this bitter defeat, Hayes resolutely stated that the setback should ultimately help his team. The program could resolve to grow stronger, by redoubling their efforts in order to rebuild from the rubble of the loss. From this valiant effort, greater triumphs could be reached, at least according to the doctrine of Hayes. As Woody said, "What's wrong with dedication? It's the first demand I made on my kids...," and now was the time for even greater dedication. Cousineau believed, "If you have not lost, then you have not played in enough games." Even Schembechler agreed, "Nothing motivates like your own failure."

In reference to Abraham Lincoln, whom Hayes idolized and termed, "The eventual winner," Woody reminded his team that this great president lost eight elections, failed twice in business, and suffered a nervous breakdown - before he was elected as our 16th president. Hayes related this saga to remind his team that they could bounce back, too.

Out of this perplexing defeat, many heroes emerged. Adkins was voted the team MVP in a vote of the squad, and also was selected as the outstanding player in the UM game. The grateful senior gave a short acceptance speech, pointing out the closeness of the '77 squad. Amazingly, Adkins had never started a game until this year, and now he was judged the greatest single player on a team with many stars. "I waited a long time for this chance and didn't want to be the weak link," he explained. Obviously, he wasn't.

David's father played for Woody at Miami, so Dave grew up in his Xenia, Ohio, town schooled solidly in the traditions and benefits of playing under Hayes. The senior Adkins, who pleased Woody further by becoming a school superintendent, reacted with unbelievable pride as his rugged son leaped at the chance to likewise play for Woody. Additionally, the OSU agriculture program which interested Dave was among the finest in the country, so he could attain a quality education, as well.

By his own admission, David arrived in Columbus, in '74, underweight (at 197 pounds), apprehensive about playing in a major program such as OSU, and somewhat overwhelmed by the fantastic talent surrounding him. As Adkins eventually put on weight and increased in confidence, the coaching staff gradually realized they had a hitting demon on their hands.

Still, as often happened in the dog-eat-dog world of big-time college athletics, of which OSU was a charter member, Dave had been labeled a back-up player, and no matter how brilliantly he played on special teams units, how fiercely he hit in practices, or how solidly he performed in limited game action, he was trapped in that reserve role. With the graduation of Ed Thompson, Dave seized his long-awaited chance and squeezed out every ounce of his hard-nosed ability.

Chris Ward was designated the offensive lineman of the year, and captured the fraternity designation as player of the year as well. Aaron Brown took the award for defensive lineman of the year. The top newcomers were defensive lineman Luther Henson, who also grappled for the OSU wrestling team as a heavyweight, and scoring sensation Joel Payton.

This award took some of the sting from the curious (lack of) use of Payton for the Michigan contest. Joel never left the bench in that game, and it seemed obvious, in view of the numerous failures in short-yardage situations during that game, that OSU could have used the talents of the plowhorse fullback.

The decision to leave the rugged frosh on the sidelines engendered much discussion in the media and in private in the weeks following, and was also the crux of many controversial complaints aimed at Woody.

The All-Big 10 team was announced later in the week, and contained some shocking selections. In what seemed like a huge slight, Gerald missed a berth on the second team by one vote, and was relegated to third team status behind Leach and Herrmann. Similarly, Dansler missed a spot on the first team by a solitary vote. More predictably, Springs, Moore, Ward, Cousineau, Guess, Brown, Cato, and Griffin were selected to either first or second team status.

The biggest slight was the complete absence of Adkins. How Adkins was left off remains a mystery to this day, for the rough and tumble senior set a then-school record with 172 tackle participations on the year. Several years later, Hayes delivered a speech on the campus of Purdue, and admitted that the OSU coaches and administrators, including himself, had been lax in promoting Adkins for honors after the '77 season. On reflection, Hayes admitted that

David deserved a much finer fate than remaining virtually anonymous following his dominating senior campaign.

Ward later also captured All-American honors, along with Cousineau, Griffin, Brown, and Springs.

Addressing a crowd of Buckeye Boosters around this time, in Cincinnati, Ohio, Hayes challenged the assembled media to accentuate the positives, such as these All-America selections. He felt the press had become too negative, particularly in their treatment of him. Since his sideline flare-up, media coverage was skewed so heavily toward wrongdoings by Woody that his good deeds were overlooked, and he for one, and for once, was growing tired of the routine. Warming to his topic, Hayes abruptly snorted, "Freedom of speech means I can quit when I want." With that, he brusquely ended his speech and left the hall.

Afterwards, Hayes had settled down somewhat and was eagerly awaiting his chance to match coaching wits with Bear Bryant. No coaching matchup in the history of college football ever pitted more wins and experience against an even greater amount of experience and victories. Bryant had 272 wins going into the game, Hayes 231, and the two had a combined 65 years of head coaching experience. Hayes cited "bullheadedness" as the chief reason he and Bryant had been so successful for so long, and Woody still got angry if he heard any mention of his impending mellowness.

If anything, Hayes was even more aggressive and hard-charging than ever, especially when it came to recruiting. As an example, Hayes flew to Miami, Florida, on an free afternoon just days before the Sugar Bowl contest, solely to sweet talk a prep prospect.

Sadly, recruiting, which had once been the forte of Woody, now more often served only to confuse and frustrate Hayes. As captured so eloquently in Robert Vare's penetrating *Buckeye: A Study of Coach Woody Hayes and the Ohio State Football Machine*, published in '74, OSU was perhaps the collegiate originator in converting the recruitment of prep players into a big business. With the specialized techniques of advanced help from increasing amounts of eager boosters and grateful former players, Ohio State turned that selling process into a non-stop, year-long affair.

Yet, until the final few years of his coaching career, the final, and usually most important, sales pitch in the involved recruiting process was basic: Woody extending the opportunity to attend a prestigious, established university. The player was presented with nothing but the chance to receive a great education and perhaps, play some for a traditional football power. Woody sold the university more to parents than to the prospective player, for that player was usually steeped in the storied tradition of OSU and leaped at the chance to be schooled by Hayes. Once Woody weaved his wonderful rapport with the parents and high school coach, the player most often willingly, and eagerly, fell in line.

More and more, however, the parents and coaches who before were overjoyed with only an opportunity for their son/player to attend Ohio State, now demanded a guarantee of playing time for that youngster. We've already seen how schools such as Michigan State, Oklahoma, and numerous unnamed others, willingly induced prep stars to attend their schools with ever-increasing enticements, often financial in nature, which tied in with these guarantees of playing time. Essentially, if one school promised a payoff to the player, and another school promised only an opportunity to receive an education, the program offering the cash incentive came off in a more favorable light.

Of course, there were many exceptions to this trend, yet Woody was growing very frustrated by the elevating demands of prospective recruits, and his own moral inability to either make or deliver on such promises.

Adkins recalls one such recruit, from the Cincinnati, Ohio, area, who made a weekend visit to the Columbus campus. Adkins was given the task of chaperoning this player and acclimating the coveted prep star to the ways of OSU. However, the prospective recruit became so demanding, asking for guarantees of playing time and cash remuneration, that Adkins blithely told the high school senior to "...get the hell out of here." In defending the honor of the program, Adkins drove away one of the top prospects in the state; increasingly, such prep stars were disdaining the Buckeyes because those guarantees were neither offered nor delivered, as they sometimes were at other institutions.

Interestingly, caught in a fierce battle with archrival Michigan for Miami Trace (Ohio) prep quarterback Art Schlichter, Woody perhaps may have conceded his traditional values and actually promised young Art a starting nod. In defense of Schlichter and his parents, it must be fairly stated that they apparently never demanded such special treatment; Woody was desperate to stave off the dreaded Wolverines, and perhaps felt this concession essential in securing the finest high school quarterback in the land. As shall be seen, this tentative step into the new order of recruiting ultimately led to the crumbling of the Hayes dynasty.

Getting back to the impending Sugar Bowl, Hayes had of course long been aware and respectful of the Bryant legend. It may fairly safely be said that if the legend and feisty aura of one man surpassed that of Hayes, then that man was Bryant. Bryant was long considered as mean and demanding as a coach could possibly be, stating, "...the only thing brutal about football is losing." Bear had a knack for taking undeveloped talent and transforming it into refined stardom, through the sheer process of hard work and adherence to his brand of football: Strong, unbelievably teeming gang tackling on defense, and quick, rugged, surprisingly daring and innovative on offense.

Of course, since his program's at Texas A&M, Kentucky, and 'Bama had been so successful for almost thirty years, Bear did not rely totally on this undeveloped talent; multitudes of superbly blessed athletes practically begged to play for the Crimson Tide every fall, much like at OSU.

The memories of Woody concerning Bryant reached as far back as seeing Bear play in the '35 Rose Bowl. Bryant was one starting end on that unbeaten Alabama team; the legendary Don Hutson was the other. By way of comparison, Hayes claimed that at his own finest level of play while at Denison, he would not have even qualified to make the traveling squad at OSU. Even in his undergrad days, though, Woody still outworked everyone. When reminded of his and Woodys' playing fortunes, Bryant offered, "I can assure you I'm not going to play, and I hope Woody does."

Hayes was eager to resume practicing, for after the Michigan game the team took nearly two weeks off, to make it through final examinations and heal up after the deleteriously brutal finale. The memories of the painful defeat still lingered. "Until that last fumble at Michigan, I still thought we could win the national championship," admitted Woody. In a meeting with ABC television representatives and Sugar Bowl officials, Woody was able to clown around a bit, posing for the paparazzi in a trademark Bear Bryant houndstooth hat. Above all, the Buckeyes looked toward the Alabama contest as a chance to redeem their season.

Senior Jeff Logan was unusually fired up to prove that this '77 team was indeed a great one. He figured this team was only slightly less talented than the '75 squad, which contended for the national championship on the first day of the '76 new year. Fellow senior Ward felt the '77 coaching staff was the best in his experience, and he also felt that the offensive and defensive units were equally talented. Only a few ill-timed, critical, and minute mental mistakes kept this '77 team from achieving their possible destiny of a national title, felt Ward and Logan.

Perhaps attesting to the importance of this Sugar Bowl game, the Buckeyes were practicing with even greater vigor than usual when workouts resumed. The intensity was at an even greater pitch than observers could ever recall, including during recent trips to the Rose Bowl. Hayes expected much more out of this team, and at least in early practices was getting more, for he appealed to the collective pride of the Buckeyes and they responded positively.

In news of the unusual, reserve defensive back Brian Schwartz was injured over the two week layoff, after the Michigan game. The native Californian was injured in a surfing mishap, shortly after his arrival back home. The only other injury of note at this time was a sore shoulder which was plaguing Payton, and threatened to keep him out of the bowl game.

Adkins merely had a proverbial chip on his shoulder, for he was eager to find out how the OSU defense matched up against the famed "Bama wishbone offense. The senior linebacker had one last chance to prove himself, and he wanted that chance to come against the best possible competition.

Alabama was led offensively by the tremendous fullback Johnny Davis. Bryant considered Davis to be the finest offensive back in the Crimson Tide history, as much for his fantastic blocking as his fine running ability. Davis led the Tide in rushing for the third successive year, and was a much feared receiver too.

The up and coming director of the wishbone/multiple motion set offense was junior quarterback Jeff Rutledge. In making a comeback from a broken wrist incurred during spring practice, Rutledge steadily improved through the course of the year. He was a capable runner, excelling in the quick, proper decisions demanded by the wishbone set, and was a vastly accurate big play passing threat, mostly on long pitches to All-American split end Ozzie Newsome.

The finest hour in the Rutledge career had come in the recent season finale versus dreaded in-state rival Auburn. Jeff connected on nine of 13 passes for 193 yards and two touchdowns, and also ran for 102 yards as 'Bama took the victory. As Rutledge fared, so did Tide fortunes: In the only 'Bama loss of the year, to Nebraska, he threw five interceptions.

On the year, Jeff was good on 64 of 107 throws, for 1207 yards and eight touchdowns. Like his father, Gary, who ran the Crimson Tide wishbone during his undergrad days, Rutledge was fulfilling his boyhood dream of being an Alabama quarterback.

Another vaunted weapon for the Tide was quick tailback Tony Nathan. Nathan led the Southeastern Conference in both average yards per play from scrimmage and in touchdowns. He also displayed an affinity for the option pass, and was a continual threat on kickoff and punt returns.

On the other side of the scrimmage line, 'Bama had started the season with a young and extremely inexperienced defense, particularly in the front five. Low ebb came in the Cornhusker loss, and improvement had been widespread and noticeable since then. Strong side linebacker Rich Wingo led the gang tackling Crimson horde, who had really jelled by season's end. Tackle Marty Lyons and end Wayne Hamilton were linchpins on the line, and Mikes' Kramer and Tucker patrolled the vicious-hitting, airtight secondary.

As always, Bryant cast his large, gravelly-voiced shadow over the entire squad, as Rutledge aptly explained. "Bryant motivates us without ever saying a word," often utilizing an old Hayes adage: "I'll tell you how to motivate. Eliminate those who aren't motivated."

As good as both Rutledge and the 'Bama defense had become, OSU appeared to be slightly better in both regards. The Buckeye defense held a big edge in keeping the opposition out of the end zone, holding eleven foes to a measly 85 points, second in the nation. The OSU national high of 22 interceptions did not seem to bode well for the passing chances of Rutledge, either.

At the quarterback position, Buckeye coach Chaump insisted that game films proved conclusively that Gerald had improved more in one season than any other player he had ever coached. The wily dasher Rod more than tripled his passing yards to a total of 913, and upped his completion percentage to 66% (60-90). Bryant considered Gerald the craftiest option helmsman ever, narrowly surpassing former Tennessee Volunteer will-o-wisp Condredge Holloway.

As a direct result of the Hayes/Freedman confrontation, in early December conference commissioner Wayne Duke concluded that Hayes had violated the Big 10 regulation governing sportsmanlike conduct. Ohio State president Harold Enarson did not disagree, yet added that Hayes had been provoked and that such a violation was antithetical to the historical actions of both the university and the Coach. According to Enarson, the incident in Ann Arbor was an accidental, admittedly avoidable aberration and would not occur again.

In light of the shocking exit of Hayes just over a year later, time would disappointingly prove this argument faulty. Duke levied a two year probationary penalty for Woody, the second time such a penalty was imposed (The first occasion was also due to sideline antics in Michigan, that being a '71 tirade involving a sideline marker and questionable officiating).

The Buckeyes were rounding into form thanks to mild mid-December Columbus weather, which afforded them several outdoor practices. On the 20th of December, Hayes transported his troops down south to the old Tulane Stadium practice site.

Since the erection and inception of the Superdome as the venue of the Sugar Bowl, the Tulane structure had fallen into a state of rusty disrepair. The venerable location was equipped with the scorned and lowly-regarded polyturf, a cheaper version of the astroturf much preferred by Hayes. To demonstrate his recently upturned spirits, Hayes jested, "I guess when you are guests - you don't criticize other people's furniture."

With the Sugar Bowl payoff for each team expected to be nearly $1 million, Hayes felt relaxed enough to clown around with Bryant at press conferences. Woody even had the wherewithal to joke with his nemesis Freedman during a practice session. Adding to the high spirits of the Coach was the selection of '69-'70 Buckeye assistant Dave McLain as the newest head coach at Wisconsin.

Hayes charmed the New Orleans newsmen with his down-home wit and homespun hospitality. His talk was peppered with tales of his favorite topics, history and war, and the many reporters encouraged this direction. To better explain his custom of heading to bowl sites at such an early date, Hayes said, "If you're going to fight in the North Atlantic, you've got to train in the North Atlantic" (a reference to the methods employed finally by the U.S. Navy just prior to the Midway battle of World War Two). When questioned regarding his certain relaxed coaching style during several Louisiana practices, Hayes readily admitted, despite contrary appearances, "We never practice easy."

Continuing on with the similarities between war and football, Hayes stated, "Football is not bloody. War is. But there are great parallels between the two - strategy, morale, and discipline." Another big influence upon Woody, former OSU head coach Paul Brown, commented, "Football is war... and wars are won by the team that's fit and ready."

The morale of the OSU team was increasingly suspect, however. As an intestinal virus swept through the ranks, striking Harrell, Lang, Beamon, and Logan especially hard, the air surrounding the Ohio State contingent seemed increasingly fraught with tension. The team appeared to be tiring of the New Orleans scene, especially as Christmas came and went with no letup in the harsh practice schedule. By contrast, Alabama did not arrive until the 29th, and the Tide seemed noticeably fresher and more enthused. Early OSU curfews prevented many late night shenanigans, though the rambunctious players were not completely denied of their fun.

Ricardo Volley recalls one afternoon when the players ventured into the infamous French Quarter after a grueling morning practice. The team had received free drink tickets from Pat O'Brien's, the world famous bar and restaurant noted for its powerful rum concoction, the Hurricane, which the founders of this establishment invented and perfected. Being the non-drinking teetotaler that he was, Hayes had no conception that such a free drink offer meant a beverage containing alcohol. Woody entered the club, along with his stable of assistants, as many players were seated at various tables sipping from a tall, ornate souvenir glass.

Woody innocently tasted the contents of one glass, and predictably all hell broke loose as he realized there was a lot of liquor in each glass. Woody began charging throughout the crowded business, also filled with dozens of people not associated with the team, throwing out drinks and tearing up the passes he had willingly passed out just hours before. Players frantically tossed down the contents of their drinks before the Coach could reach them, stashing the souvenir glass and dashing outside into the crowded streets. One terrified waiter lost an entire tray of drinks, as Hayes grabbed the load and exuberantly disposed of the demon rum.

Amazingly, Woody assembled the team together minutes later, told them to locate aide Larry Romanoff and secure their NCAA-approved stipend money, and they would then have until one a.m. to explore New Orleans, sans all coaching supervision! Predictably, the overjoyed "...crazy s.o.b.'s," as John Bozick called that era's players, took legendary advantage of such unaccustomed leeway. Hopefully, the statute of limitations have now expired!

Regardless of the normally early curfew throughout their stay, several players also snuck beer into the hotel, and surreptitiously drank in their rooms. The harsh, hot southern sun baked out the alcohol in the morning, as Hayes really drove the team hard, particularly after a few occurrences such as this. Bowl trips were always hotbeds of temptation, and the renowned "anything goes" mentality of New Orleans translated into numerous opportunities for misadventure. One can easily imagine the fun a teenager, unused to much relaxation, could cram in amidst a carnival atmosphere in the sinful city.

The fun sort of wore off, however, as the consensus seemed to be that more than three or four trips to the French Quarter was really pushing the luck that

Hayes would not discover any transgressions. Also, as on any vacation, the allure of "home sweet home" eventually rears its head, and OSU was really being worn down by the disappointments and the non-stop, increasingly hard work of the season.

With Payton still nursing a sore shoulder, and Tim Burke lost to a knee injury, the harsh practices seemed to take even more starch out of the exhausted player's psyches. The mood of gloom surrounding the OSU team became thicker and thicker. The proof manifested itself in an extremely unmotivated display on January the 2nd.

CHAPTER THIRTEEN: SUGAR BOWL

There seems no use in distinguishing between the end of the bittersweet '77 season and the halting start to the '78 campaign. The two years juxtaposed in a telling indication of the even more disappointing season to come, as what was touted as a battle for the ages, between two legendary programs and two equally legendary coaches, turned into a crushing, listless OSU loss in their very first Sugar Bowl. The 35-6 defeat was the most lopsided margin against OSU since Purdue, led by Leroy Keyes and Bob Griese, stomped them 41-6 in '67. This was also the worst bowl defeat ever at Ohio State, barely eclipsing the 28-0 loss to California in the '20 Rose Bowl. Despite the preseason contention by Woody that this '77 team had a chance to be among his greatest ever, the squad finished with a 9-3 record, the least effective since the 6-4 slate in '71.

Hayes readily admitted the Alabama dominance. "They beat us with a team that had half the talent we had. Our team had about 1/4 of the coaching their team got," a very frank condemnation of his own effectiveness in the Superdome.

In an interesting theory introduced by *Columbus Dispatch* sportswriter Bob Hunter, the recent rash of bowl defeats, crowned by this mismatch, suffered by conference superpowers OSU and UM stemmed in part from the success each school, comparatively easily, experienced within conference play. Superior reserves, greater resolve, better coaching, and basic, powerful, straight-ahead offensive and defensive tactics won out in the regular season; in bowl games, the opponent traditionally enjoyed these same advantages.

Ohio State and Michigan were unused to such equal firepower, and did not easily adapt to the more competitive nature of the bowl games. Hayes himself alluded to the merit of this theory, in his admission chokingly offered following the latest loss.

Nevertheless, all was not bleak in '77. An unprecedented sixth straight share of the conference crown was accomplished, and the only blemishes on the record were to three outstanding programs. Michigan, Oklahoma, and Alabama each ended the year in the top ten in national rankings, with the Crimson Tide landing the number two spot. With a few breaks here and there, Ohio State very easily may have been among the finest squads in the land.

The Sugar Bowl itself began on a somewhat promising note. Alabama took the opening kickoff and embarked on a 17 play drive. On a fourth and goal situation from the Buckeye one yard line, Adkins savagely met and repelled Rutledge short of the goal line. Not only had the Tide been turned away, it appeared that the tide had turned in favor of the Buckeyes. Unfortunately, it turned out that OSU had merely temporarily stemmed the Crimson onslaught.

Gerald led OSU on a short drive, though Orosz was forced to punt as the second quarter began. Alabama thereupon scored on each of their next two possessions, and OSU was effectively done for the day, especially as the first half concluded with the Buckeyes impotently stalled on the 'Bama ten. The halftime count was 14-0, and OSU appeared fortunate to be even that close.

In light of his recent probationary status, Hayes was on near-perfect behavior, despite the sad Buckeye showing. The lone outburst along the sideline, mild by his mercurial standards, came on the initial Alabama scoring drive. As 'Bama receiver Ozzie Newsome was tackled to complete a 29 yard gain, Hayes ripped off his scarlet windbreaker and threw it angrily to the turf.

More disturbingly, yet unnoticed by most because of the timing and brevity of the act, was an incident which occurred as Hayes was running off the field for the halftime gathering. Woody was jogging at a steady clip toward the locker room, and with his head lowered, he blindly collided with the padded goal post. Startled and momentarily caught off guard, Hayes reacted with a swing at the padding. A wave of sarcastic heckling rippled from the crowd, and Hayes angrily waved the taunts away. There is no greater illustration of how frustrating this day actually was.

Alabama picked right up after the intermission, marching in for a touchdown off the second half kick. Ohio State, in sheer desperation, managed to salvage some hope, traversing 85 yards, with Harrell making a diving layout catch for a thrilling 38 yard touchdown. Unfortunately, Logan was stymied in the try for two, and this was the last sustained threat by Ohio State. Alabama negated this score by driving for touchdowns on their next two opportunities, and the decisive outcome was sealed.

Indicative of the breaks which went against OSU in each of their '77 defeats was the fact that Alabama fumbled a shocking ten times, yet recovered eight of these miscues. Rutledge was charged with eight of these fumbles, and later credited most of those to middle guard Brown, whose unmatched quickness distracted and disturbed the center exchange all afternoon.

Rutledge, fumbles and all, was named the MVP of the contest. He connected on eight of 11 pass attempts for 109 yards, including well-delivered scoring strikes of 29 yards, to Bruce Bolton, and a three yard pitch to Rick Neal. Alabama ran up 389 yards in total offense, 280 of those on the ground. Davis led all rushers with 95 yards, and contributed a score. Nathan and Major Ogilvie were also major contributors in the ground domination.

The Buckeyes generated just 263 total yards, a mere 160 of those on the ground, after averaging 414 total yards each game in the regular season. Three interceptions of Gerald did not help the OSU effort, as Gerald completed only seven of 17 tosses for 103 yards, including the lone touchdown. Springs ran ten times for 74 yards, with Logan adding 57 on 13 attempts, yet the Bucks were practically forced into abandonment of the ground game after falling behind so drastically.

Alas, the attempt to catch up via the air proved futile. Cousineau and Brown led a defense which was on the field an inordinate amount of time. Tom had 20 tackles, and Aaron 16, yet their efforts were not enough to stop the Tide.

CHAPTER ONE: PRE-SEASON '78

The preseason prognostication for '78 looked good, however, as esteemed forecasters such as Street and Smith paid little heed to the two consecutive losses which ended '77. Ohio State was installed as a preseason bet for a number two ranking, with Alabama drawing an expected ranking of number one. Woody again promised another good year, as OSU looked to continue their unmatched string of conference championships. Glossed over in the preseason hype, however, was reason for concern.

Back in '74 and '75, Hayes had complained to the NCAA about violations committed by Michigan State, and had openly admitted in '76 and '77 that he wanted the Spartans nailed to the wall as these allegations proved correct. In return, MSU made accusations concerning the Ohio State program, and after extensive internal university and NCAA investigations of OSU, violations were indeed found.

It was determined that OSU committed five technical infractions, mostly in recruiting practices, during the '73-'76 time frame. The NCAA publicly reprimanded OSU for these minor violations, in what amounted to a miniscule slap on the wrist. It was determined that the infractions broke the letter of the law, although they were proven to be involuntary oversights, and not intentional or deliberate. Stacked atop the probationary status of Hayes, however, all was not coming up roses for the OSU program.

Hayes' philosophy toward these added challenges was straightforward. "If you want to win, if you want to get something out of the game when you get knocked down, you get up and go again and again. That's what I like about the game of football; nobody gets to stand up all of the time. That's how you enjoy success - when you've been knocked down."

With the retirement of Esco Sarkinnen after 32 years of dedicated coaching and scouting, and the loss to graduation (and the NFL) of Chris Ward, David Adkins, Jeff Logan, Aaron Brown, Ray Griffin, and Herman Jones, along with Jim Harrell, the Buckeyes had definitely been knocked down a bit.

Incidentally, the outside linebacker coach replacing Sarkinnen was Buckeye alumnus Glen Mason. Mason was a reserve middle guard on the '70 conference championship team, whose career was halted unexpectedly by a broken ankle one week prior to the start of the '71 season. Mason chose graduation instead of a delayed playing comeback, and went on to coaching stints at Ball State, Iowa, Allegheny, and Illinois. He had returned to his alma mater to learn from his college Coach.

Not even one month removed from the embarrassing loss to Alabama, the '78 Buckeye captains were selected. There were no surprises in the vote by players. Vastly underrated defensive tackle Byron Cato; first team All-

American inside linebacker Tom Cousineau; All-Conference tailback Ron Springs, who led the league in rushing in '77 with 108.7 yards per conference contest, and the squad in receiving with 16 grabs; and the rugged and crazy center, Tim Vogler, were each deemed worthy. These accomplished athletes captained a Buckeye squad which was possibly the fastest on record.

The team possessed decent overall size, and exhibited good depth, particularly in the backfield. Cousineau admitted the defense had really been thinned by graduation, yet boldly predicted an improved unit.

The preseason optimism of the captains stemmed in no small measure from the newly modernized and invigorated off-season conditioning program. In the Orange Bowl following the '76 season, Woody was taken not only by the outstanding weightlifting facilities of Miami, he was equally intrigued by the architect of that state-of-the-art fitness center. In essence, Hayes insisted that this individual, Steve Bliss, join the OSU coaching staff.

Predictably, Bliss jumped at the chance to work at a program the caliber of OSU, although he had a lot of work to perform in updating the OSU training regimen. The '77 strength advisor, Kevin Rodgers, had done what he could with the heretofore limited emphasis, though Hayes was just now realizing the advantages to a significantly stronger team. Bliss was hired with little of the usual formalities, i.e. interviews and references, since Hayes had seen his handiwork.

Besides, the idea of a strength coach was still a new concept, and few people really knew the minimum qualifications necessary in such a coach. Nebraska pioneered the concept behind advanced strength training for the football player, and in fact Bliss based his Miami foundation upon the Cornhusker principles. Ironically, within six years of Bliss departing, Miami won their first national title, with a weight program still centered primarily around Bliss' methods.

These methods emphasized explosion. Many older coaches argued, "I didn't lift weights when I played," though the proper rebuttal to this argument was now becoming, "...and neither did the player across from you." As the Pittsburgh Steelers popularized the concept of strong offensive linemen, and won by doing so, the concept that strength improved performance became virtually de rigueur among football teams.

As mentioned previously, Hayes had lost several recruits to Michigan because OSU had inferior training facilities, and Woody refused to allow UM to maintain this advantage. For, if one team lifts year round and grows more powerful, by necessity a competitor, to remain competitive, must lift year round as well. Hayes belatedly recognized this principle, which had already caught on at UM, UCLA, and Oklahoma, among others, and followed suit.

Bliss believed in position specific training; a lifting schedule throughout the year, including maintenance work, mostly involving Nautilus equipment, during the season itself; and the development of speed and power through explosive movements in the off season, emphasizing the use of free weights.

The four tenet system of Bliss blended the facets of stretching, lifting, running, and nutrition.

An already superbly conditioned Cousineau claimed that, due to the innovative methods of Bliss, the '78 team was the best conditioned squad ever at OSU. Woody was also pleased at the improved strength and condition of his squad as fall workouts began.

Those who thought Hayes a relic of a bygone age and unwilling to experiment with new techniques, should note that Woody was usually at the forefront of any advances applicable to football. Based largely upon the efforts of Dr. Robert Murphy, the OSU medical facilities and treatments were absolutely cutting edge. Surgery, handled by Dr. Mel Olix and capable others, was world class and set the standard for all colleges. The training staff, fronted by Billy Hill, was the envy of many, and with the arrival of Bliss, the training facet of the program became one of the finest in the country. Each of these branches of the team were continuously updated and refined, with the discretion and guiding hand of Woody.

A rather bizarre twist of this advancement characteristic was a new downhill training ramp which Hayes had installed. Due to a certain Soviet school of thought which he adopted, Hayes believed that running downhill forced a body to adapt and consequently become faster. The 25 yard steep decline may not have delivered measurable results, yet it does fantastically illustrate the Hayes penchant for perfection, no matter the cost. No detail or possible aid was too trivial to try.

The improved strength of the Buckeyes was distributed fairly evenly between the offensive and defensive units. On offense, returning seniors Rod Gerald, ostensibly at quarterback; Bill Jaco, tight end; Jimmy Moore, All-Conference tight end; Joe Robinson, right tackle; Springs; Vogler; and junior right guard Ken Fritz all returned to starting spots.

A key among these returnees was Moore, who finally seemed 100% healthy. The new conditioning program brought Moore into camp at a very muscular 242 pounds, about 20 pounds lighter than '77. Moore had been sidelined much of his freshman and sophomore years with severe knee injuries, though when healthy, he was perhaps the finest blocker in the nation. Moore also made his infrequent receptions count, witness his huge touchdown catch against Oklahoma in '77. Moore entertained thoughts of pro ball as scouts drooled over his amazing frame, athleticism, and relatively untapped potential (once in the NFL, Baltimore Colt teammate Bert Jones christened Jimmy "The Black Samson").

Still, Moore felt the OSU team came first, and thought that if the Buckeyes had a good year, his future would take care of itself. "We have to have a good year," felt Moore, and even if, in that process, he subjugated his collegiate stardom for the betterment of the team, the NFL would come calling.

The opposite end in the two tight end formation was occupied by the returning letterman Jaco. Jaco was renowned for his ability to catch a ball in traffic, and had become a much more accomplished blocker over time. Jaco was capably backed by the 6'8", 248 pound Ron Barwig, who was the tallest gridiron athlete ever at OSU. Speedy Chuck Hunter, who ended up starting in the Sugar Bowl after making a successful switch from the backfield, could play either at tight end or split end.

The status of the remaining line members was clouded, due to an excess of bodies. Right tackle was the domain of leading All-American contender Joe Robinson. The 6'2", 254 pounder was fully recovered from the dual ankle injuries he incurred the week of the '77 Oklahoma game, which troubled him throughout the remainder of the year. Joe played in that Sooner contest, though his effectiveness was greatly diminished in that game and beyond. Regardless of the hampering injuries, the powerful tackle remained an optimist.

The past was unchangeable, he felt, and, "...when things aren't going well, you just have to try to pick it up and go from there." Since Joe was at last healthy, '78 figured to be a banner season.

The left tackle slot was open, and a three-way battle between sophomore Keith Ferguson, two-time letterman Doug Mackie, and junior Tim Brown was hotly contested. Ultimately, based on his daily consistency, aggressiveness, and potential, Ferguson captured the starting nod.

Brown, the younger brother of former scarlet and gray star Aaron Brown, was a huge, 6'6", 272 pounder readily gaining experience since transferring (with Springs) from Coffeyville (Kansas) junior college. He merited much attention from the coaching staff.

The right guard slot was firmly nailed down by junior Ken Fritz, who was expected to be the standout of the line. Fritz maintained the aggressive mindset he displayed as a standout linebacker during his prep days.

Like the left tackle position, left guard was a fierce struggle between a trio of willing players. Leading the way was combative senior Ernie Andria, who enjoyed a solid '77 season after his freshman and sophomore years were marked more by injuries than playing time. Andria actually had two years of eligibility remaining, if he so chose, due to his prolonged injury-induced absences. Andria was a scrappy, combative sort, who even argued with his own tackles at the line of scrimmage, if he did not agree with their blocking calls.

Jim Savoca was making a difficult comeback from a one-year layoff due to major back surgery, and the old skills which landed him a starting role in '76 were becoming more evident as the rustiness wore off. Junior Scott Burris looked to be a capable backup, at worst, and with slight improvement would perhaps inherit more playing time.

The center of the line was anchored by Vogler, who rated among the finest at that position in the country. Behind Tim was two-time letterman Tom

Waugh and the untested sophomore, Dave Phillips, whose younger brother Larry was a promising freshman defensive tackle for the Bucks.

Vogler played with a certain reckless abandon, and had a tendency to overextend his still-growing frame, resulting in debilitating injuries. Tim was still packing on the mass, filling out a body which, at the time, was somewhat light for an offensive lineman. The responsibilities and leadership inherent at the center spot needed a strong presence, however, and the slightly berserk style of Tim contributed much to the overall attitude of the squad.

He played every down with every fiber of his being, and if injuries occasionally interfered, he felt that they were a price that must be met. Like many Buckeyes, the aggressive and reckless enthusiasm which made Vogler a fine player often simultaneously disabled him, paradoxically keeping him from the game he loved.

Plenty of speed and ability graced the wideout positions. In addition to Hunter, Tyrone Hicks readied his jets as the fastest Buckeye of this (or probably, with respect to former receiver Billy Ezzo, a 5'5" flash who lettered in '72, '73, and '74), any year. Hicks captured the conference crown in the 100 yard dash, held the conference 100 meter record, and was a scant .2 seconds from a world record in the 60 yard sprint.

Hicks came out of the aforementioned football-factory town of Warren, Ohio, where he starred at tailback, and the OSU coaching staff hoped his frightening speed would translate into a consistent game-breaking threat. Hicks had been in plenty of off-field trouble, and fervently hoped to put his stormy past behind him.

Another sprinter adept at catching footballs was sophomore Doug Donley. Donley caught a touchdown pass in his first appearance as a Buckeye in '77, yet was never at full health thereafter. Donley was a top conference sprinter in the indoor season, and if he and Hicks could get open and hold on to the ball, few defensive backs would ever catch them.

The quarterback position, despite the return of two-year incumbent Rod Gerald, was apparently wide open. A little over a week following the Sugar Bowl massacre, prep phenom Art Schlichter committed to OSU, in a recruiting coup for the Bucks. Schlichter won every game he started as the quarterback at Miami Trace, a small town on the outskirts of Washington Court House, Ohio, and was considered one of the finest prep athletes, ever, in the entire country. Schlichter was big, at 6'3" and 195 pounds, and possessed unbelievable arm strength and accuracy.

Art was a powerful, fast runner as well, and was even coveted as a basketball player by most major colleges. Indeed, after signing with Ohio State, Buckeye basketball coach Eldon Miller agreed that Art could join his squad at the conclusion of the gridiron season.

Originally, it was assumed that Schlichter would spend the '78 year as a backup to the senior Gerald, learning at the feet of the acknowledged option master, before easing into the starting role as a sophomore. Gerald had really come into his own in '77, dramatically improving his passing and leadership abilities from the year before.

Traditionally a quick, elusive runner, Gerald was slowed at the tail end of '77 by a very slight stress fracture apparently incurred in his leg while scoring a touchdown against Northwestern in the seventh game of the year. The injury did not cause him to miss any action, and in fact was not even diagnosed until the conclusion of the year, yet it had to hamper his normal pell-mell option gyrations. Gerald was really hitting his prime as a passer, hitting nearly 65% of his attempts in '77 for over a thousand yards, despite the somewhat limited Buckeye attack.

By the tail end of that year, though, the OSU offense had become almost predictable. Players recall, due to a limited amount of plays traditionally run from each offensive set within a particular situation, that the Michigan defense often knew with uncanny certainty the exact play Ohio State was about to run. Although the passing attack was greatly improved, Alabama was also able to accurately predict the routes, timing, and situations that Gerald would go to the air, with equally disastrous results for Ohio State.

Hayes desperately wanted to win another national title, and eventually seemed to determine that the path to this prize lay in a more wide open offensive attack. Such an attack, Woody came to believe, required a more conventional, drop-back passer, albeit one who could capably contribute to the ground game, too. The increased options via the air would make OSU less predictable, Hayes felt, and would probably also reduce the tendency of opposing defenses to almost exclusively concentrate on the Buckeye ground game.

Hayes haltingly began this transformation in '77, although the passing options available to the quarterback remained somewhat simplistic, and in stressful situations during a game, Hayes often seemed to react very predictably and conservatively in his play calls. With the addition of Schlichter, a quintessential pro-style passer with great rushing talents, Hayes had found the man to effect this subtle change in offensive strategy.

Somewhat unfairly and very uncharacteristically, Hayes seemed to proclaim young Art as the savior, as it were, and deliverer of this transformation, without giving Art the benefit of actually earning this role. In a shocking development during '78 spring practice, Schlichter, who of course was still in high school at the time, was actually allowed to take a few ceremonial snaps with the practicing Buckeyes.

Never before could anyone recall Woody granting a green freshman such accord and respect, especially at such an essential leadership position. Woody always felt the best man proved himself through time as worthy of the task, and had really never kowtowed to personal favorites or popularity contests in naming a starter.

In this case, many of the players felt that Schlichter was handed the position, since Woody felt four years of Art to be more advantageous than the one remaining with Rod. Recall that a similar decision was reached in the case of Skladany, when Tom entered as a frosh, yet the difference lies in the position: By its very demanding and complex nature, the quarterback spot demanded a player well-respected by his teammates, and one with a proven track record of achieving. Unlike the punter, who largely depended upon his own talents, the quarterback blended, originated, and fashioned the entire mood of the team with his play.

In fairness to Woody, who felt that the proposed slight changes in the offense permitted Rod and Art to begin at the approximate same level in fall practice, the more conventional passing talents of the younger athlete seemed, on paper, a better fit with these changes. However, a quarterback is so dependent on intangibles for success, and Art never seemed to truly rally the '78 squad with the firm leadership required, despite his obviously great athletic skills.

The signalcaller backups at this early fall juncture remained Greg Castignola and Mike Strahine. Castignola was still recovering from the puzzling blood clot which troubled him in '77, although the effects were not too detrimental. Each junior demonstrated steady, if not spectacular or dangerously striking, ability to lead the team if necessary, as both were fine athletes and capable performers. Strahine had been briefly tried at defensive back during spring ball, yet spent most of his time behind center.

The running back situation looked very promising indeed. During the early May spring game, the scarlet first team offense was led by the amazing Springs. Ron bolted for a phenomenal 235 yards and two touchdowns, one on a breathtaking 75 yard dash. Based on this performance and his efforts in the fall, Springs seemed a sure bet to surpass his '77 total of 1166 yards rushing.

The senior was already in very select company, for only Jim Otis ('69), John Brockington ('70), Archie Griffin ('73-'75), and Jeff Logan ('76) had hit the 1,000 yard mark since Hayes first came to Columbus. Springs was supported by lettermen Rickey Johnson and Calvin Murray, an avid motorcyclist.

Woody customarily spent virtually all his practice hours with the offense, and within the offense, particularly zeroed in on the running backs. Mickey Jackson thinks, deep down inside, Hayes always wanted to be a running back, although Woody was otherwise blessed with a lineman's physique, temperament, and physical abilities. So, Woody vicariously lived out his unrequited fantasy by imparting his vast knowledge of blocking to the Buckeye running backs.

Hayes instructed the backs on how to best read and react to the blocking in front of them, which was a critical skill in the formations OSU traditionally employed. According to Woody, a running back was only as good as the line in front of him, and the units must work together.

As another prerequisite in the traditional Hayes running attack, the fullback was a (sometimes) equal blend of runner and blocker, with a nose for the goal line. A troika of formidable talent was ready and willing to bust some chops from the fullback slot. Paul Campbell was the most experienced of the three, while Joel Payton had led the conference in '77 scoring with 62 points during league games, and 82 points overall. Ricardo Volley grew up with dreams of being a USC Trojan. He often fantasized about scoring a touchdown from the famous Trojan tailback slot, resulting in victory laps from the mascot thoroughbred, Trigger. Instead, he had found his niche at OSU.

Volley was a tailback coming out of high school, yet volunteered to move to wingback as he arrived in Columbus, in an effort to play some in the star-studded OSU backfield. Eventually moved to fullback, the immensely excitable Ric was a surprisingly quick, inspirational, and powerful runner, unafraid to stick his body in the line or lead the way with a devastating block.

Volley grew up in Appomattox, Virginia, near where the Civil War was concluded, which immediately endeared him to the history buff in Hayes. Not as endearing, at least to Woody, was the tendency of Volley to lead the OSU stadium crowd in cheers after a nice run, or the tendency Ric had of letting his active imagination roam, causing repeated tardiness to team meetings.

On one such occasion, the timing of Volley was especially distressful. During Michigan week, everyone in the Ohio State program knew to be especially wary of Hayes, whose emotions were so tightly wrapped up in the quest for a victory that any disruption caused a volatile unraveling. As always, when Woody was around, intensity levels picked up right now, and Michigan week was even more so. Volley happened to stroll in momentarily late to a meeting during one such week, and predictably, Hayes went ballistic.

Volley just happened to be wearing a brand new jacket, courtesy of his mother, and Woody proceeded to maul, shred, and otherwise obliterate this item in his desire to instill some punctuality in the wayward player. The other players sat watching, stunned at the temper of Woody, yet trying desperately not to laugh at the fate of the prized, new jacket.

Eventually, Woody realized he perhaps had been a little overexuberant, and casually asked equipment man John Bozick to repair the damage, which of course was irreparable. As Volley got over his initial anger, the resultant teasing by teammates caused him to later laugh heartily at the incident.

In retrospect, Volley was fortunate he was even allowed to become a member of the OSU football team. During his senior season in high school, Volley came to the OSU campus on a recruiting visit. In the course of that visit, a wild party ensued, and the young Volley was suitably impressed with the good times available to a bachelor athlete in Columbus. Impressed, that is, until Hayes himself came to the party and disrupted the festivities.

Since Volley was a minor and in essence a temporary ward of the university, if he had been caught in this reveling, the punishment for all involved would have been extreme. Realizing this possibility, Ricardo climbed onto a balcony and remained hidden there until Hayes ended his tirade and finally left the room. This incident became the stuff of legend, and contributed to the Volley mystique.

Moving to the defensive side of the ball, coordinator George Hill felt, "We've filled up the holes. We'll be really young, but we have some really fine seniors who are good leaders." Foremost among these leaders was the consensus All-American Cousineau.

Six other starters also returned: The remarkably strong senior co-captain Cato, at tackle; All-American senior end Kelton Dansler; boundary halfback senior Lenny Mills, hampered by injuries throughout his career, yet potentially one of the finest defenders in the country; senior end Paul Ross, who was as underrated as Cato yet just as indispensable to the success of OSU; junior openside tackle Gary Dulin, who really came on at the end of '77 as he spelled an injured Eddie Beamon; and rising star, junior safety Mike Guess, who quietly led the conference in punt returns with an 11.1 average in '77.

On the subject of special teams, the Buckeyes returned two fine toes. Sophomore Tom Orosz was chosen the punter, as well as again handling the kickoff chores which he was limited to, by injury, as a frosh. When healthy, Orosz repeatedly boomed kickoffs into and out of the end zone for touchbacks.

Junior Vlade Janakievski was in the midst of a school-record string of extra points; his mark of 44 straight by the conclusion of '77 had eclipsed the previous Buckeye record of 40, set in '70-'71 by Fred Schram. Janakievski was eager to atone for his disappointing showing against Michigan, and looked very strong as fall workouts began.

Also on hand was freshman walk-on Bob Atha, from Worthington, Ohio. The skinny Atha displayed shocking power and strength in his placekicking efforts, and also hoped to get a chance to play quarterback, his primary prep position.

The traditional defensive strategy employed by Hill was a three-pronged attack based evenly on aggressiveness, pursuit, and speed. The accomplishments of any defense rely on the strength up the middle, primarily at middle guard. Senior Mark Sullivan hoped to shake off his three somewhat injury-plagued years with a banner final campaign. The feisty, combative Irishman from Boston was converted from the offensive line, and Hill thought his temperament and abilities promised great things.

With Cato and Dulin flanking the plucky Sullivan, the defensive line provided a solid initial contact point. Line depth was augmented by tackle Luther Henson, senior tackle Joe Hornik, and another wild-and-crazy middle guard, the rambunctious Tim Sawicki.

The outside linebacker (end) spots looked extremely strong. Dansler was in his third year of starting, and in '77, Kelton compiled 109 tackles, four interceptions, and made ten tackles behind the line of scrimmage. Ross was a very quick, punishingly efficient tackler often overlooked, although close studies of game films revealed his outstanding qualities. In '77, Ross made 85 tackles, including nine for a loss. The backups at this spot included Dave Allen, Terry Bach, and Jim Laughlin.

The cornerstone of the defense, and the man to whom pursuit was funnelled, was the estimable Cousineau. Quickness, particularly laterally, was Tom's greatest attribute, and Tom roamed from sideline to sideline to make tackles. His textbook tackles and capacity to make the big play did not go unnoticed, either. Even allowing for the excellence of Randy Gradishar, Tom was being written up as the greatest linebacker Hayes had ever coached. The backup for this inside linebacker position was the other Vogler twin, Terry.

The battle for the other inside position elicited fierce competition. Tom Blinco, who filled in admirably after Cousineau wrecked his shoulder against Oklahoma, and sophomore Tony Megaro were barely edged out during spring ball by the hard-hitting sophomore Al Washington. Washington had mighty big shoes to fill, for Dave Adkins took his rugged style and a school-record number of tackles in '77 to the Atlanta Falcons.

The secondary was a curious mix of inexperience and talented upperclassmen. Mills was coming off a solid, at times even spectacular, '77 campaign, at least when he was not injured. Guess was acclimating himself to the safety position after a brilliant sophomore year at the boundary halfback slot, which Mills now assumed. Prep track standout Todd Bell, a long-jumping sophomore marvel out of Middletown, Ohio, had sewn up the other safety spot with a spectacular spring.

The remaining slot was rotated between three players, among them senior Duncan Griffin, the only member of his class to have appeared in every possible game. Duncan was a dynamo on special teams, customarily leading the coverage units in tackles. The former prep tight end-linebacker used his extensive wrestling background to fierce advantage in making open field tackles. Sophomore Ray Ellis, a wingback and split end sensation at Canton (Ohio) McKinley, and prep sprint star sophomore Vince Skillings, who was making a return from major knee surgery, were also coming on.

Overall, the '78 team numbered 99 as the August workouts commenced. The class was skewed to the underclasses, with the freshmen and sophomores totaling 55 between them. A wealth of experienced talent was in surplus, and very few starters were separated from their backup by an insurmountable margin, resulting in that daily competition for playing time so beloved by Hayes. The arrival of the strong freshmen class aptly demonstrated this fact, as several newcomers immediately contended for key roles.

The much-anticipated arrival of Schlichter alone generated more subterfuge, upheaval, confusion, and controversy than ever recalled for a Hayes-era squad, and the hullabaloo seemed to splinter the usual focused team effort into a puzzled jumble of uncertainties. No one, least of all the players and not even

Woody himself, ever seemed rigidly certain of the offensive leadership once the quarterback controversy began, and the resulting mess of distractions proved insurmountable to all concerned.

From the inception of fall camp, Gerald, Castignola, and Schlichter assumed almost equal time behind center. At least, that was what the press releases claimed. Actually, Schlichter mostly worked with the first team, and got in the most work.

Amid reports that Gerald was also working out at a wide receiver slot, former Buckeye Cornelius Greene (now spelled Green) offered his advice. Green, who as a senior competed against and eclipsed Rod for the starting nod in Gerald's freshman year, advised Rod to do what was best for the team. Green and Gerald were very similarly styled as quarterbacks, and Green had spent the better part of three years, after his final OSU season, bouncing around various football leagues and teams, attempting to latch on in a role as a wide receiver. Corny played in the CFL for a little over a year, and in '78 was playing semi-pro ball with the Columbus Metros.

"It is not smart for anyone to try to revolve their entire future around pro ball," Green said from experience, as he also claimed that one year at receiver would not help Rod in a bid for an NFL career. Still, Hayes and Gerald both thought that Rod could fit comfortably into the receiving mode, if for no other reason than to facilitate the placement of Art into the offense.

The initial public pronouncement on who was the top quarterback proved no help at all, though. Exactly one week prior to the season opener with Penn State, Hayes appeared on his weekly television show and said that all three quarterbacks looked good enough to, and in fact would, play against the Nittany Lions. In a later statement during this same telecast, however, Hayes did hint that Gerald would assume the starting spot because he was the most experienced. In any case, Strahine was the odd man out as the other three jockeyed for playing time.

Most likely due to the extra running demanded by his many repetitions as a split end, Gerald began experiencing very sore and fatigued legs. The pain and discomfort cut into his practice time, and Schlichter took even more snaps with the first team. Complete rest was the prescribed cure for Gerald, yet rest during the season was undeniably impossible for a man who loved football as much as Rod did.

The onset of this fatigue was merely the first in a seemingly unending procession of injuries Rod incurred during the year, and his slight leg injury was also only the first in a spate of hurts which impacted the team in a very negative manner.

Similarly, Blinco went down with a knee injury, which gradually worsened to the point that he went under the knife less than a month later. Jaco was stricken with psoriasis, a stubbornly persistent and totally unpredictable skin affliction. Mackie was the next in the morbid trek to the operating table, also with a knee injury.

Then, Mills injured his ankle in a practice just before the PSU contest. Originally the injury was termed moderate in nature, though within days the report was updated to serious, and the medical staff predicted Lenny would be sidelined at least two weeks.

During his first weekly press conference of the upcoming season, Hayes verified that Mills would miss at least the opening game, though he was the only starter who was out of commission, at this time.

The absence of Mills took a huge chunk of game experience from the secondary, and although Ellis moved into the spot, the chemistry and newfound delicate unity of the defensive backfield soon was in disarray. Individually, the unit performed well, yet the group effort was marred by inconsistencies and critical breakdowns which seemed to coincide with the absence of the senior halfback. The backfield never regained their effective cohesiveness, and played inconsistently throughout the remainder of the year, as did the defense as a whole.

Unfortunately, as soon as OSU seemed to get back on track, other critically essential players were felled by injuries as the year evolved, as a Pandora's box of similar ills seemed to open and strike at the most inopportune times.

Mostly in response to the increasingly inquisitive media in regards to the quarterbacking status, Woody barred all press from witnessing any fall workouts. He even imposed a gag rule on all the players, effective for a period of five days, until after the opener.

In a bold stroke of typical inspirational attempts, Hayes brought in former Buckeye Pete Cusick to address the team. Cusick had most recently played with the Tampa Bay Buccaneers, yet was forced to retire, due to a severe knee injury. As Cusick spoke to the team in his typically emotional manner, Hayes took over and regaled those assembled with assorted tales of the intimidating tactics the imposing Cusick always displayed in big games.

The intent was to show that injuries were merely temporary obstacles, and even if those injuries finally proved disabling, the tradition of Ohio State demanded that a supporting player step up and play spectacularly.

Hayes related the effort of Steve Myers, who played the entire '74 Michigan game with a broken hand, even though he was the center and had to painfully snap the ball on every down. Such extreme efforts ultimately led to success, which Cusick resoundingly affirmed, for he was still emotionally prepared to do battle, even if his body had finally given out.

Also circulating this week were tales of the first-ever matchup with Penn State, way back in '12. Both schools had just moved into competition with the finer and bigger programs in the country, and PSU coach and former All-American fullback Bill Hollenback brought his team to the old Ohio Field at 17th and High near the OSU campus.

After being forced to practice that November 17th afternoon on an auxiliary field littered with broken glass and strewn with rusted tools, Hollenback further fired up his emotional squad by reading to them excerpts of Ohio newspaper clippings which, he purported, belittled the Penn State program. Sufficiently inspired, a vengeful Penn State led 16-0 after one quarter.

Then the rough hijinks began in earnest. Rookie Ohio State coach John R. Richards continually berated the officials for allowing the visitors to beat up on his already overmatched Buckeyes, but to no avail. After a particularly vicious, illegal shot was delivered to a Buckeye during a PSU kickoff, Richards pulled his team off the field.

Outraged by what they perceived as unsportsmanlike conduct on behalf of Penn State, some overzealous partisan OSU freshmen tore down a goalpost with Pennsylvania bunting attached to it. The rowdy students lit these opposing school colors on fire, charged onto the field, and presented the flaming mass to the stunned Penn State gridders.

Consequently, the 37-0 score was converted into a 1-0 forfeit, with the victory still going to Penn State. Painful memories of the humiliating defeat, the heated walkout, and the subsequent near-riot lingered on the OSU campus. By the following year, Richards was gone as head coach.

Back in the relative comfort of '78, Hayes joked that this '17 debacle had been one controversy he had nothing to do with. Nevertheless, national attention was spotlighted on this '78 matchup of the two perennial powerhouses. The acknowledged masters, Hayes and Joe Paterno, led their teams into this game hoping for a fast start toward national championship aspirations. This game attracted an even larger press contingent than the '77 Oklahoma game, as it featured returning consensus All-Americans Cousineau and PSU quarterback Chuck Fusina, and a pre-season consensus All-American, Springs.

As an example of the extraordinary single-minded focus Hayes had prior to this game, a prospective interviewer called Woody's office one week to arrange a meeting. The intrepid reporter asked to speak with Hayes, and the secretary replied, "He isn't in." The reporter inquired as to when he would return, and the secretary, most likely either Trish Farwig or Sandy Trelay, allegedly responded, "I won't see him until the end of the season." Woody literally lived at the stadium throughout the season, and little intruded with his intense devotion in preparing his team.

Penn State had the advantage of already playing two games, both victories, in '78. The Nittany Lions opened early, squeaking past Temple on a late field goal by Matt Bahr (fresh off a summer spent starring in the NASL, the professional soccer league, and younger sibling to Buckeye nemesis Chris), and followed this narrow win with a lackluster, unimpressive defeat of Rutgers.

Despite the two close games, Penn State brought a typically strong team into Ohio Stadium. Led by Fusina, whom Paterno called, "The greatest quarterback in the history of the school," the Nittany Lions were deep and talented. The favorite target for Fusina was crafty Scott Fitzkee, who also doubled as the pinpoint placement punter.

The running game was punctuated by the hard-charging Matt Suhey, and included a fine set of halfbacks, Booker Moore and Mike Guman.

Linebacker U., as Penn State was commonly called, boasted Paul Suhey, brother of Matt, and Lance Mehl in those glorified 'backer spots, in addition to strong linemen Matt Millen and Bruce Clark. Pete Harris, whose older brother Franco had starred at PSU and went on to greater glory with the Pittsburgh Steelers (Penn State was renowned for their strong familial ties), roamed the airways at his safety position.

CHAPTER TWO: PENN STATE

As Ohio State ran onto the sold-out home field on Saturday to a torrent of cheers, the position of starting quarterback was still unsettled, to everyone but the team itself. After OSU fielded the opening kickoff, both Gerald and Schlichter ran out with the offense. As Gerald broke from the huddle and split off as a flanker, cheering noises and surprised gasps in the stadium grew deafening. The clamor from the scarlet and gray crowd was unfathomably loud, even in normal circumstances; at this shocking entrance, the decibels reached a higher level.

Schlichter promptly hit two straight passes, and the mood among the then-third largest crowd in school history was grippingly electric and rabid. A new age was dawning in OSU football, the likes of which had rarely been seen, and the optimism among those present was palpable.

That dreamy optimism quickly came crashing down as Schlichter dropped back to pass for the third straight time. That pass by the excited freshman was rudely intercepted, and Art suffered through four more interceptions on the ugly afternoon. The more experienced Lions harassed and perplexed the frosh all day, and the newly-revamped passing attack of OSU was stymied by a solid line of Lion defense.

In spite of the many miscues, Schlichter flashed glimpses of his awesome potential, both in passing and running the football. The gutsy, courageous style of Art was evident throughout the disappointing day, though Penn State did overwhelm him at times. The 34 passes attempted by Ohio State were the most in any one game since a '71 victory over Indiana. The 19-0 final score on this day indeed proved the old Hayes adage, "...more things go wrong when you have to pass," as OSU was shut out for the first time since the '76 Michigan game.

Perhaps the Buckeyes should have realized something was amiss when crowd-pleasing OSU drum major extraordinaire Dwight Hudson was inadvertently bumped during the pre-game entrance by the band, and dropped his traditional victory toss after the baton passed over the upright of the goal post.

Whatever the reason, the highly touted Buckeye ground game sputtered throughout, in part due to the shuffling in and out of Joe Robinson after he injured his foot and ankle. Because of the resulting constant personnel switches, the line was never able to develop a successful pattern or groove, though Ferguson played spectacular ball, being judged the best lineman in his first start. As a result of the lack of offensive punch, Ohio State lost the fourth opener in the tenure of Hayes (with one tie). According to the exasperated coach, this was, "...about as bad an opener as we've ever played."

Gerald, despite missing considerable amounts of contact work in the fall due to his aching legs, looked spectacular at times, new position and all. He caught four balls for 91 yards in his unaccustomed role as a receiver, including a nifty fifty yard catch and run. On the negative side, Rod fumbled at the tail end of this run, adding to the OSU total of eight turnovers on the day.

Doug Donley found some open seams, too, grabbing four balls for 85 yards and establishing himself as a favorite target for Schlichter to locate when in trouble.

Twice in the game, OSU was pinned deep in their side of the field, and Gerald was inserted at quarterback. Hayes wanted the senior at the helm in unusually stressful situations, since Rod had considerable experience in making crucial, pressure decisions.

Alas, Rod's lack of work at the position showed, and the only sustained drive of the game for Ohio State was actually engineered by Castignola, albeit with less than three minutes remaining in the contest. This drive eventually stalled on the PSU four with a mere 21 seconds remaining, and OSU left the contest without scoring.

Sadly for Rod, his own perceived failure to spark the offense, despite his recent lack of work in the signalcalling role, tore at him and greatly damaged his self-esteem. While outwardly Rod refused to badmouth the position switch, or his re-insertion at the helm in impossible situations, privately the sensitive young leader was devastated.

The home defense performed remarkably, considering the immense amount of time they spent in the trenches. Due to this overwork, the unit grew visibly tired in the final quarter, as the big Penn State line wore the Buckeye defenders down. Cousineau was credited with a school-record 29 tackles (assistant Dave Adolph insists to this day the total was actually 36), while Washington, Cato, and Dansler really hung tough, too.

The Buckeyes allowed only one touchdown, on a short blast by Matt Suhey, yet Penn State repeatedly got the ball within scoring range via turnovers, and Bahr connected on four of five field goals. The defense played well enough to win most games, yet on this day, the offense provided little assistance and too much harm.

That night, on his weekly television show, Hayes refused to air clips of any turnovers, apparently in a noble gesture to spare the psyche of Schlichter. "I won't allow my players to be humiliated," Hayes protested, and shocked many viewers by vowing that the unfamiliar barrage of passes would continue. Informed that OSU had not thrown more than 17 passes during any single '77 contest, Hayes replied, "He [Schlichter] is going to be a great one. I'm sure he'll end up being one of the best quarterback's we've ever had."

Receiver and quarterback coach George Chaump defended the switch of Gerald to receiver, stating that Schlichter was the most "courageous" player he'd seen in many a year, and that better times were soon to follow in Art's wake.

In a most indicative sign of the kind of day this Saturday was for Ohio State, the game films were somehow botched and portions of the contest were missing. In some ways, this was a blessing: Woody did not have to watch an apparent blown call by an official, which was the sole play of the entire contest about which Woody really pitched a noticeable fit over. The play occurred on the lone PSU touchdown drive, and a Nittany Lion appeared to go into motion illegally, although the whistle signifying such an infraction never blew. The play gained positive yardage, and the drive was sustained. A few plays later, Suhey found the end zone.

Ohio State did escape from the Nittany Lion's den with only the one major injury, the foot of Robinson. This painful sprain prohibited Joe from making the upcoming road trip to Minnesota. Robinson was joined at home by Mills, who was still unable to suit up.

In a practice for the upcoming Gopher clash, frosh receiver Gary Williams was the next Buckeye to be felled by the injury bug. Williams, who was already nursing a sore knee, injured the other knee and was forced to undergo surgery. Gary was a converted high school quarterback, exhibiting blazing speed and sure hands.

One of the lone bright spots in a fairly gloomy, dreary week was the continued emergence of Donley. Recruited as a tailback from Cambridge, Ohio, the thin speedster was judged too frail to take the pounding required by a Buckeye back. His tremendous speed and fine hands prompted the switch to wideout. Curiously, his four receptions in the Penn State game were more than he managed his entire senior year of high school. The sophomore was learning how to time and coordinate his routes with the quarterback, and Doug's sure fingers gave the flinger confidence that if the ball was delivered, he would catch it.

The week following a defeat really would not be complete without a mild uprising from the Coach, and this week proved no exception. In mid-week, Hayes contended that the grass at Memorial Stadium on the campus of Minnesota was being intentionally maintained at too great a height, specifically to slow down the speedier Buckeyes.

In retrospect, it appears that once more, Hayes was merely deflecting the pressure and attention from his players onto himself. Woody was more than accustomed to the glare of the media, although he did not always acquiesce to or agree with the source of that glare. It is ironic that a man who had gained a justly-deserved reputation for disdain of the media could, on occasion, reverse the usual pattern of his ire and actually seek out the media spotlight, if such a reversal helped his football team relax.

Hayes stopped at nothing in an attempt to gain the competitive edge, or to help his players. As Ric Volley said, "Woody would do anything, literally anything, within legal means, to help us."

CHAPTER THREE: MINNESOTA

Come Saturday, 55,200 fans crowded into Memorial Stadium (the largest Gopher crowd since O.J. Simpson led the Trojans into the land of the lakes a decade before), in hopes that their Gophers were upset bound. These enthusiastic fans had high hopes of the first Gopher victory against OSU in a dozen years, and thought that the supreme talents of tailback Marion Barber could lead Minnesota to a national ranking.

Those hopes were quickly dampened, as Dansler recovered a fumble on the home 17, on only the third play of the game. Six running plays later, Schlichter scored his very first touchdown as a Buckeye. When Janakievski tacked on the point after, Ohio State had eclipsed their meager point total of any one of their last three games. Not coincidentally, those three consecutive low-scoring games had all been losses.

Dansler again came up with a big play on the ensuing Gopher possession, picking off an errant pass for his second turnover of the day. The OSU defense dominated the Gopher offense, which had stung a decent Toledo team for 38 points just one week previously. No such good fortune existed on this day. Although Schlichter tossed an interception of his own shortly thereafter, OSU relied on a powerful running game the remainder of the half, forging a decisive 21-3 lead at the break.

Cal Stoll brought his home team out remarkably rejuvenated after halftime, and the Gophers played OSU to a scoreless standstill in the third quarter. By the final quarter, though, the deeper, stronger Buckeyes wore down the valiant Minnesota team. The offensive line of the Buckeyes took over, and the offense, led alternately by Castignola and Schlichter, battered a diminishingly effective Gopher defense for a finishing touchdown. Springs and Campbell, spelled capably by Volley and Payton at times, led the smash-mouth rushing thrust.

Overall, Ohio State accumulated 311 rushing yards on 71 carries, in a perfect example of the consistent, hammering, low-risk offense Hayes built his reputation on. Donley made the most of the very minimal (eight) pass attempts, breaking loose on a 33 yard catch and run in the opening half.

The defense again put the clamps on a seemingly strong Minnesota attack, allowing just the early field goal and a late, harmless touchdown. Cousineau, Cato, and Ellis looked particularly impressive, and Dansler continued his pattern of making climactic plays.

The only down facet of the OSU game was Janakievski. Vlade missed a short field goal, and also flubbed an extra point, ending his record streak in that area at 47. Although the Gophers played to a tie after the half, OSU came away with an all-important 27-10 win, in a contest which did not seem as close as the final score might indicate.

With OSU apparently back on the winning track, the week following this win became decidedly more upbeat and less foreboding. The week began with a wonderful yarn, reported by Dick Otte in the *Columbus Dispatch*.

According to this tale, on the August '78 eve of inaugural dedications for the brand new College Football Hall of Fame near Cincinnati, Ohio, dusk descended, as the final preparations were completed in anticipation of an immense, national audience the following morning. As the majority of the facilities workers headed home to finally complete an interminably long day, a lone car pulled into the almost deserted parking lot and stopped near the entrance. A solitary, kind-looking older gentleman tapped on the locked door of the building and somehow convinced a roving security guard to let him briefly wander around the otherwise desolate museum grounds.

After a three hour visit, the man quietly left. The guard watched, puzzled, as the older man walked to his car and reached inside. Holding something that was impossible for the guard to pick out in the darkness, the man walked back towards the guard. As the security man re-opened the museum door, the man handed him a small token of appreciation: The book *You Win With People*, signed on the inside title page "Best Wishes, [author] Woody Hayes."

When informed of this story, Woody insisted that his only visit to the shrine had come on the very next morning, after this incident allegedly occurred. According to Woody, he toured the Hall's grounds in broad daylight, with hundreds of witnesses. Despite this denial, this story adds considerably to the ever-growing mystique of Hayes, and also ties in neatly to the wide disparity of images the man presented.

True or not, this is exactly the sort of thing Hayes was noted for: Small, unannounced nuances of niceness which counteracted with his fierce, blustering public image. The true Hayes encompassed both spectrums, and it seems his dominant traits tended to the generous, humanitarian side.

Except for the rare, home-town article such as Otte's, though, the average football fan never realized this fact, something Hayes himself did not normally mind. Woody rarely concerned himself with his public image; as mentioned, he sometimes courted controversy to take the spotlight off his "kids," and most of his good deeds escaped unnoticed, except to those many whom Woody benefited.

On more mundane ground, Schlichter was deemed sufficiently settled by this week and was allowed to grant his first interview since matriculating to Columbus. Art explained that a football game was just a football game, regardless of where it was played or the level of competition involved. He felt the game itself was deceptively simple, and his biggest adjustment was not the game, but the heightened intensity of the combatants involved. His adjustment to the intercollegiate game was proceeding nicely, he felt, and the challenge of raising his game to a new level excited the competitor in him.

Art denied there was friction between he and the man he displaced, Gerald, and Art lavishly praised the unselfish senior. "Rod Gerald has been great to me. I respect him completely as a person, and as a ballplayer." Schlichter continued on to compliment Gerald and Donley with easing his adjustment to major college ball, and added that each upperclassman had contributed greatly to his frosh play, through numerous tips and hints about what to expect, both on the field and off.

Schlichter was far from alone in his glowing assessment of Gerald. As the week kicked off in preparation for a first-ever clash with Baylor, Hayes commented on the leadership qualities and amazing receiving talents of Rod. Woody also admired the tenacity and guts Rod displayed in the extensive blocking role of the wide receiver. In the eyes of the harsh perfectionist Hayes, a dyed-in-the-wool running purist, the blocking of Gerald was spectacular.

Though some of this gushing might be passed off as gratuitous appreciation for Rod's sacrifice in moving to a new position, Hayes insisted that Gerald actually was as hard-nosed and spunky as any Buckeye receiver had ever been, whether blocking in the trenches or searching out targets downfield. There is no doubt that Rod was the kind of fearless, reckless go-getter Woody admired, however thin or inexperienced at a blocking role Rod might have been.

Hayes was even in sufficient cheer to open the practice sessions back up for media perusal. Mills and Robinson were expected to be back for the meeting with the Bears, and several players were performing better than expected. Fritz, and especially Ferguson, were enjoying dominant campaigns on the line, while Laughlin was behaving like a berserker on specialty teams. The scrappy backup linebacker was drawing a lot of notice in film sessions, for Woody was quite pleased with his intensity and combativeness.

Alas, this sunny mood soon attracted some clouds. Prior to the trip to Minnesota in the previous week, a female photography editor of the OSU student newspaper, *The Lantern*, was not allowed to embark on the team flight, although a male editor from that same paper did travel with the team.

In the ensuing flap, accusations were tossed around, blaming various individuals and departments for her exclusion. One such accusation, supposedly delivered from athletic department sources, claimed that the order to keep the female off the team flight originated straight from Woody.

The validity of this theory was neither confirmed nor denied, yet OSU officials did later state that from this point on, all women reporters and photographers who wished to travel with the squad, would be permitted. No public comment on the matter was ever offered by Hayes, though his feelings regarding any sort of distraction for his team, especially on the heels of a defeat, can well be imagined.

The issue to Woody was never one of gender; the issue was always a matter of what helped, or hindered, the team. Media distractions went along with the job, yet complications such as this were never welcomed.

By midweek, the status of Mills was downgraded to doubtful, for new light was shed on his injury. According to Billy Hill, Mills had an extremely uncommon "eversion" sprain in his ankle, which was only seen "...once every five years." Also of great concern was the slow start of Springs.

Ron himself felt inexplicably "rusty," though he admitted that '77 was the first year he had begun a campaign with a bang. The loss, to graduation, of behemoth Chris Ward left a huge void when it came to drive blocking, and the line was just now beginning to communicate and work as a harmonious unit. Facing a Baylor squad which had lost two consecutive heartbreakingly-close games because of defensive lapses, Springs felt that he would finally bust loose come Saturday. Fate chose a different path instead.

On Friday, Hayes read to the squad various selections from his beloved author Emerson. Woody felt, "Anything you can do to bring the squad closer together is a plus," so Woody often educated and bonded simultaneously. Hayes was a teacher at heart, just like his father, Wayne Benton, and Woody never failed to converse in seemingly diverse subjects, then tie them all together, and relate them to the game of football.

"Football to a football player is more important than any other course," he claimed, yet only if history and literature were weaved into that teaching of football. Each of these three subjects were intertwined and virtually interchangeable in the Hayes scheme of the universe, so Woody attempted to work elements of each into his lessons on an almost-daily basis.

CHAPTER FOUR: BAYLOR

This orderly universe of Woody's survived a fantastic jolt on gameday, when Baylor quarterback Steve Smith riddled the ailing pass defense of OSU for 249 yards and three touchdowns. Hayes did chalk up a win, 34-28, his 200th in his 28th season at Ohio State, though the determined visitors from Waco, Texas, held that feat in doubt for most of the contest (The 200 victories at the same school put Woody in mighty rare company, as Amos Alonzo Stagg, at the time, was the only other coach to accomplish this feat, winning 243 games in 41 years at the University of Chicago).

The game began pleasantly enough for Ohio State. Baylor received the opening kick, and the Bears were quickly forced to punt. The Buckeyes promptly breezed down the field to chalk up a touchdown. Then, the familiar passing game foibles reappeared in the OSU attack, as Schlichter was intercepted on each of the two following Buckeye possessions.

Baylor capitalized on both of the turnovers, marching in for two touchdowns, despite losing their leading ground gainer, Greg Hawthorne, to an injury. In a cruel balancing act by the gods of football, Springs soon followed his counterpart, falling prey to a similar knee injury.

Campbell and the relatively-unknown Calvin Murray stepped up and brought OSU back. Murray played like a man possessed, totaling 93 yards on 14 carries on the day, and the offense adjusted well to the loss of their senior weapon. Campbell led the way, with 109 yards on the ground, mostly accrued on short runs behind fine blocks by Vogler and Fritz.

Despite the success of the OSU offense, the defense could not contain the Bears, and the visitors held a shocking 21-17 lead at the half. Some of the Baylor standouts included tight end Ronnie Lee, defensive tackle Gary Johnson, and running back Frank Pollard. The sold-out crowd sat stunned and restless as OSU trudged into the locker room.

The Buckeyes re-emerged from the break with a vengeance. Schlichter soon connected with Donley on a 51 yard scoring strike, putting OSU on top. The Baylor offense found the Buck defense suddenly impenetrable, and OSU added to their lead with a field goal and another touchdown in the fourth quarter. Gerald made an amazing circus catch to put the Bucks in position for this field goal, which the sidewinder Atha promptly drilled.

This touchdown followed a long, impressive drive which chewed up time and further fatigued the visiting defenders. Campbell capped the march with a short end zone plunge. Ohio State was able to move the chains, and score, in spite of the incredible efforts of Bear middle linebacker Mike Singletary. Singletary ended with 29 tackles, and even busted open his own helmet, thanks to his harsh, unrelenting hitting. As the game clock ran down to just minutes remaining, the OSU lead stood at 13.

Baylor had just enough time for one last drive, and Cousineau raced into the flat, grabbed a Smith pass, and sprinted 61 yards for an apparent score. However, a personal foul call against OSU nullified this touchdown, and Baylor retained possession. Given a reprieve, Smith led the Bears to the end zone, although time finally ran out on the comeback effort.

Ohio State sorely missed both Mills and Bell, who was forced to leave early in the contest after being injured. Smith riddled the air defense all afternoon, mostly hitting the intermediate seams between linebacker coverage and deeper backfield zones, steadily and relentlessly chipping away at the normally solid Buckeye defense.

Cousineau finished with 23 tackles, almost keeping pace with the driven Singletary, while Ross and Ellis also led the way to the slim escape from the grasp of defeat.

Fortunately, one piece of good news reached the OSU coaching staff by Monday, after a rigorous night of film watching and ear chewing. Springs would not require surgery on his damaged knee, though stretched ligaments would confine him to a cylindrical cast for at least a few weeks. The injury to Springs added to perhaps the most extensive list of injuries ever during the Hayes tenure.

In the coming week, the defensive backfield would be further depleted, as Brian Schwartz blew out a knee and frosh Mark Eberts strained his neck. At least Springs retained some hope for a '78 comeback, although he was limping very badly in his protective cast.

Due to the on-field absence of this senior leader, Hayes appointed Gerald as an acting captain. Gerald was always rather removed and somewhat aloof from his teammates, though definitely not in a conceited or egotistical sense. The sacrifices Rod made, and the extra hardships he was enduring, all undertaken with a sense of camaraderie and unity as opposed to martyrdom, endeared him to his coaches and fellow players and brought out his finest leadership virtues.

With the secondary down to precious few healthy bodies and reeling in attempting to assimilate newcomers into unaccustomed roles, the upcoming opponent, the Mustangs of Southern Methodist, had good reason to feel confident. Bell and Mills were cleared to return, though neither player was in peak form. After all, the pass-crazed 'Stangs had given the Nittany Lions all they could handle early in the season, before bowing out by a scant 26-21 margin.

For the first time since '58, when the exploits of "Dandy" Don Meredith allowed the Mustangs to compete with the nation's top teams, SMU appeared ready to make an assault on the national rankings. Head man Ron Meyer, who grew up on College Avenue in Westerville before attending Purdue University, had visions of a victorious homecoming.

A stormy cloudburst ended the practice week at Ohio State, and the deluge seemed an omen bearing ill wind for the battered Buckeyes, who looked far removed from the team which crushed SMU 35-7 just one year previously.

CHAPTER FIVE: SOUTHERN METHODIST

Sure enough, OSU narrowly averted a loss on this Saturday. Mustang quarterback Mike Ford had improved remarkably from his scatterarmed, overly bold self of a year ago, and he launched an all-out aerial assault on the thin OSU pass defense. Ford kept the Buckeye defense off balance, revealing minute coverage flaws and exploiting them to full effect as the Mustangs compiled 501 yards in total offense.

Perhaps even more astoundingly, SMU ran 107 plays from scrimmage on this day. The sophomore Ford nailed a stupendous 36 of 57 pass attempts for 341 yards, against an exhausted and beleaguered unit of baffled defenders.

Although this game was as exciting a matchup as ever witnessed in Ohio Stadium (in theatrics, passing feats, and last-second drama, perhaps only a 49-42 victory over Illinois in '80 comes close), neither school was overjoyed at the 35-35 final outcome. Ohio State was particularly upset, as much for the spate of new injuries they incurred, as for only salvaging a tie out of this matchup.

One of these injuries came as Schlichter severely bruised his right (throwing) shoulder on the final play of the game. This play served as a microcosm of the pain and ultimate shortcomings inherent in the Buckeye effort on this day. Also sidelined were Cato, who suffered a deep thigh bruise; substitute linebacker Tony Megaro, who went down with an ankle sprain; Tim Vogler, who fractured a thumb; and Campbell, Ellis, and Skillings, who each was hampered by less-severe dings and scratches.

Regardless of the severity of their pains, the diminished effectiveness and partial absences of Skillings and Ellis were particularly damaging to the task of containing the red-hot Ford. The SMU slinger capitalized on every mistake, sparing no opportunity to resolutely chip away at the thin Buckeye blanket of pass coverage.

As they had against Baylor, Ohio State stopped SMU cold to open the game, then took possession and rambled downfield for a fast touchdown. Yet SMU, following the lead of the never-say-die Bears, struck back for two retaliatory scores. A botched extra point reduced their lead to 13-7, however, presenting OSU with a window of opportunity to forge ahead.

Finding themselves in a hole at home once more, the Buckeyes embarked on an exquisite 88 yard drive. A banged-up Campbell ran in for the score, and as Janakievski converted the point after, OSU was in front by a single point. Undeterred, Ford catapulted the Mustangs downfield, running for a touchdown just before halftime. Just as importantly, Ford scrambled and connected on a two point conversion, negating the effects of the earlier extra point miss. At the intermission, OSU again trailed, 21-14.

Shortly after the break, sophomore inside linebacker John Epitropoulos, with an assist from the ever-present Laughlin, broke through and blocked an SMU punt. Al Washington alertly picked up the bounding ball and ran in untouched for a touchdown. The season of cruel breaks and near-misses continued apace, though, when Janakievski shanked the extra point attempt, leaving OSU down by one.

The immediate impact of this miss was lessened somewhat by a touchdown on the next OSU possession, as Ricky Johnson exploited his increased playing time by keying a long drive, eventually dashing in for the score. Schlichter found Donley open on the bid for two, negating the extra point flub, and things looked bright again for the home team. This optimism increased as OSU capped a short drive with an Art run for another touchdown, increasing the lead to 35-21, with time still remaining in the third quarter.

Southern Methodist fumbled on their ensuing possession, and when OSU recovered at the visitor 24, a Buckeye victory appeared imminent. Instead of salting the win away with a score, however, Ohio State fumbled and all momentum swung immediately back to the Mustangs. Hayes succinctly stated, "I feel we blew this [game]," and based on situations such as this, he was correct.

Ford subsequently led his emboldened charges on a time-consuming drive of 66 yards, culminating in a one yard scoring plunge. Meyer went for the gusto, anticipating a following score, and tried for a two point conversion. Ford was stacked up, and OSU temporarily celebrated. The OSU offense was inexplicably unable to generate any thrust, however, after appearing untracked in the third quarter, and SMU got the ball back with plenty of time remaining.

Starting from their own nine, SMU gamely marched down the field, mostly behind short passes from Ford, and eventually the Mustangs ran into the end zone again. This time, the try for two proved successful, as Ford just snuck in across the goal to tie the score with 3:47 left.

Despite the earlier success of the Buckeye ground game, led by Schlichter with 77 yards and Murray with 105 yards in only 14 rushes, the Buckeyes were now forced to pass on third down, as the Mustang defense tightened to allow little gain on two running attempts. The rousing earlier success of Murray was partly attributable to the return of Robinson, who gamely played despite his bum ankle. The Mustangs anticipated and read the forced pass, picking Schlichter off.

Ford again drove the Mustangs into OSU territory, though Meyer eschewed a long field goal attempt on a fourth and one call from the 30. Cousineau, Washington, and company stuffed the line surge on the try for a first down, stopping the play for no gain. Ohio State braced for one last possession and a chance to salvage a win by breaking the tie.

A mere three plays later, Schlichter again threw an interception, and SMU now had their final opportunity for an unlikely victory. There were still a few twists of excitement left in this rollercoaster, emotional, continuously shifting afternoon, though, as Ford passed the visitors down to the OSU 29 yard line. On third down, with only seven seconds remaining, kicker Eddie Garcia trotted out for a 47 yard field goal and the win. Thankfully, the erratic Garcia had no von Schamann tricks up his sleeve, and missed the long attempt.

The Buckeyes were therefore presented with one last-ditch chance at a win, as Schlichter had an opportunity to show off his considerable arm strength in hopes for a Hail Mary miracle. More true to '78 form, Art's long, telegraphed, pass downfield was picked off, and adding injury to insult, Art was viciously slammed to the turf and wounded his shoulder. The game clock expired as the SMU defender was tackled following the theft, leaving both teams vividly drained and disappointed.

The sold-out stadium crowd filed out in tired amazement, not really certain they had really witnessed an Ohio State team play or not. Come on, a Hayes squad blows a huge lead, throws three interceptions in the final three minutes, and surrenders over 500 yards in total offense? Not likely, until this day.

No group was more void of energy than the OSU linebacking corps, who had been all over the field, seemingly every minute of the game. Unfortunately, a lot of that time was futilely spent chasing receivers who had just caught short passes. Regardless, Cousineau recovered enough to record a scintillating 28 tackles, Dansler had 18, and Washington contributed 16, plus his touchdown. These glorious statistics did little to soothe the agony of a tie in front of the home fans.

That Monday dawned with Schlichter on the sidelines, unable to practice because of his bruised wing. Art also had a swollen right hand, and a banged-up right elbow which had bothered him since fall training camp. He would be unable to throw until Thursday, so Gerald was forced to take over at the helm. Gerald himself was still mending from his leg woes, so Castignola also got plenty of work.

In the teeth of some very harsh and very vocal fan and media criticism concerning the often-ineffective Buckeye passing game, Chaump asserted that Schlichter was merely lacking a little in confidence; with a few timely completions, the entire offense would pick up some much-needed faith and their execution would correspondingly improve. Including sacks and interception return yardage, the OSU passing game netted just 50 yards against SMU, so those few completions were sorely needed.

Even new running sensation Murray was bothered by a severely bruised toe, which occurred on his last rushing attempt in the Mustang game. Murray had not carried the ball much during his prep days in Woodbine, New Jersey, yet OSU backfield coach Mickey Jackson saw enough to see the ultimate potential in the youngster. Jackson pushed hard for Murray to matriculate to Columbus, and Cal, with 28 carries for 198 yards on the year thus far, was more than happy with the chance to contribute.

With the way Buckeye backs were being felled by injuries, especially in the last few years, a surfeit of talent was necessary at this position, particularly since the passing game was floundering.

Ohio State now had to travel to Ross-Ade Stadium and take on the youthful Purdue Boilermakers, led by former Buckeye lineman Jim Young, who was the Riveter head coach. The OSU offensive line continued to shine during workouts this week, with Moore leading the way. Robinson was not quite at full strength, and Moore had responded to the slight breach by playing his finest game as a Buckeye, according to the coaching staff, after extensive review of the game films.

On the flip side, Ross and Skillings graded very highly for their defensive efforts against the Meyer bunch.

CHAPTER SIX: PURDUE

Eager to bounce back and right their stumbling start, OSU instead fell prey to a fired-up Riveter team. Self-destructing fumbles and penalties came back to haunt the Bucks, in front of the then third-largest crowd in Purdue home history. The loss dropped Ohio State to a woebegone 2-2-1 start, which was the most dreadful beginning since '67.

In a strange twist, '67 was also the last time Purdue had beaten OSU, though this '78 loss was not quite the thrashing the earlier loss had been. As in that earlier season, Purdue emerged from this 27-16 victory atop the conference standings.

Amazingly, the OSU passing game effected a complete turnaround from the terrible fortunes of the SMU contest. Schlichter, still bothered by his various ailments yet seemingly unaffected by his imposed layoff, surprisingly came out firing and had his finest day thus far in a scarlet and gray uniform. He pinpointedly delivered his plentiful passes to finish with 20 connections in 34 deliveries, amassing 289 yards.

Sixty of those yards came on a spectacular fourth quarter touchdown connection with the amazing Gerald, who had slipped behind the secondary and gathered in the lofting bullet, dashing the remaining yards to paydirt. The only interception suffered by Art came on a last-second desperation fling into multiple coverage in the end zone, as OSU belatedly searched for a miracle with only eight seconds remaining.

The visiting team lost this game primarily because of six costly fumbles, four of which the Boilermakers recovered. Two such turnovers came in the opening quarter, ending promising drives at the Purdue 18 and 11 yard lines, respectively. Another fumble, during the final quarter, was lost deep in Buckeye territory and Purdue capitalized with an icing field goal.

Also harmful to the OSU cause were nine penalties assessed on various Buckeye transgressors. The violations cost a school-record 116 yards, and stalled many Buckeye drives while prolonging certain Purdue possessions. This gross of errors was extremely uncommon for a Hayes team, and as feared, proved costly.

Hayes literally hated fumbles; his attitude toward them is best captured in a quote by John Heisman: "Better to have died as a small boy than to fumble this football." A fumble tore Hayes up inside, and he accepted no excuses for their happening.

Injuries again took their toll, too; Cato was limited to isolated spots of action, although he did record the only sack for OSU and provided a gutty rush during his brief bouts of activity; Murray was limited exclusively to returning kickoffs; Campbell played very sparingly; and Skillings went down in the second quarter. Fortunately, his replacement, Bob Murphy, picked off a Mark Herrmann pass in his very first play.

Herrmann, who led the conference in both passing and total offense in '77, chewed up the exposed seams in the OSU defense, with a plethora of short pitches and numerous dump-off passes to his backs and secondary receivers circling underneath downfield coverage. Herrmann fared somewhat better than his counterpart Schlichter, connecting on 22 of 34 passes, for 210 yards, including a critical scoring toss in the final quarter which sealed the victory.

Mark was sacked just the one time on the day, and that came late in the contest - even this loss was negated as Gerald fumbled on the very next play and Purdue regained possession. Shortly after this turn of events, Herrmann struck for his touchdown fling.

Purdue opened the contest with a long, clock-eating drive which resulted in a Scott Sovereen field goal. Ohio State then proceeded to dominate the remainder of the opening half, yet were stymied from piercing the scoreboard on numerous occasions, because of their untimely fumbles and ill-timed penalties.

Volley was able to bust loose for the longest OSU run of the season thus far, charging 49 yards for the score which carried a 7-3 lead into the halftime break. Volley ended the day with 81 yards in 11 rushes, as the Buckeyes outgained the Boilermakers 507 total yards to 328. Still, turnovers loomed large in dulling much of the offensive brilliance.

After the half, Herrmann directed a 77 yard drive, hitting seven of ten passes in the journey downfield. John Macon capped the effort with a one yard scoring dive. Ohio State drove downfield on their ensuing possession, and Atha responded with a tying field goal. Purdue came right back, breaking free for an eleven yard pickup on a third down situation, which led to another Sovereen field goal.

On the next OSU possession, Purdue end Keena Turner broke free around the outside and nailed Schlichter, forcing a fumble. Sovereen capitalized on the fortunate field position, booting another three-pointer. This kick advanced Scott into a tie as the most accurate Boilermaker kicker of all time, yet OSU came roaring back with the scoring strike to Gerald.

Alas, this was the last gasp for OSU, and coupled with a Michigan defeat on this very same day, Purdue now led the conference. Interestingly, both OSU and Michigan suffered defensive collapses late on this day, and consequently the Buckeyes and Wolverines each lost to a conference opponent on the same day for the first time since '67. Coincidentally, UM was also beaten by the same team during both years, the Michigan State Spartans.

Schlichter spread his completions out among six different receivers, with Donley snagging six for 86 yards, and Gerald gathering in three for 72 yards. Tyrone Hicks, briefly moved back to tailback in lieu of the injured Murray, played a delightfully key role in the rushing effort, particularly after Johnson was nicked up and forced to the sideline.

Defensively, Ohio State was victimized by poor field position, due to turnovers, and a continuing inability to halt short passes to secondary receivers. The Buckeyes were halting the big pass play, which was their primary mission, yet were being nickle-and-dimed to death in long marches featuring repeated, small gains. Cousineau, Washington, Sullivan, and Dansler each had strong games, though not powerful enough to stave off the loss. Mills saw his first extended action of the year, adding five tackles, though the efforts of Herrmann and company proved a little too much.

Young had boldly predicted a victory over his alma mater in pre-game comments, and his sentiments rang true. "...Certainly the biggest win of my career," Young triumphantly declared the win.

The bad news for Ohio State did not abate after the loss. Gerald hurt his elbow sometime during the contest, and team doctors diagnosed the injury as a coronoid process, or chipped bone, in his left elbow. It was expected that Rod would miss three weeks, though the offense was in no position to lose his receiving talents, invaluable leadership, or combative blocking.

With Springs, Vogler, and now Gerald sidelined, and Robinson still hobbled, the offense was severely lacking in elderly rudders to steer the green Schlichter and other, inexperienced backups now pressed into extended playing roles. Chuck Hunter moved into the receiving spot in the stead of Gerald, and Hayes was uncharacteristically low-keyed and subdued after hearing the medical status of his acting captain.

"It seems like every game we play anymore is an exciting one, but excitement doesn't get it, you have to win," said a glum Hayes. Adding to his depression was the continued hobbling of Cato, even though, playing primarily on one leg, Byron was named the top defender of the Purdue game by the coaching staff. Cato was also playing despite a painful hip pointer, and the pride and effort demonstrated in his heroic effort was the epitome of leading by example.

Three of the four co-captains were sidelined or severely laden with injury now, in addition to the loss of Gerald, and it is easy to see how the loss of their leaders had shaken the team. Hayes candidly admitted this was an unusual situation for a team of his to be in, and his usual remedy, hard work and extra effort, was difficult to impose with so many ailing or missing players. Even the weather turned against Ohio State on this week, as electrical storms ravaged the outdoor practice fields during the early part of the week.

The costly fumbles, other blunders, and untimely mental breakdowns of the season thus far really pained Hayes. Woody's concept of football really entailed execution against the game itself, and not any specific opponent (although he perhaps occasionally strayed from this path when confronting Michigan).

Essentially, Woody thought that as long as his squad did not defeat itself, no other team could outduel the Buckeyes. Countless repetitions of routinely simple plays, performed to perfection, would work, thought Woody, even as the opponent knew what the play was. Sid Gillman, ex-OSU star-turned-legendary-coach, contended: "We're going to drill those plays and we're going to run them so well that... it wouldn't make a hell of a lot of difference if Mohammed, Moses, or anyone else was over there."

The entire philosophy of the OSU squad stemmed from Woody. Quickness, in thought and deed, yielded power, which was displayed in a mano-a-mano method. Like one of his and his father's boyhood idols, President Theodore Roosevelt, Hayes possessed a strong, "Horror of words that are not translated into deeds, of speech that does not result in action." (Quote by William James, the father of American psychology).

Hayes rarely shirked from a difficult decision, and there was no doubt he was the central figure of authority, always interacting with players and coaches alike. It was not uncommon for Woody to threaten to banish even assistant coaches from a practice, if he felt they were not living up to his exacting standards, and he even booted player's parents from tense practices.

The battle on the field was not necessarily with the other team, but with oneself. This struggle was always conducted within the concept of the team framework, for Hayes desired no glory hounds. Ara Parseghian recalls, "As long as there is unity, there is strength."

Consequently, Woody's teams were always tight-knit, and went through experiences, both positive and negative, together, as if a family. Ideally, individuals within that family were never satisfied with less than a starting slot, yet backups accepted their role in an effort to improve the overall team. Hayes taught Lou Holtz the concept, "Not everybody can be first team, but you can always put the team first."

One rare on-field leader this season offensively was the pugnacious Savoca. Like many players who originated from the defensive side of the ball, Jim was outwardly more aggressive and vocal than his purer offensive proteges. Savoca spoke his mind, no matter the situation.

In one game, an opposing player was overcome by exhaustion and lost his lunch at midfield, right in the middle of the "O" in Ohio Stadium. Jim was destined to take his stance in the revolting mess, and refused to line up until the officials toweled off the regurgitation.

In another contest, the '78 opener against Penn State, Tim Burke was being dominated by the incredibly gifted Bruce Clark (of course, what lineman wasn't during this fantastic defender's collegiate career?). Savoca savagely barked, "If you think Clark is beating you up, wait until I get hold of you," or similar words to that effect. Not surprisingly, Burke's play picked up from that point on.

In another instance, the young Schlichter was bemoaning his lack of protection, and Savoca brought the huddle to a standstill as he commanded the signalcaller: "King Arthur, just worry about throwing the ball." Whatever the situation required, Savoca provided. Jim also continually amazed his teammates by refusing to ever wear either underwear or socks.

As the difficult preparations for the upcoming Iowa contest continued, Campbell and Barwig were knocked back with injury re-aggravations, and the coaching staff heard repeated public complaints regarding the lack of playing time for '77 top scorer Payton.

His absence in the attack was explained by and credited to the glaring improvement and versatility of both Campbell and Volley, yet the question lingered throughout the remainder of the season. Joel had also never been an exceptional practice player; Hayes never took kindly to those Buckeyes who did not put forth constant effort.

These clouds of sullen discontent were temporarily replaced by a rare ray of sunshine when Springs made an unscheduled early return to a practice. Murray was also back working out with the team, as the trainers commented that his injury was one in which the soreness could be ousted if Cal continued to run on his leg, and keep it loosened up.

The Iowa team, led by coach Bob Commings, was coming off a heartbreaking loss to the Gophers of Minnesota. Commings felt that the insertion of little-used third string quarterback Jeff Green into the starting lineup had transformed the Hawkeyes into a contender, for Jeff was establishing himself as a legitimate passing threat. Ironically, Green replaced the ineffective Bob Commings, Jr., son of the coach.

To shore up the at-times porous OSU line of pass defense, Guess was moved back to his more familiar open side halfback role, while Skillings and Murphy assumed the roles of the safeties.

Another change in the lineup came along the offensive line. Tim Brown would now alternate with Robinson, whose lofty All-American hopes were dashed with his injury in the Nittany Lion clash, as the PSU middle guard fell onto his foot, twisting and tearing the connective tissue. Joe battled through the pain and reduced flexibility to play near his healthy level of excellence, only to seriously aggravate the foot in the Purdue showing.

Robinson ended up removing himself from that game as he came to the realization that his backup, Brown, could perform better. The absence of this accomplished senior further shook the stability of the offense, though Moore continued to play the finest ball of his career, in an inspired senior season.

Commenting late in the week on his own astounding senior season, Cousineau stated he would gladly exchange some of his many tackles for a few more victories. "I'm really tickled with the way I've played," said Tom. "But the season we've had so far as a team takes away from it." Tom admitted that the team sorely missed the workmanlike ethic, demonic intensity, and leadership of '77 seniors Adkins, Griffin, and Brown, confiding that the underneath, short passing game was really tearing the defense apart.

"From here on in we just have to challenge ourselves and see how good we can get," Tom stated, claiming he would do all he could to continue exerting pressure and compiling eye-popping stats.

It is ironic that these otherworldly statistics (Tom finished the '78 campaign with a school-record 211 tackles) were accrued in part because the defense was on the field longer than desired, and many of Tom's tackles occurred downfield, after positive offensive gains. Still, no circumstances or team shortcomings should obscure the brilliance of his play, which led to his selection as the very first pick in the upcoming NFL draft.

CHAPTER SEVEN: IOWA

Saturday dawned brilliant and sunny, and the Buckeyes obliged their 60th straight sellout crowd, many of them alumni in town for the homecoming celebration, with a 31-7 trouncing of Iowa. Ohio State scored all of their points by halftime, as the home team completely dominated the opening thirty minutes. In the first half alone, OSU ground out 317 total yards and 15 first downs while limiting the Hawkeyes to 55 total yards and a mere four first downs.

Unfortunately, after this awesome start, the OSU offense practically took the second half off. In a complete reversal, the Hawkeyes dominated the second half, although they could manage only one touchdown during that time, in the third quarter. The biggest downer of the day was the total of 100 yards in penalties called against the Buckeyes, the second straight week OSU was stung by flags.

On the positive ledger, OSU went the entire game without a turnover, marking the first such occasion of the year.

The contest started out rather obscurely for Ohio State, as the offense moved little and the Hawkeyes forced a punt. Then, fortunes dramatically improved. Skillings intercepted a Green pass, and the Hawkeyes lost not only possession of the ball but their quarterback as well. Green badly strained his back on the misfire and never re-entered. This knockout blow proved fatal to Hawkeye victory hopes.

At this juncture, Springs made a scintillating return, bursting 39 yards to begin the scoring. Ron looked to be back in peak form as he finished the day with 71 yards in only 11 carries.

After a short Buckeye drive, Atha opened the second quarter with a 27 yard field goal. Then the scoring floodgates opened, as Ross continued his fabulous play by intercepting new quarterback Pete Gale's errant toss. Paul returned the throw 23 yards, and Campbell capitalized on the turnover by bulling in from five yards out. Campbell shook off the effects of his injury, and blasted for 89 yards in 15 carries on the afternoon.

Two plays after this touchdown, Ross tipped another Gale toss. This time, the ball fell into the waiting hands of Sullivan, who rumbled 13 yards for his first touchdown ever, at any level of organized ball. His resulting glee was contagious, for only four plays hence, after Iowa was forced to punt, the sore-armed Schlichter combined with Donley on a 78 yard touchdown bomb.

At this time, Woody brought in Castignola, because the strength of Art's arm was not up to par, and Woody wished to avoid further compounding any of the already extensive array of Schlichter ails. Although Castignola led the

Buckeyes on several extended drives in the remainder of the game, this rapid flurry of points ended the OSU scoring.

Even considering this exciting half of play, without a doubt the biggest blast of the day was provided by the special homecoming celebration guest, Bob Hope. His antics during the halftime festivities brought down the house, and the crowd noise escalated to a thunderous peak when Hope dotted the "i" in script Ohio (Hope became just the fourth non-marching band member to dot the "i". Long-time musical composer Richard Heine was accorded the honor in '74, and retiring university President Novice Fawcett and his wife shared the task in '71).

Just as Hope finished said chore with the appropriate ceremonial flare, Hayes brought the entire Buckeye squad onto the field and circled the ageless entertainer. Woody embraced the famous man, later saying that Hope is our "...greatest American...the man is just unbelievable." (Though Hope had actually been born in England, he emigrated to America as a youth and grew up in Ohio.)

The friendship and mutual admiration between these two matchless men stemmed from June of '74, when Woody was in University Hospital recuperating from a severe, sudden heart attack. Unprompted, Hope visited the recovering Coach, and Woody never forgot this unsolicited show of friendship.

At midfield, Woody introduced his entire squad to Hope, in as telling an example of the hero-worshiping facet of the Coach's personality ever witnessed. The crowd went nuts, and the players were also sufficiently awed.

Naturally, after this well-spring of emotion, the final half proved somewhat anti-climactic. Iowa managed one touchdown, OSU none; the defenses took over and the final score was 31-7.

One other unique first was achieved during this game. For years, Hayes was an advocate of a wet playing surface, for he felt a damp field produced fewer injuries than a dry one. Correspondingly, the practice field was always hosed down prior to a workout, and the players had christened the practice field "Lake Hayes" as a testament to the wet conditions. The training staff for OSU realized the concept was grounded in good sense, though the overall effect may not have been quite as beneficial as Woody believed.

For instance, especially when the mercury dipped low, the player's uniforms would literally freeze to their skin when they landed on the turf, and concentration on anything but getting warm became arduous. The footing on the field was sometimes treacherous, especially in the cold, yet Woody was convinced that the slick surface cut down on ankle and knee injuries.

With the slew of injuries thus far in '78, Hayes chose not to take any further chances and for the first time had the Ohio Stadium surface hosed down prior to a game. Whether this action really prevented an excess of injuries was undetermined; sadly, even this measure could not eliminate all injuries. Dansler was injured during this game, and Mills re-injured his ankle.

According to Billy Hill, such re-injuries were usually not as serious as the initial wound, and recovery usually came much quicker.

Ross, the 6'1", 232 pound senior, was named the conference "Player of the Week" for his Iowa exploits. Gary Dulin racked up three sacks in a monstrous performance, and Sullivan was designated "The Buck of the Week" by the coaching staff for his empowering efforts. According to assistant Glen Mason, that was "...the best game ever played," by the sparkplug middle guard.

Cousineau and Washington also received high praise for their continued fine linebacker play. Laughlin got a chance to play extensively, in relief of the injured Dansler, and performed remarkably well.

For the offense, Campbell and Ferguson were especially singled out for their spectacular play. Ferguson was consistently grading out as the finest performer on the line, and his play seemed to improve by leaps and bounds from week to week.

Regardless of these accolades, there were preparations aplenty to be made, as Northwestern was next on the schedule. This was a very young Wildcat squad, for at times as many as thirteen freshmen were on the field, combining the offensive and defensive units. Head coach Rick Venturi's squad was winless, with a 0-6-1 record, yet Hayes mandated, "You never dare take a team lightly."

It was little more than a decade since Ara Parseghian had led his alma mater to a mid-season number one ranking, for in '62 the Wildcats started 6-0, including an 18-14 victory over OSU in Columbus. In that game, Northwestern overcame a 14-0 deficit. In '59, the Wildcats had also started off 6-0. Alas, Wisconsin defeated the Wildcats in each of these years, spoiling once-promising Rose Bowl hopes.

Nonetheless, from '59-'62 Northwestern beat fine Notre Dame teams four years in a row, and Venturi held onto the dream of re-attaining such heights. With the inconsistent play of OSU this season, the Buckeyes had no reason to feel overconfident.

Unfortunately, the season of bad breaks continued apace this week. Gerald was coming along very slowly in recovering from his chipped bone, and Barwig continued his ill-fated year by being stricken with inflammatory tonsillitis.

In other disturbing news this week, the Ohio State athletic council took a vote, agreeing to permit the football team to attend only the Rose, Sugar, Orange, or Cotton bowl games. With the current 3-2-1 record, it seemed very unlikely that a tender to any of these four major bowls was forthcoming.

When news of this meeting and consequent decision was leaked to the press, former Buckeye assistant coach and then-athletic director Hugh Hindman explained such reasoning by stating, "Going to a bowl other than the majors doesn't seem like that good an idea," though Hindman left the door open to reconsider by admitting that a recommendation either by the council or from him could alter this decision. The rationale for exclusively aiming for a major bowl seemed centered around financial considerations, as all other bowls were not yet proven, fiscally profitable ventures, as of yet.

One Buckeye not content to settle for a 'lesser" bowl was the pugnacious senior, Sullivan. Mark set his sights much higher, on especially the Rose, and he fervently believed that OSU could be in a position to contend for placement in that game by the Michigan showdown. Sullivan contended that, outside of the Wolverine game, the '77 game with Northwestern was as tough as any on the schedule, including Oklahoma.

Mark was what then-Air Force head coach Bill Parcells called a "parking lot player:" He would play anywhere, anytime, even in a parking lot, because he loved the physical aspect of the game so much.

Sullivan had spent a considerable amount of time preparing for his final year of eligibility, and was really taking advantage of his sole shot at greatness. Years of being an understudy behind Nick Buonamici and Aaron Brown had prepared him well. "They were real great players and I understood that and learned a lot from them," Mark acknowledged. "I knew that they were better than I was," he admitted, yet in '78, Sullivan was proving to be every bit their equal with his fiery brand of play. Sullivan was the quintessential example of the player whose level of play rose to the occasion as needed, and really made things happen during crucial times.

CHAPTER EIGHT: NORTHWESTERN

Thus inspired by the exhortations of Sullivan and others, the Buckeyes went out Saturday and scored the most points ever recorded by a Hayes squad, pounding the Wildcats 63-20 (The previous high for points under Woody was 62, which the '69 squad reached twice, against Wisconsin and Texas Christian). Excluding those two '69 runaways, this was the most lopsided Buckeye win since Wes Fesler's '50 squad hammered Iowa by a count of 83-21.

The Buckeye rushing attack ground out 511 yards on this Saturday, falling just shy of the school record of 517, achieved in '74. The Buckeyes accumulated 33 first downs, which tied a school record, as the record-pace day saw the offense succeed mightily.

In spite of all the records, Hayes was not satisfied. He reiterated over and over that a game this lopsided accomplishes nothing beneficial, and in some ways was harmful for a team. "It's bound to soften you," he practically snarled, and no one doubted him.

Woody never rested on his or his teams' laurels, and in fact made it a point to rarely, almost never, praise a player to his face. The majority of the instances where Woody complimented a player, came either in response to media questions, were comments addressed to opposing coaches, or were part of his many speeches in front of various organizations.

Among his team, face-to-face direct praise was a rare exception to the rule, for Hayes believed, "If someone gives you a compliment, kick them in the shins, unless it's your grandmother. They're softening you up." Once a player completed his eligibility and left the program, then Woody usually made it a point to personally compliment that person on his achievements. While a player still had eligibility remaining, Woody was never satisfied with that player's performance, for he forever felt that a player could do a little better, could squeeze just a little more out of his body.

The winless Wildcat squad, racked by a lack of experience and bereft of key personnel because of injuries, actually played a better game than the score might indicate. The game was at least a tossup until late in the first half, when OSU broke open a tight battle with their offensive explosion. Ohio State struck first, on a breathtaking 55 yard run by Murray, which was the longest run of the season.

Oddly enough, on the ensuing kickoff, Orosz, who customarily crunched the ball into or out of the end zone, kicked three consecutive balls out of bounds, drawing a penalty on each occasion. The shaken Tom was replaced by Atha, who stayed in for the remainder of the day.

On the next Buckeye possession, Atha missed a field goal, though he did slightly atone for this by later jarring a Wildcat kickoff returner with a bonecrunching tackle. The skinny Atha was never shy about contact, and Hayes was learning that the slight size of Atha did not diminish his heart of a warrior.

Prior to the missed field goal by Atha, the Wildcats used some sleight-of-hand trickery to tie the game. Kevin Strasser, who trailed only Herrmann in most conference passing categories, led the Wildcats on a long drive deep into Buckeye territory. Strasser then took advantage of the OSU preoccupation with his arm, handed off to fullback Lou Tiberi, and rolled outside the defensive containment. Tiberi flipped the ball back to Strasser, who was all alone, for an eleven yard scoring play.

This was about it for the Wildcat highlights in this lopsided contest, though, as OSU henceforth embarked on a scoring rampage. Campbell pounded in for three touchdowns; Schlichter ran in for a score and hit Donley with a 20 yard bullet for another score; and Volley, Castignola, and Hicks dashed into the end zone during a fourth quarter onslaught. The lone interception suffered by Schlichter set up a second Wildcat score, in the third quarter, and the Wildcats scored their final touchdown after time had officially expired.

John Epitropoulos intercepted a pass to apparently end the rout, but a pass interference call against the Buckeyes gave NU one last chance to make the score a little more respectable. Tailback JoJo Webb promptly scored on the reprieve play, though, appropriately enough, the point after was missed.

Interestingly, John and Ernie Epitropoulos were the second set of twins to perform under Woody. The sophomore look-alikes from Warren (Ohio) Harding were much like the Vogler twins: intense, eager, and always ready for action. John was a fine reserve inside linebacker, and Ernie displayed great potential at left guard.

The Wildcat defense was not up to par on this day, mostly because of the absence of several starters, due to injuries. Hayes offered this as the reason the Buckeyes scored so often, and Venturi did not disagree. Woody did empty the Buckeye bench very early in the thrashing, for OSU used 70 players. Ohio State avoided the pass in the second half, sticking exclusively with the run, and Hayes even refused a 15 yard penalty, a move which drew a public note of gratefulness from Venturi.

Woody even contemplated having his players intentionally fumble as they neared the goal line, yet nixed this thought because this act was patronizing toward NU. Hayes also felt it unfair to impinge on the successes of reserve players such as Strahine, and did not want their appearance marred by turnovers, intentional or otherwise.

Woody related that, as a head coach, he had only run up the score on one instance, way back on Thanksgiving Day '39. His New Philadelphia (Ohio) high school squad beat Dover (Ohio) High 49-0, and Hayes admitted that he was a poor sport concerning the margin. "I didn't feel good about it at all;" thereafter, Woody always attempted to be sensitive toward the losing side, though he also believed, "We make no apologies for winning."

Those who were feeling good about this day were the OSU rushers. Murray led the way with 103 yards, Springs added 98, Johnson contributed 84, and Schlichter compiled 74. Moore and Vogler led the line surge with some ravishing blocking, and Terry Vogler played a fine game from his reserve linebacker slot. Guess continued to dazzle on punt returns, even though a clipping call shortened his explosive long runback of 48 yards.

The defense played a fine contest throughout, led by Cousineau and Ross. Paul had two quarterback sacks and another tackle for a loss in his second straight dominant outing. Skillings roamed the passing lanes and snatched two balls, as the backfield was aided by the fierce pass rush generated by Sullivan.

After the game mercifully ended, Hayes zinged the OSU athletic council with a short, caustic, sarcastic monologue. "We don't talk about bowl games at this time if other people haven't first [initiated the possibility of an invite]," proffered Hayes. "But I'm too new around here to be consulted." Hayes seemed correct in this disagreement, since at this stage of the season none of the bowls had even approached Ohio State or even remotely raised the possibility of an invite.

It seemed odd to some observers that Hayes was not the one in this case to hasten to conclusions; Woody was exercising much restraint, diplomacy, and tact, in far greater measure than the athletic council had.

This restraint, however, did not last too long. In a much ballyhooed incident, Hayes flashed his famous temper for all inquiring minds to see. This was a highly charged, tempestuous week even by chaotic '78 standards.

The controversial uproar this week began at the weekly Monday press luncheon, held in the Jai Lai restaurant, a Columbus fine-dining venue and a Hayes favorite. Local cub television reporter Marty "The Rookie" Reid, who was involved in a similar shouting incident with Woody in '77, prompted the fireworks. The relationship between Reid and Hayes was already stormy, usually over what Hayes regarded as overzealous questions from the probing newsman. Plus, despite his status as the resident OSU man at his station, Reid customarily did not attend Buckeye practices. Hayes felt no man could criticize if he wasn't actually an informed observer.

This exchange went as follows: Reid - "Last Wednesday, talk show host Phil Donohue asked [Qube cable television viewers of Columbus] if Woody Hayes should retire, and 56% said yes. Do you have any reaction to that?"

Hayes - "You know something? Those 56% probably weren't even living when I started winning here. No, I'm not interested. It's more what I'm going to do, and I'm not going to worry much over that. Sure, people are fickle, and I don't much care. There's no one in this league or any other league that has won as many games as I have. I'm not going to let their opinion decide this thing. And if you're one of the 56%, I don't give a damn about you, either. Good day."

At this juncture Hayes was visibly upset yet still in control. On his way toward the doors leading out of the banquet room, Hayes passed directly in front of Reid, then flew into an obvious rage. "And if you don't like it, you can go straight to hell," Woody bellowed.

A stunned Reid stammered and said, "I'm sorry you feel that way."

Hayes ripped into Reid. "I just wish you were bigger and stronger... you're young enough."

As Reid tried to interject a comment, Hayes harshly interrupted: "Yeah, yeah, yeah... talk, that's all you do well."

Reid meekly said, "I'm sorry."

Hayes yelled, "Yeah, yeah, you're sorry!" With that parting remark, he stormed from the hall and savagely slammed the door, as every chair in the room was rocked by the force of the exit. A stunned audience sat, dead silent.

Shortly before this vitriolic, heated exchange, Hayes had again rebuked the athletic council for not consulting with him. "I think I've been around long enough to deserve consultation," Woody angrily stated. It appeared at this point that Hayes was already on edge concerning this slight, and the resulting clash with Reid then occurred as much because of the source and Reid's timing, as because of the question itself.

Hayes was understandably defensive because of the disappointing season, and was already very exhausted by his self-imposed workaholic schedule. He resolutely resented any suggestion that his age was any factor in the below-par season, and resented any talk of retirement, especially as there were games remaining on the schedule. The largest number of injuries Woody could recall, since at least '71, contributed to a certain sense of helplessness Hayes felt concerning the '78 fortunes. (Ultimately, Hayes and Reid patched up their differences, though neither one ever specifically apologized for this incident).

Additionally, the health of the Coach was growing increasingly unstable, and at times, Woody refused to take the several medications he was prescribed to combat his diabetes and heart troubles. Like any proud, strong man, Woody sometimes felt betrayed by the unhealthy turn of his physical condition within the last several years, and he resented being told medication was essential to his survival. Stubbornly and defiantly, he would occasionally assert control over the situation by disdaining medical instructions.

Plus, he never halted his unusually long bouts of activity, pausing only to nap from two until two-fifteen each afternoon. A vaunted influence upon the younger Woody, Earl "Red" Blaik said: "There is no substitute for work. It is the price of success."

Accordingly, Hayes literally worked from six in the morning until midnight veritably each and every day, without fail. Woody was too busy, too accustomed to hard work, and too plain stubborn to bow to health, diet, or geriatric concerns. Coaching compatriot George Allen summed up this work ethic: "Leisure time is that five or six hours when you sleep at night... if you love your work, it's really no longer work." Hayes truly loved his work, and his kids.

The following day, talk-show host Phil Donohue was immediately contrite about the untoward situation, and expressed sorrow that he had started such a feud between Hayes and the public. He respectfully asked Hayes to appear on his show, guaranteeing that Woody would be treated fairly. "Woody appeared on my show once before, and I think he enjoyed it," the talk-show host said. Donohue defended his choice of the survey, which was telecast to homes in the north, west, and northwest Columbus area, including parts of the OSU campus and surrounding neighborhoods.

Since Hayes was set to turn 66 in February of '79, Donohue contended that Hayes, being a public employee supported by taxpayers, should be held to the then-standard mandatory retirement age of 65. Hindman soon countered with the information that, although Hayes was employed by a state-funded university, his salary was actually paid from revenue generated by the athletic department (and of course the football program generated the overwhelming bulk of that revenue). Therefore, no tax money specifically went to either Hayes or to any of his paid assistants.

Interestingly, on the subject of pay, Woody was notorious for refusing pay raises as offered by the university's board of trustees, and remained one of the lower-paid coaches in the conference. However, this practice effectively kept any of his assistants from receiving raises also, for their pay remained relative to that of the Head Coach.

Obviously, Woody never cared much about financial gain or material comforts, and could not fathom how anyone involved with football might desire such prosperity. It was unconscionable to Woody that someone might grow wealthy by coaching a game so loved. Nevertheless, some of his assistants were not such Spartan advocates of a simple lifestyle, and there were some undercurrents of hostility each time Woody retained his lowly salary.

Woody customarily gave away generous paychecks, accrued from his many speaking engagements, to hospitals, churches, and individuals in need. Even his wife, Anne, felt obligated to usually pay for her own game tickets and even went so far as to pay for her own air-fare on road-trips! According to Jeff Kaplan, she declared, " My husband is the Coach; why should I benefit?"

Contrary to conventional opinion, Woody did not select exclusively "yes" men as his assistants, yet looked for a man courageous enough to express his own opinion, under fire, and a man able to transmit large amounts of usable information to his charges. If some assistants succeeded better than others at remaining independent thinkers, the players benefited even more than if blind subservience to the whims of Woody were followed. Players recall that Bill Myles and Alex Gibbs, among others, usually went out of their way to relate to their point of view.

On one memorable occasion, Gibbs happened to simultaneously board a housing elevator as several players stumbled in after a night on the town. Suddenly, Hayes was at the door, demanding to know why the youngsters were in violation of curfew. Before any of the Buckeyes could utter a word, Gibbs patiently explained to the Coach, "We were in the parking lot, working on that new play you wanted put in." Hayes took the explanation at face value and left, though the group of players was an unequal blend of offensive and defensive sorts.

In another instance, Greg Storer and Garth Cox had each been booted out of a practice, unfairly they thought, and Myles stopped by their raucous bachelor pad to see how they were coping. Myles summoned the two players to meet him outside the dwelling, explaining, "If I come into your house, I might see something I'd have to tell Coach Hayes about." In this instance, Myles stood behind his player's line of reasoning about why they were banished from practice, eventually getting them off the hook and proving to Hayes they did no wrong.

Even George Hill, whose intense hands-on manner and tremendous desire to please Woody did not always sit well with the players, was occasionally prone to ease up on the youngsters. Late one night, Hill happened to walk past a group of players exiting their dormitory, just prior to the start of curfew. Hill inquired where the players were headed, and they replied, "Nowhere, coach, just back to our rooms." "In that case," Hill casually answered as he continued walking, "You might want to turn around and walk the other way, since the dorm is in that direction."

In the midst of this survey brouhaha, Gerald practiced for the first time since his injury. Rod answered questions about his adjustment to wide receiver thusly: "I look at it as a way to improve myself," for his natural abilities to run and feint were highlighted at his new position, and he had displayed a fantastic ability to hang on to a pass delivery. If Gerald had any chance of landing with a pro team, his chance would come at receiver, yet his developing talents were also handy in benefitting Ohio State this year. Rod had caught eight passes for 193 yards, ran his patterns increasingly more precise, and as always made tacklers miss him in the open field.

"Any position, no matter what it is, is only what you put into it," he felt, and he had indeed worked exceedingly hard to become a standout blocker. This facet of the game was something he rarely was called upon to perform as a quarterback, though Rod proved a powerful, nifty blocker at wide out. Hayes reiterated that Gerald was the finest blocker at split end in OSU history, and Rod took great pride in this judgment, no matter how painful it was for him to not play his usual quarterbacking role.

The increasingly ill Barwig was now diagnosed with quinsy, a deep-seated infection of the tonsils and throat. Ron had been hospitalized for twelve days, was growing progressively weaker, and had dropped an astounding 17 pounds during his confinement. One strange ailment after another had plagued the tall tight end, and this bizarre setback was the latest and worst in his season of pitfalls.

On the brighter side, Hayes commented that the play of the defensive unit was getting markedly better. A major factor in this improvement was the continuing strong play of Skillings, especially since his move to safety. Vince loved the fact that this switch provided him with a little more time to watch the play unfold from scrimmage, so his reading and diagnostic skills had improved remarkably. The 6'0", 172 pound speedster was becoming adept at predicting offensive tendencies; as a result, an air of respectability and confidence now permeated the much-maligned pass coverage of Ohio State.

Defensive backfield coach Gary Tranquill claimed that Vince possessed all the tools necessary to be a star, particularly since Skillings continually wished to challenge himself by facing the stiffest level of competition possible. With the proliferation of great passers within the conference, including Herrmann, Ed Smith of MSU (though the Spartans were not on the '78 schedule), Kevin Strasser, and Rick Leach, each among the elite throwers in the country, Vince would have his chance.

Hayes waxed euphoric as he enthusiastically talked about Skillings. "He is just a great, great kid. I haven't dealt with a better kid. He makes me laugh. He inspires me." Coming from such a master motivator, this was rare praise indeed.

Not so rare this season was yet another tempest set to boil over. Addressing a pen and microphone media luncheon in mid-week, Wisconsin team physician Dr. William G. Clancy referred specifically to a block in the '77 Badger/Buckeye game as both "...immoral and unethical." The said block disabled Wisconsin middle guard Dan Relich, and Clancy attributed the injury to a nefarious offensive line technique known as the chop block. The chop block was a method of blocking whereby one offensive lineman stood up a defender and another blocker came in and chopped the defender down at the knees.

Relich wrecked his knee when the center, Vogler, and a guard, Fritz, executed such a block, according to Clancy. Ohio State assistant sports information director Steve Snapp also attended this luncheon, and he responded quickly and concisely. "The only comment I can make on the matter is that it's my understanding we are not using that particular block this year. We did use it last year, which was well within the rules." In fact, the block was still considered a legal, if potentially dangerous, maneuver by the NCAA.

After this luncheon session, Clancy backed off a little from his initial vehemence. The doctor emphasized that he did not feel Ohio State utilized the block to intentionally injure opponents. "I was just bringing up a sore point and I'm sure they've done something to rectify it," Clancy said.

Later in this week, OSU guard and center coach Alex Gibbs confirmed that such a block was well within the rules, although OSU neither taught nor utilized the chop block. The National Coaches Football Association had asked head coaches to refrain from the use of this effective yet hazardous method, though the Association did not go so far as to make the block illegal.

Gibbs felt that the furor erupted because the story of Relich, and his claims of intentional injury, were contained in a widely-read and highly publicized *Sports Illustrated* magazine story on brutality in football. Eventually, the two camps came to a mutual understanding, if not agreement, and OSU and Wisconsin resumed more normal preparations for their upcoming clash.

With all the extraneous and peripheral happenings of the week, this upcoming game was practically lost in the shuffle. Former Hayes protege Dave McClain and his Badgers were on a downhill plunge, and hoped to right themselves against the suddenly ascending Buckeyes. Wisconsin streaked to a 4-0 start in '78, then endured a tie against the hapless Illini, were destroyed 42-0 by Michigan, and humiliated 55-2 by MSU, which used the many bombs of Smith to flanker Kirk Gibson to vault into first place in the conference.

Compounding the defensive woes of the Badgers was the dreadful inexperience of the secondary, due to all four original starters now being sidelined with injuries. As a demonstration of the consequent lack of depth in the Badger program, no less than four walk-ons now drew starting berths (some in the dilapidated defensive backfield), which was unheard of at the major college level, particularly with the increasing emphasis on recruiting. Mike Kalasmiki had taken over at quarterback and had shifted the Badger offensive focus from the run to the suddenly-prevalent pass attack so common in the once-grounded league.

Though he did not start for Ohio State, 27-year-old senior walk-on V.K. Kellum had seen his very first collegiate action, at middle guard, versus Northwestern. The 5'8", 220 pounder was too short and too slow to play much, if at all, in a program such as OSU, yet his positive attitude and tenacity brought him back year after year and practice after practice. A former All-City prep fullback at Columbus West, as a youth Kellum was counseled and extensively influenced by a local Big Brothers Organization. Currently, the grown-up Kellum reciprocated by conducting summer camps and other helpful activities for the charitable entity.

The empowering attitude of Kellum is contained in the thought, "What the mind can conceive and believe, it will achieve." Players such as Kellum embodied the true meaning of sports as character builders, and Hayes was proud to see V.K. finally play in front of the home fans. As Hayes believed, "...the football will only take you so far. Sometime later on, you have to quit and go on to something else." Kellum had a head start on this goal, and could now end his unheralded career with some fond game memories.

Almost inconceivable was one final spate of controversy. On Friday, former OSU defensive back coach and then-Arkansas head coach Lou Holtz was the focus of a widespread national rumor. According to the gossip mill, Holtz would shortly be named the new Ohio State head coach. Understandably,

Holtz was most objectionable and upset that his name would be linked to such news, for there was no such vacancy, the season was still in progress, and Lou thought the world of his former boss.

Finally, late Friday afternoon, a courageous local television commentator worked up sufficient temerity to ask Woody personally about his possible retirement, and also inquired if Woody wasn't getting tired of constantly dealing with such possibilities. Hayes reacted very positively. Woody smiled widely, and replied in his most emphatic, affirmative voice, "...yes, I'm damn tired of it."

More privately, Woody confided that he could not imagine life without football, although he realized one day he would deal with that unfamiliar fate. "You see, this has been my whole life. I mean, all of it. I love it. I love the challenge. I love the fact that I'm busy. I love the fact that I'm never bored with it." Too soon, Woody would have to cope with life away from the gridiron, and it is to his everlasting credit that he managed such an unaccustomed life remarkably well.

CHAPTER NINE: WISCONSIN

Fortunately, game day finally arrived in what seemed to be a never-ending week. For the second straight Saturday, Ohio State clobbered an opponent in a game actually much closer, for a time at least, than the final score might indicate. The Buckeye offense was surprisingly outgained 327 to 316 in total net yards, plus Wisconsin made 22 first downs to 19 for the Buckeyes.

In front of a sold-out Camp Randall stadium, the defense and special teams of Ohio State took advantage of Badger turnovers and made the big plays which somehow propelled OSU into the victory circle. The Buckeyes managed just two sustained drives on the day, a lack which Hayes attributed to the excellent defensive scheme concocted by McClain, and the superior on-field execution of an overmatched Badger team.

On the first OSU possession, Schlichter broke off a 46 yard run and eventually capped the drive with a seven yard keeper into the end zone. Excepting a third quarter drive, this march was the only consistent offensive effort for the Buckeyes.

Fortunately, the special teams kicked their game up a notch. Barely two minutes into the second quarter, Laughlin crashed through and smothered a Badger punt attempt. Todd Bell chased the bounding ball into the end zone, where frosh Otha Watson pounced on the pigskin for his first collegiate touchdown.

Undeterred, the Badgers soon after picked off a wobbly Schlichter pass and converted the turnover into a touchdown, with a short Kalasmiki to David Charles pass. Then, on the ensuing kickoff, with only about one minute remaining before halftime, Tyrone Hicks reversed this momentum by bursting 96 yards through stunned Badger coverage for a touchdown. The long return pushed the halftime score to 21-7, in favor of OSU, and the Badger victory hopes had suffered a fateful blow.

As if this return was not deflating enough, the slim upset hopes of the home team were completely dashed on the opening possession of the second half. Skillings intercepted a Kalasmiki pass, and returned the theft 61 yards for a demoralizing score. This was the sixth steal for Skillings on the year; he later added to the impressive total with another pick late in the game. Cousineau and Washington also each later picked off Badger passes, and both Al and Tom made 15 tackles.

Kalasmiki was injured shortly thereafter, and his replacement desperately tried to effect a comeback by forcing ill-advised passes into an awaiting Buckeye defense. The Buckeyes yielded yardage, yet the points came infrequently and with great difficulty for Wisconsin, as OSU kept snagging interceptions. Cato was all over the field, harassing the passer, wreaking havoc throughout by tying up extra blockers, and finished with eight tackles.

After the touchdown return by Skillings, Murray ended a long drive with a touchdown. Holding a 35-7 lead, and fearful of injuries with the Michigan showdown approaching, Hayes then pulled the starting units.

Wisconsin blew a multitude of opportunities to get back into this game. An intercept of a Schlichter pass, and a fumble recovery deep in OSU territory, each yielded only disappointment, for Steve Veith missed field goals on each respective drive.

An especially costly mistake, paradoxically committed by Ohio State yet harmful to the Badgers, came early in the fourth quarter. A 96 yard Wisconsin touchdown on an interception return of a Castignola pass was whistled dead and disallowed, since OSU went into illegal motion prior to the snap. The Buckeyes retained possession, and on the very next play, Castignola dashed in from 15 yards out, making the penalty a 14 point swing in favor of the visiting team.

Castignola later added a six yard touchdown run, providing the final points of the day for Ohio State. Wisconsin provided the final points of the afternoon when tailback Charles Green, who finished with 101 yards on the day, plunged across the goal line for his final yard. The final was 49-14.

Castignola received his most extensive playing time of the season and capitalized on the opportunity. The entire second team offensive line looked especially impressive, even considering the lack of quality reserves on the opposing side, and the resultant weakening of the Badger defense as the game progressed. Campbell, Murray, Volley, and Schlichter preceded Castignola in a very balanced Buckeye rushing attack. Gerald led OSU with two receptions in a successful test of his bum elbow. All told, Ohio State had more than enough weapons to handily defeat the Badgers for the 19th straight time.

Considering the myriad of distractions in the week leading up to this game, OSU was understandably proud of their overall effort. Vogler, Robinson, and Fritz continued their fine line play, and Laughlin evoked memories of former OSU special team standout and ferocious hitter Doug Plank. Glenn Mason explained the controlled insanity displayed by Laughlin: "He gives so much effort and intensity that he consistently comes up with the big plays." As Walt Michaels, a former Cleveland Brown linebacker, stated: "A man who has no fear belongs in a mental ward - or on special teams."

The 6'2", 214 pound linebacker Laughlin was converted from fullback, and the Lyndhurst, Ohio, native also channeled his runaway energies and intensity into baseball, playing outfield on the OSU team. If the task was running through an outfield wall to catch a fly ball, Laughlin was the man. Jim still considered the diamond his true love, although football was crowding his plate, too.

Fortunately for Ohio State, Skillings was honing in so successfully on errant passes, for Mills was again hobbled and Ellis suffered a severe shoulder separation in the Badger game and was expected to miss the remainder of the year. The OSU players tended to come back a bit earlier than expected from an injury, not because they were necessarily rushed in their recuperation, but because Hayes continually pounded into them his belief that the strength of the human will must never be underestimated.

Strangely enough, Hayes picked up much of his beliefs on this subject from his voluminous readings on Joseph Stalin. "We all should make a more thorough study of history... we'd be a lot better equipped to handle today and tomorrow," thought Hayes, and the Coach never lost an opportunity to translate what he had learned towards football.

Woody also recalled the writing of another Russian, Alexander Solzhenitysyn, who commented on history: "Dwell on the past and you'll lose an eye. Forget the past and you'll lose both eyes." Hayes studied bygone times with a fervor, mostly to ascertain how he might improve the future. Man was not limited by his past; the decision to be great transcended what had previously transpired. The power of the human mind was so vast as to be unlimited, and, "The height of human desire is what wins," espoused Hayes.

According to Billy Hill, the players of this '75-'78 period tended, as a whole, to be a little more hard-nosed and resilient than their successors. Ohio State was renowned for having tough, mean, nasty suckers on their side of scrimmage, a direct reflection of their Head Coach and his philosophy: Punish your opponent to make him respect you. With the infliction of this punishment came much pain, which Buckeyes were known to disdain. Much of their resistance to pain emanated from the beliefs of Woody, who often refused to acknowledge a minor hurt or ache in a player. As the team joke went, "If Woody can't feel it, it must not hurt."

Hayes did not advocate anyone playing with a severe injury, although his definition of severe usually meant being unable to walk, or a bone sticking out of the skin or some other such catastrophic fate. To avoid his wrath, players often ignored or played through injuries which in later years may have excused them from practice. Even Archie Griffin, who was typically so beaten up that he could barely walk for several days after a game, steadfastly put on a gold jersey (signifying no contact) and hobbled through the weeks' workouts.

Still, Woody did not take lightly his responsibility to engender good health in his boys - he acquiesced often to the training and medical staff, and their professional opinion was gospel, at least on Saturday. Occasional differences of opinion did arise, mostly because Hayes felt that pain was something which could be overcome, and injuries did not fit into his Spartan battle ethic, except in extreme cases.

One individual who espoused many of these same beliefs was the head coach at Illinois, which was the next opponent for the peaking Buckeyes. Gary

Moeller, former OSU defensive force at linebacker, needed all the strength he could muster from any source, since his Illini squad was buried in the throes of a 1-6-2 campaign. Illinois was amazingly young, starting four freshmen and ten sophomores; this inexperience was being summarily preyed on. It was widely assumed that OSU would win, and win big, against yet another team constructed in the Hayes image.

When asked how it felt to go up against a former player or former assistant, Woody was typically blunt and straightforward. "Look, they're no friends of mine now... I don't like them at all on Saturday." Then he softened his stance a bit, and let his paternalistic side peek through this initially harsh opinion. "Really, I'm extremely proud of all these men...[who spawned from his teachings]," he proclaimed.

Once into this lighter vein, Hayes became extremely charitable. Woody respected and praised those among his brethren who had proven worthy of respect, and his own teachings emanated from a wide variety of influences, including early mentors John Brickels (Miami University), Jock Sutherland (Pittsburgh), Tommy Rodgers (Woody's college coach at Denison), Timmy Temerario (Denison), Frank Leahy (Notre Dame), Wes Fesler (OSU), Earl Blaik (Miami of Ohio star athlete, dashing World War One cavalry officer, and West Point head coach), Bobby Dodd (Georgia Tech), and Murray Warmath (Minnesota), to name just a few.

Leahy was an amazing coach, who, perhaps more than the other coaches listed above, displayed many of the same traits as Hayes. Leahy described practice sessions thusly: "I raised the threshold of pain that some young men had, and I taught them to work harder."

A former Fighting Irish star, Johnny Lujack, once offered this description of his former coach: "Leahy was a truly great coach, a great source of inspiration. He could bring a team up with his talks before the game and at the half. He was a great fundamentalist, very deliberate in all of his maneuvers. He insisted upon perfection; therefore, the number of plays we had was few. He was a very hard worker... He had great sincerity on and off the field...... he has never said anything... that he didn't honestly believe in his own heart."

Sadly, Leahy literally worked himself into a state of such weakened health, that he was forced out of coaching at the age of 45. Hayes at least lasted much longer, though he was similarly obsessed.

Interestingly, Hayes had coached at New Philadelphia (Ohio) High with Brickels, and John introduced Woody to the woman who would, six years after that initial meeting, become Mrs. Anne Hayes. Woody was therefore especially helpful to and fond of the many coaches he in turn had directly influenced. As an example of this affection, Woody stated, "I told a team to fumble once on purpose because I didn't want to see the poor guy I was coaching against get fired."

Anne Hayes was a remarkable woman, and much of the success of Woody must be attributed to her patient, unassuming personality. Woody often claimed she was as stubborn as he was; it took that sort of fortitude to put up with and genuinely love a man such as Woody. On one occasion, sportscaster Jimmy Crum asked Anne if, through the long decades that Hayes virtually lived and breathed football, she had ever given thought to divorcing the Coach. Laughingly, in as apt a demonstration of her charming humor as ever offered, Anne replied, "Divorce, no. Murder, yes."

Anne stayed in the background, never making a scene, yet always providing stability and support for not only her husband, but all the coaches and their families, and especially the players, whom she always referred to as her "kids."

One telling instance of the Anne style occurred during a particular fall camp. Offensive lineman Ernie Andria, who was among the few married players, felt the need to see his wife one night after lights out, and snuck out of the dormitory. As Ernie made his way into the dormitory parking lot, a car pulled up. Afraid of being caught in a violation of curfew, Andria dove into a surrounding clump of bushes. He noticed the customary Anne Hayes trademark, the glow of a burning cigarette, coming from the driver's side of the intruding automobile just as Anne barked out, "Ernie, get out of those bushes and get over here before you get caught."

Chastened, yet relieved it was only Mrs. Hayes, Ernie trudged over to her car. Especially during fall training camp, Woody often did not see his Cardiff Road home for days, so Anne would send over fresh underwear and clean socks for him to wear. She handed a paper bag of such items to Andria, with instructions to deliver them to the Coach. Obligingly, Andria marched to the office of Hayes, dropped off the fresh laundry, and left. Woody never said a word to Ernie about the incident.

The devotion and style of Anne was extremely similar to that of Beatrice Patton and Clementine Churchill, the better halves of General George and prime minister Winston, two heroes of Hayes', respectively. As mirrored by their unions with equally controversial and charismatic leaders, Anne put up nobly with the frailties of her husband. She prodded, nurtured, supported, and shared the search for greatness Woody spent his lifetime living.

Like those two other remarkable women, Anne was, "...extraordinary in her ability to charm strangers; she devoted herself fiercely to [her husband's] career." Interestingly, ex-President Richard Nixon, a close friend of the Hayes family, enjoyed a remarkably similar union with his faithful wife, Pat.

Churchill once remarked of his wife, "For what could be more glorious than to be united with a being incapable of an ignoble thought?" Woody also realized he was similarly blessed by Anne.

CHAPTER TEN: ILLINOIS

Nonetheless, no such affection was evident between the two football teams on Saturday, as the annual contest for the Illibuck (a wooden, carved Indian totem in the shape of a duck) was captured handily for the 11th straight time by Ohio State. The game was another schizophrenic affair for OSU, with the first half a sluggish, hard-fought, veritable standoff, while the second half became an avalanche of Buckeye touchdowns.

Ohio State struck first, as Schlichter crossed the goal line from seven yards out. Primarily because Schlichter was still sore from his season-old injured throwing arm, and partly to get Gerald somewhat re-acquainted with the position, for the Michigan battle was approaching, Hayes let Rod take over at quarterback on the next Buckeye possession.

Unfortunately, Gerald showed his understandable rustiness with the ball-handling chores of the role, and fumbled at the OSU 25. The revived OSU defense rose to the occasion, stuffing the Illini for losses totaling nine yards. The rebuffed Illini were pushed out of even field goal range, and had to punt.

Schlichter re-entered the contest, only to be intercepted after a lengthy drive. The Illini took advantage of this turnover, driving 52 yards to paydirt. This drive was capped by a two yard rush by tailback Larry Powell, and was aided tremendously by a 15 yard facemask penalty against the Buckeyes. With the touchdown, the score was knotted, and momentum had shifted toward the black and orange.

Ohio State responded admirably, with perhaps the most efficient and exciting drive of the season. Assuming possession with only 2:06 remaining in the half, Schlichter led OSU to the end zone in a masterful display of time management and passing splendor. Art accurately delivered four straight completions for 58 yards, with the key play being an unbelievable, diving grab by Gerald, good for a 20 yard pick-up. With 23 seconds left, Schlichter tucked the ball under his own arm and ran in from the seven. Art audibled brilliantly several times during this drive, ably demonstrating his expanding leadership and play-calling mastery.

That touchdown drive seemed to drive a death stake into the heart of a now-demoralized Illinois team, while vaulting OSU into a higher level of aggressive performance. The Bucks took advantage of several Illinois turnovers after halftime, the first of which was an interception by Bob Murphy. Atha booted a field goal shortly after this snag, increasing the Buckeye lead to 17-7. Minutes later, Campbell powered in from the one, for his eighth score of the year.

Ohio State really poured on the scoring in the final period, beginning with a Guess punt return of 62 yards, which set up a five yard Schlichter score. Gerald came back in under center to orchestrate two short touchdown drives.

The first drive culminated with a seven yard keeper by Rod, while Ricky Johnson rumbled eight yards for the final tally. Gerald even completed his only pass, as everything clicked correctly for Ohio State on this day, at least late in the game

The OSU defense clamped down on the Illini, allowing a mere 197 total yards, even with the absence of Mills and Ellis. Cato and Luther Henson recovered fumbles, sophomore inside linebacker Leon Ellison picked off a pass, and Cousineau also grabbed a fumble, as the ball-hawking instincts of the unit were at full force. Washington and Sullivan played their usual fine games, in the midst of an exceptionally balanced effort.

Offensively, Campbell, Murray, and Schlichter paved the way on the ground, while Gerald, Springs, and Moore hauled in two passes apiece. Even the forgotten Payton participated in this Buckeye blowout, and seldom-used senior defensive tackle Joe Hornik snagged "Buck of the Week" honors for his efforts.

That Saturday also restored good fortune to OSU bowl hopes, too. Wisconsin miraculously overtook Purdue in the final 25 seconds of their contest, putting OSU back into contention for a league title. The OSU level of play was improving each week, so the Rose Bowl, among other coveted bowls, was now back in the Buckeye picture.

Incidentally, on this Monday Penn State assumed the mantle of the number one team in the nation for the very first time in the illustrious history of the Nittany Lion program. Paterno had his squad at 10-0, and at this point, PSU was clearly the finest team in the land. This status of Penn State enabled OSU to better cope with their bitter opening loss, and the newly-hyped Buckeyes sported a sure sign that a conference title was within reach: Hayes invoked a ban on all player interviews, in preparation for the clash with Indiana. With the prize back within reach, no distractions would impede on progress.

Gratefully, the Monday press luncheon brought no scene as gripping as the Reid incident of the previous week. However, Hayes did use this open forum as an opportunity to again pontificate on the merits of instant replay.

Hayes was growing steadily more strident in his belief that some sort of review system be implemented. As Ara Parseghian believed, "There must be a way to penalize officials, too." According to Woody, "There's probably no one sicker than that official when he makes a wrong call. But that's not enough." The immense strain to the already-stressing Coach might also be lessened, if an evident, wrong call could be reversed. To limit the interruptions and ease the flow of the game, Woody continued to advocate that the opportunity for replay be limited, and come with graduated penalties if those requests were disproved.

Hayes tended to only argue a call on which he was absolutely, irrevocably certain he had a legitimate beef, so this system could only have helped a coach like him. Alas, a majority of head coaches did not share his enthusiasm for the project.

At least Hayes was able to convince the athletic council to reverse the earlier opinion concerning bowl bids. For the first time ever, an OSU football team would now be permitted to participate in any NCAA-sanctioned bowl which extended an invitation.

This reversal did not come easily for the council. It took more than an hour of in-house haggling, and some strong-arm tactics by an argumentative Hindman, for the reversal of the earlier stance. This revised decision took into account the academic welfare of the student-athlete, the complications involved in scheduling around the holidays, as well as the fact that, based on the latest projections, any and all bowls were now considered profitable ventures.

Hindman was very pleased for both his Coach, and the players. "I think they have worked hard and done a fantastic job in getting to where they are now after the way the season started, and think they should be rewarded for their efforts." Of course, Hindman vehemently backed the team, for he not only played under Hayes at Miami, he coached under him for seven years at OSU.

Archrival Michigan also received a boost when Purdue lost against Wisconsin. The Boilermakers were the next opponent for the Wolverines, and Bo's bunch was definitely not looking past this confrontation toward the OSU tilt in two weeks, at least if the eating and napping habits of Bo were any indication. On the Wednesday before the Purdue game, Bo skipped lunch entirely, then took only a two minute nap, instead of his customary five minute rest. Michigan desperately wanted a return trip to the Roses, to avenge their back-to-back losses of the last two years.

To caution his own squad against overlooking the Hoosiers, Hayes pointed out that IU had played very tough against OSU in recent years, even though the final scores were not particularly indicative of this toughness. The Hoosiers, though just 4-5, had a fine offensive team in '78, boasting some fine talent in the backfield.

Quarterback Scott Arnett was still on the mend, though not from his operation in '77, which corrected an abnormal fusing (spondylitis) of bones along his spinal column. Scott had finally recovered from that rare condition; this year, he was bothered by a sore ankle and a slight shoulder separation.

Carrying the bulk of the offense in coach Lee Corso's tailback-oriented offensive scheme was the diminutive Mike Harkrader, also of Ohio. Recall that Harkrader's father was a tailback under Woody at OSU, and Mike had inherited much of his father's talent, and then some. Mike was virtually back to his 1,000 yard form of his frosh year, after sitting out all of '77 with a severe knee injury.

Leading the Hoosiers on defense was linebacker Joe Norman, whom OSU assistant Mickey Jackson compared to Cousineau in terms of impact, importance, intensity, and the ability to create the crucial turnover. Over half of the Hoosier squad was from Ohio, so a victory over their home state program would be especially sweet.

Corso summed up his refreshing approach to this big game by only partly joking, "...If we can't run it, we'll throw it, and if we can't throw it we'll run it. And if we can't do either, we'll punt." Interest in this game was so high that OSU fans snatched up almost 11,000 available tickets for the short trip to Bloomington. Indiana had not beaten OSU in 27 years, since the inaugural Buckeye season of Woody, yet many Hoosier backers thought that the team was primed for the feat this year.

CHAPTER ELEVEN: INDIANA

As advertised, the game was a toss-up. The outcome was not settled until the very last minutes, as IU pulled out all the stops on this cold November afternoon. In the first half alone, Hoosier split end Mike Friede quick-kicked the ball on third down three times. On each occasion, the surprised OSU defense could only watch helplessly as the ball sailed over their unsuspecting heads, to be downed deep in Buckeye territory. Indiana also employed a wide variety of reverses, multiple motion plays, and many unusual, rarely used offensive and defensive formations, in a total attempt to win.

A nearly-full Memorial Stadium crowd watched as OSU quickly scored on their first possession. The Hoosiers assumed control of the ball, yet were soon forced to punt. Ohio State received the ensuing kick, only to face a fourth and one situation from their 32. Boldly, Hayes elected to try for the first down. The IU line surged strongly and powerfully, and Norman busted through to stop the play cold, for no gain.

In the aftermath of the close game, Hayes readily accepted the blame for this outrageously atypical display of foolhardiness. "Nobody made a bigger mistake than I did," he contritely said. His noble intentions were for Ohio State to break the Hoosier spirit and remove the loud crowd as a factor by converting such a risky play. As it turned out, momentum shifted totally toward the home team, when Harkrader dashed in for a score just a few plays after the Hoosiers took over.

Ohio State mustered little offense in the remainder of the half, after this aborted attempt. In fact, Indiana took a three point lead into the locker room when David Freud booted a 30 yard field goal right before the break. Freud had earlier missed a field goal attempt, which in the end proved a deciding factor in the narrow Hoosier defeat. At the halfway point, though, an upset seemed highly likely.

As was their wont for most of this year, OSU emerged from the break extremely fired up, and the offense back in synchronization. Some of this emotion was a result of Woody's hat being boldly swiped from his head, by a typically crazed Hoosier partisan, as the teams headed for their respective halftime locker rooms.

Despite the absences of Springs and Moore, each of whom exited prematurely because of an injury, and with Murray sitting down with a recurrence of his foot trouble, the Buckeyes embarked on a long touchdown march, after forcing IU to punt.

Ohio State took over on their own two yard line, and the twenty-play odyssey carried them the length of the field. This 98 yard drive exhausted the Hoosier defense and exhilarated the reeling Buckeye backfield, and was capped with a Schlichter run of three yards. Starting with this drive, Johnson, Volley, and Payton were forces to contend with the remainder of the game.

The Hoosiers were victimized again early in the final quarter, as Johnson powered his way into the end zone from 46 yards out. As usual, Gerald delivered the deadly block which sprung Ricky into the clear. Johnson ended his brilliant day with 110 yards on 18 punishing carries, many of them behind the path-clearing blocks of the exuberant Volley, of whom Hayes later said, "He's an unusual kid... a winner." It turned out that this long scamper by Johnson was the winning margin, though IU still had some fireworks remaining.

The Hoosiers rebounded by marching 72 yards in 14 plays, trimming the margin to 21-18. Perhaps the biggest play in this drive was a 29 yard pass interference call in the end zone against Ohio State, giving the ball and a first down to IU on the one. Tailback Derrick Burnett charged in for the score from there, and quarterback Tim Clifford, who had stepped in when Arnett went down to an injury, delivered a two point strike to Friede. On their ensuing drive, OSU was stopped in their tracks, and IU took over in a last-ditch effort to upset the visitors.

Indiana gained two first downs, and with only 1:37 left, Corso sent in what he hoped to be the coup de grace in his day-long bag of tricks. From the scrimmage line at the IU 42, Clifford handed the ball to Friede on an apparent reverse. Friede abruptly halted and tossed a pass deep downfield to the OSU 27, where the floating ball was caught.

Unfortunately for Indiana, Guess was the man who hauled in the pass. With the turnover, the home team's chance at victory was vanquished. Corso went to the well one too many times, although this was a valiant, gutsy effort at an improbable upset.

The heroes in the winning effort were many, led by the awesome stable of runners in the very deep OSU backfield. Johnson led the squad in both receiving and rushing in a brilliant performance, as Schlichter, Springs, and Volley contributed mightily, too. Dansler enjoyed perhaps his finest afternoon in an Ohio State uniform, and Norman and Cousineau each prospered in their anticipated matchup.

With the hard-fought victory, OSU seemed assured of some sort of bowl bid. Big 10 commissioner Duke, along with the Michigan and Ohio State athletic councils, had decried, prior to this afternoon, that if each school won on Saturday, the winner of their head-to-head confrontation the following week would attend the Pasadena festivities. The loser of the heated battle would then attend the Gator Bowl, conducted in the evening in Jacksonville, Florida, on the 29th of December. As Michigan did defeat Purdue on this day to fulfill their end of the bargain, the following week's war was indeed for the roses.

Hayes took this announcement in fine spirits, saying the commissioner, "...acted intelligently, wisely, and fairly," in determining these bowl attendance agreements. Schembechler was likewise pleased to discover that a win would clinch a third consecutive journey to the Rose Bowl.

In a post-Purdue game interview, though, Bo flashed first annoyance, then downright anger when reporters questioned him about letting Schlichter escape his clutches and attend Ohio State. "If you came here to talk about OSU, then you're in the wrong damn press room," Bo yelled.

It was well-known that Schlichter had narrowed his final collegiate choices down to OSU and UM, and Art had even attended the '77 game between the two schools as a guest of Schembechler's. Perhaps Bo was pained by the year-old memory of Art standing on the Michigan sideline, all the while cheering, occasionally loudly, for Ohio State!

The week before this year's edition of the "Game of the Year" brought renewed resolve to the OSU co-captains. Each co-captain, excepting Springs, who transferred in as a sophomore, was gunning for a fourth straight conference title. Ron was overjoyed at the chance to finally attend a Rose Bowl, assuming the Buckeyes won. "The Rose Bowl is the game I've always dreamed of playing in," Springs informed; plus, a trip to California would salvage a difficult year in what he had anticipated to be a Heisman-caliber year.

Vogler, who was also disappointed by the fortunes of '78 and his hand injury, desperately wanted to start in a Rose Bowl. Tim was, obviously, down to his final chance. Cato and Cousineau expressed the fervent desire to exit as a winner, and these sentiments were shared by every member of the program.

Again, it is worth noting that each of these captains, except Cousineau, had missed significant chunks of playing time because of injuries. Even Cousineau battled through a painful hip pointer, though he did not miss any action. Each captain experienced moments where he played up to advance billing, though only Cousineau was able to exceed lofty pre-season expectations.

Ironically, if the captains had avoided the '78 injury plague and performed at their possible (when healthy) heights, the team itself would almost certainly have fared better, and Cousineau possibly would not have attained his outrageous statistics. Even Tom acknowledged that all personal glory would gladly be exchanged for victories.

As it happened, Cousineau was a unanimous selection to every All-American team, and became the very first player selected in the NFL draft, yet was somewhat unknown nationally. Perhaps, with a slightly more successful team, he would have amassed even greater fame.... Regardless, there was no more deserving footballer in the land, based on '78 performance.

Also named to virtually every first team All-American list was UM quarterback Rick Leach. Leach was that rare combination of wonderful passer, exciting runner, dependable leader, and big-play mastermind. He continued the standard (ostensibly begun by an equally amazing all-around star, Rex Kern of OSU, as determined through both individual attainments and team successes), by which all conference quarterbacks are still measured. Thus, any statistical category Rick may have been somewhat lacking in, was more than balanced in the overall ledger by the number of wins he'd engineered.

As of this time in '78, he was responsible for more touchdowns (combined running and passing) than any other quarterback in the history of collegiate signalcalling (recall that he was one of the first field generals to start all four years, and that this era was generally before the practices of prolific run-and-shoot offenses and statistical padding, simply to secure individual awards, were in vogue). To Leach, winning was the only thing that mattered, especially when OSU was involved.

The key to winning this particular game seemed to rest on whether UM elected to abide by the traditional method of this contest. Would UM play ultra-conservatively, or would Bo allow Leach and the big play Wolverine offense to go for the jugular via a daring, bold game plan? Neither team's defense had been particularly, consistently dominating throughout the year, though each unit had flashed such potential. Each defense had demonstrated remarkable improvement, though each unit also displayed a disturbing tendency to self-destruct at times.

The running attacks for each school were high-powered, plentifully deep, and impossibly fast. The bottom-line indicator seemed to reside at the quarterback spot.

Hayes and his staff commented, to a man, that the freshman performance of Schlichter was remarkable. His 19 interceptions in 149 attempts notwithstanding, the talented frosh had demonstrated a gamebreaking tendency and leadership patterns far beyond his tender years. As the senior, Leach had thrown only four interceptions on the year, with three of those coming in one game, his experience and extensive history of intelligent field decisions seemed to irrefutably give the nod to Michigan.

On Tuesday, Hayes was in a spirited mood and was granting no quarter to this opinion. "The kids are kids," he stated. "They'll do what you make them do," and of course Woody felt he could impart his will to win into the performance of Schlichter. Since '67, with the lone exception being in the down OSU season of '71, this game had been played for bragging rights to the conference title, plus a granddaddy bowl visit. If OSU won, they would attend the 11th Rose Bowl in school history, more than any other Big 10 team. This game was the biggest of the big, and everyone involved knew it.

In contrast to Hayes, Schembechler was decidedly low-key and comical this week. At his Monday press conference, Bo was asked to name his favorite general. Without hesitating, Bo responded, "General Hayes, of course." Outrageous laughter ensued. Bo related how one UM player, defensive tackle Dale Keitz of Upper Arlington, Ohio, once had a part-time job working as a garbage collector. His trash route included the Hayes household at 1711 Cardiff, just down the road from Ohio Stadium. Bo joked about the potential covert operations of that interesting coincidence.

Despite the jocularity, Schembechler grew ominously serious when asked if this game was the ultimate in competition. "I don't know what it would be like if it were any other way," said Bo very somberly. (Interestingly enough, until '33, the OSU-UM game was contested in either the second or third week of the season. Then-Ohio State athletic director L.W. St. John was among the first to realize the awesome ramifications of the rivalry, and arranged for the game to always be the last contest on the schedule).

At the height of this '78 seriousness, former Hayes disciple Bill Mallory was fired from his head coaching job at Colorado. Hayes sadly could spare little time in solace for a man he greatly respected, and had ironically set on the path to termination with the comeback Buckeye victory on New Year's Day '77. As customarily happened during this week, OSU players honed in on the ministrations of Hayes with fervency. There was precious time for any thought that did not reveal how to surpass the Wolverines.

Getting back to his idol Patton, what set Woody apart from other coaches was, as stated about the General: "His ability to transmit to his soldiers [players] a driving will to win," despite any obstacles. Like the aggressive, single-minded tank commander, "Every activity he chose to engage in contributed to his mastery of warfare [football]." In keeping with this spirit, Springs, Campbell, and Moore, despite bothersome injuries, would all play.

The sole big adjustment was the insertion of Ernie Andria into the left tackle spot, left vacant with injuries to Robinson and Brown. Andria was an amazing specimen. A roly-poly, 6'3" mass of apparent chubbiness from Wintersville, Ohio, Ernie continually amazed fellow players and coaches alike with his spectacular blocking abilities. Looking at the wild, fun-loving Italian with a bit of a beer gut, no one seemed to think he was capable of such athletic mayhem.

Andria was deceptively fast, exceedingly mean, and was devastating in his downfield blocking assignments. Like many OSU backups, Andria often demonstrated he was every bit as good as the Buckeye listed above him in the depth chart. Ohio State was ready, and eager to do combat.

Despite this burning ambition, OSU lost their third straight game to the hated Wolverines. Never before had Hayes lost more than two in a row to the school up north, and this rankled the Coach tremendously. It also marked the first time since '45-'48 that Ohio State had dropped at least three in a row to the crew from Ann Arbor.

Both Hayes and the team were positively devastated by this loss; this was the fifth consecutive loss for OSU in front of a national television audience and marked their 12th consecutive quarter against Michigan without a touchdown. There would be no Rose Bowl trip for OSU, no seventh consecutive share of a league title. How important was this win to Bo? "This means as much as any other we've ever had over OSU," he gushed, perhaps exceeded only barely by the shocking '69 toppling of the number one ranked Buckeyes.

CHAPTER TWELVE: MICHIGAN

As expected, Michigan was victoriously led by Leach. Rick passed only in selective situations, played a very effective game, and proved to be the difference as he threw for both touchdowns in a 14-3 triumph. Ohio State burst out of the gate first, marching downfield to take an early 3-0 lead on the strength of an Atha field goal. Unfortunately, that was the only score of the day for OSU on this long, frustrating day.

In front of the largest crowd, up to that day, ever jammed into Ohio Stadium, OSU lost the coin toss and kicked off to start the frenzied finale to the strange season. Michigan clicked off eight plays, as the OSU defense held and forced a punt.

The Buckeyes assumed possession and rattled off an impressive 13 play drive, reaching the Wolverine 23. After Schlichter was flushed out of the pocket, could not find an open receiver, and wisely ran out of bounds for a six yard loss, a 46 yard field goal attempt by Atha was wide left. At this time, despite the miss, OSU felt assured that the offense could move the ball into scoring position, and eventually the points would accumulate.

Once more, Michigan was stopped after a very brief possession, and OSU fielded the punt at midfield. Thanks primarily to a stunning bolt of 21 yards by Volley, OSU had a first down at the UM 12. Unfortunately, the chilly, damp 36 degree weather, in combination with the somewhat slippery, worn playing surface made footing extremely treacherous, especially near each end zone, bothering both teams throughout the day.

In the first two of many such occurrences for both UM and OSU, first Schlichter and then Springs slipped down untouched before they could make it past the line of scrimmage, so Atha came in to convert the 29 yard three-point opportunity. This was the last real excitement for the capacity crowd on the dreary day.

It was on the ensuing drive that Leach proved his mettle. In three straight passes, Leach propelled the Wolverines forward 70 yards to the go-ahead, game-winning touchdown. The final completion in the quick-striking scoring drive went 30 yards to a streaking Rod Feaster, who ended up in the end zone. From this point, the visitors never looked back.

After a few series of defensive stands, OSU got the ball back in very advantageous field position, near midfield. The Bucks mounted a short 11 play, 37 yard drive, reaching the UM 24. Schlichter was sacked, fumbled, Michigan recovered, and this divine opportunity was lost. The Wolverines were off and running, powering down to the OSU 14, setting the stage for the most widely talked about play of this contest. Oddly, the play had no bearing on the final score.

On a third and one play, Leach drilled a bullet pass to tight end Gene Johnson, who was on a crossing pattern right in front of, and running parallel to, the OSU goal line. Johnson gathered in the hard pass and was poised to step into the end zone when a scarlet and gray missile uncoiled. Skillings ran in from nowhere, hit Johnson just as the ball arrived, and crushed the tight end with a vicious, perfectly-timed pop that separated the receiver from the ball. The ball squirted into the end zone, and somehow, in the resulting mad scramble, Skillings came up with the recovery.

With only 43 seconds left in the first half, fearful of a turnover, Hayes elected to run the clock out after this big reversal. As the final seconds of the half ticked away, so did much of the OSU momentum resulting from the stunning turnover, and their excited, emotional level was never reached again.

The second half was a fairly lackluster offensive show, with the sole fireworks being an 11 yard touchdown toss from Leach to tailback Roosevelt Smith. The Buckeyes had been very successful at running the ball in the opening half, yet could never get untracked after the intermission. Burdened additionally by very poor field position much of the final thirty minutes, Hayes attempted to ignite the sputtering Buckeye offense by inserting Gerald at quarterback. Painfully, Rod was unable to ignite the attack.

No matter who took the snap, the Wolverine defense proved impenetrable. The numerous failed ground attempts for OSU were partly due to the absence of Campbell, who ran only once on the day before being forced to the sideline with an injury.

The Buckeyes recorded only one first down in the closing half, and that came very late in the final quarter. A re-inserted Schlichter found Gerald open for a 25 yard gain, yet even this brief flash of success was rendered impotent as Art was intercepted just two plays hence. No further threat was mustered by the feeble OSU attack, and Michigan hung on to the convincing win. Leach was named the MVP of the game, based on his 11 of 21 passing display, good for 166 yards.

Afterwards, Bo called his quarterback, "...the best football player in the country." Schlichter passed only nine times, connecting on four, for 43 yards, while Gerald hit Chuck Hunter for a five yard pickup on his lone attempt.

Neither teams' rushing attack ever really displayed the ability evident prior to the game. Each defense really threw superb, swarming effort into the fray, and neither offense consistently solved the defensive plan. After Springs gained 53 yards on the ground in the first half, he was held to ten in the second half. Similarly, Volley amassed 50 yards before the break, and a mere ten after. Much of the credit for this late muzzling goes to the fantastic game enjoyed by the spectacular Wolverine monster back, Ron Simpkins, who keyed the emotional UM effort.

Perhaps the greatest thrill for OSU partisans on the day was the halftime performance of drum major Dwight Hudson, who dazzled the crowd with his twirling talents, and the "i" dotting antics of sousaphone player Tim Wallick.

Michigan sorely missed their ill starting fullback, Russell Davis, and looked more than a little hampered by the absence of injured starting tailback Harlan Huckleby. Frosh Harold "Butch" Woolfolk, with a 9.4 (100 yard) clocking which made him the fastest player at that time to ever pull on the maize and blue, and Leach enjoyed limited, inconsistent success against a vicious OSU defense. In fairness, Leach was bothered by a slight hamstring pull, possibly suffered due to the slippery playing surface.

Cousineau had another stupendous day with 21 tackles. Washington, Sullivan, Henson, Ross, Dulin, Cato, and Dansler contributed their ultimate efforts, in a generally outstanding defensive effort, considering the amount of time they held a very flammable Wolverine offense in check. Still, UM finished with 21 first downs to 14 by Ohio State, and ran up 364 total yards. Ohio State managed just 216 yards in total offense, almost all accrued before halftime. With this victory, Schembechler edged ahead in head-to-head meetings with Hayes, standing 5-4-1.

In his understandable post-game frustration, Hayes stormed out of the interview session. Writer David Israel, of the *Chicago Tribune*, was the sole object and entire focus of the Hayes wrath. "You're the guy who tried to cut Dan Devine up and almost cost him his job," Hayes bellowed. Israel had been very critical of Notre Dame coach Devine in a numerous number of his columns, and speculation had it that Devine's days at the helm of the Fighting Irish were now numbered, perhaps due in part to the scathing Israel passages. Dealing with this reporter, whom Woody despised for his critical journalistic style, was the final straw in a season as disappointing as any in Hayes' career.

The Buckeyes finished 6-2 in the conference, 7-3-1 overall. The two losses translated into a fourth place finish in the conference, behind co-champs UM and MSU, and Purdue. The Spartans had their first taste of the title since winning back-to-back crowns in '65 and '66, although this '78 share was bittersweet since they were prohibited from attending a bowl game. This, of course, was due to the probationary sentence imposed by the conference and NCAA because of numerous, repeated, flagrant (mostly) recruiting violations.

At the Ohio State team banquet that Monday, Hayes, oddly, seemed slightly more upbeat than his players. Even in periods of distress, Woody was the leader, and he recalled the words of his friend, Vince Lombardi, who said: "The greatest glory is not in never failing but in rising every time we fall." Hayes promised, "We won't fold up and quit," regardless of the disappointing finish to the regular season. Murray delivered the invocation and proclaimed the season "disastrous." Each statement was proven more true than either player or Coach realized, as the ensuing Gator Bowl spookily demonstrated.

Hayes was not one to take defeat or adversity lightly; a loss to Michigan was the worst injustice which could befall him, or so he thought. Woody, as always, prescribed more effort and greater work to dig the team out of the depths of dishonor. In reflection, it is impossible to fault Hayes for caring too much about winning, or resisting defeat with all his might. These twin passions led to his greatest faults and troubles, yet Hayes rarely compromised his beliefs, even in utter defeat.

Woody considered his job, "...as part of American civilization and a damn important one. This country is built on winning and on that alone... it is still the most honorable thing a man can do." Apathy was not in the Hayes vocabulary, and neither was the concept of permanence. If Woody did on occasion carry his passion a bit to extremes, then he dealt with the ensuing frustration and moved on. Only the harsh, long glare of public inspection dwelled on his mistakes or defeats, for Woody had already placed these in his past and was surging relentlessly forward. Action and devotion to ideals, and more work than one could sanely imagine, cured all the Coach's ills.

The honors accorded at the banquet were many. Cato received the "Jack Stephenson Memorial Award" for the most outstanding defensive lineman. Tim Vogler took home the "Harry Strobel Memorial Award" as the best offensive lineman. In an obvious choice, Cousineau was voted the team MVP by his teammates, and called this recognition, "The greatest thing that has happened to me since I've been here."

Later in this week, various organizations placed Fritz, Cousineau, Guess, Robinson, Moore, Ferguson, Orosz, Dansler, Cato, and Skillings on All-Conference teams, at either first or second string status.

In a conference studded with individual stars, this sort of recognition carried a lot of weight, and Cousineau gained further acclaim as a first-team All-American. Chances are great that had the team finished with a finer record, more individuals from the squad would have merited such status.

After the Michigan contest, in which OSU did not ever resort to an all-out passing barrage in an effort to make a fast comeback, even in the waning moments, Hayes shouldered all of the conspicuous blame for the lack of a cogent air plan. He squarely placed all the blame on his shoulders, deflecting the many criticisms aimed at Schlichter, who was assailed for not reading defenses adequately enough, suffering interceptions by passing into coverage too often, running out of the pocket too conveniently, and resorting to desperation heaves instead of resolutely chipping away at defenses. "If there are any questions why he [Schlichter] didn't pass more, ask Woody. Blame it on me."

Hayes went on to explain, "We'll get better at passing, and as we get better, we'll pass as much as we need to win. But not until we get considerably better." Hayes heeded the advice of legendary former UCLA coach Red Sanders, who warned, "He who lives by the pass, dies by the pass." Ohio State predictably died a little this year.

The years of Woody being a run-dominant coach were always predicated on winning via that chosen route, so passing as a priority could not proceed any differently. Winning superseded all other concerns, even as passing was becoming a lot more prevalent within the conference. The success of MSU, Purdue, and even UM rested largely on the unpredictability and diversity of their passing plans and execution. Hayes realized the eventual winning course for his team depended on a more balanced attack, yet Hayes felt his own talents and wisdom better suited the rushing route.

Not incidentally, the OSU coaching staff was comprised of men versed in this same style. Re-orienting their teaching and recruiting focus would unfortunately take time, something Woody never could completely reconcile with his attitude of winning right now. Schlichter himself realized the OSU offense would one day become diversified, though "...it will take time."

With a healthy squad in '78, OSU most certainly could have pounded away in the traditional Hayes style, and done very well. Yet when the passing game got off to such a horrendous start, Hayes shelved much of his intended diversification, only rarely venturing back to a less predictable offensive design, even as the running back stable was decimated with injuries.

Hayes was correct in assuming the blame for the UM display, for it was his limited array of offensive formations and play calls which put the clamps on the Buckeye air attack. If Schlichter was expected to work wonders, he could not do anything other than that which the constraints of the game plan, which often hemmed his talents in, allowed. After the bitter disappointment of the Penn State debacle, Woody pulled back considerably from his air-oriented assault. Woody (correctly) realized that Art was not yet comfortable enough to effectively direct a lot of the intended Hayes system, and scaled the scheme back.

However, as Art's decision processes and familiarity with the offense improved gradually throughout the year, the running game also improved to the point, in spite of injuries, that Woody really saw no pressing need to take the handcuffs off his budding star. Thus, against Michigan, when OSU needed a full-scale, wide-open offense, the plays and system were simply not there to utilize.

In reaction to the disappointing Sugar Bowl trip of one year before, Hayes radically revised his team's travel scenario for this bowl trip. For the first time in eleven bowl trips taken in the Hayes regime, his team would stay in Columbus past December 20th. This would also be the first time the '78 seniors were allowed by the schedule to spend some time with their families on Christmas Day. Both a bowl trip, and a holiday celebration at home, were possible for the first time. This was the best of both worlds, and the players could not be more happy. "This is what the players have been asking for," said Cousineau.

The newly-devised schedule had the Buckeyes practicing through December 17th, taking a break for Christmas, then leaving Christmas night for their accommodations in Florida. This was a radical departure from the previously rigorous bowl practice schedules Hayes normally employed.

Both players and coaches did need a break after the draining, stressful year, and for once Hayes was forced to acknowledge that his own workaholic schedule was occasionally more harmful than beneficial. "The other system didn't work," was the terse Hayes explanation for the schedule shift.

Not surprisingly, Hayes was under extremely heated pressure from a legion of disenchanted fans at this time. Rumors abounded, from tales of pervasive dissension among staff and players alike regarding the offensive strategy, to the supposed lack of morale among the team, at least in relation to other years. This criticism and rumor mongering did sting and wound Hayes severely; it did not help matters that perhaps his all-time favorite leader, Archie Griffin, a man Woody was amazingly close too, was experiencing an extremely trying year of his own with the Bengals.

Woody correctly theorized that the bulk of these complaints and gossip concerning his program did not surface when the Buckeyes were winning, and he felt somewhat betrayed after his many years of exemplary service. As for the correct criticism regarding the recent lack of OSU successs against nationally ranked teams, Hayes insisted that the Gator Bowl would present a new story.

One supporter of Woody did note that overall, the Ohio State record, under Woody, against rated teams stood at an excellent 38-24-6, a .603 winning percentage, yet recognized that this phenomenal rate was indeed slipping in recent years.

Hayes opined, after the latest Michigan game (the least mention of which set his blood to boiling), "We're not practicing as often, but with more intensity. We want to try to get ready without overdoing it," and he felt the tropical, relaxed atmosphere of the Gator Bowl to be as conducive toward winning as Miami was to the '76 Orange Bowl triumph.

For that venture, the Buckeyes were housed in comfortable, apartment-type rooms; practiced early in the morning, receiving the remainder of the day off to frolic on the beach and sightsee; and generally, were able to relax a little and enjoy the privileges, rather than the burdens, of attending a bowl game.

Due to the Sugar Bowl catastrophe, Hayes realized his old methods were not working. In order to win, thus providing satisfaction for his own urge and to stop the swelling opinion that his salad days of success were over, Hayes was willing to try what his team desired. It was the end of a long, extremely troubling season, and all Woody wanted was a victory. For once, he was tired, and not just of losing.

The opponent for Ohio State was Clemson, out of the Atlantic Coast Conference. Clemson was undergoing their own considerable stresses, battling through a sudden, unexpected coaching upheaval. The situation of their program was chaotic and critical.

Head coach Charley Pell, who had lettered under Bear Bryant and was a similar taskmaster, had recently agreed to leave his position, effective following the Gator Bowl. He was moving to Florida, to become the head man for the Gators. Pell led Clemson to a sparkling 10-1 regular season record, with the only blemish being a 12-0 defeat at the hands of Georgia.

Yet Pell was forced to step down sooner than expected, amidst widespread, intense criticism by many players and influential backers of the Clemson program.

According to his critics, Pell had begun recruiting efforts on behalf of Florida, shirking his remaining duties of coaching Clemson in the bowl game. As the heat concerning his actions increased, Pell bowed to pressure and stepped aside, rather than disrupt the program any further. The reigns were passed to thirty-year-old Danny Ford, Pell's chief assistant and offensive line coach. Unfortunately, Pell was taking both the defensive end coach and the linebacker coach with him to the Florida post, and these gentleman had also vacated when Pell did.

Consequently, Ford elected to take his newly-designated team to Daytona early in December, to both acquaint the Tigers with his methods and to fill the vacated coaching holes. To further compound the already-frightful distractions, two prominent defensive substitutes were suspended through the bowl game, for undisclosed violations of Ford policies.

Luckily, back in Columbus, OSU received very charitable mid-December weather for their practices. Hayes felt that each outdoor practice session was equivalent to three such indoor practices, so the nice weather was welcomed with open arms. Both Ellis and Terry Vogler were back from injury-imposed layoffs, so only Tim Brown was missing practice time.

After several practices, this good health scenario unfortunately changed. Terry Bach suffered torn ligaments in his right knee and was forced to the operating table. Gerald bruised his right shoulder fairly severely, and missed about a week of practice. As was the case all year long, the Buckeyes simply could not remain healthy, despite all precautions and intentions to the contrary.

Schlichter used the extra time allotted by the somewhat-relaxed Hayes practice schedule, to work out with the young OSU basketball team. Head coach Eldon Miller thought Art could handle the transition to collegiate guard, and anticipated Art would join the hoop scene full-time after the Gator Bowl.

Schlichter had thought and hoped that the football season could have gone better, both on a personal and team basis. Art was a firm believer in the Lombardi school of thought, "Winning is the only thing," so the three losses were a bitter pill to swallow.

Again, Art used every available meeting with the media to commend Gerald. Rod was very open and communicative to the freshman, so much so that Art approached Gerald throughout the year for counsel regarding the many obstacles he faced. The fact that Gerald wisely aided his usurper said plenty about the class of the senior, and his devotion to the team, above and beyond any personal glory.

One Ohio Stater who had very quietly experienced an outstanding year was punter Tom Orosz, who averaged over 43 yards per boot. As a youngster, Orosz was a dedicated annual participant in Pass, Punt, and Kick competitions, consistently placing in the high ranks on a national level. As a ten-year-old, Tom captured the national title in the widespread competition.

The native of Fairport Harbor, Ohio, parlayed this background into a successful stint as a high school punter and quarterback. As Hayes was recruiting him for Ohio State, Woody promised to take a long look at these quarterbacking abilities. Unluckily, an extremely painful back condition early in Tom's frosh year prevented such an opportunity, and Tom lost out on his chance to take some snaps as a Buckeye.

When the back failed to improve throughout the course of the '77 season, team doctors ultimately discovered that his right leg was much shorter than his left, thereby throwing his body off balance and causing severe adjustment pains. The special shoe lifts he began wearing gradually and mercifully solved this problem. Tom was sufficiently recovered to punt by the final three games of '77, although his form was understandably way off and his performance suffered.

His back healthy and intact for '78, Tom stormed to the top of the Big 10 punting charts, averaging 44.4 yards per kick during conference games. As a testimony to the skill of Orosz, OSU opponents returned only 25 of his high kicks, for a low total of 141 yards. His booming kickoffs, as with those of Atha, compared to the non-returnable status of Skladany kicks.

As the Buckeyes concluded their Ohio practices, consisting of six outdoor and two indoor sessions, Hayes held two closed door meetings with the players. Many topics were discussed in these meetings, plus Hayes threw in a spirited reading of *The Gift of Magi*. Woody was feeling a little more upbeat than at anytime since the UM loss, his mood helped by the fact that Schlichter at last seemed completely healthy.

Art's dazzling displays of passing to Donley, plus the return of a healthier Gerald, highlighted a very good run of practices. Murray and Campbell were also both back at full speed, further encouraging the uplifted spirits of the Coach.

Hayes was so relaxed, that he even sent the team on a two mile cross country run several days before Christmas, a huge departure from his normal preparations. The lone drawback before the trip south was a knee injury Ty Hicks suffered during a basketball game over the holiday break.

Meanwhile, Clemson concluded their practices in Daytona, "...as healthy as we can be," according to the settling Ford. With his senior quarterback, Steve Fuller, at the top of his game, Ford felt that Clemson could pass the ball against any competition. Fuller, a strapping 6'3", 200 pound South Carolina native, directed a balanced offense through the spectacular regular season.

Seeing as how Buckeye opponents passed for eleven touchdowns on the year and averaged 164 yards through the air each game, Fuller felt confident he could perform equally well. The heady senior connected on 92 of 167 pass attempts in '78, with a mere four interceptions, and also ran for 696 yards and nine touchdowns.

His top receiver was a fellow senior, the All-American Jerry Butler. Butler was a 6'1", 175 pound speedster, who had once defeated former world-record holder Harvey Glance in the 60 yard dash during track season. Butler gathered in 54 passes for three touchdowns in '78, presenting a constant threat to opposing defenses, who often chose to cover him with two men.

The strong Tiger running game was anchored by 6'0", 175 pound tailback Les Brown and 6'3", 220 pound fullback Marvin Sims. This standout ground game powered out an average of 296 yards each contest, greatly aided by the blocking of lineman Joe Bostic.

The Clemson defense was a stingy unit in their own right, though not when it came to pre-game hyperbole. Installed as slight favorites by the oddsmakers, Clemson came to the nation's third largest post-season classic looking to vault into the national prominence which they felt was being denied to them.

As small-but-impactful linebacker Bubba Brown stated: "We feel we're among the nation's powers and we're going to prove it." Defensive end Jonathon Brooks felt, "If we make them go to the pass, we can shut them down." It was the belief of Clemson that Schlichter was prone to throwing interceptions at critical moments, and the Tigers were eager to capitalize on what they saw as a prime flaw.

The premier athlete on the Clemson squad and the undisputed leader of the secondary, which felt they could produce these turnovers, was senior Willie Jordan. Jordan had shared quarterbacking duties with Fuller as a freshman, before converting to the defensive side. Jordan was also a dangerous return man, and used his quarterbacking instincts to read defenses and opponents' throwing patterns quite accurately. Jordan knew Schlichter was a fine talent, yet Willie judged that Art was not yet developed enough to pierce the Tiger defense, or to snatch an expected victory from the grasp of the seventh-ranked Clemson team.

The last time Hayes had been at the Gator Bowl had been in '56, when he watched Georgia Tech turn back Pittsburgh by a slim count of 21-14. Hayes had taken son Steve on this trip, and the two had made a vacation out of the scouting expedition. Then-Tech coach Bobby Dodd believed in very light pre-bowl workouts, and this unusual strategy worked exceedingly well for his teams. Dodd won an amazing 12 of 13 bowl games, so Hayes was hoping that a partial adoption of the Dodd regimen would provide similar results.

In a similar reminiscent vein, in '46 Hayes had spent time at a reserve naval base in Florida, while completing the remainder of his wartime service obligation. Consequently, Hayes took the '78 squad to another nearby Florida base housing the *USS Forrestal*. Fittingly, Hayes was presented with a souvenir hat during the sightseeing session, replete with admiral insignia.

That trip was one of the few outside excursions allowed by the suddenly uncooperative Florida weather. The temperature hovered near an unusually chilly 50 degrees, and winds in excess of 30 miles an hour whipped torrential rains in all directions. For the final pre-game practice, Clemson canceled rather than deal with the severe, inclement conditions. Ohio State was scheduled to have a run-through on the Gator Bowl field, yet bowl officials nixed this intention because of the muddy playing surface.

So, Hayes rehearsed substitution patterns and insertions, and led light calisthenics, indoors, at the Sandalwood High School gymnasium. Then, Woody led his team outside for a short review of the game plan, conducted on the rain-drenched prep field. Little did he realize, this was the final practice he would ever supervise. Game time, Friday evening, had arrived.

In light of later events, several eerie incidents of this week before the game stand out. At a press conference in mid-week, long-time Hayes friend and former legendary Clemson head coach Frank Howard sent a gag gift to Woody: A pair of boxing gloves, "...just in case." The gift was accepted in relatively good humor, though Hayes was always a little tense before big games, and somewhat resented any intrusions on the time allotted in preparing for the impending battle.

Also in relatively good spirits, Hayes later cut short his final mass press conference of the week. "I'm bad copy anymore," he resignedly stated. "So I better get back to my coaches and players before they find out what they can do without me." Disappointingly, this last statement proved all too prophetic.

CHAPTER THIRTEEN: GATOR BOWL

The circumstances of the inglorious exit to the coaching career of Hayes, following this game, have been rehashed numerous times. That matter will therefore be touched upon only briefly in these pages. Those seeking further detail are well advised to read the definitive version of the confusing events, contained in long-time Hayes confidant Paul Hornung's wonderful, *Woody Hayes: A Reflection*.

Most football fans remember the tumult and furor of this demise of a coaching legend. Few recall the magnificent game itself. The Gator Bowl presented a precise composite of the '78 Buckeye season. The game had multiple moments of great excitement, wild swings of fortune, was marred by near-misses and failed opportunities, showcased many heroes, yet in the end, Ohio State lost again. There was no more appropriate cap to such a disappointing season, though the result was not a fitting end for the exemplary senior class.

The outcome mirrored exactly the rocky, tumultuous, at times joyous, incredible, memorable, yet ultimately unsatisfying journey, at least in terms of wins and losses, which the members of Woody's last legacy experienced. More fittingly, if given an opportunity, virtually every member of the class of '78 would repeat his choice to attend OSU, if only for the lessons learned off the field.

For what turned out to be his final pre-game pep talk, Hayes came up with a classic. As Tiger partisans claimed, the South Carolina school was a relatively unknown commodity, at least to the northern viewpoint of the OSU fans. So, Woody wished to impress upon his players the heritage of Clemson. Hayes got everyone fired up as he said, "If those s.o.b.'s want to fight the Civil War all over again, we'll certainly do it." Casting especial glances at many of the entranced black OSU players, Hayes reminded them that the ancestors of the southern Clemson players had literally chained and exploited the Buckeyes' African ancestors, keeping them enslaved for a hundred years.

Finally, as the emotion was peaking in the tense locker room, Hayes presented the clincher. The long-ago families of the Clemson team had, "...killed my grandpappy [in the Civil War]!" With this shocking declaration, Hayes swirled and led his troops into battle. The Buckeyes were unbelievably psyched and ready to exact their revenge on the Tigers for this myriad of appalling injustices. Once more, Hayes had uncannily known which emotional buttons to push, to put his team in the properly aggressive mood.

Ohio State entered the contest full of optimism, based on the successful practices, despite the bad weather, of the final week leading up to the 28th. Many of the Buckeyes echoed the sentiments of Cousineau, who said, "I thought we had a real good chance to win. The attitude was good." Schlichter was at the absolute peak of his frosh ability, and he led the Bucks to a 27 yard Atha field goal, late in the first quarter. The conditions of the overcast, cool night seemed to indicate a defensive struggle was imminent; accordingly, neither defense disappointed, at least in terms of keeping the opposition out of the end zone

The offense of each team flashed moments of explosiveness, yet neither team was able to really secure a distinct offensive advantage on the scoreboard. Ohio State was able to move the ball seemingly at will in the opening half, until nearing the goal line. Pinned with their backs against the end line, the threatened Clemson defenders proved their worth on two extremely critical, pivotal goal line stands.

On a drive which preceded the opening Atha field goal, OSU disdained a field goal on a fourth and goal situation from the Tiger two. Volley instead took a wide pitchout and was smothered by a wave of orange and blue defenders, resulting in no yards and no points. Following the Atha field goal, Fuller engineered a lengthy, 80 yard drive, culminating in the go-ahead touchdown.

Ohio State responded to being down by marching right back into scoring position. In a microcosm of the many near-misses of the year, Campbell was turned back on a fourth and one situation from the Clemson 21, missing the first down by a matter of inches.

Temporarily down but not out, OSU powered back on their next possession. Schlichter led his charges on a nine play, 78 yard touchdown drive, ending with five minutes left in the half. On this comeback drive, Art was magnificently brilliant. He connected with Campbell for a gain of 11 yards, Gerald for a pickup of nine, and then nailed Barwig with a perfect 34 yard strike.

Following this score, there occurred what Ford, coaching his first game ever on any level, decreed, "...the key play of the game." The Tigers massed at the line, and broke through to block the conversion attempt by Janakievski. In a game featuring many brilliant Tiger defensive stops, Ford thought this denial turned the momentum everlastingly to his team.

Fuller capitalized on the emotion provided by the block, leading the offense on a quick drive, resulting in a 47 yard Obed Arari field goal just as time ended in the opening half. Although the Buckeyes had seemingly dominated most of the first half, at least on the stat sheet, and had threatened the goal line repeatedly, they went in at the break trailing 10-9.

Both defensive units emerged from the locker room in a heated state, and put the clamps on the opposing offense. Late in the third quarter, though, the insertion of little-used Clemson tailback Warren Ratchford lit a spark under the sputtering Tiger attack. Ratchford's speedy, elusive, fresh legs propelled the Tigers on an amazing 19 play, 84 yard touchdown drive. The Buckeye defense never broke on this drive, it just bent and bent until Clemson ultimately eked out the draining, eventual, game-winning score.

After the contest, an exhausted Cousineau explained, "When you lay everything on the line, there is no shame in losing." There were no defensive breakdowns in this clinching trek, the Clemson offense rather raised their performance to a higher level, and Ohio State fell just short in stopping them.

Seemingly undeterred by the deficit, a defiant OSU offense struck right back with an amazing 88 yard touchdown drive of their own. Needing a two point conversion to tie the game, Schlichter was stymied on an keeper, falling just short of the goal line. With only minutes remaining to be played, it seemed as if the Buckeyes were out of chances. Miraculously, middle guard Tim Sawicki forced and recovered a Clemson fumble at the Tiger 44.

Blessed with another shot at victory, Schlichter unfortunately committed perhaps his only glaring mistake of the night. On a third and five situation, Art dropped back, and looked for a secondary receiver, Springs, on a curl route in the middle of the field. Art never noticed Clemson middle guard Charlie Bauman literally fall down, then drop off the rush.

Former Buckeye Jim Stillwagon was similarly renowned for dropping off the line and falling back as an extra coverage man, thus wreaking havoc with attempted passes. Bauman, virtually by accident, duplicated this intrusion, for, as Charlie stood up and recaptured his bearings, the pass hit him in the head, and he grabbed the ball. Baumann's interception of the toss came on the 24 yard line, and capped not only this Gator Bowl loss, but the unbelievable 28 year reign of Hayes.

As Baumann was run out of bounds in front of Hayes, a nasty scuffle broke out. As order was haltingly restored, a 15 yard penalty was assessed for the actions of Hayes. Such was the anger and confusion of some OSU players, following this scuffle, that they were visibly disgusted with and almost contemptuous of Woody's actions. Tim Brown, on the bench with a cast on his leg following knee surgery, had to be restrained from confronting Woody

Ernie Andria recalls another ironic instance of the play which led to the Hayes/Bauman incident. Alex Gibbs gave the third down call to Andria, who shuttled the play in from the sidelines, with explicit instructions for Art, "...not to throw an interception." The play call, 37 Streak, was a somewhat risky maneuver, and Gibbs made sure that Andria impressed this risk into the thoughts of Schlichter. Yet, because a man fell down and ended up where he otherwise would not have been, the pass was indeed picked off.

Amazingly enough, with 1:59 still remaining, there seemed sufficient time for OSU to stuff the Tigers and get the ball back. After Clemson ran one play, though, Hayes protested too vigorously that the officials let the game clock wind down too far before granting an OSU timeout. Another 15 yard penalty was assessed, and Clemson then ran off the remaining seconds to preserve their narrow victory.

Afterwards, Hayes privately addressed his team, though he sent out George Hill to talk with the bustling media. Hill said the defense had played extremely hard, they just faced a slightly better team - "Cousineau played his guts out," as did the others.

A red-eyed Schlichter, obviously fighting unsuccessfully to choke back tears, said he never even saw Baumann when he tossed his final, untimely pass. Art played a brilliant game, finally reaching his stride in the conservative passing offense, hitting 16 of 20 throws, good for 205 yards. Art also ran for 70 yards and both OSU touchdowns. His performance in this game foreshadowed the forthcoming excellence Art was to experience, particularly in '79, under an offensive plan better suited to his unique throwing and running capabilities.

Springs contributed 42 yards rushing, Donley led the receivers with three catches for 54 yards, while Barwig caught two long passes for 51 yards. Chuck Hunter once more played superbly in a bowl, catching two passes for 44 yards. Overall, OSU piled up 355 total yards, holding a slim advantage over Clemson, who compiled 331. The Tigers ran the ball 60 times, compared to the 44 attempts by the Buckeyes, and Fuller also threw on 20 occasions.

Ford praised his quarterback, saying that Steve's stats (nine of twenty passing for 123 yards, and 17 rushes for 39 yards), may not look favorable, yet Fuller was the dynamo behind each Clemson victory. Based on the final 11-1 record, Ford felt a Heisman recount (Fuller finished seventh in the balloting) was in order. As Fuller went, so did Clemson, and in this particular game he came up with the right calls in crucial situations.

Relatively unknown prior to the game, Ratchford and fullback Tracy Perry performed admirably in their relief roles, as they determinedly dashed away from an exhausted yet stingy OSU defense for 54 yards each.

Interestingly, on a night as bitterly frustrating as any in Buckeye football history, the OSU basketball team defeated the number one team in the land. In a tremendous upset, which concluded just after the football defeat, the cagers came back from a late 17 point deficit to upend the Duke Blue Devils, in Madison Square Garden. Due to the greater emphasis placed on OSU football at this time, much more attention was focused on the gridiron loss, and this rousing roundball win went mostly unnoticed.

The Buckeyes made the sullen journey back to Columbus that next morning. On the flight home, a rumor made the rounds among the players that Hayes had physically threatened and/or abused Hindman, who evidently was attempting to discipline the Coach for his actions of the previous night. Still, no one was really prepared for the announcement Hayes made at noon over the intercom of the plane, right after the flight arrived in Columbus.

Speaking in a very subdued style, Hayes began by wishing his team a safe, happy New Year. Then, almost imperceptibly, Hayes whispered, "I regret to say that next year I will not be your coach."

With this, Woody lowered his head and walked slowly out the exit at the rear of the plane, entering a car driven by his close friend, OSU trainer Mark George. This was the first official notification the players had of his intentions, and they sat stunned and silent, some with tears in their eyes. According to Cato, at first, "No one said anything."

Finally, the overwhelmed team began to excitedly talk, and the players also exited. Many players refused to comment immediately afterwards, yet Gerald spoke for most as he said of Woody: "Next to my father, he's the greatest man I know."

BIBLIOGRAPHY & ACKNOWLEDGEMENTS

Adler, Larry. *Football Coach Quotes: The Wit, Wisdom, and Winning Words of Leaders On the Gridiron*. Jefferson, North Carolina: McFarland Publishing, 1992.

Blaik, Earl with Tim Cohane. *You Have To Pay the Price*. New York, N. Y.: Holt, Rinehart, and Winston, 1960.

Blaik, Earl. *The Red Blaik Story*. New Rochelle, N.Y.: Arlington House, 1974.

Blumenson, Martin. *Patton: The Man Behind the Legend,1885-1945*. New York, N.Y :William Morrow, 1985.

Brondfield, Jerry. *Rockne, The Coach, The Man, The Legend*. New York, N.Y.: Random House, 1976.

Brondfield, Jerry. *Woody Hayes and the 100 Yard War*. New York, N.Y.: Random House, 1974.

Brown, Paul with Jack Clary. *PB, The Paul Brown Story*. New York, N. Y.: Atheneum Press, 1979.

Bryant, Paul W. and John Underwood. *Bear: The Hard Life and Good Times of Alabama's Coach Bear Bryant*. Boston, MA: Little, Brown, 1975.

Bynum, Mike (Editor). *Woody Hayes: The Man and His Dynasty*. Gridiron Football Properties, 1991.

Daugherty, Duffy with Dave Diles. *Duffy: An Autobiography*. Garden City, New York: Doubleday, 1974.

Dowling, Tom. *Coach: A Season With Lombardi*. New York, N.Y.: Norton, 1970.

Ferguson, Howard E.. *The Edge*. Cleveland, Ohio: Howard Ferguson, 1983.

Griffin, Archie with Dave Diles. *Archie: The Archie Griffin Story*. Garden City, New York: Doubleday and Co.,1977.

Halas, George with Gwen Morgan and Arthur Veysey. *Halas By Halas: The Autobiography of George Halas*. New York, N. Y.: McGraw-Hill, 1979.

Hayes, Wayne Woodrow. *Hot Line to Victory*. Columbus, Ohio: Typographic Printing Company,1969.

Hayes, Wayne Woodrow. *You Win With People*. Columbus, Ohio: Typographic Printing Company, 1973.

James, Robert Rhodes. *A Study In Failure*. New York, N.Y.: World Publishing Co.,1970.

Landry, Tom with Gregg Lewis. *Tom Landry: An Autobiography*. New York, N.Y.: Norton, 1970.

Lewin, Ronald. *Rommel As Military Commander*. New York, N.Y.: Von Nostrand Reinhold,1968.

Lombardi, Vince with W.C. Heinz and Robert Riger. *Run To Daylight*. Prentice-Hall, 1963.

Miers, Earl Schenk. *Football*. New York, N.Y.: Grosset and Dunlap, 1972.

O'Brien, Michael. *Vince: A Personal Biography of Vince Lombardi*. New York, N.Y.: Morrow, 1987.

Parcells, Bill with Mike Lupica. *Parcells: Autobiography of the Biggest Giant of Them All*. Chicago, IL: Bonus Books, 1987.

Pagna, Tom with Bob Best. *Notre Dame's Era of Ara*. Huntsville, AL: Strode Publishers, 1987.

Parseghian, Ara and Tom Pagna. *Parseghian and Notre Dame Football*. Notre Dame, IN: Men-In-Motion, 1971.

Paterno, Joe with Bernard Asbell. *Paterno: By The Book*. New York, N.Y.: Random House, 1981.

Perry, Will. *The Wolverines: A Story of Michigan Football.* Huntsville, AL: Strode Publishers, 1980.

Posner, Barry. *Leadership Challenge.* San Francisco, California: Jossey Bass, 1987.

Schembechler, Bo and Mitch Albom. *Bo.* New York, N.Y.: Warner Books, 1989.

Snypp, Wilbur. *The Buckeyes: A Story of Ohio State Football.* Huntsville, AL: The Strode Publishers, 1974.

Steinberg, Donald, M.D. *Expanding Your Horizons.*

Telander, Rick. *The Hundred Yard Lie: The Corruption of College Football And What We Can Do To Stop It.* New York, N.Y.: Simon and Schuster, 1989.

Twombley, Wells. *Shake Down the Thunder: The Official Biography of Notre Dame's Frank Leahy.* Radnor, PA: Chilton Publishing, 1974.

Vare, Robert. *Buckeye: A Study of Coach Woody Hayes and the Ohio State Football Machine.* New York, N.Y.: Harper's Magazine Press, 1974.

Wagenknecht, Edward. *The Seven Worlds of Theodore Roosevelt.* New York, N.Y.: Longmans, Green, and Co., 1958.

INDEX

FURTHER ACKNOWLEDGEMENTS

The author wishes to extend the finest thanks to the following: My wife Bobbye and rest of family, who heroically put up with my busy schedule for the past year; Leonard Mills, who provided the inspiration for this book; Tom and Michael Skladany and their fantastic printing companies, Governor James Rhodes, Mrs. Anne Hayes for her kindness to an unknown caller, and the following former Buckeye associates: Rick Volley, Archie Griffin, Billy Hill, Lou Williott, Max Midlam, Jeff Logan, Tim Burke and Joel Laser (whose philosophies I drew upon, even if their names were not frequently mentioned), Mickey Jackson, David Adkins, Jeff Ferrelli and his gracious wife, Duncan Griffin, Ernie Andria, Jimmy Crum, Garth Cox, Jeff Kaplan (and his secretary Jane), Tom Cousineau, and Bruce Ruhl. Also, Garry Benford of World Gym, John McNeely and everyone else at the *Columbus Dispatch*, the Miamisburg crew, the Shevlins, the Allamannos, the Springers, the Smiths (both sets), the Smales, the Goodwins, the Stalters, the Rowlands, the Billiars, the Richards, the Dyes, CMI and all at Grant Life Choices, Body-Fit West members and staff, the Bells, the DeLanceys, Suzuki, Yamaha, Hank and band, Rush Limbaugh, and Black Label. Special credit extended to my parents (for everything), the Heines, the Fritsches, the Hardys, and Dan Poynter.

ORDER FORM

Please send additional copies of *A Shot At A Rose, To The Bite Of a Gator: The '75-'78 Ohio State Football Saga*

Mail check or money order to:
The Brawny Pug Publishing Co.
5829 Pinecone Court, Office Three
Columbus, Ohio 43231-2940

Cost: $22.95 each, volume discounts available
Shipping: $3.00 for the first book, .75 cents each additional book
Phone: (614) 794-2582 for further detail